PRAHA

To Lorenza, Mariana, and Marisa, who put up with me.

(ABOVE) "Wunderkhammer" by Santiago Caruso, ink & scratch over plastered cardboard, 2010.

Guillermo del Toro

Cabinet of Curiosities

My Notebooks, Collections, and Other Obsessions

by *Guillermo del Toro*

and *Marc Scott Zicree*

TITAN BOOKS
London

AN INSIGHT EDITIONS BOOK

Guillermo del Toro: Cabinet of Curiosities
My Notebooks, Collections, and Other Obsessions

First published in the UK in 2013 by:
TITAN BOOKS
A division of Titan Publishing Group Ltd
144 Southwark Street
London SE1 0UP

www.titanbooks.com

Find us on Facebook: www.facebook.com/titanbooks
Follow us on Twitter: @TitanBooks

Published by arrangement with Insight Editions, 10 Paul Drive, San Rafael, California 94903, USA. www.insighteditions.com

ISBN: 978-1-78116-926-1

A CIP catalogue record for this title is available from the British Library.

Book design by Jon Glick
Manufactured in China by Insight Editions
First Printing, 2013

(PAGE 1) A sketch of a basket star by del Toro, after a photograph in *National Geographic*. Del Toro often turns to *National Geographic* for inspiration and never takes photos, preferring to record memorable images by sketching them.

(PAGE 2) A painting at Bleak House depicting a skull full of compartments that contain assorted objects.

(PAGE 3) Notebook 3, Page 5B.

(OPPOSITE) Notebook 4, Page 6A.

(PAGE 6) Concept of the pit where Ofelia encounters the Faun in *Pan's Labyrinth* by Raúl Monge and Raúl Villares.

(PAGE 7) Sketches from del Toro's fourth notebook.

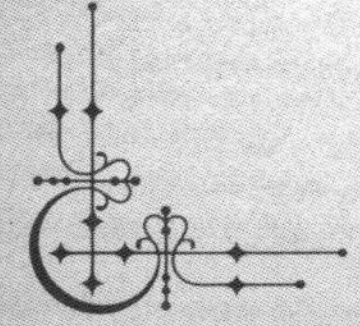

Key: t=top, tl=top left, tc=top center tr=top right, ml=middle left, mr=middle right, c=center, b=bottom, bl=bottom left, bc=bottom center, br=bottom right

Cronos artwork and photography courtesy of Universal Studios Licensing LLC and Tequila Gang, S.A. de C.V. and Ventana Films / Arthur Gorson: 63, 77tl, 77tr, 77bl, 77br, 78, 80l, 80r, 81, 82t, 82b, 83, 84t, 84b; *The Devil's Backbone* artwork and photography courtesy of El Deseo S.A. and Tequila Gang, S.A. de C.V.: 98tl, 98ml, 98br, 98bl, 98br, 101tl, 101ml, 101mr, 101bl, 101br, 108br, 111; *Blade II* artwork and photography used courtesy of New Line Productions, Inc.: 112(all), 115tl, 115tm, 115tr, 115ml, 115br, 117tr, 117bl, 118t, 122l, 125, 126tl, 126r, 130t, 130b; *Hellboy* artwork and photography courtesy of Columbia Pictures: 12br, 132tl, 132tr, 132mr, 132bl, 132c, 132bc, 138r, 141tl, 141tr, 143tl, 143tr, 143b, 145t, 145b, 149tr, 149bl, 152b, 155bl, 156r, 159l, 159r, 161t, 162, 164t, 164ml, 164b, 167tl, 164bl, 171t, 171b, 172t, 172b; *Pan's Labyrinth* artwork and photography courtesy of Telecinco Cinema, Tequila Gang, S.A. de C.V., and Producciones Anhelo: back cover, 6, 48, 54, 61, 62, 64–5, 174(all), 179t, 179b, 180tl, 180b, 183tr, 183b, 187l, 187l, 187tr, 187br, 188t, 188b, 191l, 191r, 192l, 192r, 195, 197l, 197r, 199t, 199bl, 200, 202l, 202t, 204, 207, 208tl, 208tr, 208bl, 208br, 211tl, 211bl; *Hellboy II* artwork and photography courtesy of Universal Studios Licensing LLC: 49, 50, 55, 56, 118b, 150b, 155t, 212c, 212mr, 212bl, 212br, 215, 216t, 216b, 219l, 219r, 223l, 224, 226tl, 226r, 229tr, 229mr, 229b, 235, 237t, 237b; *Pacific Rim* artwork and photography courtesy of Legendary Pictures: 238tr, 238bl, 238mr, 238br, 241(all), 243l, 245br, 246l, 247r, 249; Courtesy Basil Gogos: 10c, 136; Courtesy of Kunsthistorisches Museum, Vienna: 23; Courtesy of Mirada: 42l; Courtesy of Bridgeman Art Library, Ltd.: 47; Courtesy of Directmedia Publishing GmbH: 53; Courtesy of Ronald Grant Archive / Mary Evans: 98tr; Courtesy of the Guy Davis: 101tr; Courtesy of Mike Mignola: 138l, 223r; Photographs by Michael Collopy: 10tc, 10ml, 40b, 59, 72, 108tl; Photographs by Ethan Boehme: 10br, 15, 16m, 18t, 18b, 19, 20, 30, 33, 34, 35, 36t, 36b, 37, 39, 40t, 41, 42r, 43, 44t, 44b, 45, 66, 69

...por favor— tiene un bicho de agua que no puedo ma...

- Mercedes entra a la COCINA, ahí la niña está bebiendo un cuenco de leche con el abuelo (o alguien) de ahí se lleva a la niña a la biblioteca, sombra con rumor la acecha "eres tú" "eres tú" Mercedes le da los libros ilustrados, sale con el miedo de que Vidal los vea. Vidal las "descubre" a medio HALL y le pregunta a donde van. Ofelia esconde los libros. Vidal: La niña puede esperar. Suba a ver a mi mujer y a mi hijo. Si no ha mejorado habrá que llamar al doctor. Con la mamá poniéndole compresas calientes. Si le pone el oído se mueve, como un bicho. Una vez a un caballo le picó una mosca y la herida se le movía igual. Eran gusanos. Mercedes le da las buenas noches. Ofelia baja a leer a medianoche. Coge los libros y se como... se abre la puerta de la biblioteca. Va al laberinto. Tú eres la reina de las hadas. Va al laberinto al lado del pozo. Insecto. [illegible] a un fauno. Ella

Ⓗ

- Círculo Rojo de Melville en DVD.
- Muere y le salen cuervos de la herida abierta.

CONTENTS

FOREWORD
BY JAMES CAMERON
8

INTRODUCTION
11

COLLECTIONS
29

BLEAK HOUSE
31

GRAPHIC INSPIRATIONS
47

ANALYZING FILM
55

STORYTELLING
61

IDEA INCUBATORS
69

NOTEBOOKS
75

CRONOS
77

MIMIC
87

THE DEVIL'S BACKBONE
99

BLADE II
113

HELLBOY
133

PAN'S LABYRINTH
175

HELLBOY II:
THE GOLDEN ARMY
213

PACIFIC RIM
239

UNFINISHED PROJECTS
251

MEAT MARKET
253

MEPHISTO'S BRIDGE
254

THE LIST OF SEVEN
256

THE LEFT HAND OF DARKNESS
258

AT THE MOUNTAINS OF MADNESS
260

AFTERWORD
BY TOM CRUISE
262

ACKNOWLEDGMENTS
264

FOREWORD

ODE TO A MASTER

JAMES CAMERON

THE ARTIFACT YOU HOLD IN YOUR HANDS is an unprecedented portal into the clockworks of a wondrous mind. Guillermo del Toro's notebooks have been compared to the codices of da Vinci for good reason: Both are representations of the creative process of a genius unique in his time and perhaps in all time. There is no one out there on the film landscape to even compare him to, and in fact describing him merely as a filmmaker is far too limiting. He is an artist of enormous and precise vision who just happens to work on the most technically complex and culturally pervasive canvas of our time, the motion picture. In another age, he would have worked with egg tempera or a quill pen and made an equally great impact. Born into the late twentieth century, his brushes are lenses and animation software, his parchment a computer screen. For Guillermo, stories emerge freshly seized from the subconscious, still wet and wriggling, in a constant stream of pen drawings and tightly inscribed notes, which then form the blueprints for his films and books.

The power of his vision comes from his ability to communicate directly with our darkest places. He has the courage to squarely face that which we daily bury to get on with the ordered delusion of our lives. We are all insane to one degree or another, and the most functional of us merely hides it the best. But in our nightmares we confront the truth of our madness, fueled by fears so primal we often can't even speak their names. That land which we fear and suppress is Guillermo's playground. With his demonic glee at all things macabre and grotesque, he revels in that which we shun. He is the Santa Claus of the subconscious, the court jester of the id. He is our guide through the labyrinth of our worst nightmares, a Virgil much more suited to help us face hell than that sober Roman, because of his wit, irony, and, above all, his compassionate heart.

He will take us by the hand to confront the monster we all know is at the bottom of the stairs—our own mortality. He will drag forth our worst fears and hurl them up on the screen, knowing that to give substance to their twisted forms is to rob them of their power.

Guillermo's art fearlessly confronts life in all its beauty and horror. He sees with the wonder and stark terror of a child. His notebooks are a map of the subconscious, and his films doorways into the dungeons of our dreams, allowing us to confront our own individual hearts of darkness, to do battle and emerge victorious.

Each of his films is a jeweled clockwork of stunning detail and breathtaking design. I am privileged to be among his creative confidantes, so I have seen each one emerge and grow, even the unfinished masterpieces that the world may not get to enjoy—*Mephisto's Bridge, The List of Seven, At the Mountains of Madness*, and others. Though I mourn these unborn, I also know that del Toro conjures phantasms of stunning beauty and surreal horror as effortlessly as casting shadow creatures on the wall, using only a candle and hand movements. You can't stop him. He reaches into the whirlwind of his mind and snatches drawings and bits of narrative as fast as he can, reaping only a fraction of what roars past.

This book will give you a glimpse of that whirlwind. You will be dazzled by the artist. But I fear that by his art alone you will still not know the man, so perhaps a word about his character now, in advance, if only because we suspect that our artistic idols will always disappoint us in the flesh. Nothing could be farther from the truth in Guillermo's case.

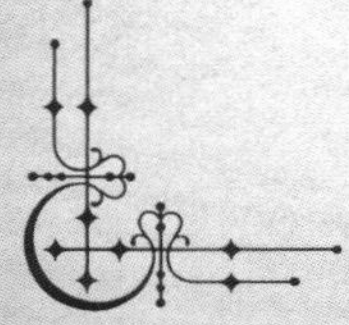

Guillermo has been my friend, and I'm proud to have been his, for twenty-two years. I met him when he first came to the U.S. with his directorial debut *Cronos*, made using his dad's credit cards in Guadalajara. I was immediately struck not only by the caliber of his work (so far superior to my own first effort) but also by his voracious appetite for life, for art, for the grotesque and beautiful in all forms, from classic literature to comics. His personality is larger than life, magnetic, profane, and utterly sincere.

As his career took off, I watched him navigate the waters of Hollywood with increasing frustration, as he tried to apply his old-world Latin honor to a business in which honor is as alien and abstract as calculus to a fish. But he remained true to his own code, to his vision, and especially to his friends, with a loyalty that is far too rare in any walk of life, let alone the film business.

He has been there for me when I needed help on my films, an honest and forthright pair of fresh eyes, and I've been there for him in the same capacity. It's less that he needs my advice than that he wants to know there's someone in his corner.

He calls me Jaimito, "Little Jim," and I am slight next to him, in many ways. Once at his house, he challenged me to punch his SlamMan dummy as hard as I could. I did, moving it about six inches and almost breaking my wrist. He bellowed "Jaimito, you hit like a little girl!" and proceeded to smash the thing across the room with one punch. Like his namesake, the bull, del Toro is a force of nature. Amazing that the same meaty fist can inscribe such exquisitely detailed drawings and miniscule calligraphy.

I know him as a true friend, a steadfast husband, a loving father, and the most original character I've ever met. His genius is protean, his moral compass finely calibrated, his humor deliciously rank, his creative passion inspirational, and his work ethic a challenge to the rest of us slackers.

If he didn't exist, we'd have to invent him, but how do you invent the impossible?

(ABOVE) Sketch of the Faun from *Pan's Labyrinth* in del Toro's fourth notebook (Page 12B).

165
* Elimina a ZACK
ZUCK!
* "I'm here to offer you a choice..."
* "Demons and Angels walk on the earth, you just have to look for them in the right places"
Radio.
Húmero
Dedo Pulgar.
Cubito
* "Ala de Murcielago" para Mecanismo Spanky.
Ala de Murcielago.
Huesos. Dedos.
* Spanky sangra color azul...
* "Maybe you're right about me Martyn"
* D.N.A. de
* El piso se agrieta debajo de Spanky
* "You wanna know something funny?!"
NOCELTICA
EUROPA DEL ESTE
ESLAVO
estética RUSA
TOLKIENESCO
HISTORIAS NATURALES
Espiral

INTRODUCTION

GUILLERMO DEL TORO
THE WORLD AS CABINET

"You have to believe the magic to see it."—GUILLERMO DEL TORO

FOR GUILLERMO DEL TORO, IT ALL STARTS WITH THE EYE—or, more accurately, the lens. His keen vision processes everything, judging it, molding it to his intellectual and creative purpose, turning it to his interests and obsessions, exquisite and grotesque, and crafting it into an endless procession of indelible, unique images—some on the world stage, some utterly private.

Most private of all are his phenomenal notebooks, full of pointed observations, random thoughts, sketches from life, and wondrous drawings. At first glance, they appear to resemble those of another polymath, Leonardo da Vinci. A true modern Renaissance man with stunning capacity, vast interests, and endless enthusiasm, Guillermo del Toro invites such a comparison. Like Leonardo, Guillermo is an artist with wide interests and talents who can be hired but not bought and who approaches the way he lives with a passionate aesthetic sense.

"One of the biggest lessons Leonardo leaves for all creators is that *man* is the work of art," notes Guillermo. "Obviously, the *Mona Lisa* is a masterpiece. The Vitruvian Man, *The Last Supper*—both masterpieces. We can all agree on that. But Leonardo—the man, the anatomist, the designer, the architect, the scientist—is the real masterpiece. *He* is his ultimate creation. So live well. Be curious and hungry and always in awe of the world."

Leonardo is far from the only titan who inspires Guillermo del Toro in his quest to create himself. "As with da Vinci, Mark Twain is the work of art. It's not the isolated novels, or stories, or aphorisms. It's the man. In the same way, in the tragic sense, that is true of Oscar Wilde or Truman Capote—both of whom, I believe, had a tragic imbalance between their artistic output and their lives as socialites."

From each of his many guides, Guillermo selects bits and pieces, playing the role of Dr. Frankenstein and the monster both, becoming the scientist who fashions himself into something simultaneously shocking and beautiful. He combines the darkness of Lovecraft, the formalism of Hitchcock, the wildness of Fellini. His distinct palette is equal parts Richard Corben, Johannes Vermeer, Edvard Munch, and his beloved symbolists—Félicien Rops, Odilon Redon, Carlos Schwabe, and Arnold Böcklin.

Guillermo is an omnivore, or more accurately, a creature who absorbs everything that draws his interest and transmutes it into something all his own. Through his sorcery we see the world transformed. His bleak and heartening vision imprints us as

(OPPOSITE, CLOCKWISE FROM TOP LEFT)
Del Toro and his partner in animation, Rigoberto Mora, with his Canon 1014XL-S Super 8 camera shooting clay animation; a bust of Mr. Barlow the vampire by Daran Holt; a study in wing anatomy from del Toro's Blue Notebook, Page 165; del Toro and Mora preparing an animation set; an automaton by Thomas Kuntz, part of the collection at Bleak House; Notebook 4, Page 20B; a gathering of childhood toys and trinkets at Bleak House; a portrait of del Toro by Basil Gogos; a dead dragon gaff at Bleak House.

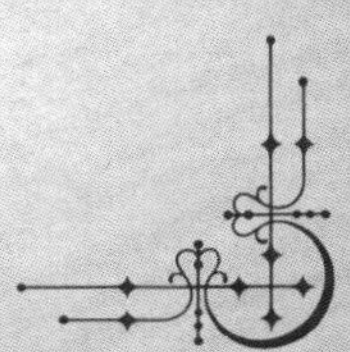

indelibly as a tattoo, its grimness leavened by compassion, its central characters—often children in emotional isolation—struggling to master a larger world.

"You write a single book and you make a single movie," Guillermo notes, but "the reality is that you graft all of them together. You do it whether you want to or not. Renoir, the painter, put it very nicely. He said, 'A painter paints the same tree all of his life.'"

For Guillermo, the accident of timing, of being born now, allows him to work in film. Combining all the major arts—painting, sculpture, photography, music, writing, performance—cinema melds them into a form and experience that is greater than its parts.

What has emerged through the alchemy of Guillermo's engagement with the cinematic medium is an artist who is utterly unique—one who blends popular culture with profound ruminations on the human condition, who juxtaposes Hollywood and Latin America in equal measure, who alternates between personal, lower-budget, Spanish-language films and Hollywood tentpoles that still manage to communicate a personal viewpoint, philosophy, and aesthetic.

In fashioning his work, his self, the things he creates, and the spaces in which he moves, the totality of the face he shows the world, Guillermo projects an idiosyncratic

(TOP) Hanging at Bleak House is the original art for the poster by Richard Corben that del Toro had over his bed as a teenager, and which continues to influence his imagination.
(ABOVE LEFT) Del Toro with child actor Bailee Madison on location for *Don't Be Afraid of the Dark*. Child protagonists often feature in films written and directed by del Toro.
(ABOVE RIGHT) A scene in *Hellboy* reminiscent of the landscapes of Arnold Böcklin (1827-1901), a Swiss symbolist painter who has influenced del Toro's aesthetic.

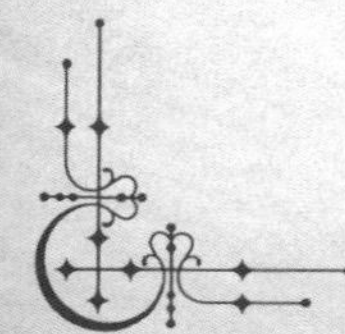

persona, one whose resistance to classification is its greatest strength. His films, too, resist classification, although strong sympathies are felt across them. Motifs such as clockwork beings, uterine caverns, and tentacled monsters travel freely through his films and his notebooks.

In his focus on these very personal obsessions, Guillermo works in a noble tradition, for the definition of a great artist often lies in his determination to fixate on things the majority deliberately ignore in order to construct an orderly life. "Eye protein" is what Guillermo calls the distinctive language of symbols and visceral figures he weaves into the tapestry of his films. "Fifty percent of the storytelling in a movie is submerged beneath the screenplay," he says. In other words, the vast freight of meaning lies in the tension between what we can and cannot control, in the play between the conscious, the subconscious, and the unconscious. "In the symbolic and Jungian sense, and in every sense," he adds, "I am interested by surface and beneath."

(ABOVE) The inside of the Cronos device, which had to be built at an enlarged scale so that it could be filmed by del Toro and his crew using the technology available to them at the time.

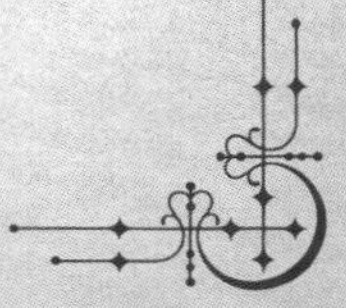

(ABOVE) Guillermo del Toro (front) and his brother Federico (back) at the steps of their great aunt's home. (BELOW) Guadalupe Gómez (del Toro's mother) and her father, Guillermo Gómez O'Colligan, on the porch of del Toro's great aunt's home, where he would spend a large part of his childhood.

BEGINNINGS

The self-invention of Guillermo del Toro began on October 9, 1964, the day he was born in Guadalajara, Jalisco, Mexico.

"I was a very strange kid," Guillermo remembers. "I was Aryan blond. I was like a German. And I was constantly ostracized because I had super-bright blue eyes and Roy Batty–white hair and was very thin, incredibly thin. I was constantly berated as a wimp, and I identified with those shortcomings; I felt like a freak. The nice, healthy kids were all those outgoing kids with dark hair and a tan. That's one of the reasons why my villains are like that."

Early in his youth, an event occurred that changed Guillermo's life forever. "My dad won the lottery when I was four years old, and we bought a bigger house. My dad's a self-made man, a very successful businessman, but he stopped going to school when he was very young, he never read, and I think he felt funny about not having a proper library now that he was rich. So he bought a collection of books for kids that I read. It was all the classics: *Hunchback of Notre Dame*, Edgar Allan Poe, this and that. But the real great thing for me was that he bought several encyclopedias, *The Family Health Medicine Encyclopedia* and one called *How to Look at Art* that was ten volumes. It took you from cave paintings all the way to what was then modern art: cubism, Klee, abstract art, pop art. I read them all, several times actually, and I consulted them a lot. Those were the beginning."

The mixture of the two—the study of great art and of all the disasters that can beset the human body—had a major formative effect. "I became a very young hypochondriac because of that encyclopedia. I was constantly thinking about tumors, and liver disease, and parasites in my brain, and I thought I was going to die really quick. And the art was great because I was learning about Degas, Picasso, Manet, Goya."

Guillermo laughs, adding, "There was a moment, I will not lie, where the family medicine encyclopedia and the art books were great because they had naked ladies. So I am very grateful to Manet, as I am very grateful to certain anatomical charts."

At the same time, Guillermo was reading comic books. "So Bernie Wrightson, or Jack Kirby, or John Romita Sr., or any of those guys were on equal footing for me in terms of how important they were. Each was as formative an influence as fine art."

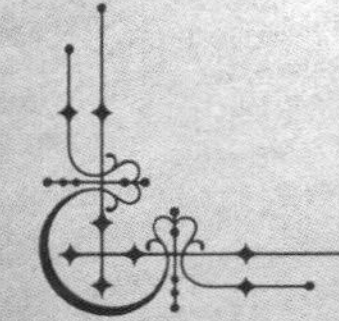

(ABOVE) The shelf in the Art Room at Bleak House where the encyclopedias del Toro read as a child are kept.

Never one for superheroes, Guillermo found himself drawn to horror comics. "I used to buy *House of Secrets* and *House of Mystery*. They did a lot of illegal reprints and ripoffs of EC comics in Mexico." Guillermo also recalls a Mexican comics magazine titled *Traditions and Legends of the Colonial Times*, "a knock-off of EC that was supposed to be based on real occurrences and legends, but that spun out of control." It was violent, brutal, and very sexy. "They started with tame nudity, but eventually went all out, and they had incredible violence. They had these rotting corpses in colonial clothing that were absolutely amazing. And eventually, they started to lie. They started to say, 'Oh, this happened in so-and-so,' and I would say, 'No, that's not true. That's a Nathaniel Hawthorne story, or an Edgar Allan Poe story, or a W. W. Jacobs story.' Because I was reading books."

The first book Guillermo bought for himself, at age seven, was *Best Horror Stories*, edited by Forrest J Ackerman. From then until he was twenty, Guillermo read a book every two days, every day if he could, thousands of them. "I read really inappropriate stuff for my age: Rimbaud, Baudelaire, Marcel Schwob, who was a fantastic symbolist writer, Matthew G. Lewis's *The Monk*, Thomas de Quincey. I read really weird stuff, at least by provincial standards. Look, my great aunt didn't want me to read Victor Hugo's *Notre-Dame de Paris* because the local church had it on its list of forbidden books!"

By seven or eight, Guillermo also started drawing and painting and building model kits (the first he ever painted was *Pirates of the Caribbean*, but he gravitated toward the monster kits). He liked eating crayons but didn't like their texture for drawing, so he used colored pencils.

"I started drawing very young because I was illustrating my horror stories," he recalls. "I started with the illustrations and sometimes never finished the story! Normally my clients were my mother, my grandmother, and my dad, and I would sell them the issues with a *great* color cover. There was a story I remember called 'The Invader,' and it had an invisible dome covering a city, with a giant tentacled monster eating everybody in sight, and people trying to drill a hole in the dome. And I did these epic Prismacolor pencil illustrations and sold out the three issues to my captive audience."

At the same time, Guillermo was drawing three monsters obsessively: the Creature from the Black Lagoon, Frankenstein's monster, and Lon Chaney's Phantom of the Opera. "And I really loved sculpting. My brother and I would do full human figures with clay and Plasticine—liver, intestines, the heart—fill them with ketchup and throw them from the roof. So I was an artistic but very morbid kid."

Morbid, but not passive. "I was speaking at a film school in Hollywood, and I said to them, 'Go have a life. Live. Get laid, get into a bar fight. Get knifed in the fucking thorax. Lose all your money. Make all your money back. Jump into a train.' When I was just a child, I was observing the world, but I lived a lot, too. We used to break into abandoned houses. We explored the entire sewer system of Guadalajara on foot. And then I became really crazy as a teenager."

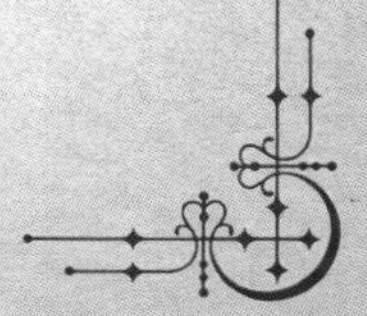

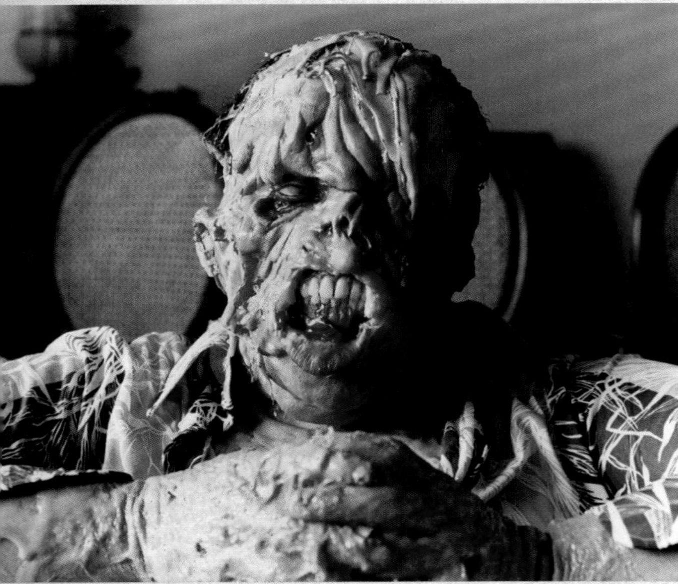

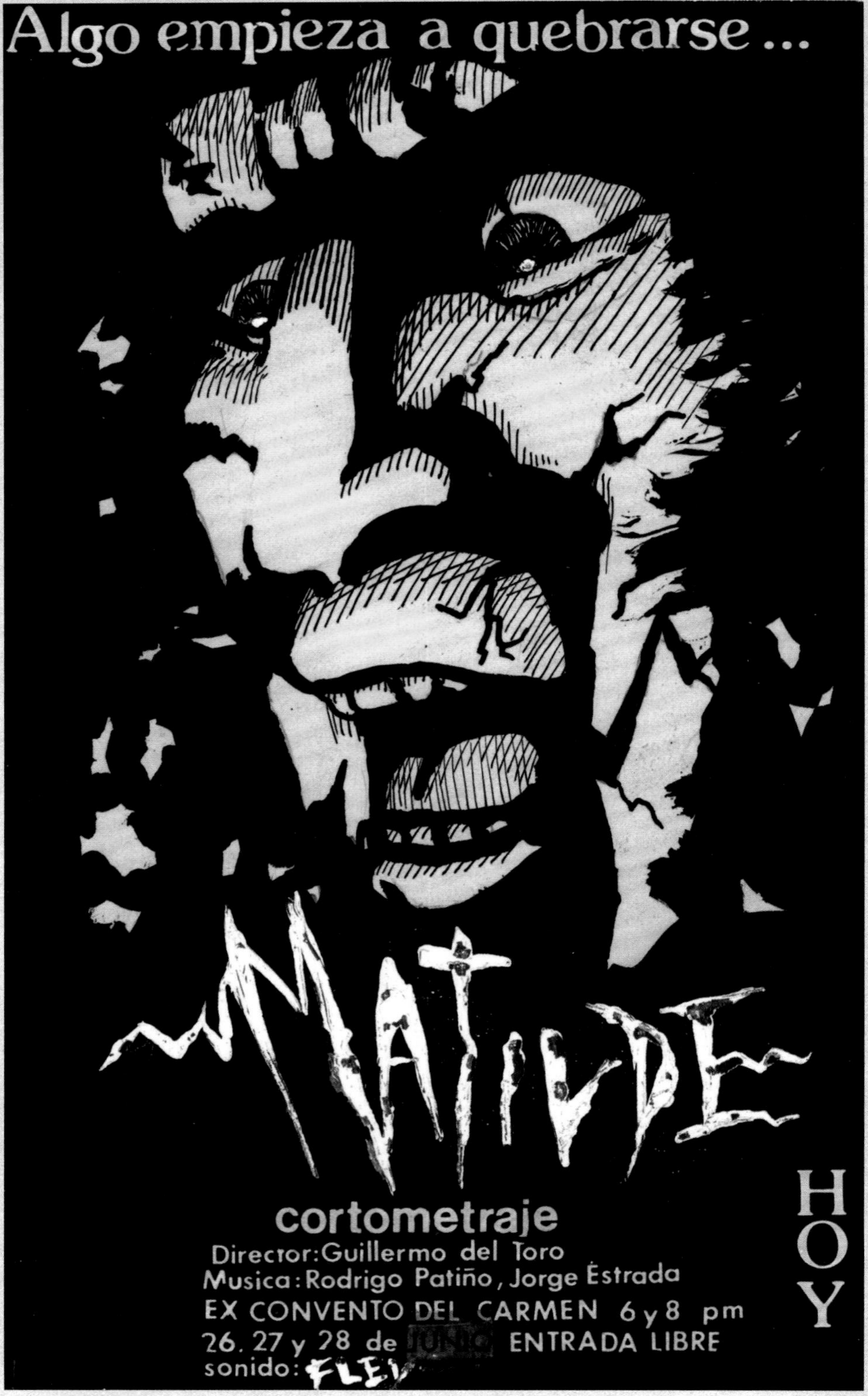

Algo empieza a quebrarse ...

MATILDE

cortometraje
Director: Guillermo del Toro
Musica: Rodrigo Patiño, Jorge Estrada
EX CONVENTO DEL CARMEN 6 y 8 pm
26, 27 y 28 de ENTRADA LIBRE
sonido:

HOY

(ABOVE, CLOCKWISE FROM TOP LEFT) Del Toro shooting his short film *Geometría* with his Mitchell camera; a poster promoting *Matilde*, one of del Toro's short films, featuring art and typography by the director; del Toro wearing sculpted and molded gelatin makeup, including fake hair and acrylic dentures and gums; a business card from del Toro's special effects company Necropia S.A. de C.V., surrounded by other mementos.

From age eight on, Guillermo also began making short films. Around age twenty, he fell under the tutelage of filmmaker Jaime Humberto Hermosillo, for whom Guillermo served as executive producer on *Doña Herlinda and Her Son* (1985), which starred Guillermo's mother, Guadalupe. (Hermosillo saw Guadalupe in a short film Guillermo made; he thought she was a good actress and cast her in her only feature film role.)

A key piece of advice from Hermosillo was to have faith in oneself. He would often tell Guillermo, "If a road is not presented, you build one." Embracing this advice, Guillermo worked for ten years to establish Necropia, a special effects and makeup company in Mexico, a country that previously had no such facility. Necropia provided the makeup effects for his first feature, *Cronos*, in 1993.

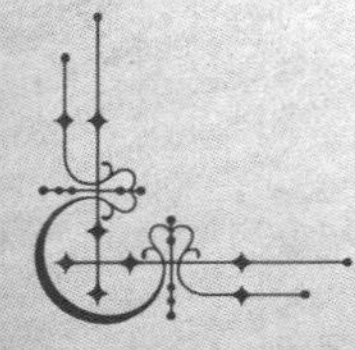

◈ ◈ ◈

Running through all Guillermo's work like the hum of a high-voltage current is *fear*, the menacing, cold beauty of a knife's edge. Rod Serling once observed, "The greatest fear of all is fear of the unknown, which you can't share with others." Nevertheless, Guillermo has explored and shared that fear with millions, his films evoking a sense of communal isolation on a grand scale.

Guillermo's films are most easily defined as horror or dark fantasy, but not of the exploitative or escapist type. Instead, he crafts a particular brand of fear-tinged fantasy that interprets the world we live in, rather than offering a separate time or place where the audience might luxuriate in imaginative denial. As Guillermo observes, "When people say, 'Oh, fantasy's a great escape,' I reply, 'I don't think so.' Fantasy is a great way of deciphering reality."

Guillermo utilizes the tools of fantasy and horror to open our eyes, as a way to see the world in its totality. His films constantly play with the border between what can be seen and what remains invisible, tackling the literal and metaphorical implications of blindness and vision.

"Spiritual blindness and physical blindness, I'm afraid of both," Guillermo says. Whether it's the Pale Man of *Pan's Labyrinth*, the Angel of Death in *Hellboy II*, or the other myriad characters who choose to see or not see what is right in front of them, Guillermo invites us to consider the conscious and unconscious choices we ourselves make.

Interestingly, while existential dread has been a major theme in Guillermo's work, a different kind of fear attends his career. "The thing I'm most afraid of is success. The second thing I fear the most is failing. But I think success is more scary. I tell you, and I'm being completely honest—people may think this is PR or me bullshitting—but the day I didn't win the Oscar for foreign film for *Pan's Labyrinth*, I was happy. It's not a reflection about the Oscar. Any prize that I don't win fuels the fire, and every prize I win quenches it. I always say, when you're young and unsuccessful, you don't have the money, and if you're not careful, when you're old and successful, you don't have the passion. To be put in either of those two positions is a tragedy. I think one of the toughest times in any man's life is his twenties, because in your twenties you're fiercely screaming who you are, but you have only half a notion of who you are. Then as you grow older, you whisper who you are, but people are closer to you, and they listen. By that time, you have half a notion, a quarter of a notion, of who you are. I think the tragedy is when you finally have all the people that you need surrounding you, and you have nothing left to say."

For now, Guillermo's fears have not materialized. He is a passionate artist working at the height of his abilities. At various times, Guillermo has stood at a creative crossroads, tempted by the sort of success he fears could lead to tragedy. But in each instance, he has drawn a line, claimed himself, seen past the illusory, and chosen his voice, his calling, his singular form of expression.

In building the edifice of his life and work, it's only natural that he'd erect a structure to hold his dreams and creations—a place called Bleak House.

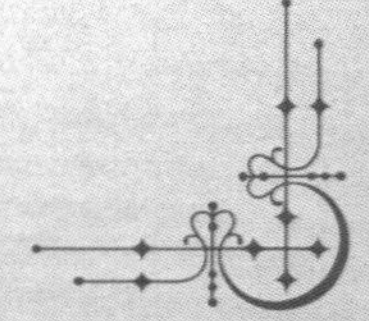

AT HOME

As I approached Bleak House for the first time, a house with an oddly Gothic air located in a subdivision outside of Los Angeles, I couldn't help thinking of the opening lines to one of Edgar Allan Poe's short stories:

> During the whole of a dull, dark, and soundless day in the autumn of the year, when the clouds hung oppressively low in the heavens, I had been passing alone, on horseback, through a singularly dreary tract of country; and at length found myself, as the shades of the evening drew on, within view of the melancholy House of Usher.

(ABOVE) The upstairs hallway at Bleak House, cluttered with framed art, books, and sculptures. The collection grows daily and is periodically rearranged by del Toro. (BELOW) The name plate that adorns the exterior of Bleak House.

I had come to Bleak House to begin the series of conversations that would form the foundation of this book. The sky was slate and intermittently rainy, and as I drew near the door, the rambling edifice towered over me, the storm clouds sweeping across the dragon weather vane like a leprous hand.

This is BLEAK HOUSE lodging the Del Toro collection since 2007

I regarded the heavy iron knocker like Marley's ghost, raised it, and struck three times. A moment later, the thick oak door swung wide. There stood Guillermo.

"Come in, come in." His big hand waved me inside.

Across the threshold, I found myself in a realm of wonders. In the foyer was what appeared to be an enormous figure of Sammael, the outrageous demon from *Hellboy*. To my left was apparently an antique oil of Saint George killing the dragon, to my right busts of Uncle Creepy and Cousin Eerie. Gleaming wood detailing flanked walls incarnadined as if infected by the mysterious plague from Poe's "The Masque of the Red Death." There was a life-size

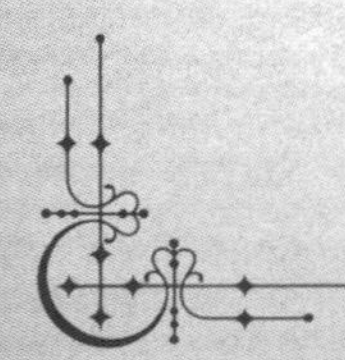

figure of the pinhead from *Freaks* and of Karloff's Frankenstein, plus samurai armor, automata old and new, and the skulls and skeletons of creatures real and imagined. And in every square inch, filling room upon room, were framed insects and original art by Arthur Rackham, Bernie Wrightson, Edward Gorey, Drew Struzan, and Basil Gogos, along with first editions of Twain, Dickens, L. Frank Baum, and Andrew Lang, plus rare treatises on magic, the occult, and vampirism, on the monstrous and the dream-born.

It is a collection Guillermo describes as "every book I ever read and most every toy I ever bought," all of it as meticulously designed as a Tiffany egg. Bleak House is Xanadu, if Charles Foster Kane had been thirteen years old and the most brilliant geek ever.

"The fact is," Guillermo says, "that what I do is not fan art. My films are not fan films, even if I am immersed in pop culture. That is just one facet of what I do, what I draw upon, and who I am. I am influenced by literature as much as I am by comics, and by fine art as much as I am by so-called low-brow. But I am not trapped by either extreme. I transit between these parameters in absolute freedom, doing my own thing. I try to present myself as I am, without apologies and with absolute passion and sincerity. I study my subjects and plan my work meticulously. Think of *Cronos*, *Devil's Backbone,* or *Pan's Labyrinth* and you will see that what I do is not only to recontextualize artistic forms but reflect on the genres or subgenres that they belong to. I try to deconstruct through love, through appreciation, not by referencing, but by reconnecting the material with its thematic roots in a new approach. The vampire film, the ghost story, and the fairy tale are re-elaborated in my work, rather than just reenacted or imitated. I never want to follow a recipe; I want to cook my own."

As for Guillermo, he likes to call it his "man cave."

(BELOW) Bleak House is a mixture of predominantly Victorian and Gothic elements by way of Hollywood, with real and imaginary skeletons scattered throughout.

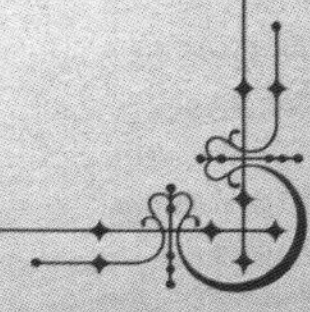

(ABOVE) An alcove at Bleak House devoted to Charles Dickens.

I've had this feeling three times before in my life.

When I was seven, I visited the Ackermansion, Forrest J Ackerman's stupendous collection of monster and sci-fi memorabilia. Uncle Forry's home was filled with articulated dinosaurs from *King Kong*, the latex alien hand from *The Thing*, Spock's pointed ears, original art by Frank R. Paul and Virgil Finlay, a copy of the robot from *Metropolis*, and thousands of other items. The second time was when I was in my early twenties and literally crawling through Rod Serling's attic while researching my book *The Twilight Zone Companion*. The attic housed heavy leather volumes holding every article and snippet printed about Serling, files with notions finished and unfinished, a box full of unproduced *Twilight Zone* scripts, and plastic airplane models still in their boxes. The third time was when I visited Ray Bradbury's canary-yellow house in Cheviot Hills, which overflowed with mementos and touchstones from his miraculous life. From original Joe Mugnaini artwork for *Fahrenheit 451* and *The Martian Chronicles* to the toy typewriter he'd first started writing on at age twelve, everywhere there was wonder.

"Never throw out anything you love," Ray said on many occasions. In each of these homes, a brilliant man's head and heart had seemingly exploded to fill a house, inviting visitors to scrutinize, linger, and be nourished. But Guillermo's house, by dint of sheer passion and obsession, tops them all.

Guillermo charmingly refers to Bleak House as his "collection of strange crap." In a more serious mood, he adds, "You're God as an artist, and it's really just the way you arrange. I think a director is an arranger. I direct this house, and everything goes somewhere, and I can tell you why, and there are thematic pairings, or there is a wall with all blue on it. There is nothing accidental. And my movies are like my house. I hang every painting, and if the frame shows a clock or a watch, or shows an apple, or shows a piece of furniture, I chose that, and I ask the art director and

the production designer to show it to me before, and I walk the set and I say, 'Take this out' or 'Bring this in.' It really is the beauty of the director, I think, in the way I understand the craft."

On that first visit, Guillermo led me deeper into the house. I was agog at the cinematic, literary, artistic, and zoological feast—akin to the food piled high to tempt Ofelia at the Pale Man's table in *Pan's Labyrinth.* Wandering Bleak House is a *Through the Looking-Glass* experience, as if one has actually stepped into one of Guillermo's films.

Through glass doors leading to the backyard, I spied the life-size bronze of Ray Harryhausen, one of Guillermo's spiritual godfathers. Then we turned down a hallway lined with wild art, gleaming weird mechanisms—some insectile, others mechanical—tin toys, Pez dispensers, anatomical models, and a miniature of the Time Machine from the eponymous 1960 film by George Pal, another member of Guillermo's pantheon. Hovering as if in benediction, now tied permanently to a wall as he'd once been strapped to Ron Perlman's back in *Hellboy,* was the torso and head of the Russian corpse, a role voiced in the movie by Guillermo himself. Just off the hall were the *How to Look at Art* volumes that started it all, and at the end of the corridor, in a glass case, was the first *Pirates of the Caribbean* model Guillermo so lovingly assembled and painted as a child.

And then the pièce de résistance. Like a character out of Poe or Dickens, Arthur Machen or M. R. James, or any of the legion of outré writers of whom Guillermo is an acolyte, my host beckoned me to enter his *sanctum sanctorum,* the room where Guillermo writes his scripts at a big old wood desk or, more often, on the overstuffed leather sofa. Best of all, at the flick of a switch, lightning flashed, thunder rumbled, and rain cascaded down false windows looking onto endless night.

We settled into the leather sofa and began to talk.

A LIFE FULL OF WONDER

In fashioning his house, Guillermo credits Forrest J Ackerman as a key inspiration, but there is another guiding principle that predates Ackerman and gives a deeper meaning to Bleak House.

Call it Guillermo del Toro's cabinet of curiosities.

After all, everything surrounding this fabulous, larger-than-life character, from his films to his house to his notebooks to his speaking engagements, is chock-full of extravagant, peculiar, and extraordinary items—his world is an overflowing credenza of marvelous things. Further, the term's provenance makes it particularly fitting.

Originally, *cabinet of curiosities* referred to a personal collection of spectacular, eclectic, and outlandish objects accumulated by a wealthy person, often an aristocrat. Also known in German as *wunderkammer* ("wonder room") and *kunstkammer* ("art room"), these "cabinets" were not pieces of furniture but entire rooms full to bursting with every unusual and attractive bauble that could be found in the natural world or realms constructed by humanity.

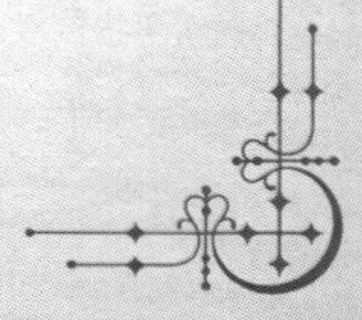

Hitting their peak of popularity in the seventeenth century and spurred by the discovery of the New World, these cabinets might house clockwork automata, Chinese porcelain, the crown of Montezuma, a madonna made of feathers, chains of monkey teeth, a rhinoceros horn and tail, conjoined twins, a mermaid's hand, a dragon's egg, real or supposed holy relics, vials of blood that had rained from the sky, an elephant head with tusks, carved indigenous canoes, an entire crocodile hanging from the ceiling, a two-headed cat, and as one list concluded, "anything that is strange."

At the time, science had not yet developed standardized methods of classification, and museums had not yet been established for public consumption, so these cabinets of curiosities grew at the whims of their owners in bizarre and breathtaking ways, each its own deformed, magnificent, unique universe.

Sporting titles redolent of their times, those famous for their cabinets included the Holy Roman Emperor Rudolf II, Archduke of Austria Ferdinand II, Peter the Great, Augustus II the Strong, King Gustavus Adolphus of Sweden, John Tradescant the elder, Elias Ashmole, and the deliciously named Ole Worm.

In some fascinating way, these wild, untamed accretions were autobiographies of their owners, spotlights playing over the darkest corners of their minds, Dorian Gray portraits they could display without ever admitting that these collections revealed true images of themselves.

Francesca Fiorani wrote in *Renaissance Quarterly*, "The Kunstkammer was regarded as a microcosm or theater of the world, and a memory theater. The Kunstkammer conveyed symbolically the patron's control of the world through its indoor, microscopic reproduction."

In a modern context, what better possible description could you have for a motion picture?

Without a doubt, Bleak House is Guillermo del Toro's great cabinet of curiosities, deliberately so. It is a microscopic reproduction of the world seen through his own lens. But it is not his only one. Guillermo has crafted an even more personal and miniaturized domain.

At the beginning of his cinematic career, Guillermo's mentor Jaime Humberto Hermosillo insisted he keep notes. "I started with a tape recorder," Guillermo recalls, "and I would record every idea that came to mind. I had it in my pocket. But I never transcribed those thoughts, and I lost the tapes. Then I started carrying the Mexican equivalent of the Moleskine book, and it was a very poorly put-together spiral notebook, so the leaves started to get loose. Finally, around 1986 or '87, I bought what was then a revolutionary thing, the Day Runner. They were like eighty dollars when they first came out, and I thought they were the equivalent of a portable computer. I fell in love with the blue notepaper, and I still have sixty or seventy packets. I said, 'I'm going to buy enough blue paper for the rest of my life.' I started keeping notes in there, and I found it really great because it was very well put together, very sturdy. I carried it on location. It rained and it didn't get wet. It was fantastic. So that was the beginning of the notebooks."

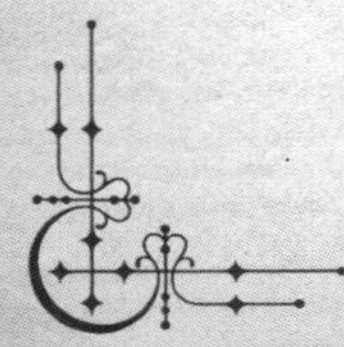

Initially, Guillermo jotted down notes and illustrations mainly for himself and for those he was working with. “Usually those notebooks were used only to communicate with actors or designers, to show them the world.”

With the birth of his first daughter, Mariana, Guillermo began to rethink the notebooks as mementos to leave his daughter—as something that might interest and entertain her in the future. “I gave myself the luxury of buying inks and pens, and I thought, ‘I’m going to make it an art project that she will find fun to look at.’ So I changed my handwriting, did the elongated *T*s and elongated *L*s to give it an old-fashioned feel, bought a quill. I wanted to make it fun for her, like finding letters. So every note that is there is not to myself, but to her.”

With the birth of his second daughter, Marisa, this determination only strengthened. “I instructed in my will that those notebooks are for them. They can quarter them, sell them, keep them, frame them, throw them out, burn them, whatever they want to do. But what they will have is a testament to curiosity. I think they indicate, not how much I know, but how much I *want* to know, how much I was thinking about this or that.”

(ABOVE) Frans Francken the Younger’s *Chamber of Art and Antiquities* (1636), a painting depicting a seventeenth-century cabinet of curiosities made up of art, collectibles, and oddities from the natural world.

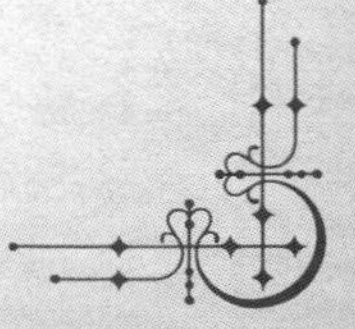

He also built a conscious whimsicality into them. "What I love is the idea that the deepest stuff in these notebooks is the stuff that looks the quaintest, and the stuff that looks the deepest is the stuff that is much more playful and crazy and not necessarily meaningful."

In designing the notebooks, Guillermo was intent on rendering flaws into the weave, deliberate stains and blemishes. "In the end," he says, "perfection is just a concept—an impossibility we use to torture ourselves and that contradicts nature. We pursue it—God knows we have to, as artists—but ultimately, like [Friedensreich] Hundertwasser says: A straight line is pure tyranny. In art, as in life, the love of imperfection is the perfect love."

More than valuable objects, mementos, or artworks, the notebooks possess an almost magical significance for Guillermo, who explains, "It's really important in our life to have talismans. Everybody has one or two or three. In my case, I have dozens. You have to imbue things that surround you with power."

In this way, one of the notebooks played a direct role in perhaps the most important juncture of Guillermo's career. "I lost the notebook at the end of shooting *Hellboy*, right before *Pan's Labyrinth*. It was a very important moment because I was considering doing a big superhero movie. Avi Arad [then head of Marvel Studios] had seen pieces of *Hellboy* and had liked *Blade II*, and he offered me *Fantastic Four*. It was a big, big, big movie for me. And I was thinking, 'Do I do *Pan's Labyrinth*, or do I do *Fantastic Four*?' And I was in London, and I left the notebook in a cab.

"I always say everything that happens is a ciphered message. Like Freud said, 'There's nothing accidental.' And I was thinking, *Why did I lose the notebook*? I spent all night meditating—I do transcendental meditation now and then—and I cried a lot. I really cried and cried and cried because these books are for my kids; I want my kids to have something from their father.

"And finally I said, 'I get it. It's because I was about to lose myself. I'm going to do *Pan's Labyrinth*.' And at *that moment*, the phone rings, and it's the cab driver bringing it back to the hotel. I had given him an address for a comic book shop in London, and he had seen the logo of the hotel on the piece of paper, and he remembered."

◈ ◈ ◈

Guillermo continues to draw and write in the notebooks, and in truth, he does so for both his daughters and himself. "When I start a screenplay or a movie, a shoot, I carry all of them with me, and I browse through them because it's like having a dialogue with a younger me. I see the stuff that was important to me at twenty-nine or thirty. I view them with great curiosity. 'Oh, this kid was interested in this; this kid was interested in that. That's funny.' And ideas will spark that you wouldn't have had before. At the end of one notebook, I made a list of what I was going to achieve in the next five years of my life. I was twenty-nine or thirty. I look back at it, and I have done all of that and more."

While the early notebooks record an avid mind capturing impressions and developing ideas in an exuberant, spontaneous way, the later ones are increasingly self-aware, done with the knowledge that others will ultimately scrutinize them. They

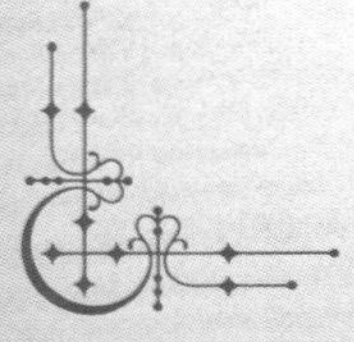

have been crafted with precision, each page composed as its own work of art, although images and words are now often disconnected. "I do the drawings first," Guillermo explains. "I write around them. These things are not chronologically intact."

The notebooks form a piece with Guillermo's house and films, but they exhibit one key difference: With those other works of art, we see the end results brought fully to fruition, presented to us wholly formed, the edges neatly planed off. The notebooks are both process and product, expression and rumination. They are Guillermo's creativity laid bare.

In these notebooks, we see the private man and his stance toward a public world—processing problems and working out solutions, viewing present and future with guarded optimism and counterbalanced by painful experience. On these pages, Guillermo's projects intermingle in the most intriguing ways. *Mimic*, *Blade II*, *Hellboy*, *The Devil's Backbone*, *Hellboy II: The Golden Army*, *Pan's Labyrinth*, and *Pacific Rim* all crash into each other. They bleed together, inform one another. It's as if the toy shop came alive when the toy maker was sleeping. The extravagant vampire design first considered for *Blade II* reaches full expression in *The Strain*, Guillermo's trilogy of novels with Chuck Hogan; notions of clockwork mechanisms and tentacled nightmares migrate from one project to the next.

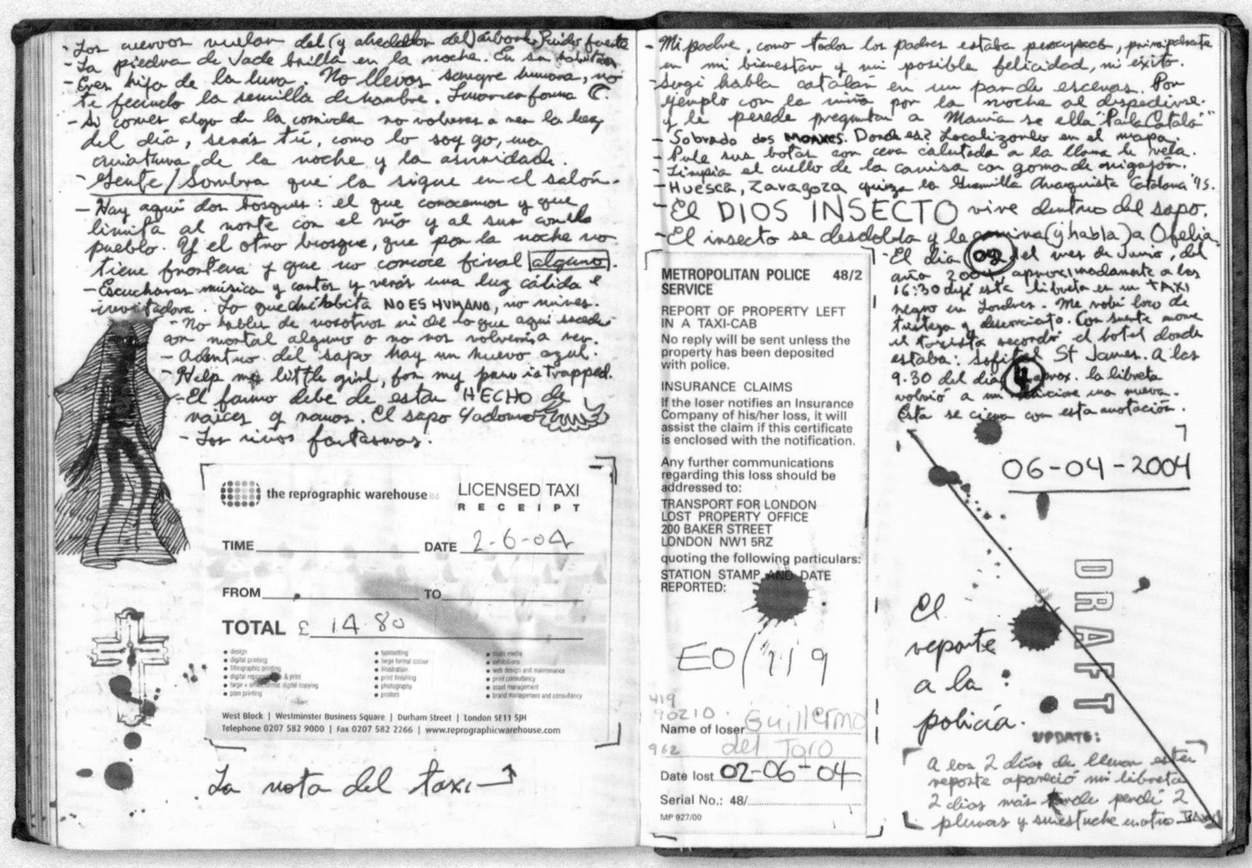

(ABOVE) Notebook 3, Pages 48A and 48B, which include the receipt for the taxi ride in London during which del Toro lost his notebook (*left*), as well as the record of the police report del Toro filed (*right*).

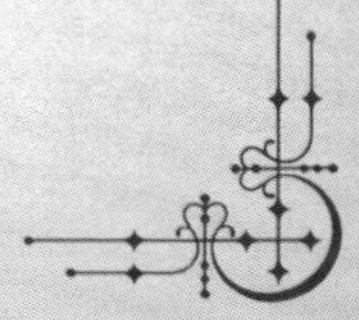

Most of all, Guillermo's notebooks present the same creative generosity one finds in the man himself. Whether he's talking in the room where it always rains, or adding to his notebooks, or sharing his fantastic visions on-screen, he gives the gift of his whole self, and in this way makes our world a little more messy, visceral, boisterous, and exalted.

The thing about great storytellers is that they are full of great stories. Pretty much everything Guillermo says or writes is by turns fascinating, surprising, appalling, hilarious, enchanting, or moving. And like all truly great storytellers, he's also a great soul. His stories can't help but instruct, impart, and illuminate. In Hollywood, a dark vision is often merely a faddish pose. But you can tell when a writer-director has never seen a dead body, never spied anguish up close. With Guillermo, his heart of darkness is authentic, born of a fully lived life. He not only observes deeply but *feels* deeply, and he has survived to tell the tale.

"You try to make the right choices," Guillermo notes. "I'm not a fatalist. I think that the plan, the universal plan and the universal energies, have a direction for everything. I don't think there is a design that we can comprehend, but I think that we are all agents of destruction or construction in our lives, and one must try to make the best choices within that. When people talk about heaven and hell, I always think of *Defending Your Life*, the Albert Brooks movie. I think that you have a responsibility not to propagate the cancer of despair, resentment, and envy. You have the responsibility to make the right choices for the people around you and yourself. We are not going to be important, but I think the collective choices that we make are. We are going to be extinct or not by the accumulation of those choices."

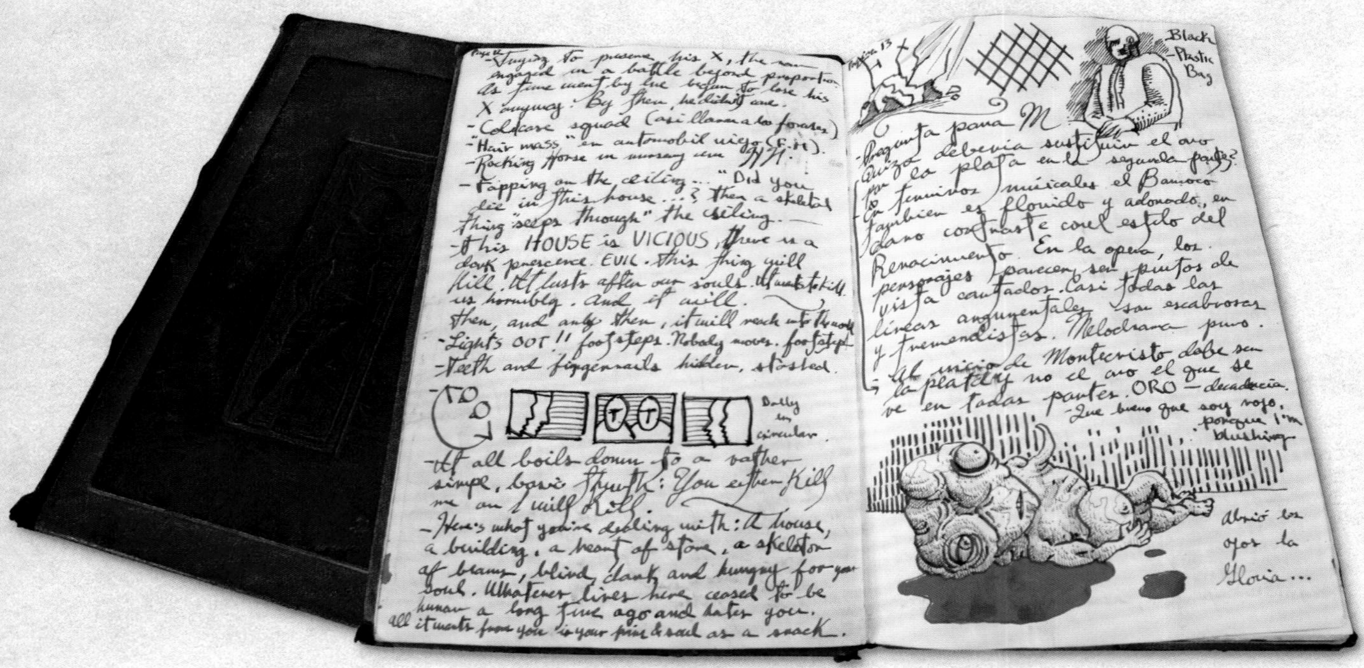

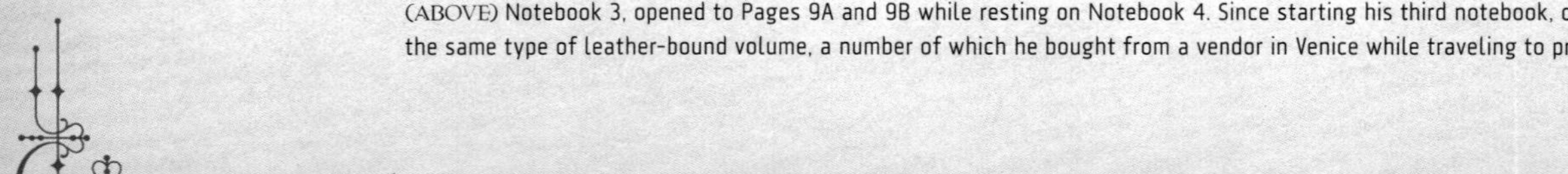

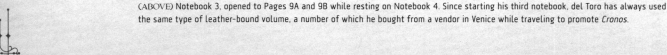

(ABOVE) Notebook 3, opened to Pages 9A and 9B while resting on Notebook 4. Since starting his third notebook, del Toro has always used the same type of leather-bound volume, a number of which he bought from a vendor in Venice while traveling to promote *Cronos*.

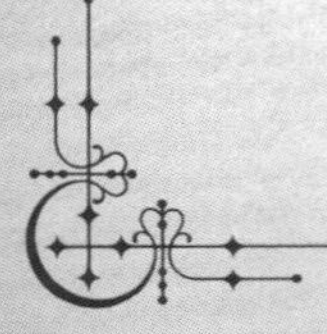

On one of the notebook pages for *Pan's Labyrinth*, Guillermo has the Faun giving Ofelia a volume that reads, "The book contains every possible destiny, every possible future which your decisions could create. It was made just for you, written in your father's blood, and will reveal its secrets to your eyes alone. Infinite and limited."

Of this, Guillermo says, "That's very Borges and is 'The Garden of Forking Paths.' Because the whole movie is about choice, and every choice gets defined when it's made, and the choices are revealed only at that moment. So the Faun gives her a book where essentially the book tries to guide her one way or another, and she takes her own choice. This is the book that writes itself, a riff on a famous Borges story called 'The Book of Sand,' where every page you turn fuses with the rest and is both infinite and limited."

Through the images in this book and the conversations with Guillermo, you'll be given the opportunity to see the world through different eyes. There is wisdom here and heartache, exaltation, exhaustion, joy, and deep compassion.

When Guillermo began writing in the notebooks, they were for himself, then for his daughters, and now we have been invited to share in them. And at the very last, these notebooks are addressed to the boy Guillermo once was, to his past and future, a love letter of hope and of the impossible made possible. As he puts it, "If I were a kid in Mexico and I read this book, I'd be inspired."

At this stage of his life and career, Guillermo knows full well that whatever path he chooses, it will be the journey he is meant to be on . . . the road he has built for himself.

(ABOVE) Notebook 3, Pages 17A and 17B.

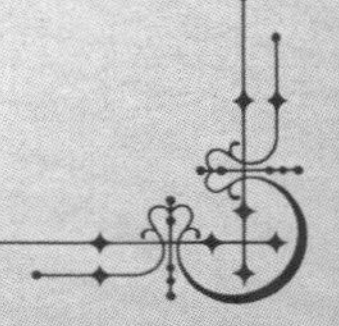

mi más
tierna infancia
aclarado de
una vez
por todas
con este
bosquejo del
Sensei
Tenada-San
durante la cena
con Shige y
Nirazawa-San
en el sushi
del papá de
Shige-San
Tokyo
5/29/02

Nombre Japones
キャプテン
ウルトラ

Capitan
Ultra en
ingles. Le
clavaba la
bayoneta
a los
monstruos
en el centro
de la
cabeza con
lujo de
violencia

Este personaje,
usaba una
bayoneta
y se llamaba
el Capitán
Infinito

GUILLERMO DEL TORO

Cabinet of Curiosities

COLLECTIONS

BLEAK HOUSE

"Anything to vary this detestable monotony." —CHARLES DICKENS, *BLEAK HOUSE*
"They're my friends. I made them." —J. F. SEBASTIAN, *BLADE RUNNER*

"TO ME," GUILLERMO CONFESSES, "the beautiful thing about Bleak House is that when I come in and go out of the house, it is cleansing for me. Catholics go to church, Jews go to temple. I come here."

He adds, "Spiritually, my life is here. I exist in this house, really."

Bleak House is Guillermo's second home and working office, his artistic masterpiece, his cluttered attic, his pride and joy. It's where he goes to draw and write, to recharge his batteries, to explore unfettered his creative whims. When in Los Angeles and residing at his family's home nearby, he visits Bleak House at least two hours every morning and one hour at night, seven days a week. He delights in giving tours to luminaries from around the globe, including other noted directors.

The moment you step inside, you are dazzled by the extent of the visual delights. Bleak House bursts with "over 550 pieces of original art," Guillermo notes. In fact, Bleak House has recently grown, so extensive is the collection. What began as one house has now expanded to include a neighboring structure, which is still finding its own distinct identity. Like the first, it features Guillermo's prize possessions. For instance, the second wing's living room is filled with magnificent preproduction maquettes of creatures from *Pacific Rim* (2013), which are flanked by a stunning bronze by Stanislav Szukalski and a full-size replica of Robert Picardo's Meg Mucklebones from Ridley Scott's *Legend.*

"When I was a kid," Guillermo says, "I read *Vathek* by William Beckford. In it, Fonthill Abbey was mentioned. That was his personal treasure: an entire building—or series of Gothic buildings—created to lodge his collection of strange artifacts, oddities, and scientific anomalies. He inherited an obscenely large fortune, so he was able to secure every treasure he could dream of. And dream he did. Within my means, I have also indulged in collecting. But I do it because it is the world as I understand it; as it exists in my soul."

Guillermo is quick to point out that neither Bleak House is intended to be a museum or storehouse. Both homes are working spaces, with each room serving a different purpose. "For example, I have a room where I assemble models," he says. "The reason is as banal as the fact that it is well-lit and is set up so I can put the actual place where I assemble the models close to a window. Because I need to ventilate when I prime. Otherwise I get really high."

However, creative inspiration, not base practicality, is what Bleak House is made for. In the main house, Guillermo says, "The Rain Room is literally my favorite place. I spend 90 percent of my time at Bleak House there, writing. But my second favorite room is the Sun Room, the Manga Room, the cabin in the back. I love to draw there, more than in the real drawing room, which is upstairs, because the Manga Room has really good energy. It's so peaceful."

Sometimes, though, where Guillermo works is more a question of what feels right on any given day. "If I want to write a scary story, I don't necessarily go into a scary room," he explains. "If I want to write a light-hearted story, I don't go into a light-hearted room. It's just whatever feels comfortable on the day. I do most of my writing on sofas. I sit exactly like my mother—one leg under my other leg, leaning. I have every form of desk known to man—I collect them as objects—but I never write on a desk. Except for the desk in the Rain Room. I can put my elbow on an adjacent desk, so it's comfortable."

It's hard not to wonder: Will Bleak House continue expanding until it consists of, not one or two structures, but an entire block? Guillermo says no. "Most of the time, it's just my personal office," he elaborates. "I don't want to expand because I think it would be unfair to the house and the neighbors. It needs to remain a home."

And *what* a home! A journey into Guillermo's imaginative world would hardly be complete without a tour of one of the most remarkable residences in the world. Beckoning warmly, Guillermo bids us to accompany him into the hallways, rooms, and recesses of Bleak House. . . .

(PREVIOUS PAGES) Notebook 4, Pages 43A and 43B. (OPPOSITE) The Comic Book Library at Bleak House.

THE FOYER

Entering the Foyer of Bleak House, the first thing that confronts you is an enormous head of Boris Karloff as Frankenstein's monster, fashioned by former Tussauds sculptor Mike Hill. Hill had considerable difficulty making the head that massive. It took numerous attempts to get the proportions right. But since this is one of Guillermo's favorite monsters—along with the Gill-Man from *Creature from the Black Lagoon* and Lon Chaney's Phantom of the Opera—it was no surprise that Guillermo snapped up the sculpture when it was exhibited at Monsterpalooza in 2011 and installed it in his home.

On one wall above the entryway are prints of Manhattan in troll language from *Hellboy II: The Golden Army* ("because," he says, "the conceit was that the Troll Market was underneath the Brooklyn Bridge"). Taking center stage is a full-size figure of the demon Sammael from *Hellboy,* made for Guillermo by Spectral Motion.

Throughout Bleak House, other original props, concept art, storyboards, and preproduction maquettes from Guillermo's films have been carefully selected and artfully scattered, but they do not dominate the collection. Were Guillermo to house everything designed and built for his films, he'd need a series of warehouses rivaling Charles Foster Kane's. Instead, only those mementos from Guillermo's films that hold a special fondness or significance for him are included among the wealth of glittering objects.

Certain artists make regular appearances throughout the house. A perennial favorite is Basil Gogos, the famed cover artist for the magazine *Famous Monsters of Filmland.* His portrait of Guillermo is featured prominently in Bleak House's entryway.

Dominating another wall is a large painting of Saint George killing the dragon that looks old but is actually a recent painting by Russian artist Viktor Safonkin. It holds special significance for Guillermo: "It's one of my favorite images: (a) it speaks of impossible tasks, (b) it's a great image because of the way the dragon is rendered."

Guillermo adds, "I love dragons. They are my favorite fantasy creatures and are the most beautiful animals in all of mythology." He cites a theory he likes, articulated by David E. Jones in *An Instinct for Dragons,* that proposes the dragon "is an imaginary amalgam we, as a species of primates, made from the predators we feared the most—the reptiles, the birds of prey, and the big cats."

(OPPOSITE) The Foyer at Bleak House.

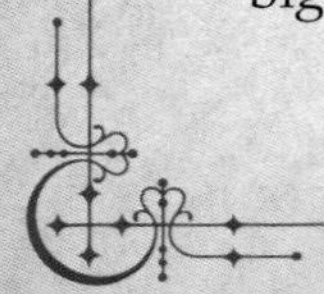

Once upon a time . . .

hives of Evil
PRESENTED BY
RISTOPHER
LEE

(OPPOSITE) A life-size sculpture of H.P. Lovecraft by Thomas Kuebler watches over the Horror Library at Bleak House. (ABOVE) The Horror Library is also home to one of the original Cronos device props, clasped by a silicone hand used for some of the film's special effects.

THE HORROR LIBRARY

To the right of the Foyer is one of Bleak House's many libraries, where a full-size—and utterly convincing—figure of H. P. Lovecraft stands perusing a volume. Lovecraft is one of Guillermo's most cherished icons, a spiritual godfather, and Lovecraft's *At the Mountains of Madness* is Guillermo's most-longed-for, unmade film project.

The Lovecraft statue was sculpted by Thomas Kuebler. "I had it commissioned," Guillermo says. "I approved every stage of the sculpt. People think his likeness is very easy; it's actually very difficult. He has a few quirks, the fold by the mouth, the lantern jaw. They can be cartoonish."

The Lovecraft figure stands watch over Guillermo's beloved books on horror, including the first book he ever bought—an anthology edited by Forrest J Ackerman, which Guillermo purchased in 1971 when he was seven. The Horror Library is filled with classic stories by such outré and macabre authors as Arthur Machen, M. R. James, and Sheridan Le Fanu. "Everything that is in Spanish means that I bought it when I was very young," Guillermo explains. Ravenous for knowledge, Guillermo began teaching himself English as soon as he could, so he could read more broadly: "I was very young. I was less than ten, and I was bilingual. I started with a dictionary and all the movies from America, which were subtitled, not dubbed."

In the Horror Library, Prince Nuada's sword from *Hellboy II* rests quietly a few feet away from the baby bug prop from *Mimic*. "And that's one of the real Golden Army soldiers, life-size," Guillermo says. "Next to it is the chopped-up head from *Blade II*." Another familiar figure from Guillermo's oeuvre stands out. "That's the first concept maquette ever done of Hellboy," Guillermo notes. "That was done by Matt Rose. And this is the Cronos device on one of the silicone hands we used in the movie."

Guillermo avidly collects items from cherished movies and TV shows, including the Devil figure featured in Tim Burton's *The Nightmare Before Christmas*. "That's my favorite character in the whole movie," Guillermo says. Scattered throughout the room are also visual touchstones from *20,000 Leagues Under the Sea, The Phantom of the Opera, Lost in Space,* and *Night Gallery*. The replica figure of Baron Boris von Frankenstein, based on Boris Karloff, from the stop-motion-animated *Mad Monster Party* was made for him by the animation crew on *Blade II*.

This library also holds a miniature scene from Disneyland's *Pirates of the Caribbean* ride. Disney, in particular, has been a towering influence on Guillermo. But to really appreciate that, we need to stroll down the hallway and find a certain bookcase, which slides to reveal a secret room. . . .

THE DOWNSTAIRS HALLWAY

The downstairs hallway of Bleak House is lined with a cornucopia of wonders, gathering together framed insects, cameos, nineteenth-century anatomical drawings, a fake mummified rabbit, weird objets d'art, and stunning artwork. These pieces include concept art for *Sleeping Beauty* by famed children's illustrator Kay Nielsen, original work by science fiction and horror illustrator Michael Whelan, and illustrations by Charles Doyle, the father of Arthur Conan Doyle.

"These are my magic books," Guillermo says, pointing to tomes on the art of illusion, prestidigitation, and misdirection from across several centuries. Then he gestures toward a row of busts depicting famed magicians: "And these are Thurston, Houdini, Chung Ling Soo."

Favorite works of literature also line the shelves—volumes by Charles Dickens, Victor Hugo, Jorge Luis Borges, and Edgar Allan Poe, among others.

Guillermo indicates a large framed insect. "That's the bug I bought as a kid when I first visited New York. I always wanted to use it in a movie, and it ended up in *Pan's Labyrinth*."

Nearby are other touchstones of Guillermo's life. "This is my grandmother's cameo, which I've used as a prop in a couple of movies, and which I want to use again in *Crimson Peak*. And this is the first model kit I painted as a kid, *Pirates of the Caribbean*."

THE HAUNTED MANSION ROOM

"I first went to Disneyland when I was three years old," Guillermo recalls. "It was life-changing for me. My mind became what it is. I'm a big Disney fan. I believe the man changed the way we tell stories. He was doing transmedia before anybody talked about transmedia."

The Haunted Mansion Room—also called the Fairy Tales and Folk Tales Library—replicates many elements from Disney's unique attraction, including the wallpaper from the mansion's foyer by Bradbury and Bradbury, gargoyle sconces, and Marc Davis's original acrylic painting of Medusa. Also notable is the life-size figure of the Hatbox Ghost, a ghost no longer seen on the

ride. "It was on the Haunted Mansion for only a few days, then they took it down," Guillermo relates. "The legend was that it was too scary. The reality is, it wasn't working."

Recently, Guillermo committed to make a new film version of the Haunted Mansion: "With Disney, when I took *Haunted Mansion*, one of my conditions was that they would let me tour the mansion by foot and that they would open the vault, so we could see all the preproduction art by Marc Davis and Rolly Crump and all the Imagineers. So we did. I spent the morning there like a kid. Amazing stuff."

Guillermo had Spectral Motion construct "The Ghost Theater," which resides here. It's a miniature tableau of a ghost whose head vanishes from his shoulders and reappears in a hatbox, while thunder rumbles and music from the Haunted Mansion ride plays. Guillermo has long been a fan of dioramas. As a child, he built a sprawling scene in his walk-in closet from *Planet of the Apes*, with sixty-five figures, AstroTurf, and an illuminated moon.

"That was, in many ways, my first Bleak House," recalls Guillermo. "I art directed that room within an inch of its life. Back then I had drawers full of Plasticine props and 'makeup effects' for the action figures: prosthetic wounds or gouged eyes; set dressings; monsters; horses; and a slew of Russ Berrie jigglers (my favorite toys growing up). I mended, patched, and repaired everything as needed. I still do! I keep my 'hospital' at Bleak House busy, repainting, gluing, or patching anything that breaks in the house. I am pretty good at restoring toys, statuettes, and books in equal measure." The dark corners of this room are havens for all sorts of eerie things, but some Guillermo found in unlikely places. For instance, he stumbled upon a macabre illustration of death on a horse, subtitled *Sooner or Later*, in a Hallmark store.

Presiding over the Haunted Mansion Room is a mask of Algernon Blackwood, one of Guillermo's favorite horror writers. Nearby, the collected Oz books by L. Frank Baum and *Arabian Nights* mingle with a sign from the Troll Market used in *Hellboy II*, along with miscellaneous limbs from Guillermo's films. "This is the hand made for the Prince in *Hellboy II*, for a close-up with the mechanical egg," he says. "That's the leg from *Cronos,* where he pulls the glass out of the foot."

(OPPOSITE, TOP) Wall sculpture by T. Gore. (OPPOSITE, BOTTOM) An example of one of the many displays at Bleak House, this one in the Haunted Mansion Room and home to the original sculpt of Santi from *The Devil's Backbone*. (RIGHT) The golden grenade housing the bean that gives rise to the elemental in *Hellboy II*.

Look closely and you can find more personal, less ghoulish talismans, such as Guillermo's first studio drive-on pass. "This is from my first meeting at a studio for a job—Universal. That would be 1992, '93."

Though most items from Guillermo's films are judiciously placed and "not prominent," he says, there is one artifact that is given pride of place in the Haunted Mansion Room: the original design for Santi from *The Devil's Backbone*. Says Guillermo: "It was important to me for him to be here."

THE RAIN ROOM

The Rain Room is the house's heart, for it holds Guillermo's heart. It is where he comes most often to write, on the big comfy sofa or at the corner desk. Beside the desk is a list of "things I have pending, things that I need to write," Guillermo says. "I fill it up, and then I sit down and start hammering them out. It's really ideal working this way. I usually write in the dark. It helps a lot."

As he enters the tenebrous space, Guillermo flicks a switch. Thunder rumbles and rain from a projector cascades outside a perennially night-lit window. The illusion is perfect and sets the stage for what lies within.

"This is also my library of occult references," Guillermo explains. Included are volumes of the landmark set *Man, Myth, and Magic*. "When I was a kid, it was very important."

As inspiring as the books are, it's difficult to tear one's attention away from the lifelike sculptures that inhabit the room. Most dramatic of all is the astonishing re-creation of one of the greatest on-set photos ever: of Boris Karloff, bare to the waist in a makeup chair, his head fully detailed as Frankenstein's monster, daintily sipping a cup of tea.

In the Rain Room, this surreal moment has come to life: a life-size silicone statue of Karloff takes his tea break, the black lipstick from his makeup staining the cup as he drinks. "I love the detail of the cup and the lips," notes Guillermo.

Attending Karloff is a sculpture of the genius makeup artist Jack Pierce, designer of Frankenstein's monster, his Bride, the Wolf Man, the Mummy, and the silver-eyed, blue-skinned replicants from *Creation of the Humanoids.*

A replica of the doll from *Night Gallery*, sculpted by Thomas Kuebler, also graces this chamber. "The scariest moment of my life is that doll," recalls Guillermo. "When she appeared on the screen, I literally—physically, biologically—peed my pants. I started screaming and lost control of my bladder." Joining it are a cane and helmet from *Bram Stoker's Dracula,* a cover painting from *Famous Monsters of Filmland,* and stunning illustrations from Bernie Wrightson's *Frankenstein.* All are originals.

A custom-made box holds stereoscopic photographs of the maquettes from the as-yet-unmade *At the Mountains of Madness,* a memento of eight months of intense artistic development and preproduction planning. The original sculptures are too large for the Rain Room. "I'd need a whole Lovecraft room—which I'll build if we make the movie," says Guillermo.

The Rain Room also displays the original Good Samaritan gun from *Hellboy* and Big Baby from *Hellboy II,* along with Kroenen's mask and Professor Broom's rosary.

Not every memento and artwork on the walls recalls the occult. "That's by a painter from my hometown," Guillermo explains, indicating a serene painting. "That's exactly how the light falls in the afternoon in the area where I had my office. So it brings great memories from home."

And why a room with a storm that goes on forever? "It makes me happy," Guillermo says. "That's all I know. I just love the sound."

(TOP) The Rain Room features a sculpture of Boris Karloff being made up by Jack Pierce (*left*) and a window that generates the effect of perpetual rain at the flick of a switch (*right*).

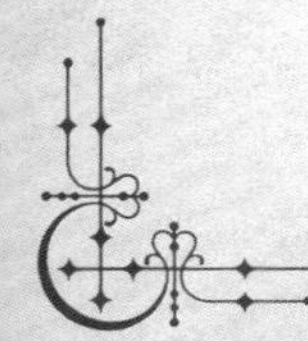

CASA DEL TORO

JOHN LANDIS

FORREST J ACKERMAN, the creator and editor of *Famous Monsters of Filmland* magazine, lived in a big house in the Hollywood Hills known as the "Ackermansion." There he worked surrounded by his huge collection of books, cinema posters, stills, and movie props. Visiting Forry's house was a pilgrimage made by thousands of fans over the years, including a certain young Mexican whose visit clearly made a deep impression.

My friend Guillermo del Toro's passion and enthusiasm for fantasy, horror, and science fiction burns as brightly now as it did when he was a child in Guadalajara. And like the five-year-old Guillermo, who read *Famous Monsters of Filmland* and made models of monsters to decorate his room, the adult Guillermo continues to create and collect images of the fantastic.

Guillermo now lives with his beautiful wife and daughters in a very nice home in a lovely neighborhood in Southern California. Just a couple of blocks away is another respectable suburban house in which his very large and constantly expanding collection of strange and wonderful objects—books, paintings, drawings, toys, movie props, sculptures, intricate clockwork dolls, and wax figures—dwells. A plaque on the front door reads "Bleak House."

From the exterior of Bleak House, the only hint of what is inside would be the full-scale working replica of the satanic automobile from the insane 1977 Universal picture *The Car*, which is parked in the driveway. And there is that life-size bronze of the great Ray Harryhausen standing by the swimming pool in the backyard.

Guillermo's own notebooks, which he has meticulously kept for many years, reveal the complex del Toro thought process and aesthetic. Drawings, diagrams, and ideas recorded in da Vinci–like detail. And like his notebooks, his collection is in constant evolution. There are works by famous painters, production designers, illustrators, prop makers, and makeup artists; one-of-a-kind statues of every size; mass-market action figures; and garage kits. Every classic monster is represented, plus denizens from Guillermo's own films and many creatures that only exist within the walls of Bleak House.

There is an entire room to honor the Haunted Mansion attraction at Disneyland. It is filled with Haunted Mansion memorabilia and, like the original, is rigged so that it is always a dark and stormy night outside its windows. A dark and stormy night complete with lightning, thunder, and rain!

Guillermo was an early patron of the extraordinary sculptor Mike Hill, who created the amazingly lifelike, full-scale tableau of Boris Karloff sipping tea while being transformed into the Frankenstein monster by makeup maestro Jack Pierce. Hill's work is disturbingly realistic, as is the work of Thomas Kuebler, whose sculpture of the midget Hans from Todd Browning's *Freaks* lurks at the end of a long hallway. Kuebler posed this exact duplicate of actor Harry Earles so that he is holding an open straight razor. Trust me, this is not something you want to stumble on unawares.

Guillermo's fascination with the work and career of men like H. P. Lovecraft, Walt Disney, and Ray Harryhausen is profound, and his collection is a riot of both high and low culture. He has taken the inspiration of Forry's Ackermansion and created Bleak House, his own private kingdom filled with items both sacred and profane. That Mexican kid has grown up into an author, artist, and world-class filmmaker. Forry would be proud.

(LEFT) Del Toro's early drawing of Hellboy's crib from Notebook 3, Page 10B.

THE ART ROOM

As everywhere, the Art Room contains items both expected and unexpected. True to its name, this is where Guillermo keeps books on art and photography; one cabinet also holds biographies. Guillermo ticks off the accretions gathered from auction catalogues and galleries around the world, then he points to a sculpture and explains, "This is a Victorian casting of an old lady's skull made in bronze. These are masonic lenses, to read their secret documents."

(ABOVE) Big Baby has its own chair in the Rain Room. (TOP, RIGHT) The Art Room is watched over by Thomas Kuebler's sculpture of Johnny Eck from *Freaks*.

A few items from Guillermo's own work are sprinkled into the room's arrangement. "This is the Abe Sapien box in *Hellboy*," he notes, "and that's a mask for *Hellboy II* that was never used in the movie." Nearby rest the seed that hatches the elemental in *Hellboy II* and a maquette of an albino penguin for the as-yet-unmade *At the Mountains of Madness*.

Throughout the house, these juxtapositions and arrangements provide tangible evidence of the dance in Guillermo's life between his inspirations and formative experiences and what he himself creates. These influences span from childhood to the present day. "This is the original art by Richard Corben for a poster I had on my wall as a kid," Guillermo points out. "I really loved it, and I hoped to one day own the original art."

The guardian of the Art Room is Thomas Kuebler's hyper-realistic sculpture of Johnny Eck from Tod Browning's *Freaks*. Though in its totality the house seems filled with spirits and presence, Guillermo says this was literally true for one particular object: "This cabinet came with a ghost. It was here for a while. So my mother cleansed the house, and now it's gone."

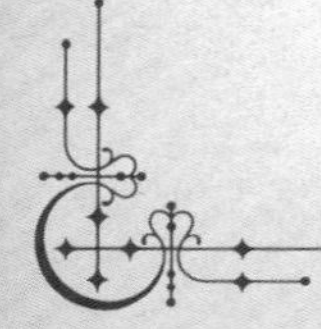

THE STEAMPUNK ROOM

Adjacent to the Art Room is what Guillermo calls the Steampunk Room. Here, he gestures to another familiar figure from *Freaks*: "That's Koo Koo the Bird Girl." Nearby is Hans, the homicidal dwarf, from the same movie, both sculpted by Thomas Kuebler.

The Steampunk Room contains a supernatural bestiary: Along with a figure of Lovecraft's Cthulhu and a morlock from George Pal's *The Time Machine* is a superb figure of Oliver Reed as the Werewolf, from the Hammer Films production. "My favorite werewolf in history," Guillermo notes. "Roy Ashton's design is almost like a cubist painter's. It has that square head. There's something ridiculously beautiful about it. And savage—Oliver Reed is an animal."

Here, too, are Hellboy's original coat and Rasputin's robe from *Hellboy*, plus art by Mike Mignola for *Pan's Labyrinth*. Prints by the brilliant French artist Moebius grace the wall and more art books line the shelves. "At the bottom," notes Guillermo, "are all the symbolists," and perhaps most important of all, "the encyclopedia of art I read as a kid."

Two more of Guillermo's heroes have strong presences here—James Whale and Ray Harryhausen. "This is an original drawing by James Whale," Guillermo comments. "And that's a brush from his paint kit."

A sweep of his hand takes in model kits, a skull clock from the 1700s, Japanese *netsukes*, representations of the Gill-Man from *Creature from the Black Lagoon*, and finally an odd little container—a vial of blood from Steve Brudniak, an artist who sells his own blood as art. "We all do," Guillermo notes.

(ABOVE) The Steampunk Room, presided over by a sculpture of Oliver Reed's Werewolf from Hammer Films' *The Curse of the Werewolf*.

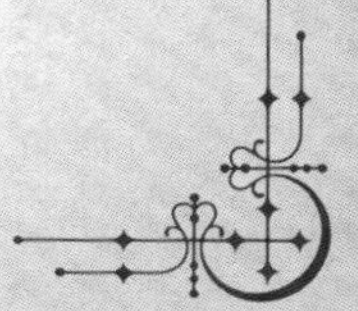

THE STUDIO

Guillermo renovated Bleak House's garage to serve as his art studio, where a quote from Albert Einstein sets the tone: "Imagination is more important than knowledge."

The Studio is the most utilitarian of all the rooms in Bleak House. It's where Guillermo invites concept artists to work together on his projects. "Normally it's empty," Guillermo notes. "But when I bring people in for preproduction, it can accommodate up to eight artists without any problem."

On display in this room are some of Guillermo's many awards—"The Hugos, the Nebula, Mexican Oscars, . . ."—along with mementos from fellow filmmakers. Of one, he remarks, "This is a letter from Miyazaki, thanking me for a book I sent him."

However, most of the inspirational items in the Studio are meant to be directly related to the work at hand: storyboards and concept art from Guillermo's films, which line the walls in greater quantity here than in the rest of the house. There is art from *Cronos, Devil's Backbone, Mimic, Hellboy, Hellboy II,* and more. An illustration from *Pan's Labyrinth* bears the inscription "In our choices lies our fate." Maquettes and props are scattered about, along with terrific presentation boards from the unmade *At the Mountains of Madness.* Indicating a figure, Guillermo comments, "That's one of the guards from *Hellboy II* with a crushable head, so you can see the dented portions. Mr. Wink grabs it and crushes it. So we had a wire inside. You pull that, and the head crushes in."

The framed insignia from Guillermo's company, Mirada, is prominently featured: "We wanted to make it sort of a baroque little piece that has death, rebirth, imagination represented by imaginary animals, octopuses—which we all like—and dragons. The owl is the gaze and the wisdom to look at things a different way. The company name, *Mirada*, means 'the gaze.'"

THE STAIRCASE

At the far end of the Foyer, a winding staircase leads to the second floor. Upstairs are the Screening Room and the Comic Book Library. As we reach the landing, Guillermo points to an image and says, "This is the first concept drawing of Hellboy we ever did." Next to it are illustrations by classic fantasy illustrator Hannes Bok, an original cel from the landmark 1914 Winsor McCay cartoon *Gertie the Dinosaur,* and a Ron Cobb design for *Aliens*, which was given to Guillermo by James Cameron. Continuing the *Alien* theme is artwork by H. R. Giger.

As in other areas, standing guard is a Thomas Kuebler sculpture from *Freaks*. This one is a life-size figure of Schlitzie. "This is my favorite, probably, because it usually puts me in a very good mood," notes Guillermo. "I need to be very grumpy for it not to work."

Two other notable items are originals of the posters Drew Struzan did for *Hellboy* and *Pan's Labyrinth*, which were released only as limited editions. "The studios didn't want to use them," explains Guillermo. "I think Drew is a genius. Such a shame the marketing departments have their own ideas."

(TOP, LEFT) The logo for Mirada, del Toro's production company. (TOP, RIGHT) Sculptures of skulls and human expressions, meant to aid artists working in Bleak House's Studio. (OPPOSITE) The staircase leading up to the second floor of Bleak House.

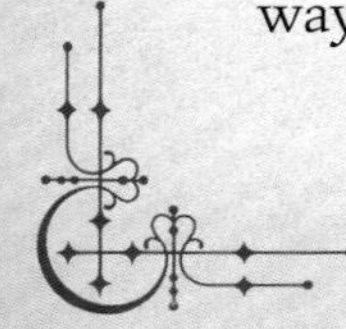

THE SCREENING ROOM

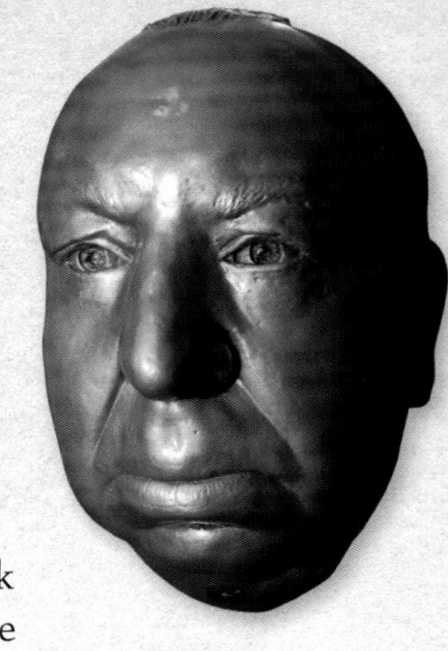

Indeed, the primary function of the Screening Room is to watch films, but it is also a shrine to Guillermo's favorite filmmakers—a place where he can come to study and be inspired by their work. In particular, Hitchcock and Disney, Guillermo's eternal favorites, vie for wall space: "Everything on the wall is original art from *Fantasia, Sleeping Beauty, Alice in Wonderland, The Adventures of Ichabod and Mr. Toad*. . . ."

The books in this room are predominantly biographies and retrospectives of four directors Guillermo holds in the highest esteem—Stanley Kubrick, David Lean, Alfred Hitchcock, and Luis Buñuel. "I also have some texts on Kurosawa," he elaborates. "What I try to do is, before I watch a movie, I read a little bit about it."

Guillermo owns film prints of only two movies—*Cronos* and Brian De Palma's *Phantom of the Paradise*—which are housed in their film cans beside a vintage Chinese desk.

An original Virgil Finlay illustration from *Weird Tales* hangs on the wall alongside Mike Mignola's first drawing of Abe Sapien for *Hellboy*. The concept maquette of Mr. Wink from *Hellboy II* sits side by side with a figurine of the Gill-Man from *Creature from the Black Lagoon*. "Second-greatest monster ever made," Guillermo proclaims.

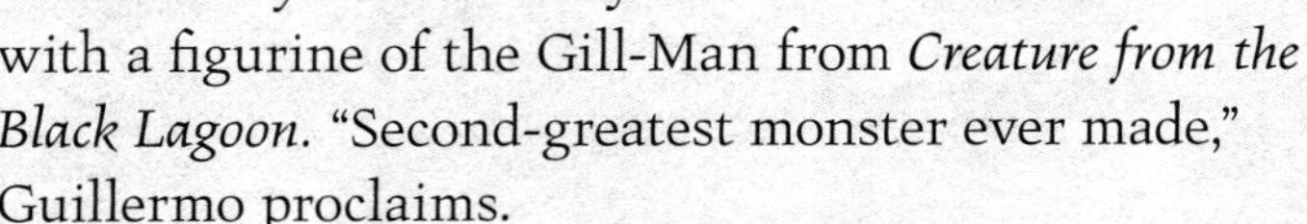

Nearby, incongruently, is a figure of Jesus. "It's a Jesus that was in my house when I was a kid," Guillermo explains. "It's a pretty gory Jesus. Pretty brutal, but his face is so serene. This explains a lot."

THE COMIC BOOK LIBRARY

Though he has a library dedicated to them, Guillermo admits, "Every closet in the house has comics." He's read all of them, but he tends not to buy publications of recent vintage: "I only buy the new collected editions of *Dick Tracy*, the *Spirit*, or *Little Lulu*."

Covering the walls are more originals by Mignola, Corben, Wayne Barlowe, Mike Kaluta, and Gahan Wilson. "The final pages of Alan Moore's *From Hell* are over there," gestures Guillermo. Then he notes, "This is one of the last drawings Charles Doyle did." Doyle was a popular illustrator who went mad and was sent to a mental institution, where he continued to draw until his death in 1893.

Atop a drawing table rests a strange, furry creature. "It's a toy from when I was kid," Guillermo exults. "It's an action figure of an insect warrior. I started collecting vinyl art long before people were into it. This is a real toy. It's not a postmodern reflection. Somebody said, 'This would make a great toy.'"

THE BACKYARD

The backyard shared by the two wings of Bleak House is surprisingly sunny and pleasant, and Guillermo admits he doesn't work here. "I don't like the outside. But I like sitting here in the shade, just enjoying the silence."

In truth, Guillermo wishes he had gnarled trees like those his neighbors down the block have planted. A bit of Victorian topiary would lend a more somber mood to Bleak House's yard and complement the rest of the decor.

But that's a dream to be realized another day. For now, the backyard is a serene place where Guillermo can contemplate his next projects in the company of a life-size bronze sculpture of Ray Harryhausen, one of his creative patron saints.

One final question remains: Was this exactly the house he wanted when he was a kid?

"Yes," Guillermo affirms, "if I ever finish. . . ."

(OPPOSITE, TOP) A bronze mask of Alfred Hitchcock hangs in the Screening Room (OPPOSITE, BOTTOM). (ABOVE) A Japanese toy stands guard over mementos from his past in the Comic Book Library. The photo is of del Toro at age nine, pretending to suck blood out of his sister, Susana.

J·R·

GRAPHIC INSPIRATIONS

(OPPOSITE) Julio Ruelas's *The Critics* (1906), a print of which hangs in the entryway at Bleak House. (BELOW LEFT) A sketch of Odilon Redon's feathered eye motif in one of del Toro's early notebooks. (ABOVE) *The Winged Man* (1880), by Redon, a classic symbolist image that has inspired del Toro.

MSZ: Your work involves such a melding of influences. Is there a specific fine artist that you might say is your favorite?

GDT: Well, the guy I connect with most viscerally is Francisco Goya because I just find him incredibly powerful.

But I love the symbolists and I love some of the surrealists. Of the symbolists, I love Marcel Schwob, Félicien Rops, Odilon Redon. I was very influenced by Rops. And I love Mexican symbolist artists. I have two original drawings at Bleak House by an artist named Julio Ruelas. He did one of my favorite engravings. I have it right in the entrance. It's called *The Critics*, and it is a self-portrait where Ruelas has a parasite with a long beak and a top hat on his head.

Ruelas was really incredible. He was influenced by Arnold Böcklin, who is another favorite of mine, but he was also influenced by Félicien Rops. Ruelas is very lewd, but he's also very sensual and sort of a necrophiliac. He is a very strange guy. One of his drawings that influenced everything I do is called *Profane Pieta*, and it's a crucifixion with the virgin at the foot of the cross. It looks like a really great religious illustration. You can show it to your grandmother, and she'll go, "Oh, what a beautiful religious painting."

But then, if you observe carefully, Christ has an erection—the shadow of death has taken him over—and the virgin has one breast out and a snake is suckling or biting her. I learned from this painting that you can make things with one apparent surface meaning and have them work as a symbolist piece that is completely counter, depending on the way you organize the symbols. I was fascinated by that drawing. I discovered it when I was sixteen or seventeen, and it had a big impact on me.

After that, I started to really get into the methodology of how to read a painting, and I started to appreciate the little symbols that medieval and Renaissance portraits would use, the symbology in Gothic cathedrals. And then I got into alchemy. My mind has always been guided by curiosity.

MSZ: With respect to the symbolists, you really can see resonances from those guys, such as Redon and Rops, in a lot of the visual elements that you explore.

GDT: Yeah, Redon and his feathered eyes. Fantastic. Proto-symbolist, actually.

MSZ: He's an interesting bridge between the symbolists and the Pre-Raphaelites just in terms of his style.

GDT: I'm also fascinated by the lives of the Pre-Raphaelites and their ideas. They certainly are very interesting characters that start with the same spirit and, as you read about their lives, they get co-opted by the society that they set out to overturn. It's a very interesting artistic moment.

MSZ: Why, then, do the symbolists have more power than the Pre-Raphaelites for you?

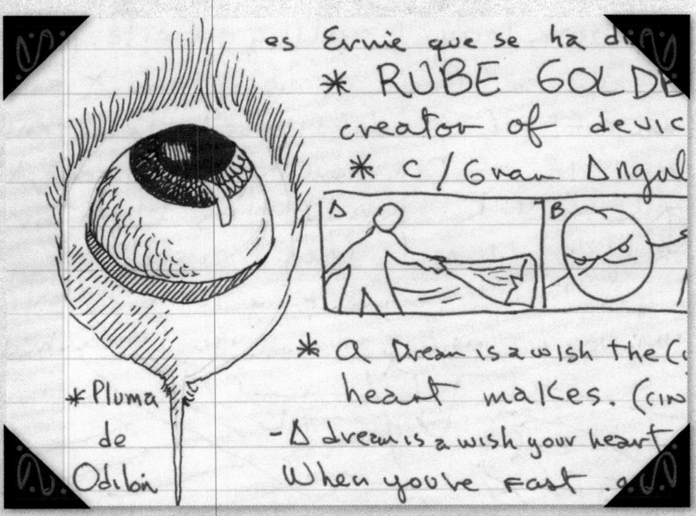

GDT: To me, the Pre-Raphaelites are more surface driven. More superficial. Vanity and aesthetics eventually overpower their spirituality and otherworldly power. The symbolists, on the other hand, tried to organize stuff, like medieval painters did—where they would organize every detail in a painting to tell a story. Like a portrait of a young woman—she would be holding a peach, which would represent the ephemeral nature of beauty. Because the peach rots very fast. Then, by the same token, there would be flowers. And there would be a skull. They would organize things so you would read the painting. But the symbolists take all that much further. And they start bringing in elements of subterranean eroticism, buried, unconscious desires. In some ways, they prefigure Dada and Surrealism in that they tap into concepts and ideas and spirituality but are driven by impulse!

MSZ: I see them as an arrow right into your work because your work puts beauty and sensitivity right alongside grotesquerie and death. You don't sugarcoat stuff.

GDT: That's what surprises me a lot when I read reviews of my work. I read one criticism on *Pan's Labyrinth* in which somebody said, "Well, it's a very simple dichotomy. Fantasy is beautiful, real life is hard." And I thought, *What movie did they watch?* The fantasy in *Pan's Labyrinth*, except for the ending, is super grimy. The fairies are these little imps that are dirty, naked, and kind of evil looking. The Faun is incredibly ambivalent, even menacing. I cannot think of the frog as a pleasant piece of fantasy. Or, much less so, the Pale Man. And having to feed the mandrake with blood, and the fetal implications of the mandrake? I mean, I tried to make the fantasy as gritty as reality because that's what it's supposed to be.

When you seek beauty only within a world of perfection, you end up with illustrations of fairies dressed in pink tutus, sprinkling dust, with cherubic babies and a flower garden. And then the images really, in my mind, don't have any weight, any gravity. But when you have seen something horrible and you choose to create something beautiful, the work comes out with a hefty weight, and I think that's why I like Rops, who was undoubtedly a guy who was tragic and fascinated by war, tragedy, destruction, and sex. He creates something beautiful out of that.

MSZ: The feeling with Rops is that he really indulged in a lot of vices.

GDT: Such was the life of the bohemians and the life of the symbolists. They would explore pleasure no matter what the consequences. After a certain moment in the history of art, the artist and the work become indivisible. For example, you can see the essence of Van Gogh in his paintings.

(ABOVE LEFT) An illustration for *Mephisto's Bridge*, one of del Toro's unrealized projects (*see page 254*), done in the style of a medieval illustration. (ABOVE) The Faun (Doug Jones) in *Pan's Labyrinth* is intentionally both inviting and menacing. (OPPOSITE) Prince Nuada (Luke Goss) provides one of the best examples of del Toro's fascination with pale, translucent skin, a feature he admires in the work of Édouard Manet and in medieval painting.

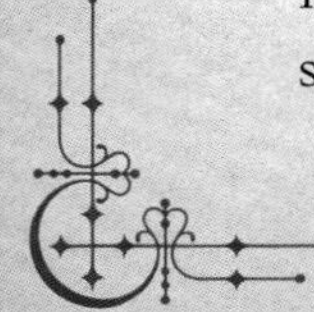

MSZ: That goes for Goya, too, at least in his later work. The interesting thing about him is his duality—he did these beautiful court images, the portraits, and then he finds his real power in all the grotesquerie.

GDT: With Goya, you really have a compulsion. He is literally chronicling the compulsions within him, the darkest phase of his life. The engravings and the "black" paintings are such a contrast to the luminous paintings, the court paintings, and all the parties in the garden. I don't like the colors in those in the same way that I'm not attracted to Renoir because I find him too colorful. I'm attracted to pale—for example, Édouard Manet. I'm very much attracted to pale palettes or dark palettes.

MSZ: You've talked before about how on *Blade II* you were influenced by Caravaggio and chiaroscuro.

GDT: I wish. [laughs] I was trying for a very deep saturation of colors and dense blacks and I discussed Caravaggio with Gabriel Beristain, the cinematographer on *Blade II*, because he had shot Derek Jarman's *Caravaggio*. So we talked about chiaroscuro quite a bit. He said, "A lot of people think that chiaroscuro is just about creating one source of light, and the rest is darkness. But it really is incredibly thoughtful and very, very regimented and a very calculated, painterly approach." In the same way, nothing is casual in Vermeer. A lot of people think, *Vermeer is going to be a big window with soft light streaming in and certain textures, silk, and plaster walls.* But, really, all those guys codified their paintings and approached painting and light very carefully.

Too, there is a narrative quality to the art. There was a moment when art made it very clear, as we approached the modern concept of art, that there was a refutation of the narrative in art, and this function was given over to mere "illustration." Some people I admire, like Edward Hopper, are constantly demeaned as "just a great illustrator."

MSZ: When discussing *Blade II*, you've also referenced Andrew Wyeth's *Christina's World*. I don't know if you know the story, but she is actually a crippled girl, and the only way she can get around is by crawling. So while a lot of people see *Christina's World* as a very idyllic image, there's actually a grotesquerie to it.

GDT: *Christina's World* can never be confused with a mere illustration. What I always say is that illustration is a piece of art that doesn't tell you a story. It needs the text to complete it. It's incomplete art. *Christina's World*, though, is a world unto itself.

I try to do the same in film. I always say that 50 percent of storytelling is "eye protein," which is very different than eye candy. They look the same to the untrained eye, but they are fundamentally different. A master of eye protein, especially in his early films, is Ridley Scott. Half of why *Blade Runner* is important is not in the screenplay or the story.

MSZ: A moment ago you were talking about how the artists you tend to gravitate toward have somewhat muted palettes. But *Blade Runner* and your films have very bright palettes. Yours in particular are supersaturated, making them almost like comic books.

GDT: It's true. The films I'm the proudest of are the *Hellboys*, *Pan's*, *Devil's Backbone*, and *Pacific Rim*. I think they are absolutely beautiful to look at. I try to work with very contrasted palettes in the movies and in the design of the monsters, and sometimes it works really well.

I base a lot of my color composition on a primary clash between blue or cyan and gold or amber. This over a thick layer of blacks and then the rest of the colors come in an absolutely punctilious, obsessive manner. I am particularly careful with red. I use it only in calculated ways. Even on *Hellboy*.

But if you look at *Devil's Backbone*, the film is saturated, but it is divided into almost monochromatic episodes. And *Cronos* is very controlled. *Pan's Labyrinth*, too, has a really controlled palette, although it is saturated.

I'm attracted to and influenced by some things that I don't do. For example, I was always fascinated by a translucency of the skin. Many, many artists, going back to the Middle Ages, depict a translucency of the skin. There is a fascination with pale skin in European art that, for me, is really attractive. And there's a moment where it becomes almost iridescent. There's a hue of green, an almost fishlike quality in certain paintings that has had a huge influence on me. But I don't know if that's come through in the movies. I've tried.

MSZ: We've just covered quite a lot of Western art history. Your parents had art books in your home when you were a kid, and you were able to look at the entire history of art, right? It's very interesting. You were really studying a lot of different styles and soaking up a lot of different influences at the same time.

GDT: Yeah. And at the same time, I was reading comic books by Bernie Wrightson, Jack Kirby, and John Romita Sr.

MSZ: In contrast with some of the fine artists you gravitated toward, those guys were dealing with extremely vivid colors, extremely vivid expressions. With respect to Bernie Wrightson, was it *Swamp Thing*?

GDT: Yeah, I never bought many superhero comics. I used to buy *House of Secrets*, *House of Mystery*.

So I have a very strange mix of art, movies, books, and magazines. I don't like compartmentalizing. The mind is flexible. If you are rigid and you say, "I am a scientist," or, even worse, "I am a nuclear scientist, and that's my only area of interest," it's a tragedy. Or "I'm a serious literate. I'm a serious writer. I'm a serious filmmaker. I do only drama." Obviously, you can find an amazing range in drama, but by not being rigid you really discover things and end up enjoying yourself.

As an artist, I think that you have to be as free as a kid: In the morning you can be an astronaut; in the afternoon an Indian or a cowboy; and at nightfall an Antarctic explorer. And you play, enjoy, and grow. Inevitably as you play, you grow.

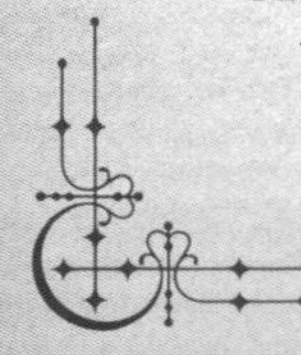

MSZ: Let's talk, then, about how you started drawing—how you started synthesizing all these influences and finding a voice that was your own.

GDT: Well, I started drawing very young because I was illustrating my horror stories. But the three creatures I drew obsessively were the Gill-Man from *Creature from the Black Lagoon*, the Frankenstein monster, and Lon Chaney's Phantom of the Opera. But obsessively—when I was eating ice cream, or on a bicycle. . . .

I remember there was a panel by Jack Kirby, from the period when he was doing Etrigan the Demon for DC. It was a story about Farley Fairfax, who was an actor who got his face taken by a demon, and Kirby quoted from *Phantom of the Opera*. The original art, which I always wanted to buy, is in the hands of Mike Mignola, and he constantly tortures me with that fact. But that panel of Farley Fairfax—his mouth open, his eyes, and the tongue—and he's saying, either in that panel or shortly thereafter, he says, "He took my face! He took my face!" Oh, I drew that panel like a Lichtenstein. I mean, I drew it small, I drew it big.

MSZ: How old were you when you started drawing?

GDT: As far back as I can remember.

MSZ: And was it always in color?

GDT: No, no. I did all the doodles, and all the little balls and sticks and all that stuff, in black and white. But color was very important because I'm very attracted to color, instinctively.

MSZ: So when you first started working with color, was it with crayons or markers?

GDT: I've always hated crayons because I hate the texture. What I did with crayons was eat them, like every kid. I loved the taste of crayons when I was a kid. But I always drew with colored pencils. I find them very soft. Now, if I had the time, I would do alcohol markers all the time because that's such a gentle medium.

MSZ: And where did you get your color sense from? It's very strong.

GDT: I think it's expressive. The colors of youth are gold, blue, and white. Those are the colors of hope and untainted promise. Then, to me, cyan is always a very subterranean color. And death is black, revenge is red, and tarnished gold or blue for memories. But it varies from picture to picture. They all dictate their own palette.

I taught myself to mix colors because I started painting models when I was a very young kid. So I was assembling models, all these monsters.

Part of me dreams of what would have been if I had become an illustrator. There is a saying, "Those who can't draw, render." And I can't draw. I really am a self-taught guy, so my drawings are very deficient, and the way you mask a deficiency in a drawing is by overrendering, so what you see in the notebooks are not very good drawings.

MSZ: You're really skilled, though. Did you ever take classes as a kid?

GDT: Well, the ones at school. But I was always drawing the wrong things, so I never got good grades on that, because they always found the subjects objectionable. For example, they would say, "Choose a moment in the life of this president and make it in clay." And I would do the president when he was shot in the head, with blood on the table.

When some people saw my drawings and my paintings, they told my mother, "You've got to take this kid to a psychologist." And she took me to a psychologist, and the guy gave me some clay and he said, "Do whatever you want." And I did a skeleton. And then I asked the psychologist, "What does 'bastard' mean?" That didn't help my case.

But I was truly—I mean, I knew stuff when I was a kid that I just don't know how I knew. There are proclivities in my life that I just don't try to understand.

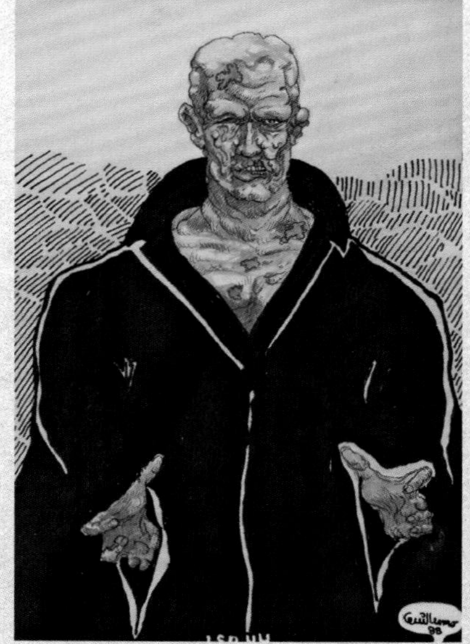

(OPPOSITE) The illuminated book from *Hellboy II*.
(ABOVE) Drawings by del Toro from his early twenties.

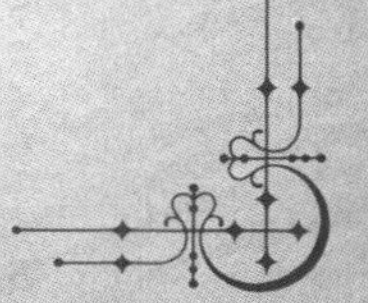

GUILLERMO'S
MUSINGS ON SYMBOLIST ART

I HAVE ALWAYS BEEN partial to the symbolist and Pre-Raphaelite artists, because they go against the avant-garde. To them, the past was a source of awe and mystery. But unlike the Pre-Raphaelites, the symbolists also cast their gaze inward to find the root of the stain on the human soul: lust, violence, corruption. They connect our human impulses—good and bad—with the mystical, mythical, and supernatural elements that represent them in art (for example, satyrs, skulls, centaurs, demons) and in that they are, in my opinion, truly modern and timeless.

There are a few key words to understand the symbolist movement: paganism, mysticism, Romanticism, and decadence. Not all artists in the movement share these in equal measure. Félicien Rops fits decadence perfectly, Carlos Schwabe embodies paganism quite well, Redon tended toward mysticism, and Arnold Böcklin ascribed, without a doubt, to Romanticism.

I first became aware of the symbolist movement through a Mexican artist who was not exactly a contemporary of Rops, but rather a spiritual twin: Julio Ruelas (1870–1907), a multitalented artist obsessed with two of the symbolists' staple themes: sex and death. In the late 1970s, while walking through a flea market in Puebla, Mexico, an art book with a startling cover caught my eye: a forensically detailed oil painting of a drowned satyr being pulled out of a river. Its body was purplish and bloated and its tongue hung loosely to the side. The book was Teresa del Conde's monograph on Ruelas, which to this day is the best, if not the only, authoritative source of Ruelas lore.

Although he is not formally considered part of the school, Ruelas is a bona fide symbolist and his work seems heavily influenced by Rops, to the point that they share some shockingly similar vignettes and tend to gravitate toward a consistent array of imagery and themes: blind faith, Circe, satyrs, Socrates.

(ABOVE) *The Supreme Vice* (1883) by Félicien Rops.

(OPPOSITE, TOP) *Isle of the Dead* (1880) by Arnold Böcklin.

FÉLICIEN ROPS (1833–1898)

I was first exposed to Rops when in Cannes promoting *Cronos* in 1993. A young French critic urged me to seek him out so, while staying in a crappy hotel in Paris, I bought a book or two on Rops and was blown away by his sensibility.

The similarities between Rops and Ruelas made it all click for me. The nineteenth century was a period of enormous moral contrast. Nobility, honor, and good manners, all of which were supported by the "academic" art of the age, started to be sabotaged by a wild and perverse notion: that life was full of pagan pleasures and savage impulses. Our flesh made us weaker, yes, but it also made us human.

Sex for these artists is a savage, almost demonic, task. And none of them is more accurate in portraying the hopelessness of male desire than Rops. In his paintings are abundant, detailed, and deformed genitalia that stand side by side with images of death, evil, and decay. Like his century, Rops was a prisoner of dread and desire.

It is a fact that sex and politics go hand in hand, and Rops was also blessed with a sharp satirical eye that yielded some of the best political cartoons of the time—all of them mordant portrayals of the changing social climate. Incessantly drawing, etching, and painting, Rops strived to capture a "tainted" century where the entitlements of royalty and the excuses of nobility were about to be supplanted by more mundane rights and ambitions.

Savage and sensuous as his themes may be, Rops's line work is supremely elegant—even exquisite. His use of drypoint is testament to the precision of his draftsmanship.

ARNOLD BÖCKLIN (1827–1901)

Böcklin's treatment of light has always fascinated me. The way he captures the soft, dying sunlight and uses it to cast deep, ominous shadows in his forests and rocky outcrops is exquisite. The jewel-like

quality that his overcast skies confer to the green ocean waves is mesmerizing.

Böcklin's superb technique makes his creatures and landscapes seem absolutely real. Hooves, roots, glazed eyes, and fur all appear to be accurate depictions of actual, living things. Look at any of his beasts and you will see that their eyes are wild and stunned by instinct, their bodies sensual but animalistic, their mouths agape and lubricated. They all have the strength and savagery that I associate with Arthur Machen, Algernon Blackwood, and—in the case of Böcklin's sea creatures—with H. P. Lovecraft.

If Rops excelled at portraying the human form, then Böcklin is the single most gifted landscape artist of the symbolist movement and the best at creating a sense of atmosphere. Böcklin's landscapes are characters themselves—full of dramatic gloom, trees, rocks, and seas that reek of antiquity. In his most famous painting, *Isle of the Dead* (1880), for example, the darkness in his woods lurks like a sentient creature, and the majestic vertical rocks and cypresses form a perfect mausoleum. It's no wonder his painting was "paraphrased" by another Swiss artist almost a century later: H. R. Giger.

To me, Böcklin is perfect proof that art does not reproduce the world; it creates a new one.

ODILON REDON (1840–1916)

Most art movements are comprised of such a variety of artists and techniques that it becomes difficult to define the borders that separate one from the next, or the qualities that fuse them into a movement in the first place. If you think of Schwabe, Böcklin, or most of the other painters associated with the symbolist movement, you'll evoke a sense of realism. By way of contrast, Redon's diffuse pastels and line work seem weightless and luminous—sometimes almost abstract. Both his technique and concerns remain unique amongst his peers. He is the sublime anomaly.

Even so, Redon was part of a more general movement amongst painters working at the end of the nineteenth century to turn away from technical realism and to begin to value the strength of a brushstroke, the immediacy of an emotion. But these new values were typically developed with respect to the outside world, whereas only Redon looks to the inside.

Distinctive motifs in Redon's work are: the feather, the eye, prisons and bars, botanical shapes, feathery line work reminiscent of animal fur, and spidery forms with human faces—every one of these comes straight from the id and a sense of pagan frenzy. If one needs any persuasion to find a strong connection between the Surrealists, the Dadaists, and the symbolists, one doesn't need to look any further than Redon. Most of his images go beyond the pagan contemplation of Böcklin or Schwabe and become iconic, striving to capture not only the essence of a symbol but its direct link to the human psyche. Jungian and Freudian images populate his work and remain elusive, slippery, and hellish, but then his color work has a nimble, vital energy that captures mystic rapture and the true light of paradise.

After I die, if there is life beyond this one and I go anywhere—either up or down—I am pretty sure that both places will be art directed by Redon.

CARLOS SCHWABE (1866–1926)

The two artists who inspired me most while working on *Pan's Labyrinth* and *Hellboy II: The Golden Army* were Schwabe and Arthur Rackham. Their interpretations of the fairy world are not at all similar, but both men seem to approach it as explorers attempting to document a world only revealed to their eyes.

Schwabe did splendid graphic work based on texts by Zola, Mallarmé, and Baudelaire, but his drawings, etchings, and paintings should not be regarded as mere illustrations for these works. Each one of them is suffused with a mystical energy and with pantheistic conviction.

In this day and age, we confuse hip smartness that does not fully endorse any idea with intelligence, and consider callousness the product of an experienced point of view of the world. Naturally, this attitude leads us to value artists who seem to know it all. But Schwabe and the rest of the symbolists were the exact opposite: They celebrated not knowing, the twilight of our knowledge. To them, the supernatural was absolutely real, and mystery was the supreme goal of art.

(ABOVE) According to del Toro, one of the great mysteries of cinema is its ability to reverse time, a technique he employs at the beginning of *Pan's Labyrinth*, depicted here in storyboards by Raúl Monge. (OPPOSITE) Del Toro on the set of *Hellboy II* with Hellboy's gun, The Good Samaritan.

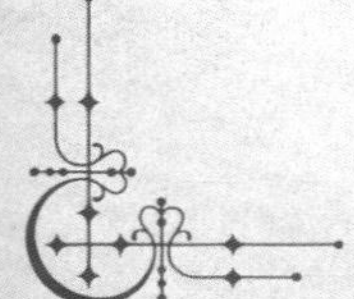

ANALYZING FILM

MSZ: One very distinctive quality about your film work is that it's enormously tactile, textural, lyrical. There's a sense that every moment, every image, is handmade, as if you're sculpting every shot. Viewers can revisit your films over and over again.

GDT: Well, if they want to. I do put a lot in the audiovisual coding of a movie. Some is rational, but then another 50 percent is instinctive—the way you arrange things. I think a director is an arranger. *Alien* is the perfect example. It's an absolutely mind-boggling feat of filmmaking. People can say, "Oh, well, it's Giger." No, it's not Giger because Giger was a painter before Ridley Scott called him up to sculpt and design.

And lest we forget, Scott grouped him with Moebius [Jean Giraud], Ron Cobb, Chris Foss, and Roger Christian. Each of those men brought a syntax, but Scott created the context. I think that's what directing is—saying, "I'm going to use this photographer, and I'm going to use this musician." It's a fantastic feat. Directing is the orchestration and the arrangement of images and sounds and also of people and talents.

MSZ: When you see films that come out well, behind them is a process in which ideas have become better and better, whereas with bad films it's the exact opposite—they just get worse and worse, progressively.

GDT: Well, but you never know. You never know. You have no idea. If we knew what our destiny is, we would be great. Everybody would be great. What I do think is that there is a myth—the myth of the director as this inflexible creature that has it all figured out from the get-go, as if they are a mechanical master who arranges everything perfectly.

Some people can point to Stanley Kubrick, and I'll tell you this: The more I read about him and the more I talk to people who worked with him, it's only mostly true. He had 80 percent of it figured out. But the 20 percent that he didn't have figured out, he found—through the same process that every director uses, which is finding perfection in compromise. Because you compromise with the weather, you compromise with the schedule, you compromise with the budget, you compromise with the fact that an actor is sick. You're figuring it out. You are reorganizing. You don't necessarily say, "I cannot take this out because the movie will be compromised." At some point you might have to, but not always.

I remember very clearly an anecdote about Kirk Douglas having an accident during one of Kubrick's movies. I think it was *Paths of Glory,* but it could have been *Spartacus*. The anecdote I read was that he was out of commission for over a week, and he got a letter from Kubrick, or a phone call, and Kubrick said, "Could you claim that you're still not able to work so I can get a few more days? Because I'm just figuring the movie out."

Or take James Cameron, who is arguably one of the most precise filmmakers in the world and the smartest, most disciplined artist I have ever met. The myth is that he is an inhumanly precise filmmaking machine. But the beauty of Jim is that he is all too human. I've seen him toil and sweat and, in the middle of the night, ask himself, "What do I do here? What do I do there?" That's the beauty and power of it: Jim is human but he demands more of himself than anyone else.

Why enthrone the myth of the perfect, infallible superhuman if it's always more beautiful to know that the humanity that creates beauty is the same fallible species that can create horror or misery? Bach, when explaining his genius, used to modestly say that he just worked harder and that all you have to do is press the pedals on the keyboard and the notes play themselves. Here you have one of the greatest geniuses ever and yet this was a guy that had personal flaws of one kind or another and who created in the face of self-doubt and adversity.

I always say it's more interesting to think that the pyramids were built not by aliens but by people. People go, "Oh, they're extraordinary things. They were built by aliens." No, the extraordinary thing is that they were built by people. Normal people.

When people say that cinema is life, I say, "Impossible." Any cinema that strives to be realistic, in my opinion, is

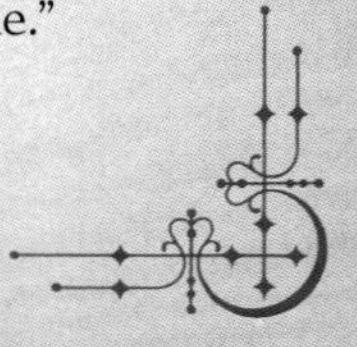

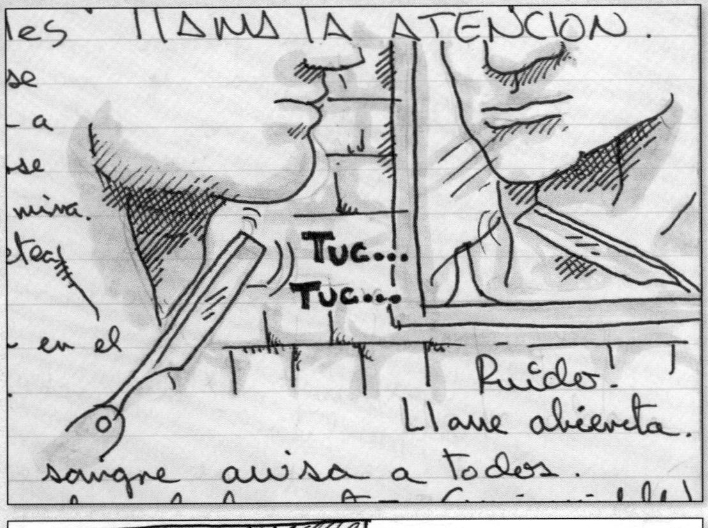

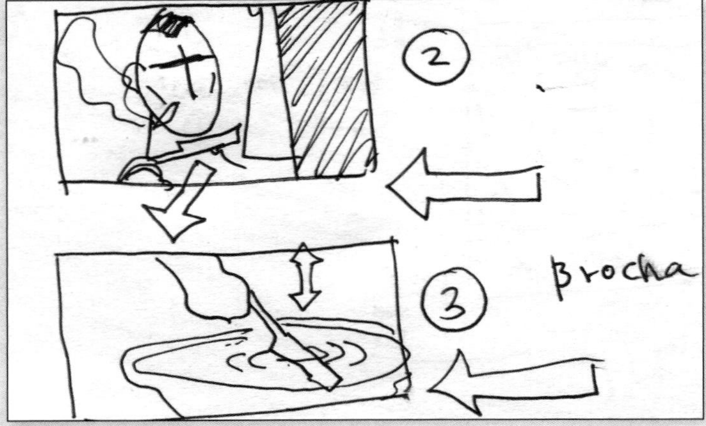

For del Toro, the notebooks are a place where he can record and develop ideas to use in his filmmaking endeavors. Frequently, they change over time. Here, an image of a man shaving with a straight razor first drafted for the unmade *Meat Market* (TOP, *and see page 253*) was realized in different ways in both *Pan's Labyrinth* (ABOVE) and *Hellboy II* (ABOVE RIGHT).

going to be confused with a theater play. But any cinema that attempts to be truthful is not afraid of assuming that it is not life. It's an impossible endeavor.

Like René Magritte used to say, "The vocation of art is mystery." That's why one of the quintessential beauties of cinema is the spilled cup coming back to the hand by running film in reverse. I don't care how many years go by, that's pure magic. Why? Why is it so great?

MSZ: Because it's impossible.

GDT: Because it's impossible. In the same way, what the eye of the camera can see is so much more powerful than what the human eye can see. Think about this: We have such a fascination with slow motion. It's primal. It doesn't matter—it never goes out of style if you use it right. There are programs on the Discovery Channel that are dedicated to making you drool at a balloon being perforated by a bullet. Because you're trying to stop time; you are trying to stop life.

I think cinema resonates with a piece of our brain that is way, way in the back. Because the way you watch a movie is not the way we watch life. When you go to a mall, yes, you're absorbing, subliminally, *Drink Coke*, and *Buy this*, and *Buy that*. But cinema is different because when you go to a theater, it's like you are going to church. You sit in a pew, and you look at an altar, and the reception is completely different.

MSZ: You often present screenings of movies and give talks on the nature of film. Does participating in these events help nurture you as an artist?

GDT: Oh, yes. If you dedicate yourself only to the business of film, your soul dies. I have come to the tragic conclusion that you have to be a mediocre businessman in order to be a good artist. I'd rather not make as much money and be at peace with my decisions and be free and not dependent on a big apparatus.

I think it's really important to do things that make you no money, that give you no apparent benefit except they renew your little love affair with cinema. Seeing those movies with an audience is great. I mean, I introduced one of the movies I produced at the LA Film Festival, and I said, "This is as close as it gets to me taking you out for cookies and milk like Andy Kaufman."

MSZ: What about producing? I've noticed you've taken a lot of young filmmakers under your wing. What do you look for?

GDT: When I look at short films, and I look at a lot of them, I don't bother with the originality. Originality is one virtue that, without context, means nothing to me. Originality in context is valuable, but I think that, when you're learning to write, you always follow an example. Like learning to write cursive. All the short films by kids, or young adults, whatever, I think they are like cursive. They need to imitate somebody.

Alfonso Cuarón and I, until we were in our twenties, every time we shot a piece of fiction, we would say, "I'm going to try this." Like, I remember we were doing a TV series, and I had seen Scorcese's *Life Lessons* with Nick Nolte [in the film *New York Stories*]. And it's not that I had any rhyme or reason, but I said, "I'm going do a sequence with those chain dissolves he does so beautifully. I want to learn them!" That became the sole reason why I did that TV episode.

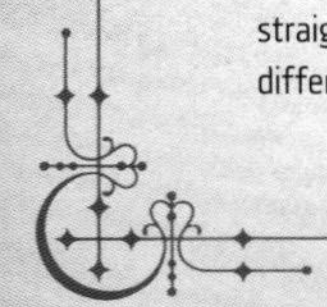

GUILLERMO AND ME

ALFONSO CUARÓN

IN THE LATE EIGHTIES, I had just directed my first gig for a television show called *La Hora Marcada,* a Mexican anthology series of horror stories modeled on *The Twilight Zone.*

I was waiting in the production office to have a meeting with the producer. I had just finished making a very loose adaptation of a Stephen King short story. Everybody had praised it, and I felt proud. I had painstakingly storyboarded it, and even though I was aware of its shortcomings, I felt it was better than the norm.

Across the waiting room there was this guy sitting on a sofa looking at me with a mix of curiosity and mischief. I immediately knew who he was, since I had heard so much about him. He was the special effects makeup artist from Guadalajara who had studied with Dick Smith; he had worked on designing corpses, mutilated hands, and bullet wounds for a couple of people I knew working in film. He loved his work and was always ready to lend a hand to a production in need. Everybody described him as smart, funny, and very, very strange.

Now he was smiling at me from across the waiting room.

"You're Alfonso, right?"

"Yeah . . . ? You're Guillermo?"

"Yup. You directed that episode based on the Stephen King short story."

"Yeah, you know it?"

"It's a great story."

And so we went on to praise King and embarked on one of the first of many lengthy conversations we were to have about literature, film, and art. We became excited—it was immediately clear that we shared the same eclectic taste, that we spoke the same language. Suddenly, out of the blue, he asked: "If the Stephen King story is so great, why did your episode suck so much?"

There was no malice in his statement, just an honest opinion. I burst out laughing. When I could finally speak again, I asked, "Why do you think that?" And he went on to explain, in a very eloquent and well-informed way, what he thought was wrong with my show. And he was right.

That was the beginning of a beautiful friendship, one which has provided insights into my work and life that have become invaluable.

Guillermo went on to direct episodes for the same TV show, and he did the prosthetics for my episodes. We were certain that we were doing amazing stuff. One day he discussed an idea he had for an episode. It was the story of a little girl living with her abusive alcoholic father and the child-eating ogre that was haunting her. He said that he wanted to design the ogre and that he would be too busy working on the prosthetics to direct, so he asked me to do so instead. I agreed, and Guillermo cast himself as the ogre, enduring his own prosthetics. We were very self-congratulatory about the end result, which everybody else also praised. We thought we'd achieved greatness.

Several years ago, Guillermo re-watched the episodes we directed for *La Hora Marcada* and later told me over dinner, in words that can't be printed, how awful they all were—both his and mine. Once again, I'm sure he was right.

At that same dinner, he went on to tell me about an idea he'd had for his next film. It was a story very similar to the one he'd told me about many years before, with a little girl and a child-eating ogre. He went on to make that film, which he called *Pan's Labyrinth.*

(ABOVE) A drawing in the Blue Notebook, Page 141, of Sagrario—the Count's friend from *The Left Hand of Darkness*, del Toro's adaptation of *The Count of Monte Cristo* (*see page 258*).

I think that when people ask me about the notebooks and why I use them, it's because they are a record of those sorts of ideas. You can see where it started, but then it bounces to another idea, and then a third one comes up, and page by page you see an evolution.

MSZ: I came upon a note in the notebooks where you talk about the way you have to work with an actor to remove aspects of their initial performance in order to get it right. Comparatively, when you have an abundance of ideas, I imagine deciding which ones not to use is just as important as committing to some of them.

GDT: What you subtract is very important, as is what you leave in. For example, the mistake most people make when designing a monster is they literally put in everything they can think of that is scary. It's like Homer Simpson designing a car in that *Simpsons* episode. "I want a giant cup holder, and I want a bubble where I can see 360!" And the car that comes out is horrible because it has everything he wants.

With an actor, it's the same thing. You let the actor act first; you don't give him much direction. I like the first or second take to be his. And you observe. A director is not dictating, he is observing. I think the best job you can do at directing can be achieved in ten words or less. You have to give the actor something to do—or something to not do—that's very specific. "Don't do that," or "Do this." That's great direction.

But you always have to ask, "Why?" Always try to think about the opposite of your instinct. In between, you'll find the direction for everything. Color, light, monsters, acting. The first instinct, and then the complete opposite instinct, and then you decide, "I'll go with this."

MSZ: At what point does one develop the courage to speak with one's own voice?

GDT: Well, I think you need to be blind, a little bit. I mean, I think you need to be willfully ignorant.

For example, I had the opportunity to direct many times before *Cronos*. They would offer me—because they knew I shot TV—little exploitation movies to do, in the horror genre and all that. Alfonso Cuarón and I always had each other to persuade the other not to do that. Alfonso used to say, "Don't do that. Wait. Do your own thing." And vice versa, because Alfonso was a very famous first AD [assistant director] in Mexico and a very good director of TV. They offered him a lot of crap, and we were very good friends with an exploitation producer who was adored in Mexico.

I think it's important that, when you make your choices, you always make them by instinct at the end of the day, and that you fuck up sometimes. I recently made a mistake, but I've got to go with it. Whatever happens, that's my decision, you know?

MSZ: You don't always succeed, but the goal is to find your truth.

GDT: That's right; you don't always succeed. But very often you find people that guide you. You've got to recognize that they are wiser in certain ways than you. They become teachers, or partners, or whatever. There are very smart people that are fiercely alone, and I admire them. But I don't want to be them.

MSZ: There is also that interesting tension between a filmmaker and his or her audience where, to a certain extent, you have to give them what they want, but to really be an artist, you have to go beyond that in service of your vision.

GDT: I believe very much in screening for friends, really harsh friends, or screening for an audience but not asking them anything. Because you see how they react, you see what they like, you see what they don't like. But I don't believe in asking about their opinions afterward. You don't have that relationship with any other art. You don't say to Robert Louis Stevenson, "I don't like Dr. Jekyll dying at the end. I think you should kill Hyde and go into the sunset with the girl." I think it's a very corrupt exercise.

But I also think that critics are a genuine part of the art. As long as there has been art, there have been critics in some form or another. What I think is not genuine is to make the creation of art an open process.

MSZ: There's a great line you wrote in the notebooks: "A critic is a man of whom you ask guidance, who instead offers you an opinion."

GDT: In the process of creation, the one thing you've got to remember always is that if you ask for an opinion, no matter from whom, you'll get one. So you've got to be very careful to be inclusive, but not to be so inclusive that you start listening to seventy-five versions of the same story. There's always a different way of telling a story.

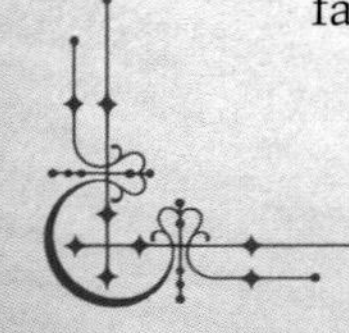

(ABOVE) Del Toro with his life-size sculpture of Sammael from *Hellboy* at Bleak House. For del Toro, the secret to designing a good movie monster is knowing what to leave out.

So, as a storyteller, one thing you want to say is, "I'm locking into this track until I'm proven wrong." Or, "Life is a labyrinth and death is the only way out: the solution." A labyrinth is a transit. You turn, and turn, and turn, and turn, but you will reach the center. In a maze, you get lost. A labyrinth is an instrument of meditation, and it is supposed to be a spiritual journey.

MSZ: And then you also write, "Criticism gives one the illusion of participating in the act of creation by way of an autopsy. The act is there and it exists and moves and challenges you while criticism fights to approve and validate."

GDT: I feel that way. I was a critic for many years in Mexico and Guadalajara. Amateur, but I was on TV and radio. I think that the only times I felt really useful were when I was helping people understand a work of art.

It's very easy to feel oneself smarter than the work you're analyzing, as if that made you better than the work. But the moments where you're really, really helping are so much more rewarding. The way we were raised in film school, they said, "A critic needs to show you where the work is, what the work's intentions are, how the work fails to deliver on those intentions; to put it in context." It's not an opinion; it's a construction. And when you read, really, the pillars of criticism, you see real analysis.

I mean, I think some critics are very happy to be critics. And blogs should, in theory, give people the freedom to review only stuff they like or that they want to talk about. So, ideally, today critics could claim a smaller stake and say, "We want to talk only about movies we feel passionate about, one way or the other, and take the time to analyze them."

84

* Un monstruo que mata como c/un toro cuernas.
* S/M Al manifestar poderes usar un efecto c/de túnel d'viento MERCEDES.
* We shut ourselves down, we face the best & the worst alone, how to react? Our needs are emotional not social.
Con los griegos era lo inverso.
Los Griegos veían la pasión como algo peligroso.
Agamenón regresa a Argos (de Troya) sacrificó a su hija y por ello Cligmenestra lo matará
"In every FAMILY there is a struggle"
Need to liberate — Need to belong. (to identify)
Drama Griego: "No era personal o artístico, Era ético, religioso.
La Tragedia muestra las condiciones para la catástrofe.
Sistemas de pensamiento en choque: la materia prima de la tragedia.
No importan los actores — MASCARAS.
Se propicia la respuesta RACIONAL al drama.
Sólo una sociedad sólida tolera la tragedia.
Esto no solo como género sino como acontecimiento. Con los Griegos el estado no garantizaba la ciudadanía sino la condición de ser humano.
No importa el SHOCK sino la consecuencia.

* *A monster that kills with a bull's horn.*

* *S/M when they manifest their powers, use effect with wind tunnel MERCEDES.*

* We shut ourselves down, we face the best & the worst alone, how to react? Our needs are emotional not social. *The Greeks were the opposite. The Greeks thought passion to be a dangerous thing.*

Agamemnon returns to Argos (from Troy)

he sacrificed his daughter

Clytemnestra will kill him because of it

"In every FAMILY there is a struggle."

Need to liberate—Need to belong. (to identify)

Greek drama: "It wasn't personal or artistic, it was ethical, religious."

Tragedy shows the conditions necessary for catastrophe.

Clash of differing systems of thought: the raw material of tragedy.

The actors didn't matter—MASKS.

It provides the rational response to drama.

Tragedy is tolerated only by a cohesive society.

This not just as a genre but as an event. With the Greeks, the state didn't guarantee citizenship but rather one's status as a human being.

SHOCK *doesn't matter, only its consequences.*

STORYTELLING

MSZ: Let's talk about your screenwriting teacher.

GDT: Two teachers were important for my love of cinema: Daniel Varela in high school, who was my film teacher and a dear friend—a very visual and sophisticated guy. And Jaime Humberto Hermosillo, who was a very literary, script-minded director. In America he became famous for a really brilliant gay comedy called *Doña Herlinda and Her Son*, which I produced for five thousand dollars. It starred my mother, which led to some very interesting and fun speculation in my homeland.

The decision to cast my mother came from Jaime Humberto when he saw my short films and said, "Your mother is a pretty good actress." He also saw what I was doing with my short films for very little money, and he said, "Would you like to be the line producer?" So one of my best friends and I were the producers, and they gave us five thousand dollars. I didn't know anything about anything. I had never seen that much money at once. I was twenty-something, nineteen, I don't remember.

I said to the producer, the guy who gave out the money, "What if I give you change?" And he said, "Well, if you give me change, I'll give you a bonus of five hundred dollars." So, in order to give him change, I ended up driving the grip truck and the electric truck on my own, back and forth, between Mexico City and Guadalajara, and then taking the bus back. I was like a thousand dollars under. So the guy gave me five hundred dollars, which I immediately put into my next short film.

MSZ: That's great. Your screenwriting teacher, from what you say in some of your audio commentaries, sounds like he was really smart and didn't say, "Well, you have to hit plot point one," and all that nonsense.

GDT: Right. Let me make a good point about why people who say things like that are full of it. I won't name any names, but I have read their books, so I'm not talking blindly. Some of them, they take a published screenplay and they say, "As you can see, character so-and-so does this, and plot point one, etc." And then you realize, they are actually talking about the movie, the finished movie. They are not talking about the actual document that is the screenplay. With 90 percent of the movies that are made, 20 percent of the stuff that was written ends up on the cutting-room floor. Twenty-five percent of what was shot ends up living in a different place than it was written. And that is why, I always say, analyzing the movie is not analyzing the screenplay.

But that is now institutionalized. People talk about these things like they're talking about Aristotelian theory, and even the Aristotelian core is valid only in Western storytelling. Eastern storytelling jettisons most of that stuff.

Jaime Humberto was a really good teacher. He encouraged us to read James, Chekhov, Tolstoy—not just "biz" books on screenplay writing. Some of his rules were very simple. He used to say, "You can't write what the character can't describe with actions or looks." So when I open a screenplay and it reads something like, "Jack enters a room. You can see that he is a man to be reckoned with. He has the world on his shoulders, but he will take it by the throat and shake it until its end," I say, "This is a terrible screenplay writer because the only thing that the camera can do is show Jack coming in. That's it." Humberto used to say, "If you put an adjective on the page, a qualifier, you've got to prove to me how you're going to shoot it."

The second rule he gave us—and I think he misread something somewhere about how every draft of a movie is different colors—is the first draft of any screenplay had to be on pink paper. That was him going completely wrong with the color paper theory. But the reason he used to do it is because you cannot photocopy pink paper. And back then, if you wanted to distribute a screenplay, you had

(ABOVE) *The Book of Crossroads* prop from *Pan's Labyrinth*. (OPPOSITE) Reflections on the nature of ancient Greek drama in one of del Toro's early notebooks. Del Toro often writes in his notebooks using a mixture of Spanish and English. Translations of the Spanish-language text and transpositions of the English-language text have been rendered in the margins of the notebook pages reproduced throughout this book.

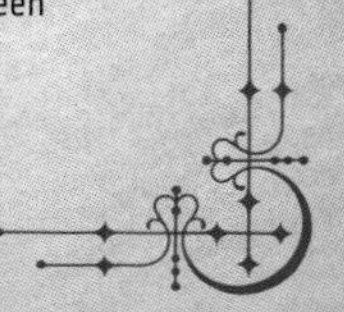

to photocopy. He used to say you never, ever, ever show anyone, or distribute, the first draft. He would say, "If you like it so much, you type it again on white paper, and then you distribute it. And if you are able to type it again and not change anything, that means it's really, really good."

Now, this was misguided and all, but it was really good discipline. He was a really tough guy. I always tell the story of how back then, you didn't have even word processors, and he made us typewrite everything by hand. So formatting became an act of discipline. Take *The Devil's Backbone*. Before I did *Cronos*, I wrote *Devil's Backbone* as a feature. It was a very different screenplay. He took the screenplay, which was pink, and he flipped through it. He flipped through it, and he threw it in the wastebasket, the original. He said, "It's badly formatted. If you cannot take the trouble to write it well, why should anyone take the trouble to read it well?" It was too Mr. Miyagi for me, so we kind of fell out of contact for several years after that. That's when I wrote *Cronos*. I said to myself, "I can retype *Devil's Backbone* by memory, or I can start over and do *Cronos*."

MSZ: You've mentioned that he used to say, "If a road is not presented, you build one."

GDT: Yes. He always said that. He would give you rules that you understood immediately. One of those things he used to say was, "Look, it's bullshit that a character needs to change through the movie. Sometimes the greatest character is the one that doesn't change." Like Candide, or Forrest Gump. Those are characters that, whatever they do, they stay the same. It's not like Forrest Gump becomes smarter in the end. Sure, there is a journey, there is a pilgrimage, but there is not necessarily what Hollywood understands as an arc.

Another thing that Humberto used to say was, "In writing for a film, there is the star of the film and the main character. And sometimes they are very different things." For example, the main character of *Fight Club* is Edward Norton's. But the star of *Fight Club* is Brad Pitt. Or take *The Shining*. Tom Cruise said to me that Kubrick told him he cast Shelley Duvall because he found her irritating, and he knew that the star of the film, the main character he was painting, was Jack. So all the big moments, they all go to Jack. Kubrick said, "The only way to make people understand him is to share some of his darkest emotions in spite of themselves." So if he made Jack's wife grating enough, the audience would enjoy him going insane because they dislike her. I find that misanthropically fascinating.

In my own films, in *Pan's Labyrinth* and *Mountains of Madness*, I identify with the assholes as much as I identify with the good characters. Why? Because we are all assholes, many times, during the day. You have to write them all from inside. Both of them have to contain things that you would be ashamed to discuss publicly, aspects of your own person that you can socialize only by fictionalizing them.

MSZ: In your work, one consistent theme that runs throughout is that your characters triumph if they hold true to themselves when put to the test. And often, they are silent victories.

GDT: That applies to all the things in life that are important. That's why I find it so hard to write dialogue. Dialogue is the most challenging thing for me. In Spanish or English, I don't care. The rhythm of it is easier for me in Spanish, obviously. But really good dialogue, which eludes me most of the time, has to be about something while being about nothing. I don't mean the ramblings that you find in brilliant pieces of work like Barry Levinson or Quentin Tarantino. But I mean really, truly, in the same way that body language tells you a lot about the person. It's very hard, but dialogue needs to communicate things, but not the things the characters are talking about.

If I had to, I would love to have lived in the time of silent film because I think it's the purest cinema. Chaplin said, when sound came, "Film has died." At some point he was very, very reproachful about it, and it was because, right at that moment, the black-and-white film was perfect. I mean, you

(ABOVE) As a screenwriter and director, del Toro is able to identify with all of his villains, even the menacing Vidal (Sergi López) in *Pan's Labyrinth*. (OPPOSITE) Jesús Gris (Federico Luppi) strikes a pose reminiscent of Lon Chaney's Phantom of the Opera. In many ways, *Cronos* is indebted to silent film.

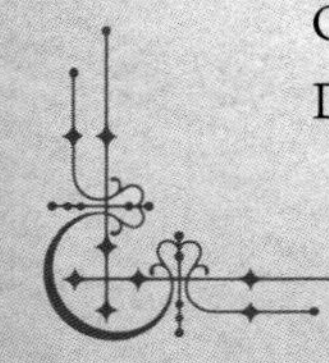

were getting really beautiful hues of gray, and the visual language of silent cinema was completely absorbed.

MSZ: *Cronos* is very much like a silent film.

GDT: It is. I like writing silent. I mean, I can come up with stuff I like, such as, "In the absence of light, darkness prevails." Or, "There are things that go bump in the night. We're the ones that bump back." Or things that I'm proud of, like in *Pan's Labyrinth* where the Faun says, "I've had so many names. Old names that only the wind and the trees can pronounce." But that's it. If I attempt to be naturalistic, I often fail. Most of the time I fail completely.

Some people develop their own style, like David Mamet, who has a rhythm and a style that is inimitable. I suspect—I may be wrong—that part of his writing style comes from the theater theories of Sanford Meisner, with their famous exercises in repetition, like where you go, "I'm okay." "Oh, you're okay?" "I'm okay." "You're okay." It's a rhythm that is meant to be about listening. I think that at some point maybe Mamet realized, if you really want the audience to listen to the dynamics, you have to hammer it three times. "I'm alone." "You're alone?" "I'm alone." "Alone?" "Yes, I am alone." "You are alone."

But it's funny because I always say a screenplay is almost like a partitur, but it's missing half of the musical notes and annotation. Ultimately, when the director fills those in, he's also directing the orchestra while completing the partitur.

I've always written my movies, but I have a real problem with writing them the way they should be written.

MSZ: In what way?

GDT: In the way that I read every screenwriting book growing up, but I couldn't help but disagree constantly. Because I would always think of how many times Truman Capote, or Ernest Hemingway, or Saki, or Isak Dinesen, or so many of the writers I admire don't follow or portray their characters through any of those devices. A lot of the stuff that we leave in as screenwriters—like the "rules of the game," the antagonist's plan, and finally, the character's arc—is contradicted by majestic works of fiction that contradict and question those rules.

This translates to difficulties down the line if you follow their examples. *Pan's Labyrinth,* for instance, was a difficult movie to finance. Nobody wanted to give us the money. I remember a meeting where some producers said, "Well, this is a very interesting movie. But we can't put money into it because we think it's not going to be appealing to a lot of people."

They gave me a few notes, and they said, "If the girl really loves books, we should see her reading more often." But you don't need that. I mean, I love books, but you never see me with a book on the street. I read them at night, or I read them in the morning. I didn't carry them around. I said, "The way I show the depth and the breadth of her imagination is when she makes up a story to the baby brother in her mother's belly." Because she's not reading the story, she's telling it. So that tells you how much she has read, but without doing it directly.

MSZ: Let's talk a little bit about your storytelling techniques. There is a great thing you once wrote: "The epic is a vital genre for humanity."

GDT: A lot of people think that in epics one character almost represents an entire race; the whole race is imbued in one character. Borges does that a lot. Borges talks a lot about a man who is "the" man that represents Argentina at a certain moment. In a strange sense, for me, *I Am Legend* is an epic because it really represents both the rise of a new civilization and the falling of another one, becoming a legend.

MSZ: It's the microcosm that speaks to the macrocosm.

GDT: Yes. But the interesting part of that book, for me, was the fact that Richard Matheson brings the urban into horror, revitalizing it. This is not Transylvania; this is not a castle. This is the streets of an American city. What was really incredible is that *I Am Legend* is a very metaphysical book, in the same way that his *The Shrinking Man* is a very metaphysical book. The fact that somebody we have empathy with is not the winner, historically, and therefore they become the monster, the loser, the legend: "If you're not good, the human will come for you at night." I mean, there is a whole society of vampires outside, which he manages to show us are the antagonists. But at the end of the book you realize, "Holy crap! We are the anomaly. We are the legend." That's fantastic! I don't think it's ever been done in the movie versions.

The ending of *The Shrinking Man* is almost like Albert Camus. The final notion in the book is that you abandon yourself to the cold embrace of the cosmos. It's really fantastic.

MSZ: In that regard, two interesting things about Matheson are that he has a very strong belief in an afterlife—a very strong belief in a larger reality than the prosaic one—and in many of his books he uses himself as the main character and his family is the family in the book. He'll often name the wife Ruth because his real wife's name is Ruth.

GDT: Well, everybody does that. I mean, everybody that writes. Anybody that doesn't do it, I don't understand

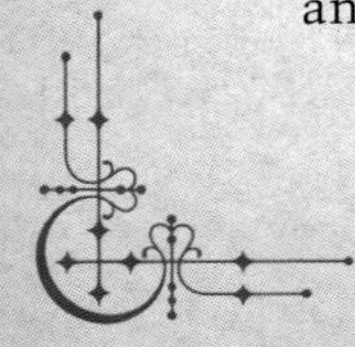

how they write. The same can be said of most everyone. Borges, certainly. And in a strange way—very, very twistedly—I think all the children in Dickens are sort of him in a shoe polish factory thinking, *I deserve better.* I think Mary Shelley is in *Frankenstein* big time, and so on and so forth. That is beautiful. Roald Dahl does it. H. P. Lovecraft more than anyone. And Stephen King.

King and Matheson are two writers I really love because they not only bring the urban and the suburban to horror, they bring in, brilliantly, family dynamics. This is interesting because horror, during the pulp years, was always about superlative characters: a professor, a reporter, an archaeologist. They were not regular people. Fritz Leiber does a little bit more urbane characters. But Matheson, starting with the family man in *The Shrinking Man*, is talking about the dynamics in a marriage, how they change. He becomes a child, a baby, and his desires are no longer acknowledged. He becomes a toy. The family dynamics in *I Am Legend* are gorgeous—how he loses everything, and how his best friend is every night outside of the house screaming his name. Matheson and King bring you people that go to the supermarket, fill their car with gas, take their children to school. And they put them in situations you can be absolutely scared shitless about.

MSZ: You mentioned Roald Dahl. He seems, in some ways, to be a spiritual relative of yours because, even in his writing for children, his work has enormous darkness.

GDT: Most of the great writers of children's literature have a very dark side. Some of them are very repressive. Carlo Collodi is very repressive, for example, but I still love him. I also think Oscar Wilde and Hans Christian Andersen deal with a lot of identity issues, and they are present in a very dark and fascinating way in the tales. Strangely enough, both have these almost psychosexual dramas in their stories. Like Andersen's "The Snow Queen." As a kid, I found it enormously sensual. I remember reading it and being vaguely disturbed and aroused as a kid. It really has a lot of strange images of snow, and it almost portrays death as an erotic goal, an experience. I mean, it's really, really weird.

But Dahl, Saki—they all have something in common, which is that they create really, really great children's tales that are really, really disturbing for parents. Parents often give children the Roald Dahl books thinking, *Oh, they're safe*. But they're full of great violence. I mean, *The BFG*? There's more descriptions of ways to consume a child, and brutality, than anywhere else. It's fantastic. And *The Witches*, where the witches sing something like, "Boil them, fry them, chop 'em."

The reality is that kids are not bothered by these things. So I was sad that *Pan's Labyrinth* didn't get a PG-13 [it is rated R]. I think it should have gotten a PG-13 because the violence in the movie is part of the tale. As disturbing as it is, it is part of the flavor. We couldn't get it. But, in my mind, *Pan's Labyrinth* is a movie done from me to young readers, so to speak.

(OPPOSITE & ABOVE) Concepts by Carlos Jimenez for the frescoes that array the Pale Man's lair in *Pan's Labyrinth*. The almost hyperbolic depiction of violence against children hearkens back to a tradition of children's storytelling that is not afraid of the dark side.

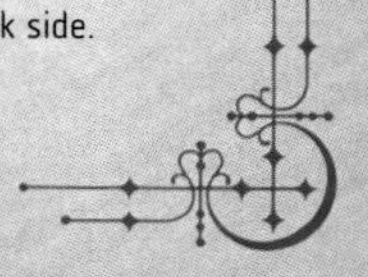

GUILLERMO'S
MAINSTAYS OF HORROR

TO LEARN WHAT WE FEAR is to learn who we are. Horror defines our boundaries and illuminates our souls. In that, it is no different or less controversial than humor, and no less intimate than sex. Our rejection or acceptance of a particular type of horror fiction can be as rarefied or kinky as any other phobia or fetish.

Horror is made of such base material—so easily rejected or dismissed—that it may be hard to accept my postulate that within the genre lies one of the last refuges of spirituality in this, our materialistic world.

But it is a fact that, through the ages, most storytellers have had to resort to the fantastic in order to elevate their discourse to the level of parable: Stevenson, Wilde, Victor Hugo, Henry James, Marcel Schwob, Kipling, Borges, and many others. Borges, in fact, defended the fantastic quite openly and acknowledged fable and parable as elemental forms of narrative that would always outlive the much younger forms, which are preoccupied with realism.

At a primal level, we crave parables, because they allow us to grasp the impossibly large concepts and to understand our universe without and within. These tales can "make flesh" what would otherwise be metaphor or allegory. More important, the horror tale becomes imprinted in us at an emotional level: Shiver by shiver, we gain insight.

But, at its root, the frisson is a crucial element of this form of storytelling—because all spiritual experience requires faith, and faith requires abandonment: the humility to fully surrender to a tide of truths and wills infinitely larger than ourselves.

It is in this abandonment that we are allowed to witness phenomena that go beyond our nature and that reveal the spiritual side of our existence.

We dislocate, for a moment, the rules of our universe, the laws that bind the rational and diminish the cosmos to our scale. And when the world becomes a vast, unruly place, a place where anything can happen, then—and only then—we allow for miracles and angels, no matter how dark they may be.

MARY SHELLEY (1797–1851)

Much like Matthew G. Lewis, who was only twenty years old when he wrote *The Monk*, Mary Shelley was painfully young—a teenager, in fact—when she first published *Frankenstein, or the Modern Prometheus*, and into the monster and his tale she was able to pour all her contradictions and her questions—her essential pleas and her feelings of disenfranchisement and inadequacy. The tale spoke about such profound, particular feelings that, irremediably, it became universal.

While reading the novel as a child, I was arrested by the epistolary form Shelley had chosen (and which Bram Stoker would use in *Dracula* to good effect many decades later), because it felt so immediate. I was overtaken by the Miltonian sense of abandonment, the absolute horror of a life without a reason. The tragedy of the tale was not dependent on evil. That's the supreme pain of the novel—tragedy requires no villain.

Frankenstein is the purest of parables—working both as a straight narrative and as a symbolic one. Shelley utilizes the Gothic model to tell a story not about the loss of a paradise but rather about the absence of one.

The novel is so articulate and vibrant that it often surprises those who approach it for the first time. No adaptation—and there are some masterful ones—has ever captured it whole.

Taking its rightful place among the essential characters in any narrative form, Frankenstein's creature goes beyond literature and joins Tarzan,

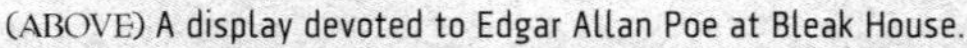

(ABOVE) A display devoted to Edgar Allan Poe at Bleak House.

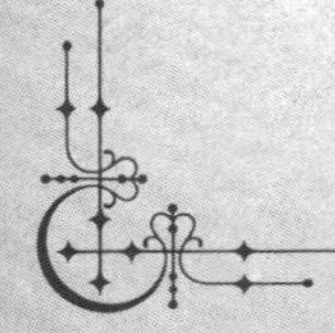

Sherlock Holmes, Pinocchio, and Monte Cristo in embodying a concept, even in the minds of those who have never read the actual book.

EDGAR ALLAN POE (1809–1849)

Clearly, the horror tale deals with the essential duality of mankind, a topic that has proved irresistible to philosophers, prophets, and saints. The Adamites, the Dulcinians, and other savage orders advocated salvation through Bosch-like excess and violence—and they all situated the root of all evil in the soul. It is not until Poe that the seat of evil is transferred back to its proper place: the human mind.

It is in Poe that we first find the sketches of modern horror while being able to enjoy the traditional trappings of the Gothic tale. He speaks of plagues and castles and ancient curses, but he is also morbidly attracted to the aberrant intellect, the mind of the outsider.

Poe grappled with the darker side of mankind, with the demons that reside within us: our mind, a crumbling edifice, sinking slowly in a swamp of decadence and madness. He knew that a rational, good-hearted man could, when ridden by demons, sink a knife in the eye of a beloved cat and gouge it out. He could strangle an old man or burn alive his enemies. He knew that those dark impulses can shape us, overtake us, make us snap—and yet, we would still be able to function, we would still presume to possess the power of rational thought.

ARTHUR MACHEN (1863–1947)

It is a rare breed of fabulist who transcribes and records—rather than invents—a reality invisible to most of us. These scribes, like St. John the Divine, are possessed of a near-religious certainty that such worlds exist. Arthur Machen was one of these.

Much like Algernon Blackwood, Machen had no doubts about ancient worlds beneath us and the power their inhabitants exert over our souls and, ultimately, our flesh. There are, he knew, barbarians at the gate, hiding somewhere in the darkness below.

Much like Borges, Machen was an acolyte of Robert Louis Stevenson, one of the most painstaking writers in the English language. And also like Borges, Machen seemed to believe that reading and writing are a form of prayer, each an extension of the other. But where the world was a library to Borges, to Machen it was an all-encompassing concrete geography, even as he was fascinated by traces of pre-Roman cults. Today, as then, his words are neither scholastic nor philosophical, but rather an alarm, a frantic denunciation.

Machen recorded his articles of faith with great zeal as an explorer in a lonely spiritual universe. He abandoned the safety of his humble quarters, the sanctity of his God-given name, and the veneer of metropolitan sophistication to achieve an ecstatic vision. Much like Lovecraft, he believed in the transitory nature of our agency in this world and the unyielding ferocity of the cosmos.

Machen knew that to accept our cosmic insignificance is to achieve a spiritual perspective and ultimately realize that, yes, all is permitted. And that no matter how wicked or how perverse we can be, somewhere in a long-forgotten realm a mad God awaits, leering—ready to embrace us all.

H. P. LOVECRAFT (1890–1937)

One hot summer afternoon (I must have been eleven or twelve years old), I stumbled upon the text of the Lovecraft story "The Outsider." I was riding in the family car, and the text was included in Spanish in an anthology for my older brother's lit class. I started to read, and almost an hour later, I was left behind in the car, still reading, oblivious to the inclement heat, mesmerized and moved by this story.

Starting that afternoon, and for the rest of my life, I have devoted more time to Lovecraft than virtually any other author in the genre. His mannered, convulsive prose, so antiquated and yet so full of new ideas, is very compelling to a young writer for the same reason Bradbury's is—it *seems* easy to forge. It is so clear, so full of evident quirks, that you long to imitate it, and it is then that you find out how full of secrets his prose can be.

Lovecraft's crown jewel is, in my opinion, "At the Mountains of Madness." Reading this tale in my mid-teens was a revelation. I had never been exposed to any literature that so dwarfed our existence and hinted at the cold indifference of the cosmos. I became entirely enamored. Making a film of it became my quest.

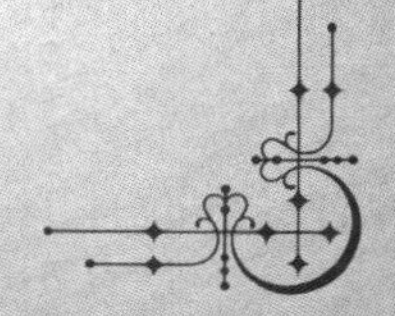

IDEA INCUBATORS

MSZ: These notebooks are very personal, of course. What prompted you to have this material published?

GDT: I started the notebooks a long time ago. More and more, people have heard about them and become curious about them. I started putting a few pages on some of the DVDs of my films because we were running out of extras. I think the first time we put the notebooks on a DVD was *Blade II*. People reacted very well. At one point I thought, there are a few personal moments in them, but they were moments that were public in some way because I seldom record stuff that is truly personal.

MSZ: I love when there are little personal asides. They give context to all the ideas that are in the notebooks.

GDT: One of the really, really great ones is on one of the first pages of the lost *Cronos* notebook. It says, "March 3, '93." That is the day when Bertha Navarro, my producer, spoke with Imcine, the Mexican film institute, and the guy in charge said, "*Cronos* is a horrible movie. It will go to no festivals, it will win no awards, nobody will ever want it, and it will be forgotten soon enough." And instead of getting angry or whatever, I just wrote it down and said, "This is an important day in case I can ever prove the guy wrong." And it was 3/3/93, and it's in that book. But unfortunately, the book got lost.

Losing things is part of the process, too. That's why, every time I talk publicly, I always say it's really important in our life to have talismans. Like my car. We call him the Handsome One. Every day, when I'm riding in it, I'll have a moment where I love my car. I go, "I love you." You imbue these things with power.

If you have a really great relationship with an object, if something happens to it, it's part of the story. Because you're collecting memories, or experiences, and that event becomes part of the tale.

MSZ: That raises a question I've had: Who are you writing these notebooks for?

GDT: For my daughters. When they are grown-ups and they have lives of their own, children of their own, or whatever, they can look at the guy that was their father when he was young. I want them to understand that being a grown-up is not being boring. It's being alive. I want them to know that grown-ups are people, too.

MSZ: Have they seen the notebooks? Have they had a chance to look at them?

GDT: You know, they look at them now and then, but they draw manga-style, so they find my drawings absolutely reprehensible and horrible. But it doesn't matter. I told them, "I want you to enjoy them if you can."

MSZ: There's a wonderful playfulness in the notebooks. For example, you write about the need to fill empty space. Is that something that you still do with your notebooks? Do you sometimes just try to fill up the page, to make a beautiful page?

GDT: I do. There are definitely moments when the writing becomes part of the design. I'm very glib about it. I'll write things like, "This means nothing. It's just to fill the space."

MSZ: Well, you write, "No doubt the need to fill all available space is Freudian and very serious."

GDT: Yeah, because I do it out of compulsion. Literally, I just say, "I need a line over here," and I don't want to wait for an idea to write the line, so I fill the space.

MSZ: Speaking about the composition of the notebook pages: Do you ever sketch something in advance in pencil?

(OPPOSITE) "Fear at the Foot of the Bed," an image that has haunted del Toro since his childhood, as it appears on Notebook 3, Page 28B. (ABOVE) The Handsome One, del Toro's car, which he regards as a kind of talisman. (FOLLOWING PAGES) A spread in del Toro's fourth notebook (Notebook 4, Pages 37A and 37B) mixes ideas for *Hellboy II* with a more playful drawing for a series of illustrations del Toro calls "Children with Problems." Frequently, del Toro skips from project to project in the notebooks, illustrating and writing about a variety of ideas that are at different stages in his creative process.

- Nuestra vida es siempre igual a nivel cósmico. presencia montaña, ausencia eterna. Porque al final de cuentas la nada es el mar y lo es todo y nos reclama a todos y a todo. Siempre.
La ausencia es la madre del amor.
- Vamos a ver si la WIKIPEDIA tiene la respuesta al cosmos o la soledad
- Y se acaban los días, y se acaban los años y la piel cede a la gravedad y que queda? Quedan galletas que no dejó nadie, que a nadie le importan pero que. únicamente forma así.
VERTICAL.
- La vida mirada de frente les una, de perfil es la muerte.
un saludo a Mantequilla.
- La muerte, de frente, es terrible, de perfil es la vida.
- La secuencia de ilusiones son distraccione momentáneas: fama, sabiduría, etc.
- El universo es líquido
- Mongolia, bicicletas abandonadas y cosas oxidadas. La terrible, inexista y eterna poesía del OXIDO.

-La lanza del Príncipe en / vertical como VENTILADOR

E P I L !

·Los ojos son las partes más ÍNTIMAS del cuerpo y los únicos órganos que no podemos cubrir ante el M.
-M.A. el Tigre más bello que el aire nunca vió.
Hoy sin garras, sin dientes, sin huesos, convertido en alfombra para ser pisada por una gorda rica e indiferente. pero no hay tragedia en la presa sino en el hecho de que no hubo cacería. La rendición voluntaria, la VOCACIÓN de alfombra, la atracción de la chimenea.

神户 -Did you know that every cell phone now has a camera. Every one of them. They're pretty good too. You imagine what that does to our budget?

a dame
and
you can
does to

-Agua Elevantal con
-En usar edificios scaffold para

cuando de la [illegible] la calle soldada. detrás con dom[illegible] muy teatro a la ext

sale el alcantarilla explosión del E. en los de un plástico

LUZ
como
MUSICAL
MIMIC

Red de luces. noche.
Lente gruesa de acrílico.

-Es muy importante que lo de adentro sea plano p/anular cabeza.

6.1416

Niño con Problemas III
happy. Full of life.

Johann

-Un fulano está haciendo la traducción a otro, se ve [illegible] y la saliva y la sangre que se agolpa en las sienes y luego el traductor dice las cosas más dulces: "He said it's O.K."

-El Fascismo es el culto a la figura del padre imposible y es por su esencia latentemente homosexual NO GENITAL pero anal/orden.

(ABOVE) Del Toro at work on his current notebook in the Comic Book Library at Bleak House.

GDT: I do. I sketch, write notes in pencil, and then, if I do a drawing, I try to organize the notes around it.

MSZ: So you're typically writing in pencil, and then you fill it in with ink as it becomes a finished page?

GDT: I draw faster than I write. Like, I might be five pages ahead of the writing with the drawing. So I write around the drawings, which means the images and text connect only tangentially.

Sometimes I'll even do a drawing just to try a new set of colors, which has become a lot easier. When I started the Blue Notebook after *Cronos*, for example, I had zero money, and I would draw with four Prismacolor pencils. If I wanted a purple, I needed to shade that purple by combining colors, and if I needed a certain hue of green, I would find a way to do it with the same four pencils. It was very time consuming, you see? But it actually made me appreciate and learn the value of each of the basic colors of the spectrum and now, when I do film color correction, I am fast and precise.

Then, if you look at the *Pan's Labyrinth* pages and some of the *Hellboy II* drawings, you'll see I used acrylic. It's a very heavy medium, and you need to put time aside for it, too.

I now have these alcohol markers, and they're very quick. They are my favorite medium. Not only can I do a drawing fast, but I can start a drawing, put it aside, and then come back to it.

MSZ: Has that change in medium affected how you approach the notebooks?

GDT: Yeah, because now, with the markers, I can do a drawing in thirty minutes, whereas before, with acrylic, I would need, like, an hour. I'm self-taught, so the way I figured out how to use acrylic was to start with the darker shade and then add highlights. But with markers, you start with the lightest shade, and then you start adding darker, and darker, and darker colors. At the end, if you need it, you can put a layer of highlights on. It's much faster.

MSZ: Besides experiments with color, how do you determine what you put in a notebook and what you don't?

GDT: Honestly, I don't think about it. If I've already given instructions to a sculptor, or I've already talked to the designer about a concept, I don't put it in the book because it's not a journal, really.

MSZ: What about the blood splotches and so forth, those elements that give the notebooks a sort of vintage quality?

GDT: What I was trying to do in the third notebook, in particular, was make it feel like a found object. I was doing these long, drawn letters, with long bottoms and flourishes. But it became very tiresome, and after a number of pages, I said, "Oh, screw this." But during that time, I found the right color for the blood, and I thought it looked good to have it, so that it started to look like a found grimoire.

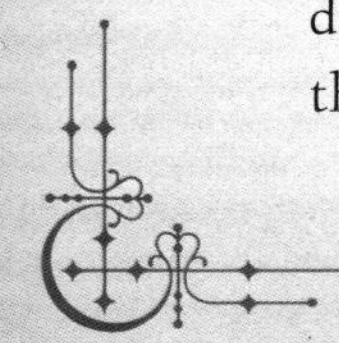

What is interesting is that I tried, most of the time, to do a little composition on each page. That's why the blood helps now and then, or a little Lovecraftian symbol here and there.

MSZ: So your composition is really localized to a single page.

GDT: Yeah. And I actually try to do a composition across facing pages a lot of the time, although I'm often working with multiple projects at once. I don't always succeed, but I try to make it coherent.

I like to say that we make only one movie in our lifetime—a movie made of all the images of all our movies. I believe this is true of Hitchcock, for instance. Hitchcock made a single, giant, symphonic movie. You can see Hitchcock trying a thing in one movie and cannibalizing it later. I think this is true of many great filmmakers that I admire. But I also think it's true of guys that are consistent with themselves. Not that they're good or bad; they're just consistent.

I think these books are important to me because they narrate the story of that single movie I'm trying to make. So the composition in them, the colors, everything is important to me in the same way that Bleak House is. The house is in all of my movies—not only the ones I've done, but the ones I want to do if I'm lucky enough to survive a few years.

MSZ: Looking at Bleak House, your notebooks, and your films is like walking through your head.

GDT: Exactly. When you see a photo of Francis Bacon's studio, for instance, the floor is thick with colors. You see not just the color, but the vigor of the brushstrokes. You go, "This is a single, forceful, incredibly precise beautiful brushstroke, or a passionate brushstroke." In the case of Bacon, I think they should exhibit the studio and the paintings because you're going to see just how much paint ended up on the floor. Or when you see a Van Gogh in person, the reason they are impressive is how thick with paint they are. You can imagine the guy almost unable to stop himself to get there with the next brushstroke full of paint.

MSZ: To get back to the notion of the single film: I really love the juxtaposition of projects in your notebooks, where you migrate inspiration from one project into another, or you'll find a motif for one that doesn't show up in that movie, but then you use it later.

GDT: Before I start shooting a movie, I read all the notebooks. They travel with me. I consider the notebooks a catalog, and that's why I try to explain to people that these are not necessarily the organized notes of a linear thinker. They're the opposite. The notebooks are a catalog—like a mail-order catalog of ideas that I turn to when I'm low on ideas.

I've always got five projects because, statistically, if you have a number of projects, one eventually happens. When I concentrate on a single thing, that's when I get blocked creatively. The mental promiscuity of having four or five things going at once in the notebooks makes them feed off one another. So I go, "That idea is great for *Mountains of Madness*! That idea is great for—" And I can keep the ideas and the projects alive that way.

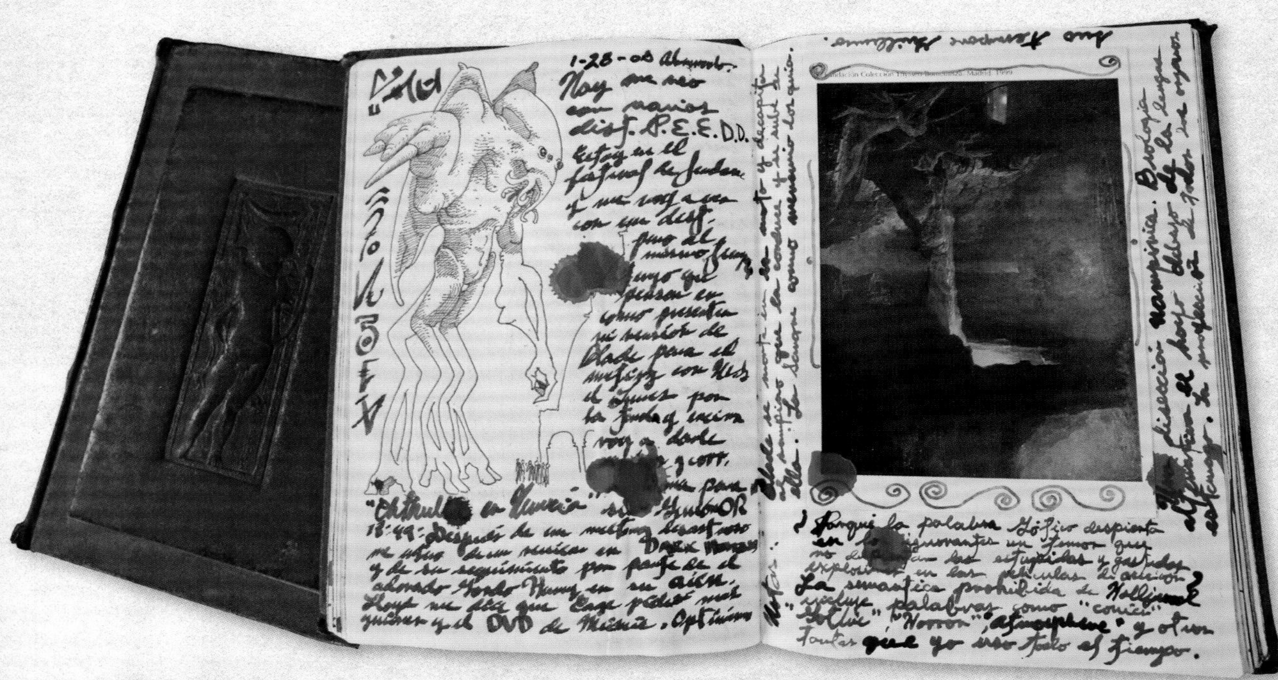

(ABOVE) Del Toro embellished Notebook 3 (here open to Pages 22A and 22B) with splotches of fake blood and Lovecraftian symbols.

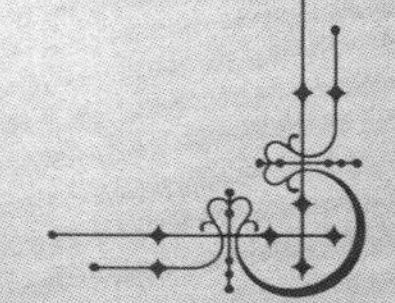

GUILLERMO

CABINET OF CURIOSITIES

NOTEBOOKS

DEL TORO

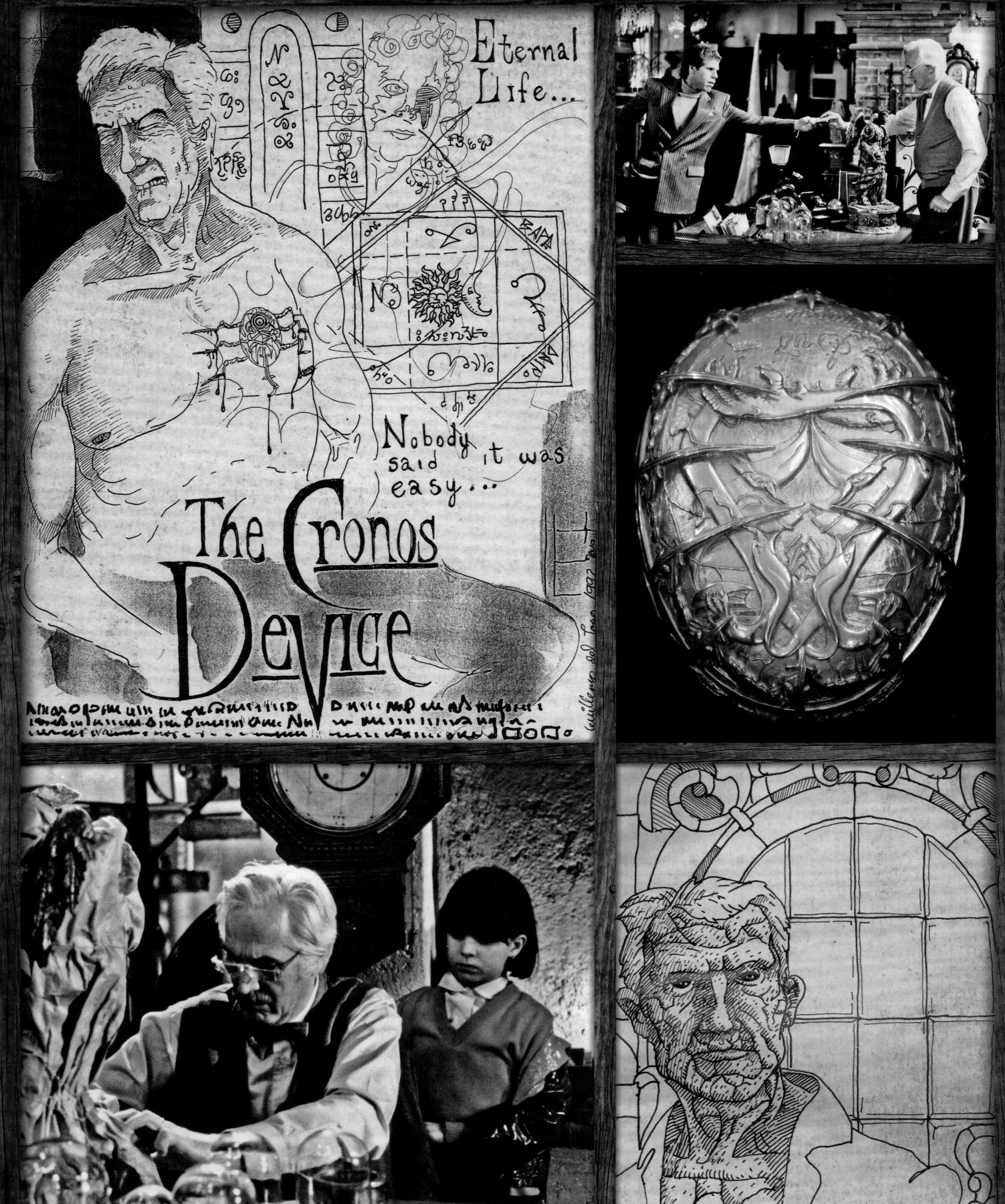
Eternal Life...
Nobody said it was easy...
The Cronos Device

CRONOS

WATCHING A FILM in a theater holds a unique power. Guillermo del Toro works and has worked in many media, but he prefers movies because in the theater the image is vast, all-encompassing, inescapable—forming the totality of the viewer's experience in that moment. In a theater, the audience is propelled along a time frame that the director dictates. Unlike at home or in other contexts, viewers can't pause the story, step away for a few minutes, read a paper, call a friend, and then return at their convenience. Guillermo is a maestro who insists on full attention and immersion, and this is what the movie theater provides. In addition, film allows Guillermo to unite all his artistic proclivities in one singular vision, and so movies became his medium of choice.

Cronos (1993) was Guillermo's first foray into feature film. For many novice filmmakers, their first film is an embarrassment they want to put behind them. Commenting on *Fear and Desire*, his first feature, Stanley Kubrick once said that he didn't want the film to be remembered or shown again because it was a "bumbling, amateur film exercise . . . a completely inept oddity—boring and pretentious."

Not so with Guillermo and *Cronos.* This astonishing film reveals an already-mature visionary. It is a personal, profound philosophical rumination on the choices unconditional love demands when faced with the facets of our nature we cannot control—sexual obsession, hunger, mortality. It forces us to ask where we draw the line on our actions.

A vampire film where the word *vampire* is never used, *Cronos* presents a merciless world where mercy survives in the face of uncontrollable appetite but only at a grave cost. The characters face hard choices and are pushed to ever more extreme actions. All of it unfolds in a fantasy realm that blends the Jalisco of Guillermo's youth with the Grand Guignol world he soaked up from books and films.

In the film, it's initially easy for Aurora (Tamara Shanath), like any granddaughter, to love her gentle grandfather, Jesús Gris (Federico Luppi), who stays reassuringly the same. But what do you do when your grandfather inexplicably gets younger, more vigorous—and then, astonishingly, returns from the dead, growing ever more horrific looking? In Aurora's case, you see the soul within and cherish

(PREVIOUS PAGES) Notebook 3, Pages 4A and 4B. (OPPOSITE, CLOCKWISE FROM TOP LEFT) Sketch of a poster idea del Toro made when trying to find an American distributor for the film; Angel de la Guardia (Ron Perlman) and Jesús Gris (Federico Luppi) in Gris's antique shop; the bottom of one of the original Cronos device props; a sketch of the aging Dieter de la Guardia by del Toro; Jesús Gris (Federico Luppi) examines the statue of the angel while his granddaughter, Aurora (Tamara Shanath), looks on.

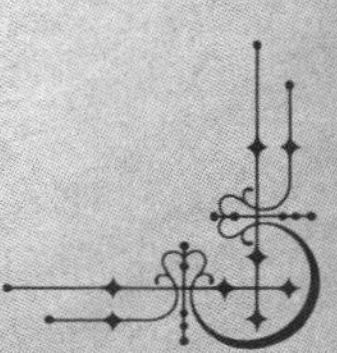

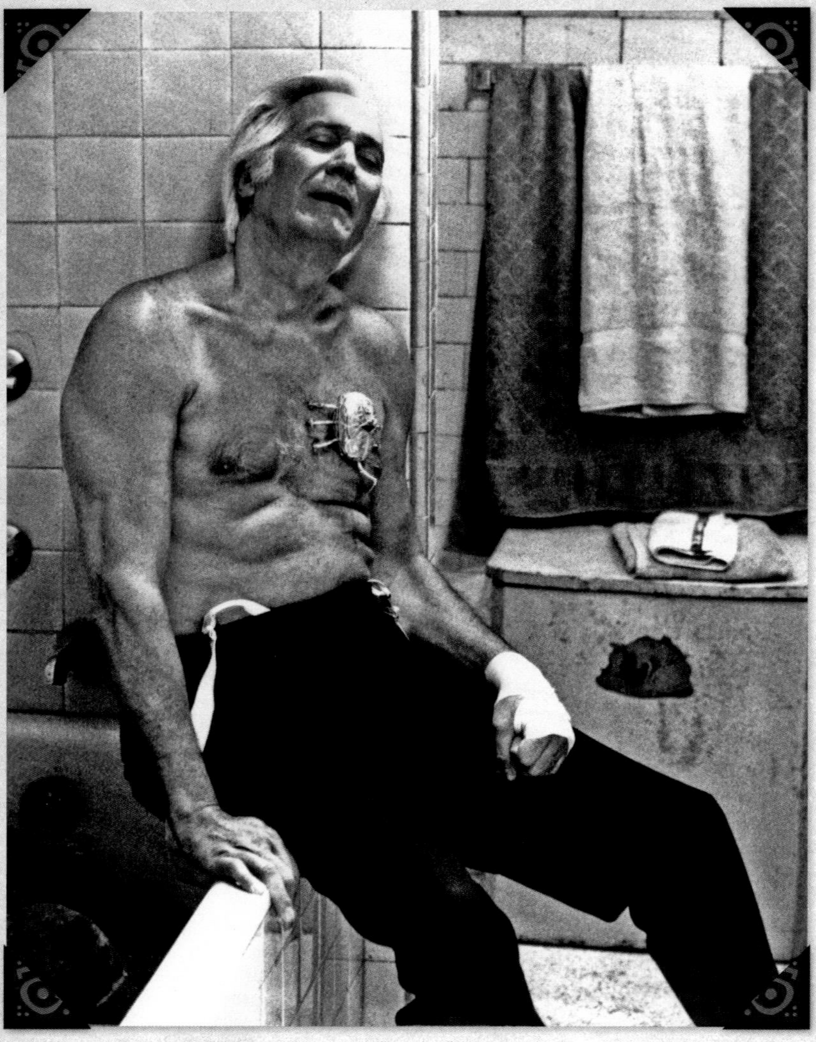

it, regardless of outside appearances. You tuck him into your toy chest with your plush bear; you shield him from the light and witness his final moments of existence. As for Jesús Gris, who is transformed by the exquisite, monstrous Cronos device into a deathless addict, he chooses to destroy both himself and the device rather than sacrifice his granddaughter on the altar of his need.

With these characters, their monstrous circumstances, and their difficult choices, Guillermo confronts his audience with an inescapable truth of life: that those we love, and we ourselves, will ultimately be made horrible by either accident or illness, and certainly by death. Constancy and devotion are possible only by virtue of love, which alone endures.

In his first film, Guillermo announced his singular aesthetic: his desire to utilize classic horror tropes to strip away artifice and show us clear reality—albeit *his* reality, *his* world. With *Cronos*, Guillermo gave voice to the world inside himself.

Guillermo took ten years building the makeup and special effects infrastructure (through his company Necropia) that would allow him to make this film, and its production was fraught with trouble. At one point, financing collapsed during shooting, and Guillermo had to tell star Ron Perlman, whose agent advised him to quit, "I can't pay you now, but I promise you *will* get paid." The time and attention to detail paid off. In *Cronos,* many of Guillermo's major themes are on display, particularly child/parent and especially child/grandparent relationships, the fragility of innocence and its inevitable dance with corruption, and the sociopathic impulse that spoils for an excuse to let loose unbridled violence.

While working on *Cronos,* and as he would do with all his films, Guillermo kept a detailed notebook full of his illustrations, concepts, and thoughts. These are suggested by the storyboards, sketches, and production stills that follow, but none of this artwork is from the notebook itself.

For that, blame James Cameron.

"When I was finishing *Cronos*, Jim and I went to an Italian restaurant in Santa Monica," Guillermo explains, "and it was a very, very, very dire time. I was staying

(ABOVE) Jesús Gris (Federico Luppi) succumbs to the device in *Cronos*.

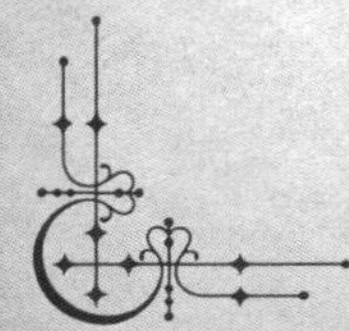

in a hotel that was three hundred dollars a month, so it was very, very economical. With that hotel, most of the time the plumbing did not work, so I had to go to another hotel every three days and rent a room just to take a shower—or I could have a hot dog at Pink's. Those were my choices. The day I took the shower, I couldn't eat lunch.

"So when I met Jim Cameron, I was really filthy. I was a disaster. And he said, 'Order what you want.' And I thought, *Oh my God, I'd better carve up for the whole week.* I ordered like a madman, and wine kept pouring, and I got completely bloated and drunk. I said to Jim, 'I want you to have my notebook for *Cronos*,' which was a Day Runner full of notes. I gave it to him, and Jim received it, and I think he was also not completely sober.

"The end of the story is that the notebook—he says that he placed it *somewhere*. He still lives in the same house, so I have hopes, but he says that he hasn't been able to find it since."

As a result, the pages that follow can only hint at what the *Cronos* notebook held, at what it *still* holds, like a snippet from a lost work of Sophocles quoted in a play by Aristophanes or snapshots of the Ark of the Covenant that is itself crated and buried in the closing-credits warehouse in *Raiders of the Lost Ark*.

What's clear from the surviving *Cronos* storyboards and sketches is that, from the beginning, Guillermo possessed a bold creative vision and the ability to communicate it. In the years to come, Guillermo would make bigger films, more ambitious ones, but from the first he staked out a territory that was all his own.

(ABOVE) The top of one of the original scarab props.

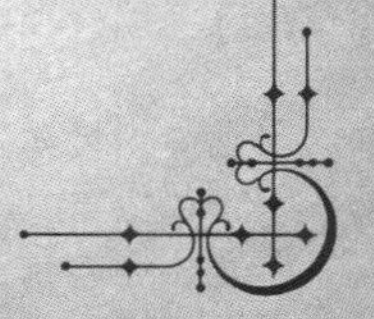

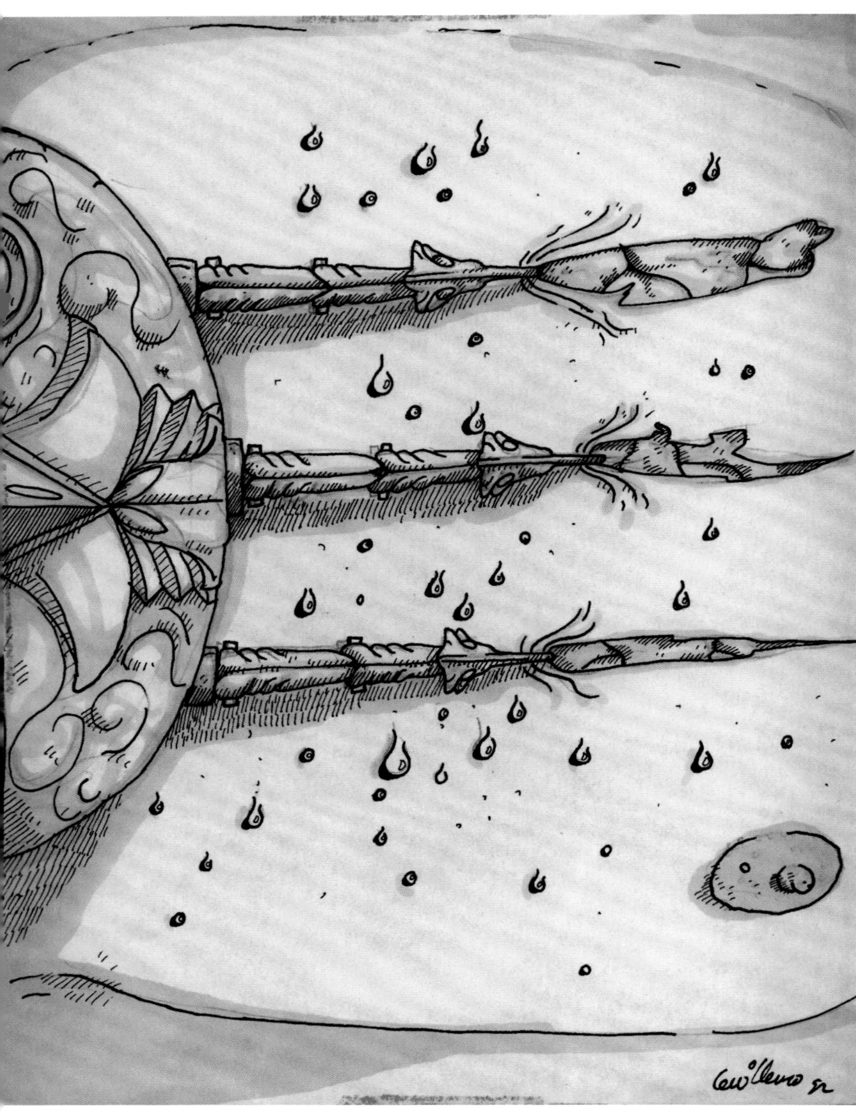

● **GDT:** I did this illustration of the Cronos device tearing into the skin [*above*] to show a possible idea for a poster for the film's release. At the time, we were sending the movie out to American distributors, and I wanted to convey the idea that *Cronos* could be marketed. I was particularly happy with this image and the distributor, October Films, liked it, but they changed it for an image of a woman—like a girl having an orgasmic reaction to the device.

And the storyboards here [*right*] are rare—very few storyboards for *Cronos* survived. These particular storyboards were for an original prologue that I discarded, which was to start in the dark and then show the alchemist harvesting the insects.

MSZ: I know storyboarding is something you do on an ongoing basis while you're working on your films. Can you talk a little bit about how you use them?

GDT: I now just doodle because it serves the same function as a more elaborate drawing. Even if you're just using shapes, you can still communicate how you want to organize the frame—you're still able to share the composition. I'll give my doodle to someone who can interpret it and make it useful for preproduction. For example, if it's for a VFX shot or a makeup effects shot, they'll do a better job rendering the scene for budgeting.

I also use storyboards when I'm shooting. I call it the poor man's Avid. Because I can edit on the page while I'm shooting. If I have sixteen or twenty setups I can put them all out on a sheet of paper and decide if I want to go from this one to that one, or if I have to skip one—you know, as time gets tighter. Storyboards are a great tool for making decisions like that.

MSZ: But this particular storyboard seems much more detailed. Was there a time when you drew more elaborate storyboards?

GDT: This one is so detailed because we were trying to budget for the effects we needed. I wanted to show the insect moving in the foreground, but I didn't want to show its shape. So the storyboard was important for communicating how much we really needed to reveal to my guys at Necropia.

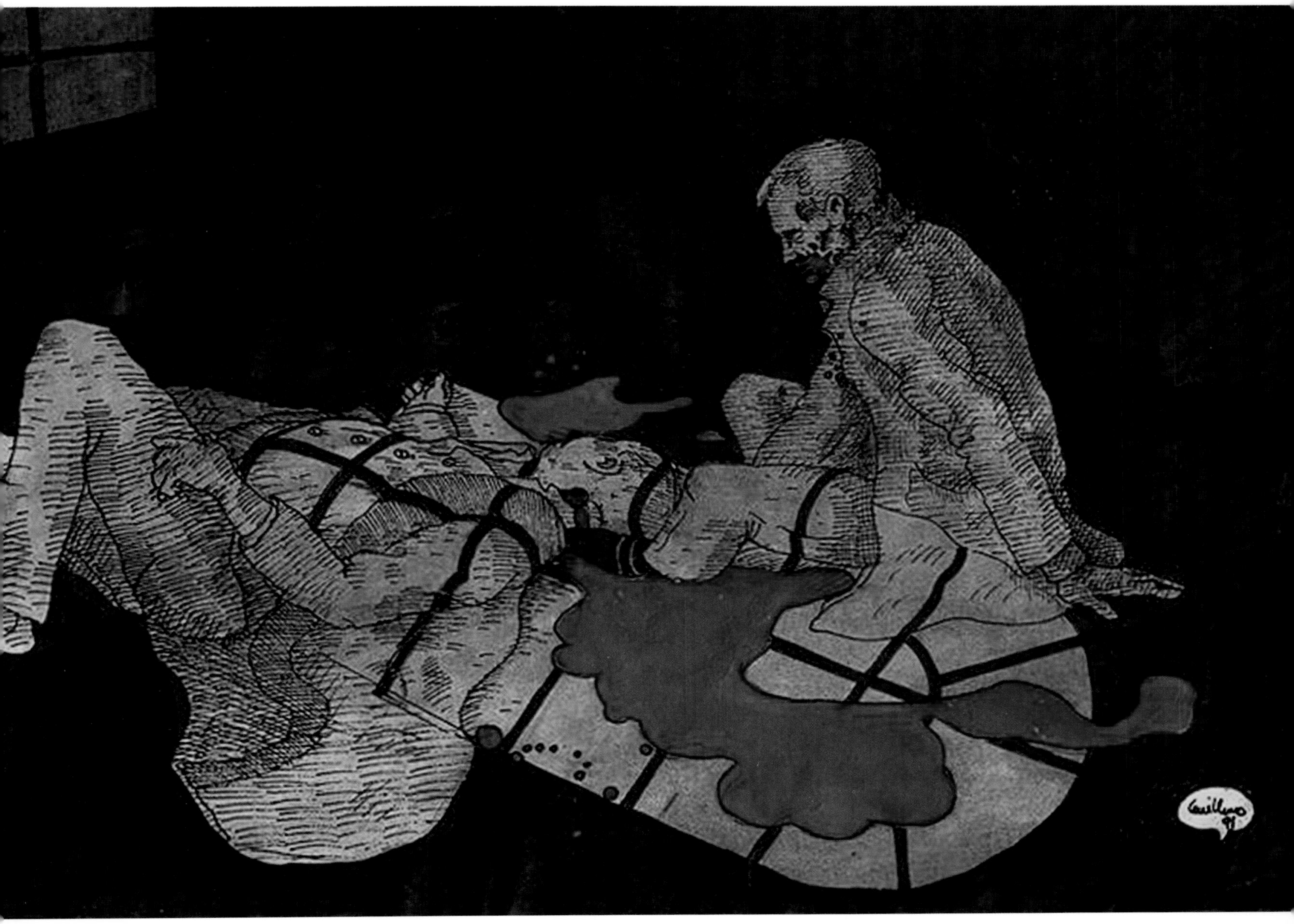

MSZ: And what is this color piece over here [*above*]?

GDT: That is a preproduction painting I did to show what I wanted to happen to de la Guardia when Gris bites him and drinks his blood. I wanted it to be all in blue and red, but I didn't know how to do it with the budget we had.

MSZ: The colors are reminiscent of the contrast of the red and the blue in *Hellboy*, of Hellboy and Abe Sapien.

GDT: I normally mix a warm color with a cold color. I think red and blue is a color scheme that is a lot more 1990s at this point. But I also like to combine cyan with gold or amber, because there is a lot of gold in cyan. And if you use the right shade of amber, there's some green in it, so they can be complementary colors.

MSZ: Something I noticed in this artwork—in both the poster and the color pieces—is the signature.

GDT: The signature is my take on Will Eisner's signature. I'm a big Will Eisner fan, and I tried to combine his name with my name, because you know "Will" and "Guillermo" are the same name. And I used to add that little comic book bubble, too.

(OPPOSITE, LEFT) Sketch of a poster idea del Toro made when looking for an American distributor for the film. (OPPOSITE, RIGHT) One of the few surviving storyboards for *Cronos*, this one for an unfilmed introduction to the film. (ABOVE) Concept by del Toro of the scene where Jesús Gris bites Dieter de la Guardia and drinks his blood.

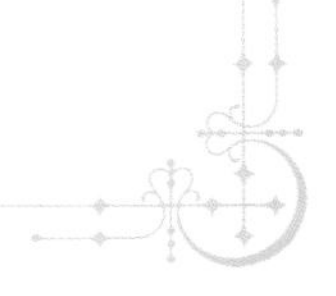

(RIGHT & BELOW) Excerpt from the manual that describes how to operate the Cronos device. These pages, designed by Felipe Ehrenberg, influenced del Toro's approach to his future notebooks. (OPPOSITE) Storyboards by del Toro of an unfilmed scene introducing the alchemist who originated the Cronos device.

GDT: These pages are from the diary in the film, which were drawn by Felipe Ehrenberg, who did a fabulous job. I've always been obsessed with the props in my films looking the right way, and this prop was perfect.

MSZ: Each film of yours seems to have a special book.

GDT: I try to put books in all of my movies so I can keep them. This particular one also has patterns I ended up using in my diary.

MSZ: Yes, I wanted to ask about that because the *Cronos* book prop predates the diaries you acquired in Venice and your new approach to recording your thoughts in the notebooks.

GDT: I love the contrast of the crimson and the sepia, which comes from medieval and Renaissance diaries. I tried to adopt that in the first *Hellboy* notebook.

MSZ: And what about the storyboards [*opposite*], which depict the alchemist making notes in the book?

GDT: These are for the sequence in the movie where we show the alchemist in his workshop. Originally, we were going to go to a monastery to shoot the scene. But we didn't have the money to pay for transportation to go to a separate location. So the final alchemist scene, if you want to call it that, ended up being shot against a backdrop in the same house where we shot the rest of the movie. And all we had was a piece of fabric and a stove. So it was much less elaborate.

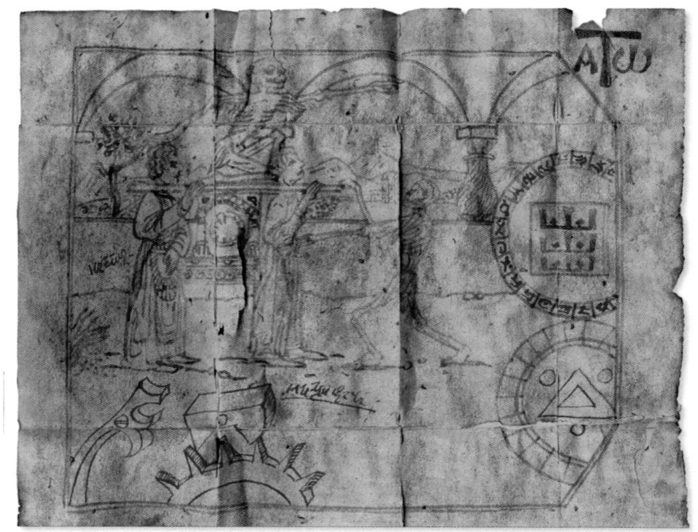

MSZ: You've spoken, too, about admiring Vermeer and his compositions. There seems to be a strong resonance here, particularly in this first frame of the storyboard.

GDT: I wish! We tried to do this sort of beam of light but we realized that we couldn't, because you need distance for the light to travel to produce that effect. The light needs to have enough of a "shoot," and you need to have atmosphere on the set—to put a lot of smoke in the set—to get that "ray of light" effect. I wasn't able to do it here. I was able to do it when Gris encounters the sunlight upstairs in the attic, though, when all the little holes create pins of light. The lights on that set were very, very high.

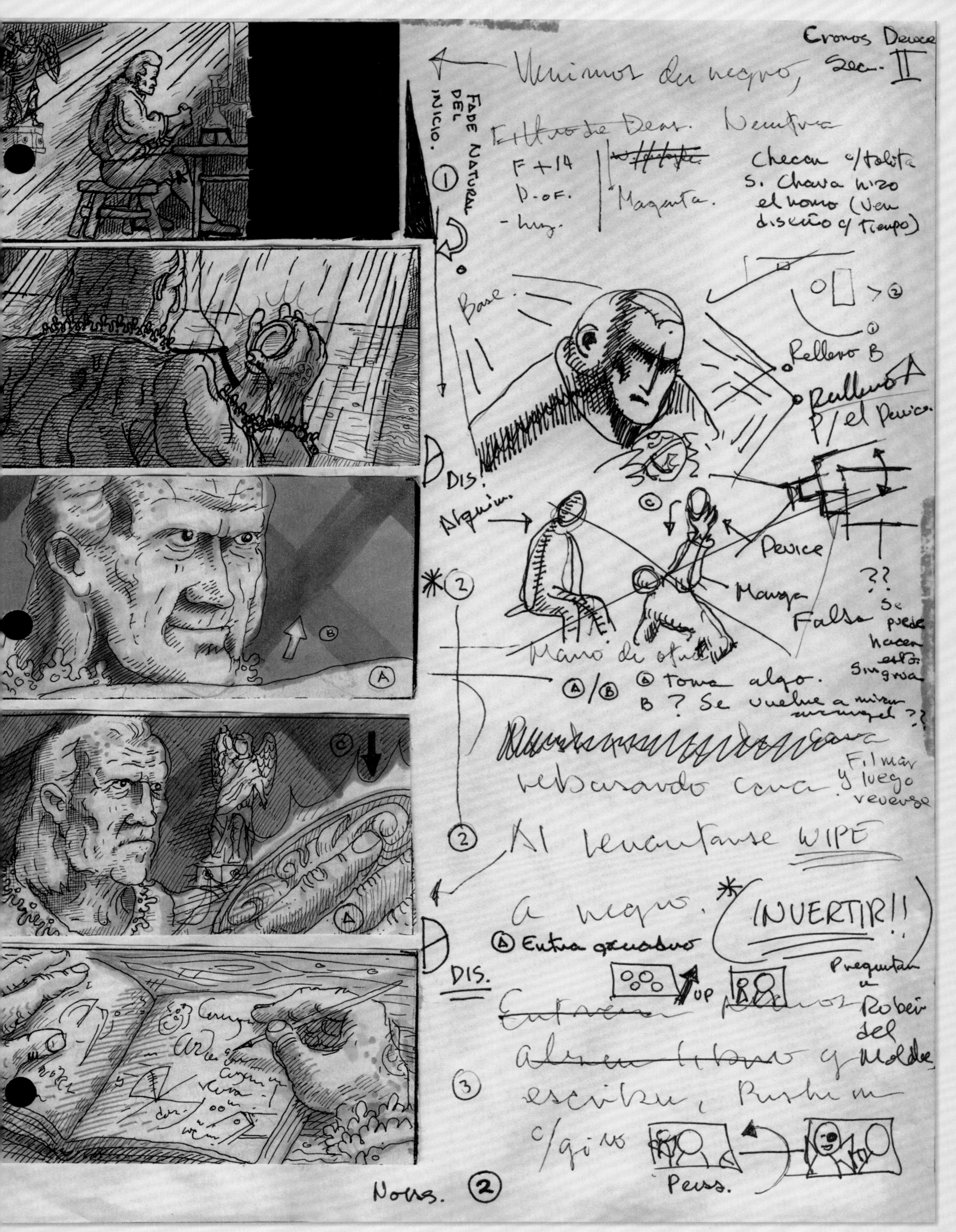

Cronos Device
Sec. II
Venimos de negro,
FADE NATURAL DEL INICIO.
Neutra
F + 14
D-of.
Magenta.
Checar c/Talita
S. Chava hizo
el humo (ver
diseño c/ Tiempo)
Base.
Relleno B
Relleno A
P/el Device.
DIS.
Device
Manga
Falsa
??
Se
puede
hacer
esto
sin grúa
A/B
A Toma algo.
B ? Se vuelve a mirar
??
rebasando cara
Filmar
y luego
reverse
Al levantarse WIPE
a negro.
(INVERTIR!!)
A Entra grabado
DIS.
UP
Preguntar
a
Robert
del
Molde
escribe, Rush in
c/giro
Pers.
Notas. 2

(TOP) Concept by del Toro of the final scene where Angel de la Guardia and Jesús Gris face off in front of the massive sign at the top of the de la Guardia family's building. (ABOVE) Gris (Federico Luppi) and Aurora (Tamara Shanath) walk along the sign in the final film.

GDT: This [*above*] was done in preproduction, and it was supposed to represent what I wanted for the sign in the finale. I wanted these guys to fight in front of a huge, broken clock, to show that Gris is immortal.

Also, in the drawing, Gris's hair is black. Originally, the idea was that he would use black shoe polish to paint his hair, and in the end the front of his hair would be all white and the back would be all black, with tears of black streaming down his face. But that would have meant a lot of time in the makeup chair, which we didn't have.

MSZ: Is there any association between the stopped clock and the gears of the Cronos device?

GDT: Yes, of course. *Cronos* is about immortality and how we want time to stop. All these characters are seeking immortality or fearing it, but the only immortal character, in a sense, is the granddaughter who simply does not care about it. Therefore she is immortal.

Also, I love gears as an image. In *Cronos*, they are literally time and mortality—the transition between life and death. But I like that they can mean many things: the universe as a mechanical model; the cycle between good or evil; or between creation and consumption. It's a huge machine, precise but nonlinear and made of flow and flexibility. But like with anything big, if you zoom back enough, there is order in chaos and chaos in order. Gears symbolize that, amongst other things.

For instance, in *Pan's Labyrinth* they signify history. And, at the same time, very literally, the fact that the captain is trapped inside his father's watch—there are these giant gears behind him in his office. In terms of the story, they come from the mill, so it's logical, but symbolically, he keeps obsessing about this watch, and time, and being remembered, and being important. So gears mean different things in the movies I've made.

RESURRECTION

RON PERLMAN

IT WAS TOWARD THE END of the second year of the biggest malaise of my life—which was both artistic and personal. It was a midlife crisis of dynamic proportions. Whatever creative fire had once driven me had long since been extinguished. I wasn't even answering the phone. Then, a parcel arrived in the mail. It was a parcel that, for me, would come to have near mystical dimension. Inside was a script and a handwritten letter from an unknown Mexican filmmaker asking me to participate in a little experiment that was to be the first film in his oeuvre—*Cronos*. Up until then, I had been doing esoteric projects that I thought nobody in the entire universe had even noticed, particularly my minor contributions. Then, all of a sudden, this beautiful handwritten love letter arrived describing in minute detail the most subtle nuances of my work in these little fringe projects. I was stunned.

I began reading the screenplay while working out on an exercise bike at the Hollywood YMCA; a fairly prominent indie filmmaker was reading over my shoulder. Aside from complaining that I was reading too slowly, she commented about how strange this little screenplay seemed. What was it and where did it come from? And I said, "Well, it's the weirdest little vampire movie I've ever seen. But it's also the smartest. Never in a million years would it ever get greenlit in Hollywood. And just for that reason alone, I'm going to fucking do it."

Shortly thereafter, Guillermo came to Los Angeles. We had dinner, and by the time we finished, it seemed like we were two guys who had known each other for thirty years. There was just this immediate ease.

The only problem was that Guillermo had sent me the script in beautifully written English, so I never imagined it was going to be filmed in another language. I didn't know that until I met him at the Mexico City airport. A tiny lightbulb went off, and I said, "Can I ask . . . what language are you shooting in?" And he said, "Spanish, my friend!" I said, "You do realize I don't speak Spanish?" And he said, "Let's go eat!"

I went back to the hotel after a sumptuous meal and said to myself, "I'll show him! I'm going to give this performance in perfect Spanish." I began to prepare two of Angel's longer speeches. I called Guillermo the following morning, not having slept, and arranged to meet him at his production office. I read the first speech. When I finished, he said nothing. So I read the second speech. I thought I was phenomenal! Again he said nothing. So finally I said, "How was that?" And he said, "That was bad, very, very bad. You sound like an idiot." So I said, "Well, what are we going to do? We start shooting tomorrow!" And he said, "Let's go eat!"

When filming *Cronos*, his first big movie, Guillermo was very humble about the responsibility he was charged with. And being somebody who has a true passion and reverence for the medium, he put a lot of pressure on himself. But once he started filming, it seemed like he had been doing it his whole life. The minute I saw the imagery, I knew I was dealing with somebody in the same class as Luis Buñuel and François Truffaut.

Cronos was the first time I experienced truly independent cinema. It was the first time I'd ever worked on a non-studio, non-mainstream movie. Since then, I've appeared in over forty low-budget films for first-time directors. There was a magic that took place as I watched Guillermo do his thing in a setting that didn't involve a big corporate organization. He was surrounded by people who loved him, believed in him, and enabled him—under some very compromising conditions—to make his movie.

I give Guillermo credit for jump-starting the entire second half of my life, which I have continued to try to make about independent cinema. I give him total credit for opening my eyes to what real cinema looks like. The impact Guillermo has had on my life goes far beyond the credits on my resume. That is nothing compared to how profoundly knowing him has changed the course of my life.

[TOP] A sketch of Ron Perlman as Hellboy from Notebook 3, Page 44A.

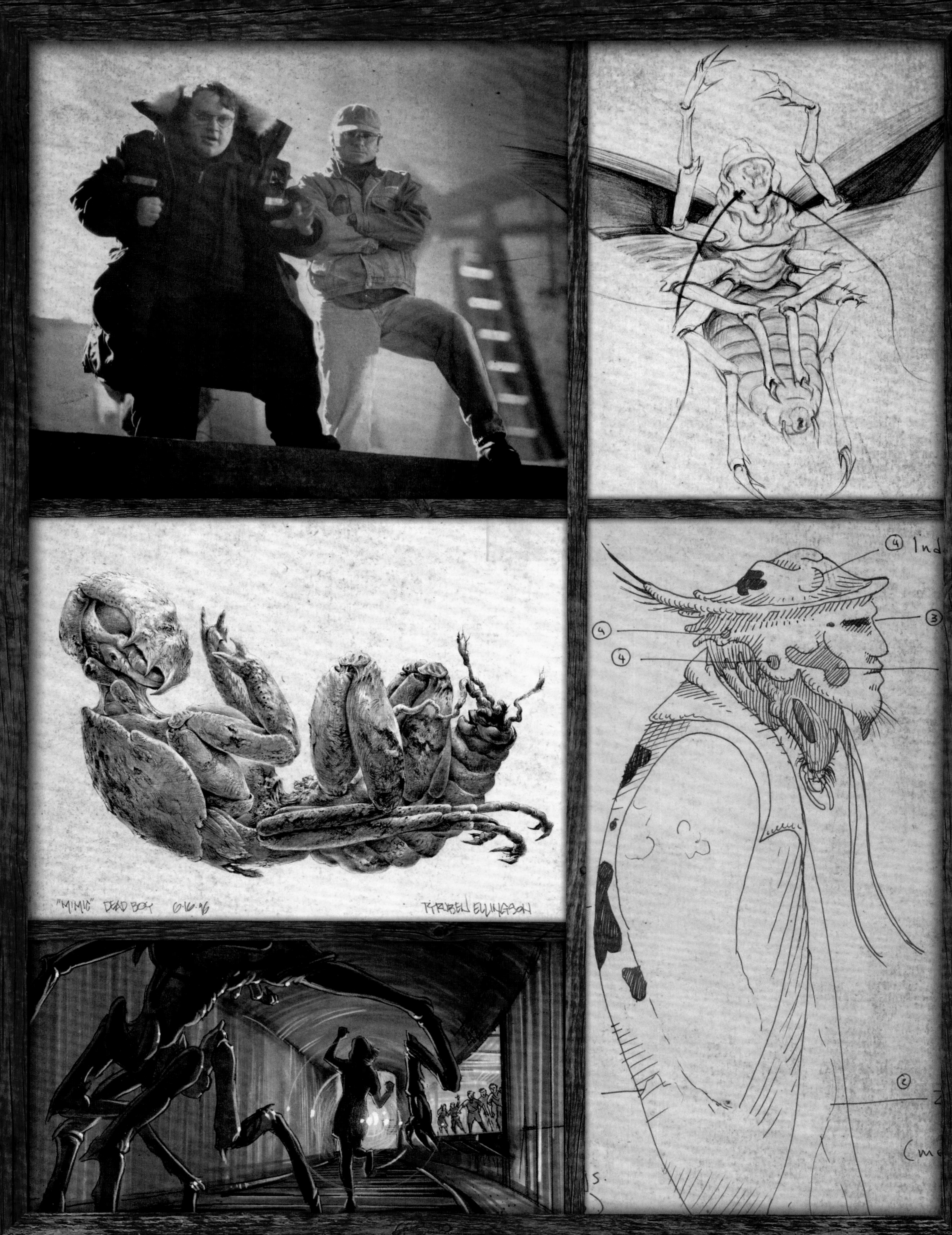
"MIMIC" DEAD BOY 6.16.96
TyRUBEN ELLINGSON
4 Ind
3
4
4

MIMIC

"AN EVOLUTIONARY LEAP. Evolution's on their side." This comment by Guillermo in his *Mimic* notebook sums up his second film's key question. In *Mimic* (1997), New York entomologist Dr. Susan Tyler (Mira Sorvino, fresh off winning her Best Supporting Actress Oscar for *Mighty Aphrodite*) inadvertently alters cockroaches' genetic code so that they evolve into six-foot-tall creatures that mimic the appearance of human beings.

For Guillermo, *Mimic* had an ironically apt title, as it's ostensibly about a creature trying to imitate something utterly alien to its nature. This was Guillermo's fledgling attempt to shoot a studio film as a studio director, to assume the role of a commercially minded technician while maintaining his artistic core and instincts. Like many of the bugs in the film, Guillermo got squashed, in this case by the studio machine. Eventually, the film was taken away from him and recut, with sequences added by another director. For Guillermo, it was a soul-crushing experience.

In the end, he learned vital lessons for the future. Afterward, he would consistently favor artistic choices over commercial ones as he built a singular and successful career. "This is a struggle you have as an artist," Guillermo notes. "Hellboy in *Hellboy II*, when he shoots the elemental, he's shooting it because he wants people to like him. He goes, 'Well, okay, I'm going to do the right thing for these guys to like me because they don't like me.' And he comes out and delivers the baby like, 'I did a great thing,' and they boo him and they throw stones at him. As an artist, I've gone through that. You say, 'Okay, I'm going to do what people like.' I go and do a commercial movie like *Mimic*, and it's a huge hurt in my life. Then when you go and do the hard choice, there's a reward in there."

Thankfully, in 2011, Guillermo released a "director's cut" of *Mimic* that gives audiences *his* version of the film (or as close to it as it's possible to get now). Filled with unforgettable images and powerful scenes that were not in the theatrical release, Guillermo's version includes a stunning opening sequence in a church hospital, dreamily white, its long arched hall narrow and high, with rows of patients' beds—all children—draped in opaque fabric lit from within, like embryonic sacs or insect chrysalises.

(OPPOSITE, CLOCKWISE FROM TOP LEFT) Del Toro and assistant director Walter Gasparovic on the set of *Mimic*; a concept of one of the giant insects by TyRuben Ellingson; sketch of a mimic profile by del Toro; keyframe of a chase scene in the sewers by Ellingson; Judas breed "dead boy" concept by Ellingson.

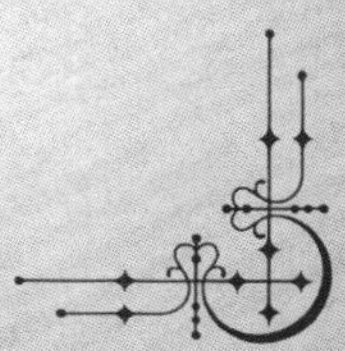

"It was the first day of shooting of *Mimic*, and I thought it was a very beautiful, a very striking image," Guillermo recalls. "It was the first image that got me into deeper trouble because some of the producers hated that image from the start. They said, 'It doesn't look like a real hospital. It looks like something off another planet. What are you doing? Are you making an art film out of a B-movie bug picture?' And I said to them, 'Well, I think they are one and the same. I think that the movie needs to be sumptuous, look beautiful, but have a real emotional sense,' and so on and so forth. It was a losing proposition from the get-go."

With *Mimic*'s restoration, one can perceive how incredibly *beautiful* the film is when considered shot by shot, with its rich golds and blues, its textures of brick and coursing rain. Restored to a lyrical and patient pacing, it's now unmistakably a Guillermo del Toro film, exhibiting his attention to detail and his tendency for observed, held moments.

Even without these amendments, many of Guillermo's dominant themes and motifs feature prominently in *Mimic*, notably his fascination with mechanisms and insects, which are presented almost like living mechanisms. By cloaking his creatures in protective camouflage as *faux* humans, Guillermo urges us to consider humans as organic mechanisms, too—this visual alignment becoming a paradox that mixes physical sameness with spiritual difference.

"Insects are really well-engineered by nature," Guillermo observes. "They are awe-inspiring, but I don't find them admirable in their function, socially or spiritually. And I think that's why we fear them, because they have a complete lack of emotion. They are the true living automatons of nature. That's why they work as symbols of so many things. . . . They're completely alien."

The character of the little boy Chuy (Alexander Goodwin) also raises this question of what defines humanness. Due to his autism, Chuy is unlike other people, and at first he quietly observes the giant insects and reacts with curiosity, rather than disquiet or fear. The film itself takes a similarly ambivalent perspective on the creatures, showing them in both understandable and repulsive ways.

As in *Cronos,* central to the story is the emotionally moving child/grandparent relationship between Chuy and the shoeshine man Manny (Giancarlo Giannini). The other main relationship is between Susan Tyler and her husband, Dr. Peter Mann (Jeremy Northam). While the human couple struggles with issues of fertility, the faux-human insects have no such difficulties or doubts and multiply at a staggering rate.

Interestingly, it was because of *Mimic* that the public got its first glimpse of Guillermo's notebooks. Guillermo and Mira Sorvino were on the *Charlie Rose* show promoting the film. "Mira said, 'You should show him your notebooks,'" Guillermo recalls. "And I showed the book for the first time in that interview. I actually made a fool of myself. I think they edited it out, but I was really nervous about Rose putting a thumbprint on it. I'm very anal-retentive about my stuff. I was telling

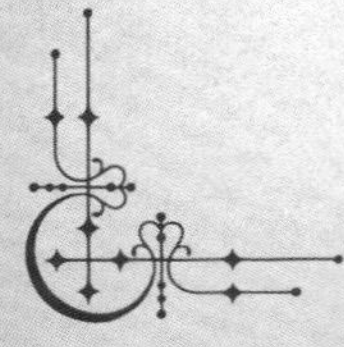

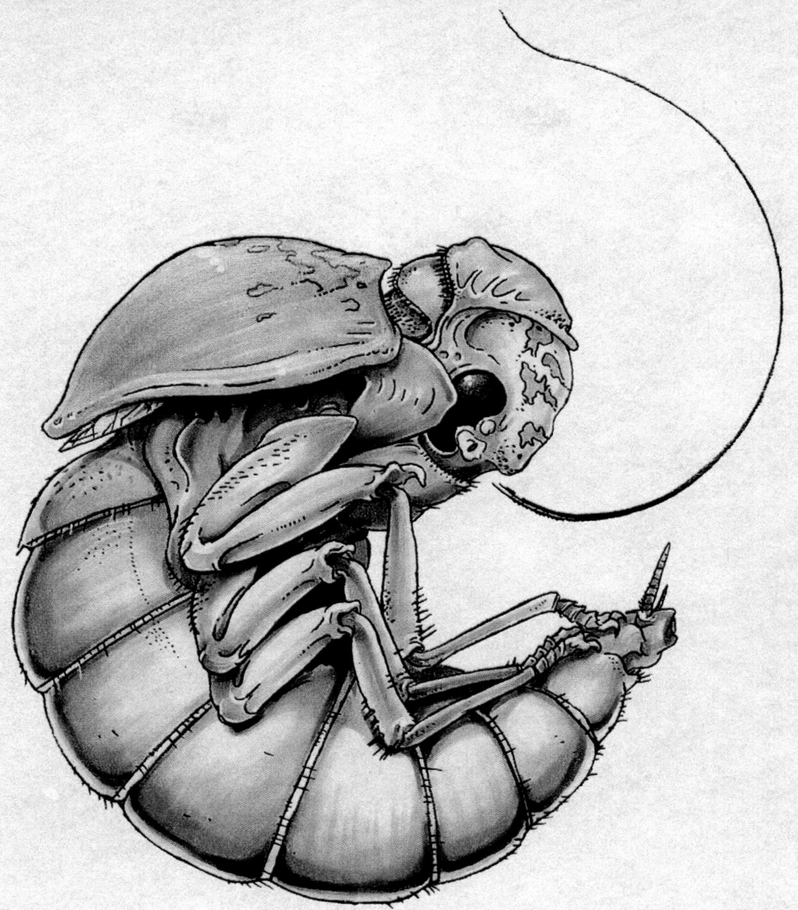

(ABOVE) Judas breed "nymph" concept by TyRuben Ellingson.

Charlie Rose, 'Oh, give it back to me.' And I'm like this stupid guy who had no idea how to behave in media or whatever.

"People reacted very well on seeing the origins of those things, and eventually the notebooks became a really strong point of contact with the people that like my movies. However small that group is, it's a very devoted, very loyal group that likes the freaky stuff I do, and they love the notebooks."

In the notebook pages that follow, we see Guillermo first wrestling with some of the key notions and images for *Mimic* before the film was actively in production. Most spectacular and central of all is the image of the man prostrating himself before the godlike figure of the man-shaped insect, a shaft of sunlight sweeping diagonally across them from on high, as if God were passing judgment. This single image presents the core atmosphere of the film—mystery, awe, the unknown, the mystical, and the subtly horrific.

The *Mimic* notebook pages make clear that light is very important to Guillermo, as are dramatic tableaux. On certain pages, Guillermo might weigh a certain shot, a segment of storyboard, a snatch of dialogue, or how the mechanism of the insect's face makes it appear human. Interspersed are Guillermo's thoughts about other projects, especially *Mephisto's Bridge*, an unmade film based on the novel *Spanky* by Christopher Fowler.

Then, like the clouds parting to reveal an epiphany, two words appear that sum up the entire structure and theme of *Mimic*: *Doomsday/Rebirth.*

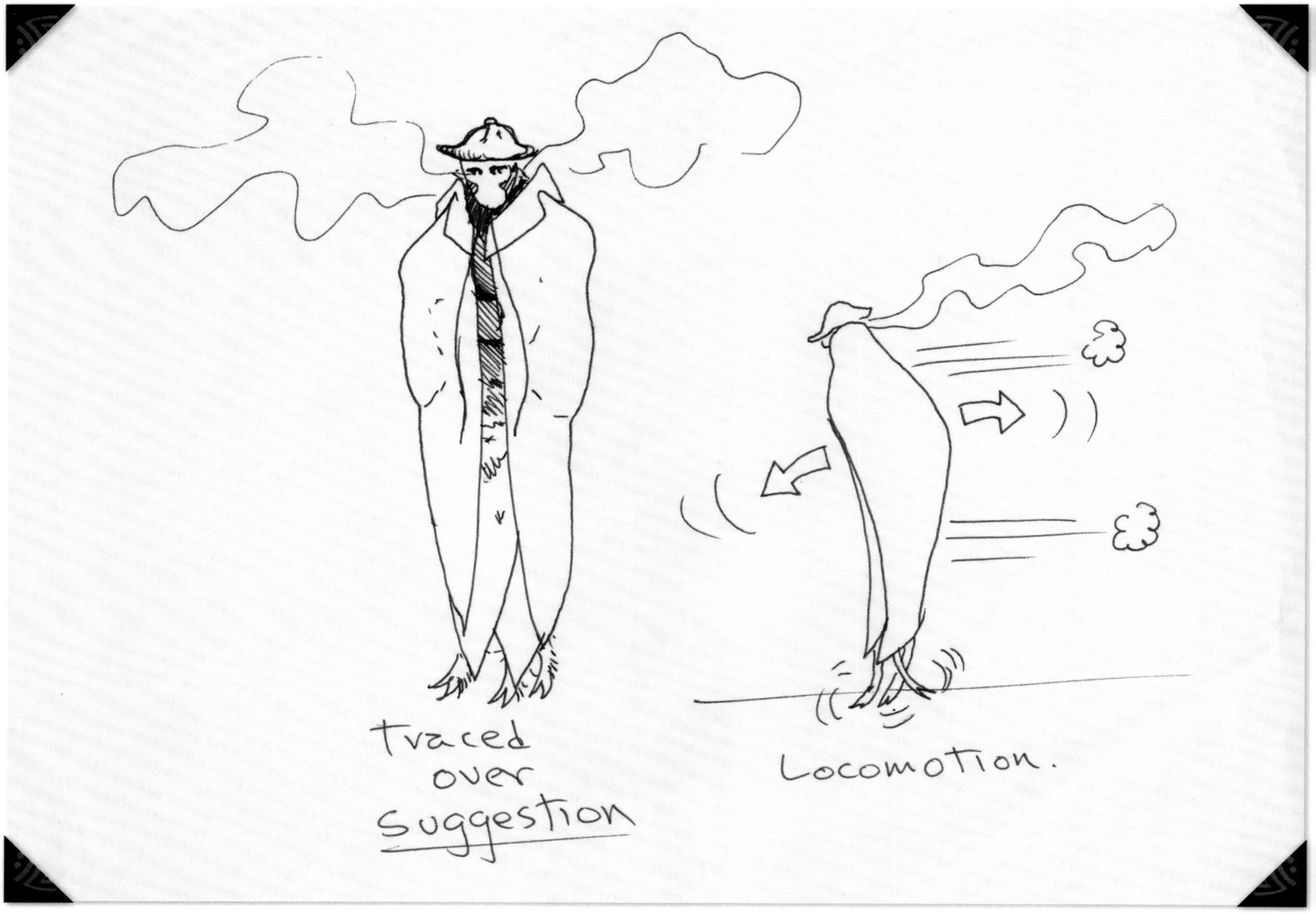

traced over suggestion

Locomotion.

GDT: This was my first illustration [*opposite*] of the mimic before the film started. I wanted to make them God's favorite creatures, angels. I wanted very much to indicate that God supported our downfall as a species.

The idea was that people in the sewers, the mole people, worshipped the mimics; they really loved them, and they aided them, and the insects didn't kill them. It was the same idea with Chuy, the autistic kid. I wanted to have him not pose a threat to them, so they wouldn't kill him.

At the end of the movie, I was hoping you would see the albino silhouette [*below, left*], which would move like a man, move exactly like a naked man. It was going to come close to the character and say, "Go. Leave." That was the scariest possible ending for me. But I think Dimension wanted explosions. So we ended up having an explosion rather than an explosion of ideas.

MSZ: And this image here [*above*] says "traced over suggestion." What was traced over?

GDT: The idea was that you would be able to trace the body of a human over the insect silhouette. It's almost like if you backlit this, you could see the wings, but if it was silhouetted, it would look like a man. And if you looked a little closer, it would seem like the guy had his hands in his pockets, but in reality it was just a bump in the wing. Back then CG was not that advanced, so we couldn't do that on our budget, which was about $30 million.

And I love the idea, which we also couldn't do, of steam escaping through the vents on the side of the head. The mimics were going to be super hot, because they were making a huge effort.

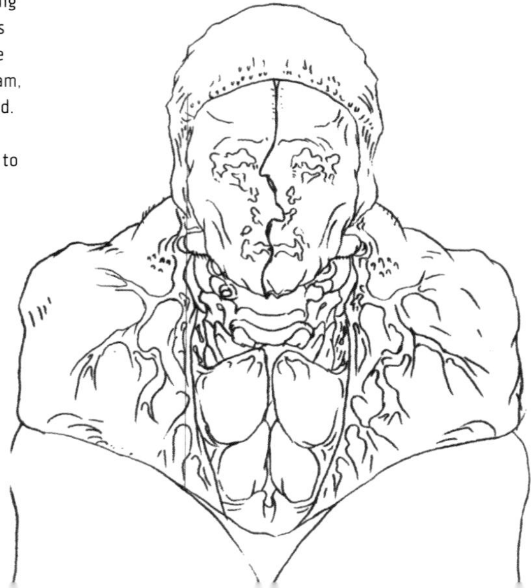

(ABOVE) Sketch by del Toro illustrating several key components of the mimic's design—the human-like silhouette, the mode of movement, and a trail of steam, the last of which was not implemented. (RIGHT) A concept of the final facial architecture for the mimic, which was to be uncannily close to that of a human being, even when seen up close.

* Paper
Bag
Man
prays
to The
Dark
Angel.

* An evolutionary leap. Evolution's onTheir SIDE
* Perro la mordió por quedarse quieta.
* La cebolla sin olor, olor sin cebolla.
* Actor: Jhon C. Reilly: chato, burdo.
* They've dibloxivuanded poxes: thougt so.
* POKING TRASH with stick.
* IT'S FAKE POTATOES: TASTES just as good.
* Signo de Neón [illegible] †
* I should've STARTED when I was younger (she's 30!).

* Paper Bag Man prays to the Dark Angel.

* An evolutionary leap. Evolution's on their SIDE

* *A dog bites her to keep quiet.*

* *The onion without smell, smell without onion.*

* *ACTOR: Jhon C. Reilly: snub-nosed, rough.*

* They've dibloxivuanded poxes: thougt so.

* POKING TRASH with stick.

* It's FAKE POTATOES: TASTES just as good.

* *Neon Sign:*

JESUS SAVES †

* I should've STARTED when I was younger (she's 30!).

THE COLLECTING INSTINCT

ADAM SAVAGE

I'M MADLY IN LOVE WITH GUILLERMO'S FILMS. He holds to Elmore Leonard's axiom, "Don't ever write a villain you don't like." It makes for terrific drama when you're not sure who you should be rooting for. Especially when you manage to identify—even in some small way—with the bad guy.

I think the first del Toro film that I saw was *Mimic*. Although it's well known that Guillermo's vision for the film was compromised by studio interference, there are many images from the movie that have stayed with me over the years. The idea that the "villain" of the film is not driven by evil motivations but is simply a bug that has learned to look like a man is a stunning reveal. As an audience member, you always want to ascribe an intelligence to the villain; for there to be a reason for their villainy. The cruelest trick of the natural world is that there is often no motivation for a creature's actions save for its biological impulses. In the animal kingdom, evil is truly banal. For me, this makes the villains in *Mimic* even scarier.

It's a shame that *Mimic* was a disappointing experience for Guillermo, but his director's cut of the film, released in 2011, went some way to reinstating his original vision. Having worked in the movie industry as a model maker, it's so funny to me that Hollywood is an industry where they hire people specifically for their vision and then persistently interfere with it. Fortunately for all of us, Guillermo wasn't cowed by the experience. Quite the opposite. He's gone on to create a powerful and singular body of work.

We first met in 2010 when I was at San Diego Comic-Con promoting *MythBusters*. After a sixteen-hour day, my wife, Julia, and I pulled up at our hotel to find Ron Perlman standing outside. "Look, sweetie," I said to her, "it's Hellboy." In 2008 I actually walked the floor at Comic-Con in a full Hellboy costume, complete with prosthetic makeup, so needless to say I am a bit of a fan of the movie (you could say rabid). Julia pointed out that another of my heroes was standing right next to Ron—Guillermo del Toro! To this day she makes fun of the fact that I (allegedly) clambered over her to get out the door to meet him. As I was approaching, he looked at me, his ever-present smile grew twice as big, and he greeted me like an old friend. "I love your show!" he said, and gave me the biggest bear hug I've ever experienced. We talked briefly but enthusiastically, and as we were parting ways, he said, "Come to my man cave."

As anyone who has seen *MythBusters* is aware, I too am obsessed with collecting and re-creating esoteric ephemera from movies and elsewhere, so the chance to visit Bleak House was not to be missed. I discovered, however, that I am an amateur compared to Guillermo. Bleak House is a wonder. We spent hours walking around the various rooms, trading stories, and talking about our obsessions with props and the unobtainable treasures we hope to track down or build one day.

Like Guillermo, I have a strong belief in the talismanic power of objects. Collecting and making movie props is, on one level, a way to connect with the films that inspire me. There's a power to those objects, and my weird passion for them and the films they're from is the engine that drives me as a maker and as a man. Feeding those passions is the engine of everything I have. Like the innate drive of the Judas bugs in *Mimic*, it's simply in my nature to behave this way.

I think it's the same for Guillermo. He spends a lot of time at Bleak House painting models and assembling pieces to put on display. Just to have them around, feeding his creativity. For us, it's an important meditative practice. I get asked, "Why are you doing this?" and all I can say is that if I didn't do it, I wouldn't be nearly as happy. I also wouldn't be me.

Sharing these passions with Guillermo has been a real joy. Since that first visit to Bleak House, we have ended up becoming patrons of each other's collections. His enthusiasm and generosity are overwhelming and truly infectious to be around. I don't think I've ever been around him when it hasn't felt like he was having the time of his life.

(ABOVE & RIGHT) Sketches of the human brain and heart by del Toro from Notebook 3, Page 3A.

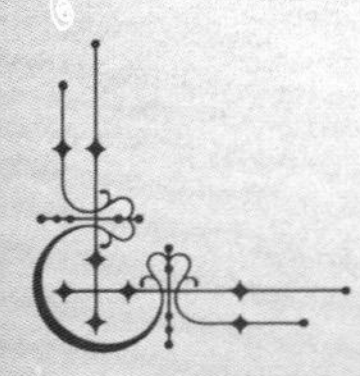

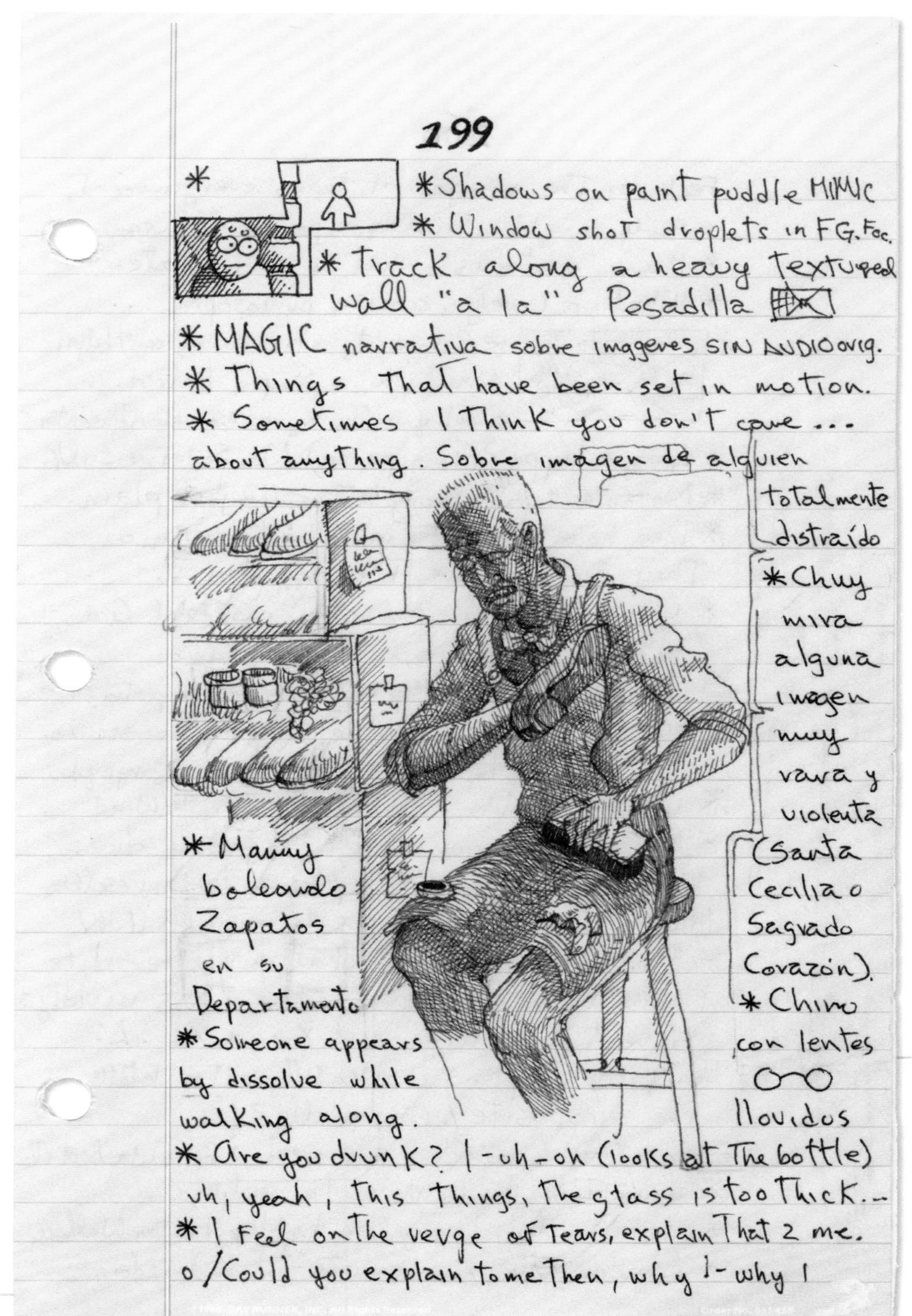
199
* Shadows on paint puddle MIMIC
* Window shot droplets in FG. Foc.
* Track along a heavy textured wall "a la" Pesadilla
* MAGIC narrativa sobre imageves SIN AUDIO orig.
* Things that have been set in motion.
* Sometimes I Think you don't care...
about anything. Sobre imagen de alguien
totalmente distraído
* Chuy mira alguna imagen muy rara y violenta
(Santa Cecilia o Sagrado Corazón).
* Chino con lentes
llovidos
* Manny boleando Zapatos en su Departamento
* Someone appears by dissolve while walking along.
* Are you drunk? I-uh-oh (looks at The bottle) uh, yeah, This Things, The glass is too Thick...
* I Feel on the verge of Tears, explain That 2 me.
o/Could you explain to me Then, why I- why I

Blue Notebook, Page 199

* Shadows on paint puddle MIMIC

* Window shot droplets in FG. Foc.

* Track along a heavy textured wall *"a la" nightmare*

* MAGIC *narrative about images without orig.* *AUDIO.*

* Things that have been set in motion.

* Sometimes I think you don't care . . . about anything. *About image of someone who is totally distracted*

** Chuy looks at a very rare and violent image (Saint Cecilia or Sacred Heart).*

** Chinese man with glasses on*

** Manny shining shoes in his apartment*

* Someone appears by dissolve while walking along.

* Are you drunk? I—uh—oh (looks at the bottle) uh, yeah, this things, the glass is too thick . . .

* I feel on the verge of tears, explain that 2 me. o/Could you explain to me then, why i—why I

MSZ: The grandfather figure in *Mimic* is interesting because there's a resonance with the grandparent/grandchild [*see page 88*] relationship in *Cronos*.

GDT: I wanted Federico Luppi to play the character (you can see it in the art), but his English was not very good. When we talked with him, we realized he would have trouble with abundant dialogue. So we had to cut a lot of the vignettes between the grandfather and the grandson in the original screenplay. In one, he said, "This god cannot see," and he cut his own throat. It was too much for him to see the kid that he loved sort of happily living with the insects. And the grandson didn't react to the grandfather's death in the script, which was doubly shocking. They were good ideas, but I don't know if I would've gotten away with them even in the best of circumstances.

MSZ: That's interesting, because in *Cronos*, I think of the relationship as the granddaughter observing the grandfather, as opposed to the grandfather watching the grandson.

GDT: I love the idea of somebody watching a loved one doing something unforgivable but still loving them. Or in *Hellboy*, I love the fact that Liz Sherman comes to terms with who she is by allowing Hellboy to be who he is. I think that's a very beautiful love story, better than the "Beauty and the Beast" idea of the beast having to look like a prince. Instead, the princess has to accept her own bestiality so the love story can happen.

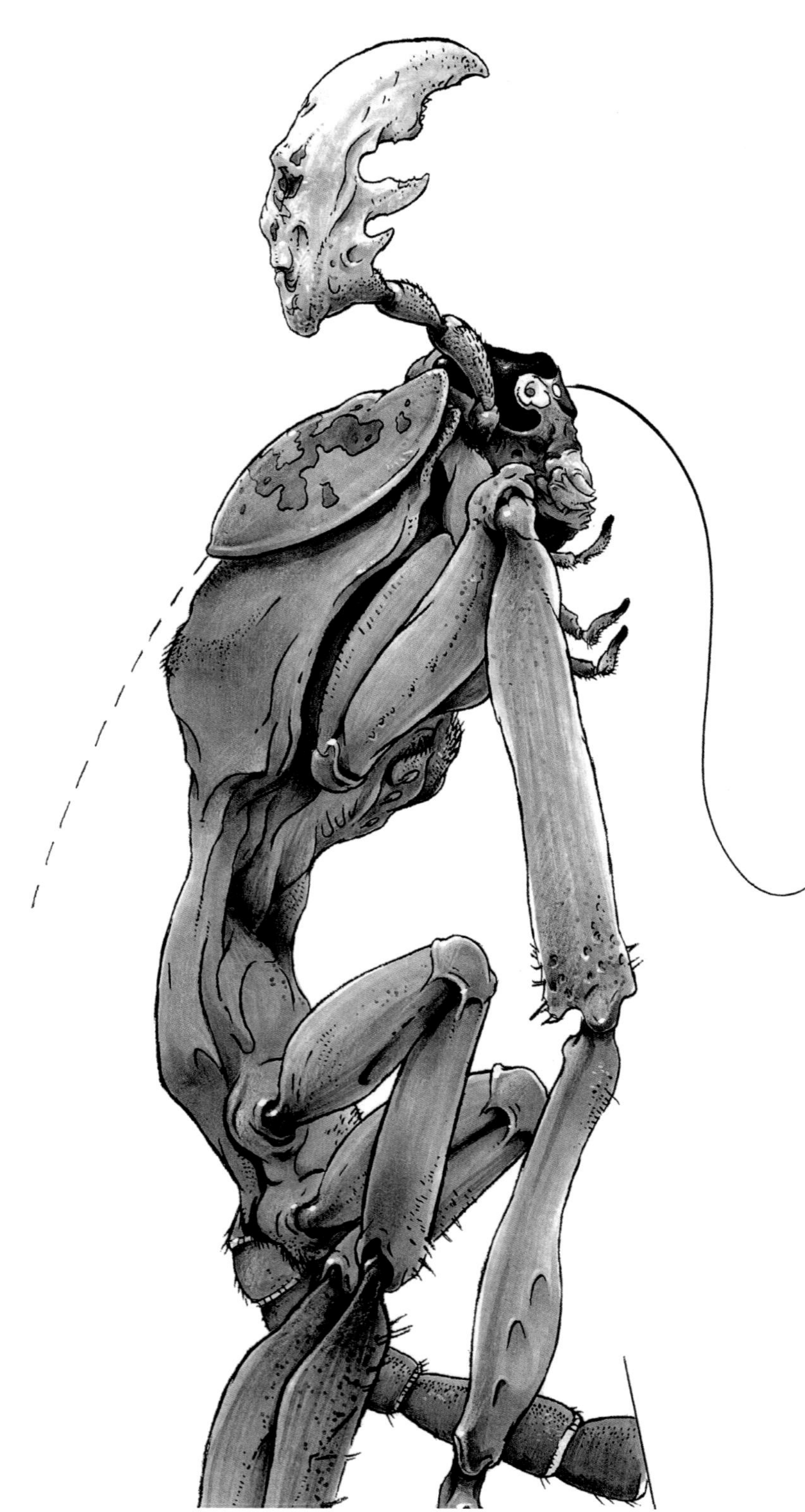

GDT: A big, big win for me was that Jeremy [Northam] would wear glasses. The idea was that his character was a scientist—an arrogant guy who thought we could control everything. So then his glasses break, and he cannot go to the optometrist. There was a great line that we shot, when Mira Sorvino was putting the hormones all over Jeremy, and he says, "All I need is a pair of pliers." And the problem is that they're under the sink at home. And it just gives you an instant idea of how screwed they are. They are close to home, but the pair of pliers is just so far away. He might as well be in Moscow.

MSZ: Looking at your later work, a strong motif is the absence of eyes, including the covering up of eyes with lenses.

GDT: I like the idea, maybe because I wear glasses. But the most effective use of glasses is in *Lord of the Flies*, with Piggy and his broken glasses. And then you have *Battleship Potemkin*. Broken glasses are just a great image of downfall for me. I use it again and again. Or an aneurysm in a single eye—I love bloodshot eyes, but only on one side.

(ABOVE LEFT) Jeremy Northam and del Toro on set. It was crucial to del Toro that Northam's character, Dr. Peter Mann, wear glasses. (ABOVE) "God roach" concept by TyRuben Ellingson.

205

* A counterfeiter quit. He couldn't make enough money.
* LOTTIE mira a Marty bailar solo
* Martyn tiene archivo de LOTTIE.
* Mantas FLOTAN in pool con Ray
* Ben Van Os: Orlando, Macon, Vince & Theo
* Dennis Gassner: B. Fink, Miller's crossing.
* Lentes Jeremy Rotos
* Ciego a tientas en pared.
* No end to doubting.
* MUSIC OVER imagen en silencio y slo-mo.
* There is no end to doubting Martyn
* BOTA
* WATER Drips Through old planks
* MARTYN mira hechizado su calentador (o el del Hospital)

Resistencia electrica

* A counterfeiter quit. He couldn't make enough money.

* LOTTIE *watches Marty dance by himself.*

* *Martyn has an archive on* LOTTIE.

* *Sheets* FLOAT *in pool with Ray*

* Ben Van Os: Orlando, Macon, Vince & Theo

* Dennis Gassner: B. Fink, Miller's Crossing.

Jeremy's broken glasses

* *Blind, he gropes along the wall.*

* No end to doubting.

* MUSIC OVER *image in silence and slo-mo.*

* There is no end to doubting Martyn

* *Boot*

* WATER drips through old planks.

* *Bewitched,* MARTYN *watches his heater (or the hospital's)*

Electric resistance

* *Lame man's crutch*

* Spanky: Nothing to Fear but Fear itself.

* The implications are staggering

* I'm lazy, judgemental, whimpy and too thin, I don't know where to begin. S: The OUTSIDE, that's it.

* Backlit *with flares*

* the BLIND WATCHMAKER

* Stained Glass

* Ambition is a perverted form of Hope (FAITH)

* Flesh Colored Machinery

* HIS LIFE is in sindication.

* Oct 27–28/96 Doomsday/Rebirth

MSZ: What was this image of the crutch for [*opposite, top*]?

GDT: I'd been wanting to do an artificial limb since *Cronos*, to show the inhuman elements of a human character. I like the idea of showing how imperfect mankind is. The insects in *Mimic* were all organic, but mankind needed glasses, artificial limbs. The mimics are the perfect ones; not us.

That's why I tried to populate the church with statues covered in plastic, almost cocooned, like the eggs of a cockroach, which are translucent. I work instinctively by finding elements that rhyme, and I just organize them in my movies as elements that echo each other, not necessarily intellectualizing the resemblances. I think that the whole of art can be summed up in the two concepts of symmetry and asymmetry. And I am very attracted to playing with both. I love symmetric images. But I also love the asymmetry of a design, like one broken glass, one bloodshot eye, one missing arm.

On *Mimic*, I was very into symmetry and wanted to have the guys who secure the place, the ones who wear the gas masks, look a little like the insects. So here you see me playing with that visual rhyme and the question of who is more human, the insects or the guys? Then there is this composition where I put Chuy between two insects. It's like the Holy Trinity of the Father, the Son, the Holy Spirit. I wanted to put Chuy in the middle and make it look like a religious icon of a holy family of the future.

(OPPOSITE) Del Toro wanted the human authorities that secure the subway to wear gas masks, rendering them disturbingly similar in appearance to the mimics. (ABOVE) Keyframe elaborating on this resemblance by TyRuben Ellingson.

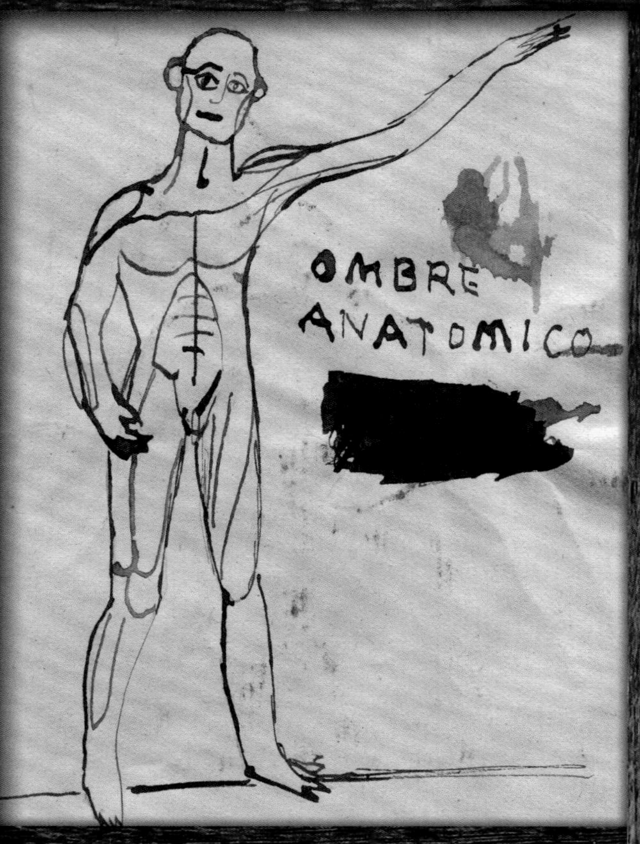
OMBRE
ANATOMICO

SIRENAS, SILBIDOS, EXPLOSIONES... LOS MOTORES de los AVIONES SE ALE-JAN... LAS EXPLOSIONES ILUMINAN LA BOMBA CON COLORES DIABÓLICOS...

THE DEVIL'S BACKBONE

"I WANT TO DO A FILM ABOUT SOME KIDS in an orphanage during the Spanish Civil War—and oh yeah, one of them's dead." So Guillermo describes his studio pitch for *The Devil's Backbone* (2001), and one would be hard-pressed to think up a synopsis less likely to enthuse a Hollywood executive. However, with *The Devil's Backbone*, Guillermo planted his flag, declaring himself something other than a Tinseltown work-for-hire—he was a true writer-director.

After the disappointment of *Mimic,* Guillermo felt certain such a distinction was a moot point for him. His career, he thought, was over. "Pedro Almodóvar resurrected me from the dead after *Mimic,*" Guillermo says. "He gave me a chance at life again."

They had met some years earlier during the Miami International Film Festival. "I was standing on a balcony near the pool at the hotel, when I heard a voice from the next room over saying to me, 'Are you Guillermo del Toro?' I turned, and he said, 'I'm Pedro Almodóvar. I love *Cronos*, and I would love to produce your next movie.'

"Years later, I called him to do *The Devil's Backbone*, and the movie saved my life. Pedro Almodóvar gave me a second chance in film and in life. He was absolutely hands-off, protecting me, giving me everything I needed to make the movie I needed to make, and not having the least amount of ego."

Guillermo had actually written a version of *The Devil's Backbone* years earlier, before *Cronos.* He was in his early twenties, learning his craft from filmmaker Jaime Humberto Hermosillo, but Hermosillo destroyed the draft. At the time, Guillermo decided to pursue *Cronos* rather than re-create the lost screenplay.

In the end, the extended gestation of *The Devil's Backbone* resulted in a wonderful film. "Depending on the week, I like it as much or more than *Pan's Labyrinth*, never less," notes Guillermo. "I seriously think it's the best work I've ever done. It is not a visually flamboyant movie, but it's incredibly minutely constructed visually. *Pan's Labyrinth* is more like pageantry; it is very gorgeous to look at. But I think *Devil's Backbone* is almost like a sepia illustration."

In *The Devil's Backbone*, Guillermo explores his personal past and present, coming to conclusions about where he has been, who he has been, and who he chooses to be as an artist. Some of Guillermo's core themes come to stark clarity in his third feature: heroes and villains defined by their actions, their choices, and how far they will go; restraint as a value held in high esteem, as in *Cronos*; and holding on to one's sense of self in the face of evil, desperation, and despair, as later epitomized in *Pan's Labyrinth.*

(OPPOSITE, CLOCKWISE FROM TOP LEFT) Illustration from Jaime's sketchbook by Tanja Wahlbeck; the ghost Santi (Andreas Muñoz); sketch of Santi by del Toro; storyboard illustrations of Santi and the undetonated bomb by Carlos Giménez.

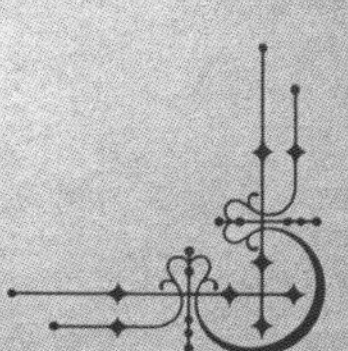

In addition, a fascinating breed of villain specific to Guillermo's films emerges. "I love the character of the fallen prince. Jacinto, the villain in *The Devil's Backbone*, is a fallen prince. I can completely relate to Nomak in *Blade II*, because he's a fallen prince. In *Hellboy II*, the main villain is a fallen prince. And I think, to a certain degree, the captain in *Pan's Labyrinth* is a fallen prince. He's a guy that has the shadow of his father suffocating him."

Exiled princesses also figure in Guillermo's films, but as heroines, not villains. This figure is exemplified by Ofelia in *Pan's Labyrinth*, Nyssa in *Blade II*, and Princess Nuala in *Hellboy II*.

Guillermo's ability to sympathize with his villains in no way mitigates or excuses their actions. "Because, the fact is, there are people in this world that are fragile inside, God knows, but 100 percent of their actions are antisocial," Guillermo adds. "There are guys that truly may have a hurting child inside, but they're stabbing, gouging, raping, and robbing everything that crosses their path. And whoever thinks that's not true has probably encountered evil a lot less than I have."

Guillermo's notebook pages show him working through some of the most iconic images in *The Devil's Backbone*, in particular the murdered ghost. This starts out as a dead caretaker who looks rather like Lurch in *The Addams Family* and ends up a sad child with white-irised black eyes and cracked porcelain skin—perhaps the most beautiful, disturbing ghost in all of cinema. We also find the unexploded bomb and the supersaturated gold and blue lights illuminating the long stone corridors.

These pages also reveal a rare personal note from Guillermo, who takes pains to point out that these notebooks are "not really diaries." However, bits and pieces from his private life do creep in occasionally. Guillermo writes of his parents, "I've found that simply being with my father is two hundred times better than speaking with him. My mom, on the other hand, is extremely intelligent. She's my soul mate. Even in her sins."

And as usual, the notebook contains Guillermo's ruminations on a number of other ongoing and future projects, most notably *Hellboy*. "People say, 'You juggle too much stuff.' I tell them, 'It's always been like that, except now it's public.' Back in the day I was doing *Devil's Backbone*, I was preparing *Hellboy*, and I was working already on ideas for *Blade II*. At the same time I was trying to polish a screenplay called *Mephisto's Bridge*, and I was writing *The Left Hand of Darkness*."

Through all this juggling of images and notes, some destined for other projects and some left to dwell in the realm of private reverie, the notebook pages for *The Devil's Backbone* chart Guillermo's return to himself—to valuing his own beliefs, his aesthetic, his voice. With *The Devil's Backbone*, Guillermo moved beyond the removable pages of a Day Runner. He self-consciously recorded his thoughts in a more permanent fashion, turning them into works of art within the pages of a totemic book marked by his signature style.

(OPPOSITE, CLOCKWISE FROM TOP LEFT) Illustration from Jaime's sketchbook by Tanja Wahlbeck; concept of Santi by Guy Davis for the Bleak House collection; Jaime (Iñigo Garcés) caresses the unexploded bomb; storyboard illustrations by Carlos Giménez; part of the set for Dr. Casares's laboratory; storyboard illustration by Carlos Giménez.

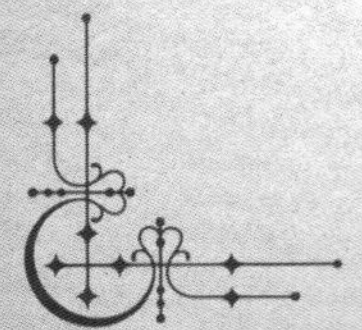

G He was a doddering, sickly old man. With the crisis he gets better and moves up in the world.*

6 * Era un viejito que ya chocheaba y traía pedos. Con la crisis se recupera y revalora.

G Someone is watching soap operas and reacts to everything he sees (it would be better if this character is a villain).*

6 * Alguien ve Telenovelas y reacciona "en vivo" a todo (Sería mejor si este personaje es el villano).

** A hand shaped like a crab's claw.*

* Una mano como pinza de cangrejo.

G Speak with the portrait of their departed.*

6 * Hablan c/el retrato de su difuntito.

G Where did I put my glasses? They're on your forehead.*

6 * Donde puse mis lentes? los trae en la frente.

*THE OLD MAN WITH THE NEEDLE

*EL VIEJO DE LA AGUJ

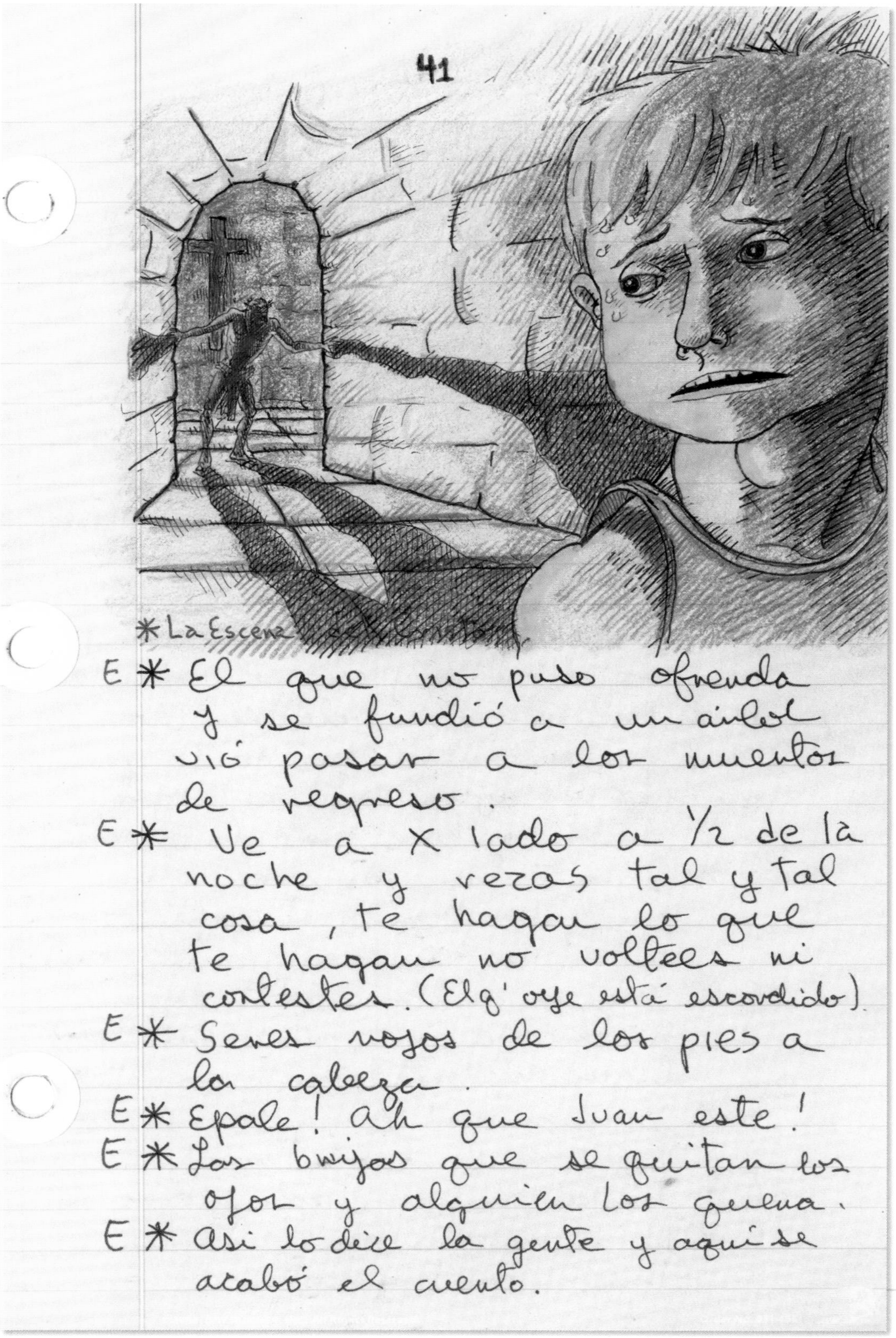

41

*La Escena del Cristo

E* El que no puso ofrenda y se fundió a un arbol vió pasar a los muertos de regreso.

E* Ve a X lado a ½ de la noche y rezas tal y tal cosa, te hagan lo que te hagan no voltees ni contestes. (El q' oye está escondido)

E* Seres rojos de los pies a la cabeza.

E* Epale! ah que Juan este!

E* Los brujos que se quitan los ojos y alguien los quema.

E* Asi lo dice la gente y aquí se acabó el cuento.

** The Scene of Christ*

E He who made an offering and merged with the tree saw the dead ones pass by as they returned.*

E In the middle of the night, he looks to one side and prays, whatever they do to you don't turn around or answer them. (The one who's listening is hidden)*

E Beings who are red from head to foot.*

E Hey! I bet Juan is there!*

E The warlocks remove their own eyes and then someone burns them.*

E That's what people say; the story is over.*

Blue Notebook, Page 41

● **GDT:** The original *Devil's Backbone* had this character that was this old man with a needle, which is really a terrifying character that one day I'll do. And here [*above*] is essentially the operation of the ghost in *Devil's Backbone*, at the end of a corridor, except in the original here it was Jesus Christ, which makes a big difference.

NOTEBOOK THOUGHTS FROM ABROAD

NEIL GAIMAN

THE FIRST TIME I met Guillermo del Toro, I was in Austin, Texas, and he sent for me. I have no idea how he arranged it: It was, in truth, all rather dreamlike. I know that I was there to present a film, and suddenly I was in Guillermo's house, and he and his wife were feeding me a magnificent lunch (she is a remarkable cook). Along with his wife I met his little daughters, and then, in the manner of dreams, he was showing me around his man cave, introducing me to the statues and the props, the pages of original art I knew from my childhood by Bernie Wrightson or Jack Kirby, the beautiful things and the grotesques and the things that inhabited the places where beauty and grotesquery collapse into something peculiar and singular and new. Guillermo delighted in pointing out all the strange and nightmarish treasures he had gathered and telling me their history.

And then, when I thought I could no longer be impressed by anything else, he showed me his notebooks and I began to marvel anew.

Once it was all over (I do not, I admit, remember who took me away from that place or where I went), I could not entirely recall the contents of the notebooks. I remembered colors and faces and words and clockwork and insects and people and nothing more. The feeling of dreaming intensified. If ever anyone had brought anything back from the place where we dream, those notebooks were it.

The next time that I spent really good, quality time with Guillermo, we were in Budapest, Hungary, a dreamlike place in its own right, and his daughters were ten years older and his wife had not aged a day. I stayed with him for many days, shadowing him on the set of *Hellboy II*. He let me listen when he talked to actors. He let me understand each decision he made. I learned so much about making movies and I learned so much about Guillermo del Toro: how he did what he did, why he does what he does. He told me of making monster TV shows in Mexico when he was young. He played the monsters. Of course he did, I thought.

He showed me his notebooks, and this time I understood more of what I was seeing. He explained the way he chose a specific palette for each film. He would start with colors; the colors that would become the keynotes for the film. There were words. There were drawings and paintings, so haunting, so resonant. It was as if Guillermo had made a secret film, and that everything the audience would ever see was only the innocent, jutting-out top of an iceberg. They would never know how huge the *Titanic*-sinking world beneath was; the world of Guillermo's imagination, filled with fairies and demons and insects and clockwork—always clockwork.

Often I suspected that the true art, the place the real magic lived and lurked, was in those notebooks, because the stories in them seemed infinite, fragmentary, perfect. And if I was sure of anything, it was that nobody would ever see the notebooks, because the notebooks took you backstage, into another world. One of the world's rarest and oddest books is the *Codex Seraphinianus*. I found a copy in a rare bookstore in Bologna in 2004, having looked for it for years. The *Codex Seraphinianus* is a strange book written in unreadable code-like writing, filled with pictures that almost make sense, and reading it is like dreaming while awake. Guillermo's notebooks are stranger than that.

My conversation with Guillermo feels like it began, in a dream, in Austin fifteen years ago and continues, in the manner of dreams, in strange places across the world. The last time we spoke, unless I dreamed it, we were in Wellington, New Zealand, in a café, and we talked about everything under the sun. We were older, and the food was not as good as the food that Guillermo's wife cooks, but we were the same people as when we first met; even if, these days, I have had a secret pocket sewn into my jacket to allow me always to carry a notebook of my own.

(ABOVE) Del Toro's drawing of a stick bug from Notebook 4, Page 3B.

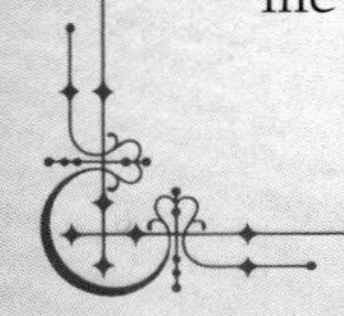

–1645 Mary Kings Close Bubonic Plague

All residents are bricked in there and died of hunger and disease. No food. Local butchers were hired to quarter and dispose of the corpses. *This happened on a street in Edinburgh (according to the frightful bartender upstairs) called "Mary Kings Close." The residents of this street were infected with the bubonic plague. A decision was made to seal the street off with brick walls and let the people inside die from starvation and the cold. They weren't given water or food*

18:43 seated p. EdTV in the Paramount.

–Use objects in the foreground to create black "wipes" for a continuous dolly shot and change the angle during the shot!!

Brick archways painted white and black ironwork.

Window is a CURVING SHAFT.

"Window" is really a curved shaft.

See EdTV in Austin with Robo.

NOTEBOOK 3, PAGE 16B

GDT: This is me trying to find a look for the ghost in *The Devil's Backbone*. And there were many, many different iterations of the story. There was an iteration where the ghost was the caretaker. It was an adult character. Because there was a version where they killed the caretaker halfway through the film with the lances, like a mammoth, and then he came back as a ghost. With many projects, you're talking two or three years, and you go through many, many things that don't make it. So this [*above*] was the rendering of the caretaker as a ghost, and it's already veering away from a real corpse in that it's really desiccated, and it has some of the features of the final ghost, with its black eyes and clear irises, but it is not yet porcelain.

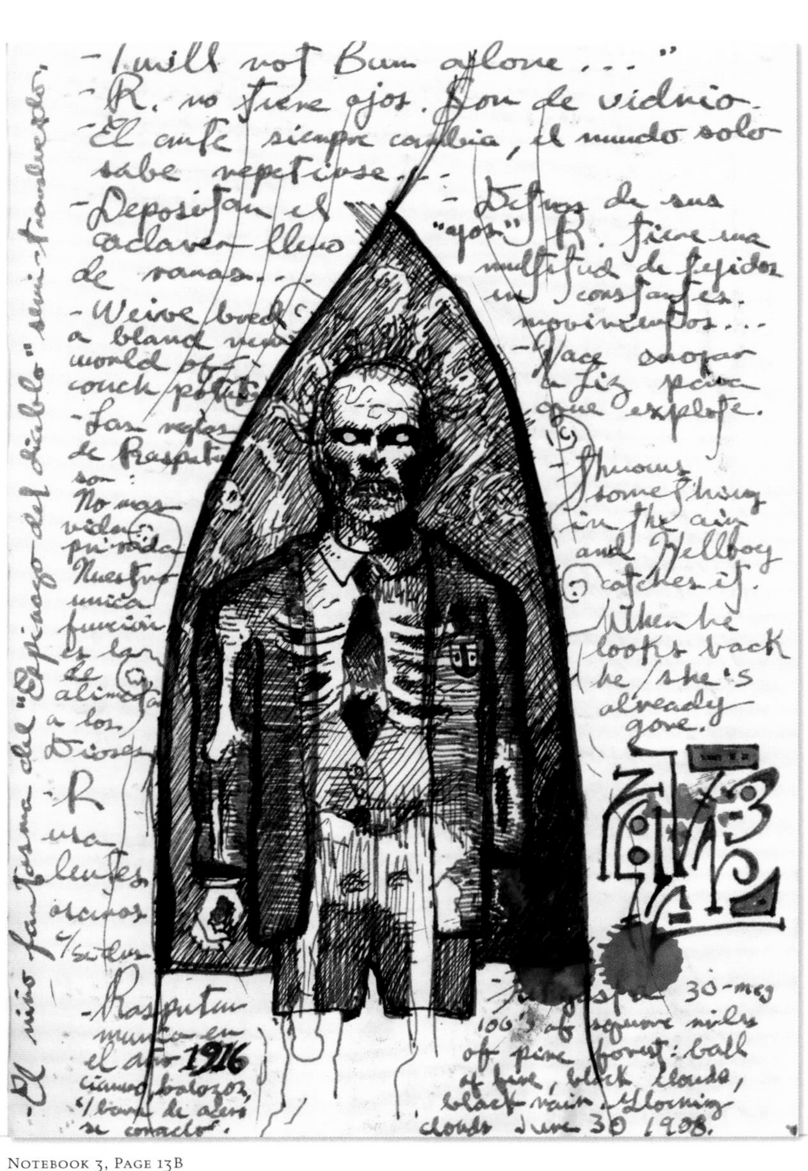

The boy ghost from "The Devil's Backbone" *is semi-translucent.*

–*Rasputin's rules are: No more lives for nothing. Our sole purpose is to feed the gods. R. wears dark glasses*

–Throws something in the air and Hellboy catches it. When he looks back, he/she's already gone.

–*Rasputin died in 1916: cyanide, gunshots with steel bullets. He froze to death.*

–I will not burn alone . . ."

–*R. doesn't have eyes. They're made of glass.*

–*Art is always changing, the world just repeats itself . . .*

–*Morgue filled with frogs . . .*

–*Behind his "eyes," R. has a web of tissue in constant motion . . .*

–We've bred a brand new world of couch potatoes.

–*He makes Liz angry so that she'll explode.*

–Rasputin 30-meg 100 of square miles of pine forest: ball of fire, black clouds, black rain. Glowing clouds June 30 1908.

Notebook 3, Page 13B

MSZ: So now, is this [*above*] *The Devil's Backbone*? Because I noticed a similarity, but I wasn't sure what you were illustrating.

GDT: At this point, I didn't know exactly what the story of *The Devil's Backbone* was going to end up being. In one incarnation or another, it had been with me since the 1980s, when I first wrote it. And then I attempted it again in 1993, after *Cronos*. So it was something I had been working on for over a decade. This is just one attempt, then, at the ghost of *The Devil's Backbone*.

I had been toying with the idea of a translucent ghost for a long time. I wanted to do a heat distortion around the ghost, and I wanted to see the ribs, and the femur, and the pelvic bone. There was also this idea of it being framed by a door. I really don't know if I was thinking of a teardrop shape, or a Gothic door that is out of whack in a crumbling building.

MSZ: How did you eventually pull off that translucency?

GDT: Ultimately we were able to do it fairly easily because by the time I shot the movie, CG was much more advanced. So what we did is we made the bones visible only when he crosses a haze of light, a little ray, a little beam of life. And they were able to animate a skeleton inside of the body.

MSZ: And the blood coming out of the ghost in the final film, was that also CG?

GDT: That came later. Originally I wanted the distortion in the air, like shimmering, and that's what the drawing indicates. But a little later I came up with the idea that he had drowned with the injury to his head. The blood was easier to produce with particle effects.

I really wanted him to look like porcelain. Here [*opposite*] he is still a corpse, but then one day I said, "Well, why doesn't he look like a broken doll?" Because it doesn't have to make sense. And DDT, the effects guys, they really, really resisted the idea. They wanted very much to do a rotting corpse, and I understood them, as sculptors and all that, I understood their impulse.

MSZ: It goes back to an idea we've talked about previously, which is that every really great monster is beautiful. Grotesque and beautiful.

* M.C. puede [illegible] c/pintura o MANO en roca. Rupestre.

* Lluvia de ceniza ardiente en c. lenta

* lento viaje por los cielos de José Mª Velazco hasta descubrir la manada allá a lo lejos c/nube de polvo.

* La aparición del pequeño Joey.
* Valle de Geysers / Aguas t. en desierto M.C.
* En la cueva-marina palomas / murciélagos. apoyar c/ haz de luz muy marcado
* La celda de M.C. lentamente consumida por las sombras del atardecer.
* Escenas "Raging sea" tras est. shot TODO en c/lenta.

** M.C. perhaps [?] with paint by HAND on the rock. Cave painting.*

** Rain of burning ash in slow motion.*

** Jose Maria Velazco's slow journey through the sky until discovering the [?] there in the distance with a cloud of dust.*

** The apparition of little Joey.*

** Valley of Geysers/Holy waters in the desert M.C.*

** Pigeons/bats in the marina-cave, support with a very strong beam of light.*

** M.C.'s cell slowly consumed by the dusk's lengthening shadows.*

** "Raging sea" scenes after this shot EVERYTHING in slow motion.*

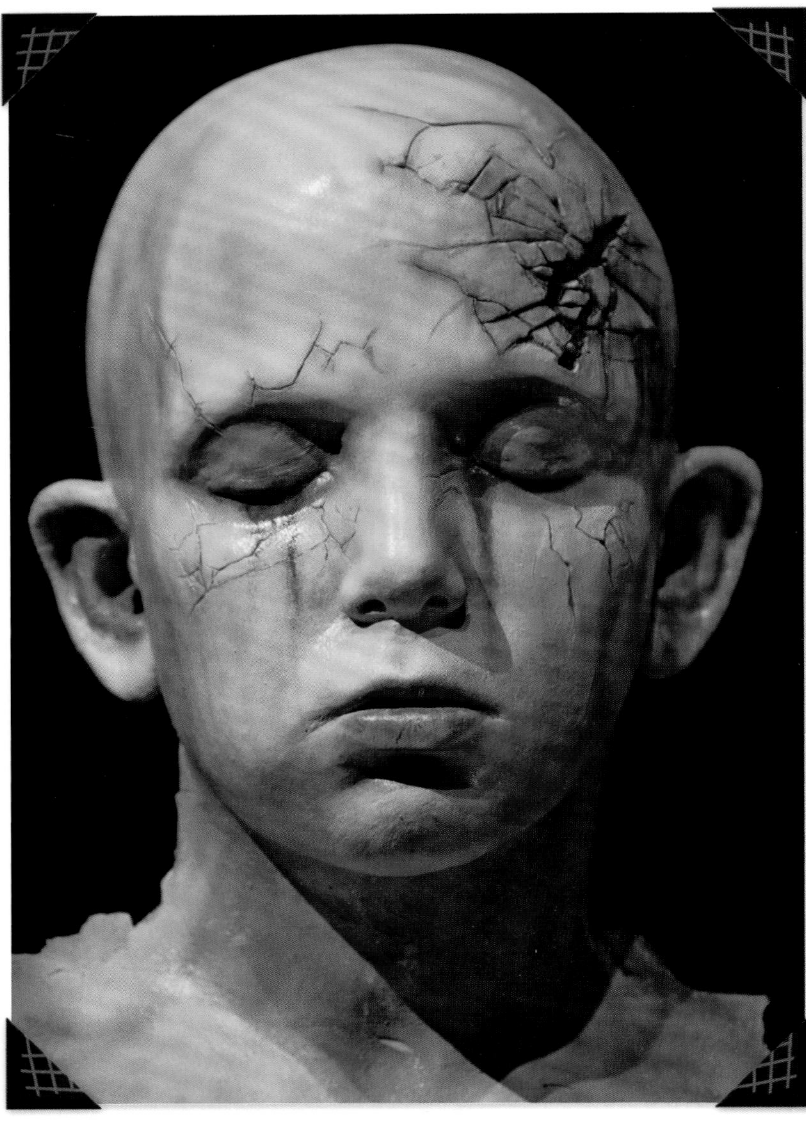

(LEFT) Close view of the sculpt of Santi's face created by DDT, based on del Toro's notebook illustration (OPPOSITE). (BELOW) The ghost (Andreas Muñoz) as he appears in the film.

it's a crying ghost. All those things are meant to evoke your sympathy rather than your terror. The ghost can function as a horrifying figure only very briefly in the beginning, but then, by repeatedly showing him, it becomes clearer and clearer that he is not a pernicious presence.

And the heart at the bottom is from *Blade II*, which you can see only in the outtakes. Then, because it didn't make it into the release of *Blade II*, I took it and put it in *The Strain*.

But in another way, the jar ended up being the jar of tears in *Hellboy*. That's exactly the design of the jar. I remember reading Raymond Chandler in his entirety and realizing that he cannibalized his stories. He would take a paragraph from his first detective, who was called John Dalmas, and he would reuse that paragraph, and make it better, like fifteen years later. He'd change one comma, or one adjective, and it was completely different. And I always think I have a similar way of cannibalizing ideas over and over.

MSZ: So here [*opposite*] is a drawing of Santi, a more elaborate one.

GDT: You can see how it evolves. The first one featured a crumbling edifice, or another alternative was for there to be a curtain. But I wanted something that felt womblike, like the fetus in the jar, the baby in the womb, the kid in the pool, amniotic fluid, amber water, all that stuff.

MSZ: So how did the design evolve from here?

GDT: I sent this drawing to DDT. You can see now the eyes are black, the iris is white. Now he's a porcelain doll. And DDT and I made a very long chain of emails, sending drawings and literally, literally counting the number of cracks. I would say, "Take this one out, put one over here." We art directed exactly the number of cracks, exactly the position of the tear.

You know, I say to people, "We deliberately made the ghost a figure that evokes things that are fragile." And there are echoes in the movie: the shell of an egg, the broken porcelain of a childhood doll, and it has tears of rust. I mean,

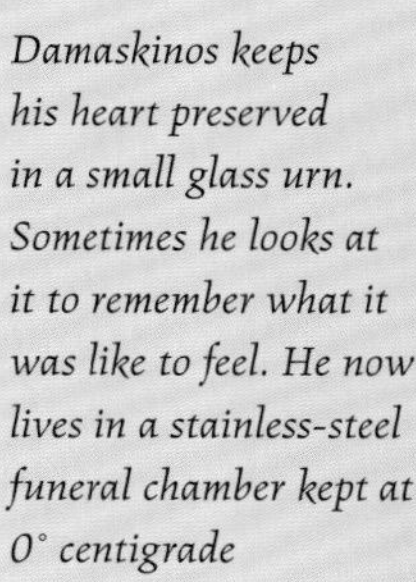

Santi en El Espinazo del Diablo
Damasquinos conserva su
corazón humano en una
pequeña urna de vidrio.
A veces lo mira para
acordarse de lo que era
sentir. Ahora habita en
una cámara mortuoria de
acero inoxidable que conserva
a menos 0° centígrados

Santi in The Devil's Backbone

Damaskinos keeps his heart preserved in a small glass urn. Sometimes he looks at it to remember what it was like to feel. He now lives in a stainless-steel funeral chamber kept at 0° centigrade

–Hellboy calls Liz to read her a letter he wrote. He goes for a coffee with Mayers.

–The story's basic triangle in Hellboy is that of the student who falls in love with his teacher's wife. Hellboy is, above all, a noble and primitive guy.

–How difficult it is to talk with Spaniards about The Devil's Backbone. It's easier for me to chat in English than in the Spanish spoken in Spain, the motherland. That said, I'm confident that the fable is universal. The characters are really, really iconic: Luppi with his "black" hair, his little tie, and his handkerchief, is the old, impotent dandy. Marisa, blonde, dressed in black, with two canes and yellow glasses. The children all in uniform, the school made up of arches, the empty, dead landscape. And God, like the sun, screws everything up, and completely burns everything He doesn't.

–I've found that simply being with my father is 200 times better than speaking with him. My mom, on the other hand, is extremely intelligent. She's my soul mate. Even in her sins.

- Hellboy llama a Liz para leerle una carta que él escribió. Va a tomar café con Mayers.
- El triangulo básico en la historia de Hellboy es el del alumno que se enamora de la esposa del maestro. Hellboy es ante todo un tipo noble y primitivo.
- Que difícil es llegar con cualquier Español sobre el Espinazo del Diablo. Los diálogos en Inglés me son más accesibles que en Castellano de la madre patria. Sin embargo estoy seguro de la universalidad de la fabula que estoy contando. Los personajes son muy pero muy iconicos: Luppi con su pelo "Negro" y su corbatita y su pañuelo, es un dandy viejo e impotente, Marisa, rubia, de negro y con dos bastones y gafas amarilla. Los niños de uniforme todos ellos el colegio formado por arcos el paisaje vacío y muerto y Dios, como el sol, lo jode todo y lo que no, lo quema por completo.
- Realmente me encuentro conque hablar con mi padre vale 200 veces menos que simplemente estar con él. Mi mamá en cambio es inteligentísima y es mi alma gemela para mí. Incluso sus pecados.

Notebook 3, Page 21A

The undetonated bomb, illustrated by del Toro in his notebook (OPPOSITE) and as it appears in Jaime's sketchbook (RIGHT).

MSZ: So now we come to this page [*opposite*] with the bomb from *The Devil's Backbone*. You write, "How difficult it is to talk with Spaniards about *The Devil's Backbone*. It's easier for me to chat in English than in the Spanish spoken in Spain, the motherland. That said, I'm confident that the fable is universal. The characters are really, really iconic: Luppi with his 'black' hair, his little tie, and his handkerchief, is the old, impotent dandy."

GDT: What is funny is all that went away. I wanted Luppi, like Professor Aschenbach in *Death in Venice*, to have black hair that he put shoe polish on, because I wanted him to be bleeding black, and because I wanted him to be really fastidious about his appearance. And that's in the movie. He's very fastidious. He presses his ties with books. But we made a budget, and we made a schedule, and we started breaking it down, accounting for the cleanup time with bleeding hair versus not-bleeding hair. And it went away.

The moment we started color-coding the movie, I realized Marisa's hair needed to be red, not blonde, and that's because the color of the school, the mosaic, and the doors, would look really, really narrow if you had a blonde. Then I said, "I'm gonna give her only one wooden leg, so I'll give her one single cane."

Everything evolves. It was the same thing with the kids. We started thinking about school uniforms. But with the reality of the Civil War, we found that uniforms would exist only in a private school. So out they went. And the only thing that remains is God and the sun.

The same with *Hellboy*. Here I wrote, "The story's basic triangle in *Hellboy* is that of the student who falls in love with his teacher's wife. Hellboy is, above all, a noble and primitive guy." There was a time when there was a different story for *Hellboy*.

MSZ: What about this great image of the little boy with the bomb?

GDT: An earlier incarnation of the bomb was that I wanted it to be rotting in such a way that you could see the mechanism inside. And then you do research and realize that's impossible, and you go, "Oh, all right." The only thing that remains of that, which is a complete fantasy, is that it ticks.

MSZ: So what was the research that proved that you couldn't show the mechanism?

GDT: We started doing the research, and the bombardment in the Civil War was done by the Condor Legion, which were German planes, and they were testing blanket bombing in Spain. And the bombs were very small. I mean, size-wise, they were very small. But I had this image in my head of the American blanket bombings and *Dr. Strangelove*, with a giant bomb and the dropper. So it's inaccurate. The planes were not able to have that dropping system. And I said, "You know what? To hell with it. It's a great image."

What I explained to the designer is that the bomb is the mother of the children. The bomb is like a fertility goddess, and that is the way the children see it. It's huge. And they put little flower pots around it. In that way, it's like the head of the pig in *Lord of the Flies*, something totemic. And it's the size they'll remember it. The bomb is the size they'll remember it. But it's entirely inaccurate. There were no bombs of that size. I always say, "You can break the reality as long as you know." If somebody tells you, "There were no bombs that size," you can't go, "Holy shit!" But you can say, "I know," and it's fine.

The opposite is true in *Pan's Labyrinth*, where people say that the raids are inaccurate. But they are not. We did research that proves they were, and exactly at that time, and exactly in that area. The guy that gave us all the research had studied extensively. He was obsessed with Fascist campaigns. And he was not a guy on the left, with an agenda. He was a historian who was obsessed with the Spanish Civil War not from the side of the Republicans, but of the Fascists. And the fact is they won; the Republicans won some skirmishes in the north because they were using guerilla tactics, which were very, very new. It's fascinating to me that some people say, "Oh, he took too many liberties" about *Pan's Labyrinth*. But nobody has said that of *The Devil's Backbone*, which took the most enormous liberties with history.

3
above
CHUPA
Reapers
out
behind
mist
MIGNOLA -
Pan up from
blood to Nomak
on the
Frazetta-style
Pile of Carnage
ART
2
--- slowly throws
8
MIGNOLA -

BLADE II

"*BLADE II* WAS DONE, partially at least, to be able to do *Hellboy*," Guillermo readily admits. "And then because I loved the idea of the bad vampires, the Reapers. I mean, literally, my agent at the time called me and said, 'Do you want to make *Blade II*?' And I said, 'No, I don't want to do *Blade II*.' And he said, 'Do you ever want to do *Hellboy*?' And I said, 'Yes.' 'Well, if you want to do *Hellboy*, you gotta do *Blade II*, because no one's going to hire you to do *Hellboy* based on *Mimic* or *Cronos*.' And he was absolutely right."

Guillermo elaborates, "The way it happened was great because they wanted me to do *Blade*, but I never met with them. Then they called me for *Blade II*, and I liked *Blade* all the way, including the ending. Especially that phrase, 'Some motherfuckers are always trying to ice skate uphill!'"

Guillermo knew he could not take on *Blade II* (2002) without finding a way to dive into it heart and soul. He needed to balance the demands of working on a studio film with his need to express himself artistically, to explore the images and ideas that ignite his passions. At his first meeting with executive producer and screenwriter David S. Goyer and star Wesley Snipes, Guillermo proposed his notion for the Reapers, a new group of voracious supervampires whose mouths would split wide open, revealing horrors within.

This reflected Guillermo's desire to present a vampire unlike anything seen before. He'd been mulling over this notion since his childhood in Mexico, watching films and reading about vampires in legends and folktales from around the world, including the *strigoi* of eastern Europe. From the first, Guillermo displayed a morbid fascination with the biological minutiae of how the vampire actually functioned—how it infects, how it feeds, how it survives—peering closely at what others might avoid or gloss over.

In his twenties, the ideas developed further, as he fashioned *Cronos* around a most unlikely vampire. "The vampires in *Blade II* came from me figuring out vampirism for *Cronos*, and also for a pitch that was not successful for *I Am Legend*," Guillermo explains. This was years before the 2007 version that was ultimately produced starring Will Smith.

"I went to Warners," Guillermo recalls of his *I Am Legend* pitch, "and I met with a junior executive, first of all, which means that no one else ever heard the pitch. It didn't travel on. He said, 'Arnold [Schwarzenegger] is attached as a star.' And for me, that is the opposite of the novel because Richard Matheson makes his

(OPPOSITE, CLOCKWISE FROM TOP LEFT) Concepts of Chupa's death by Mike Mignola; Blade (Wesley Snipes) pursued by Reapers in the sewers; concept of Nomak's fight with the security guards by Mike Mignola; concept of Blade, enshrouded in the mist of a disintegrated Reaper, by Mike Mignola; Nomak (Luke Goss) scouts the sewers.

hero the everyman, makes a point of making him a common man, because *that's* the monster. He is the monster to the vampire race because he could be any man. He's not meant to be extraordinary. And Arnold is, in every way, extraordinary. So I am a guy who just did a movie called *Cronos*, a twenty-eight-year-old twerp from Mexico, and I do a pitch for *I Am Legend,* and I say, 'I don't think Arnold is right.' Not exactly the way to get the job."

Fortunately for Guillermo, the work he did to develop a new kind of vampire for *I Am Legend* was exactly what he needed to bring a fresh take—and monster—to *Blade II*. Guillermo saw the challenge of the Reapers in *Blade II* as a series of surprises. "You think you know the Reapers. You know what they look like, and then the jaw opens. It's a completely new shock. Then when we see them in the sewers, they're upside down. Every time, they evolve. I think that it's very important not to make the creatures a single entity, but have aspects of them that you discover. You need to really play with perspective and have layers that open and reveal something else."

At that first meeting with Goyer and Snipes, Guillermo laid his cards on the table. "I said to Wesley Snipes, 'I don't understand Blade at all because, if I met those vampires, I would like them. You take care of Blade; I'll take care of the vampires.' And that's the way the movie was shot. I never told Wesley what Blade would do or not do, because I didn't know. I was like, 'Whatever makes you tick. I don't understand you.' But Nomak, Luke Goss's character, I directed with all the love I could, as sort of a Frankenstein's monster, tragic. For me, Nomak is the hero of that movie."

Unlike *Mimic,* where he submerged key aspects of his nature to try to dance to Hollywood's tune, Guillermo deliberately made *Blade II* into the kind of film that would have delighted his teenage self. And so *Blade II* is exuberant, vivid, unrestrained. Feelings are *intense,* actions full-out, colors comic-book lurid.

The same goes for his *Blade II* notebook. A pasteboard of youthful enthusiasm, these pages chart the evolution of the Reapers from their earliest incarnation many years before into a spectacular, near-final design for *Blade II*. Also featured are snatches of dialogue, discarded vampire guard uniforms, colorful tattoos, Gothic architecture, drawings of the Prague sewers, suggested action sequences, and thoughts for composing shots.

In the end, only the smallest percentage of what Guillermo had in mind was put into *Blade II*. But seven years later, he and Chuck Hogan collaborated on *The Strain* trilogy of novels, painting a grim vision of the vampire apocalypse Guillermo had been meditating on for decades. "I'm very surprised and happy that they were successful," Guillermo says of the books, "because I wrote them with Chuck, I wrote them for our own pleasure, and I wrote them because I wanted to put all that stuff on paper."

(OPPOSITE, CLOCKWISE FROM TOP LEFT) Concepts illustrating how a Reaper disintegrates when hit with silver nitrate- and garlic-infused bullets by Mike Mignola; concepts of Nomak's fight with the security guards by Mike Mignola; Caliban Industries autopsy doctor concept by Mike Mignola; storyboards by del Toro; Wesley Snipes as Blade in a publicity photo for the movie.

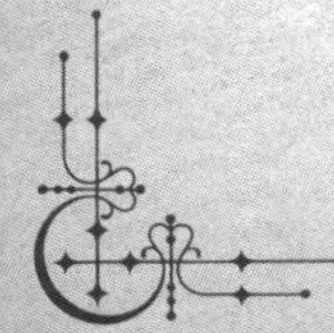

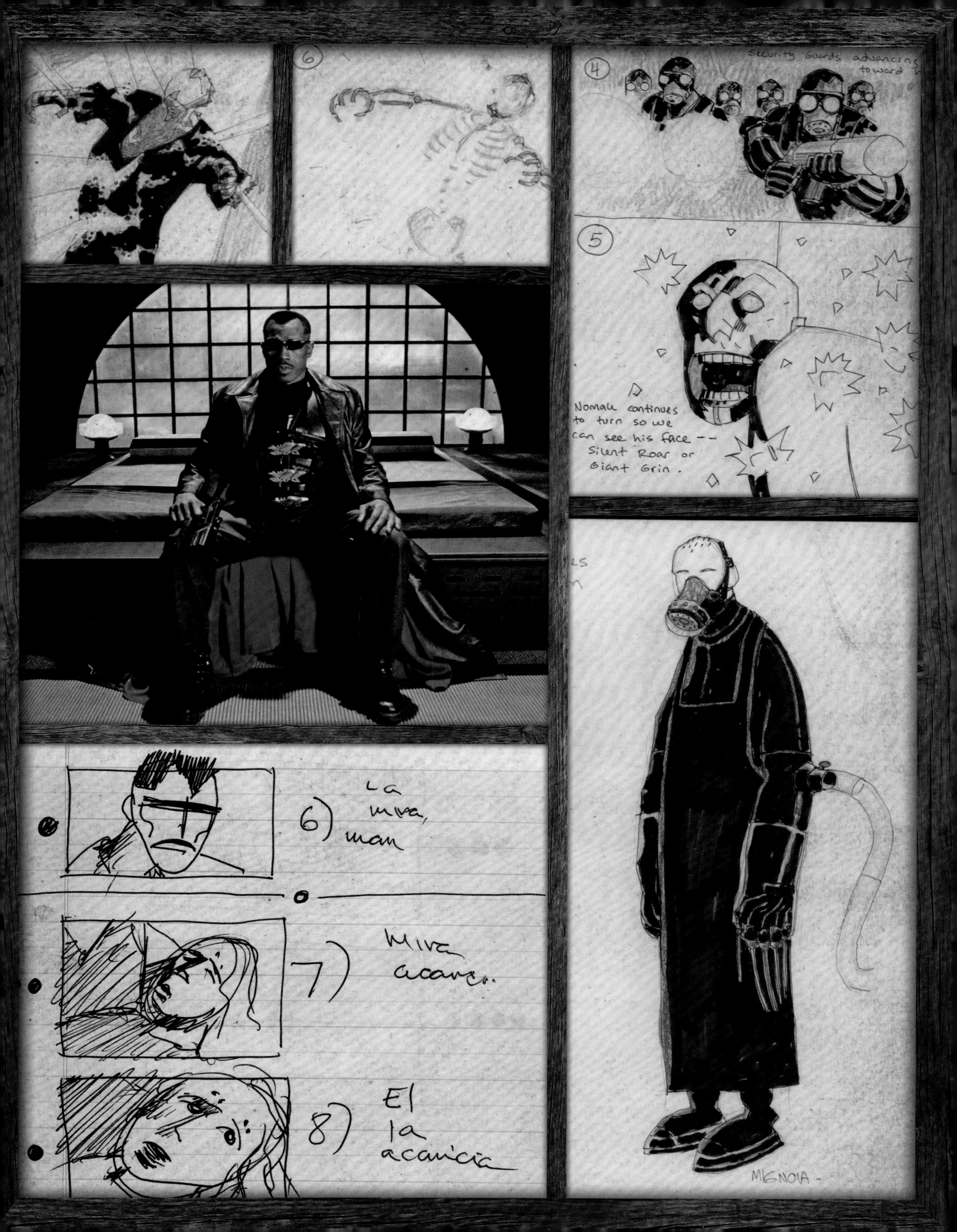

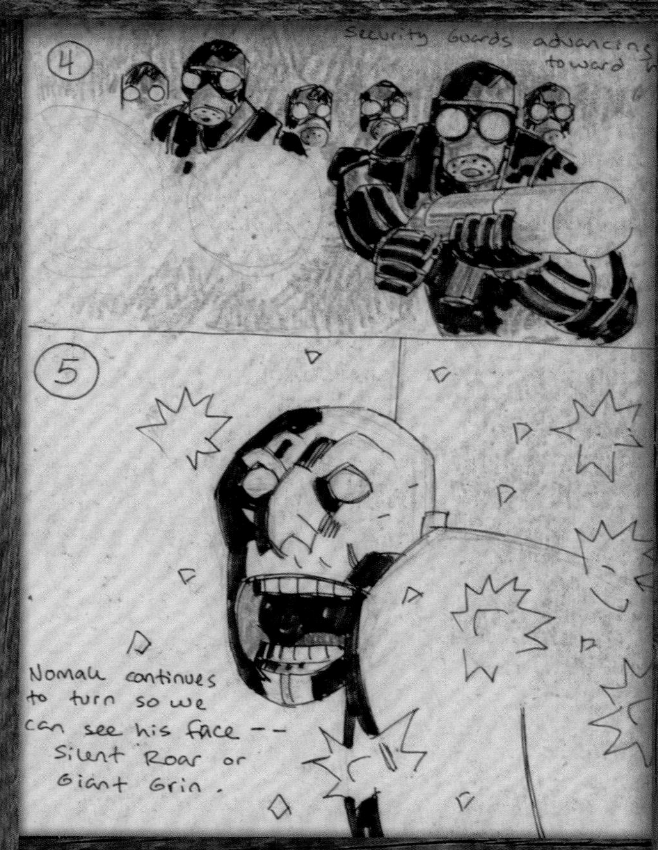
4
Security Guards advancing toward
5
Nomak continues to turn so we can see his face -- Silent Roar or Giant Grin.

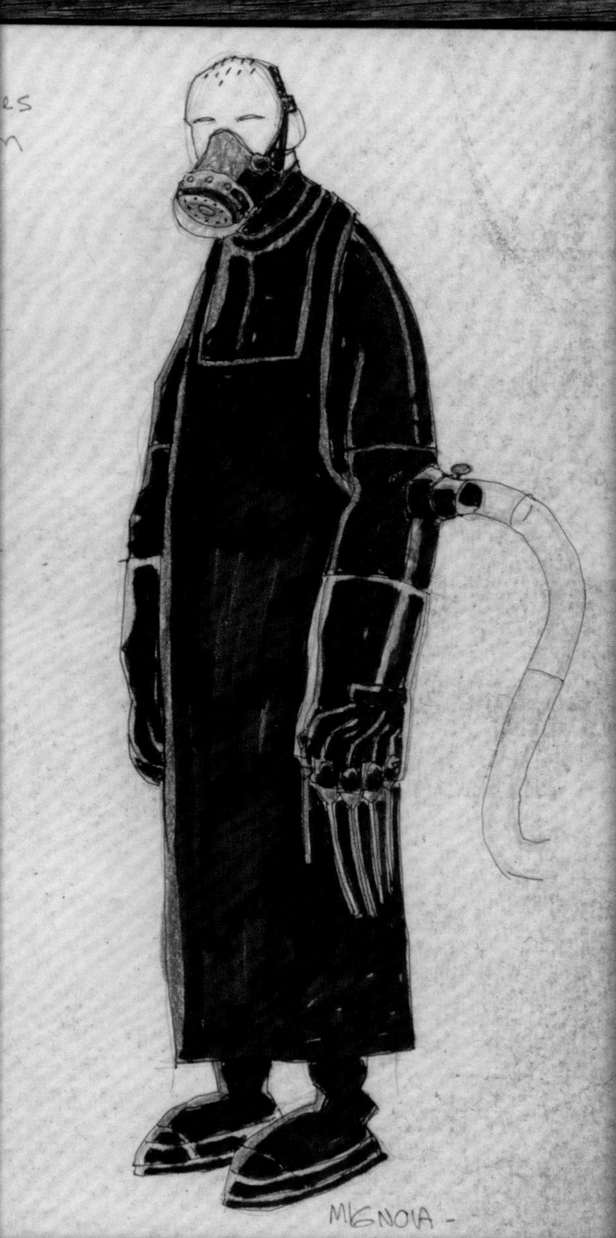
MIGNOLA -

–When Nyssa enters the lair in Blade, her temperature is -30° and she avoids UV damage to her eyes thanks to the fact that she wears special goggles with mechanical irises that close shut to keep it from reaching her retinas. Blade turns on a UV reflector strong enough to light up an entire stadium and the camera receives the "flow" full on. They're silhouettes fighting with 100% backlight.

Sometimes life offers us "tragedies" so that we might learn from them. God sends us the message but never the dictionary.

Long, narrow teeth

"Scud" gives Whistler a set of false teeth, with two silver and two gold teeth. After this kind gesture, the old man develops a certain affection for the young man. The film depicts Blade's enlightenment

● **GDT:** When I went into *Blade II*, I was very afraid. I was very afraid because I'm not a hip guy. I'm not a guy that is aware of the latest MTV music or whatever. The way that I find I'm very current is in manga, anime, and video games. I went to Mike De Luca and I said, "You realize I'm the most unhip motherfucker you can hire?" And he said, "That's fine." He said, "We want you to bring other stuff, not that."

I started to think I needed to make this movie different than the rest, because the movies I've done, they can either be movies that look like they're signed by an eight-year-old director or by an eighty-year-old director. I think *Cronos* is my oldest guy movie. It's the point of view of a very old guy. *Devil's Backbone* and *Pan's Labyrinth*, sort of in the same way. They have that sense. *Hellboy* is like an eight-year-old movie, and *Hellboy II* is the same thing. It's me at a very young age.

On *Blade II*, I said, "I need to be a teenager, so this needs to be a six-pack-and-a-pizza kind of movie." Like the kind of thing I would have loved to see when I was that age—almost like a musical of violence. I started ciphering some stuff that comes from manga and saying, "Well, I want the iris glasses," which will eventually also

(OPPOSITE) Del Toro envisioned iris glasses as central components of the lightproof outfits Nyssa and Asad wear during their initial confrontation with Blade (ABOVE). (LEFT) TyRuben Ellingson refined the concept.

(OPPOSITE) Del Toro played with the idea of basing some of the Bloodpack costumes on samurai armor but abandoned many of the details for *Blade II* (ABOVE), eventually applying them to the design of Prince Nuada in *Hellboy II* (BELOW).

find their way into Abe Sapien, and a really fetishistic rubber suit [*see page 116*]. For example, when you see the design of the suit on the right [*opposite*], it has a center that is rolled silk with a center medallion that is very Japanese.

In the end, I couldn't do it in this movie, but this exact color and pattern are found on Prince Nuada in *Hellboy II*. I like very much the fact that you can have a look that is very armored, but the true design of a really good warrior is to have a very, very exposed area. Now, what a lot of the Japanese samurai did is they layered the silk so dense that it would take longer to cut through the silk than it would take to cut through the armor. It's a very curious notion.

But as I started investigating this for *Blade II*, the teeth of Chupa on the left came to me [*see page 116*]. He has two golden teeth. He was going to be a Mexican vampire. Eventually, we cast a nice guy called Matt Schulze, who is as Mexican as a hot dog, y'know?

And you can see the idea of the row of lights on the right, next to Nyssa [*see page 116*].

And there [*opposite*], next to the armored figure, is the corroded concrete wall that ended up in the church.

The little eye is more or less the beginning of how we started playing with the contact lenses of the Reapers.

–It hides in your spinal cord and then it migrates along your nerves.

–Speed Bumps by cuts to give "speed"

–Bite and then run away <u>FAST</u>.

–We've been training in the abstract, but as of tomorrow things get real. You wanna know just how real? I'll tell ya . . . It's my guess that a lot of us won't make it through the day.

–"Stray dogs growl at Chupa in alley

Wall in HOP.

–Everybody wears goggles for daylight.

–Low [?] for sunlight.

–Light [?] frame.

–Reinhardt CORNERS HIMSELF by punching light holes in the ceiling.

Make the iris smaller or much bigger.

Long and thin teeth.

My eyes without your eyes aren't eyes at all. They're two lonely holes—.

Notebook 3, Page 24B

–There are things in life which are beautiful. To enjoy them is heaven. Not being capable of it, that's Hell

–It is impossible to outwit a stupid person. They never realize that they've been outwitted.

–You need space? Well, asshole, look out the window, see all that space? Well, so, go get the fuck outta here.

–Even I've been infected by time.

–You can choose a destiny. I was born into one.

–I've known you a long time, watch you become a man over the years I thought I knew who you were. So did I. But there's something inside.

–Scud watches I. CH. Talk 'bout it.

–When the sword stops, the air "blows" his/ her hair.

–The fight, use their leg to break beams

To stand up.

Blood Pack.

Notebook 3, Page 25A

GDT: Here [*above*] you can see a lot of stuff that made it, and a lot of stuff that didn't. On the left, I really wanted speakers that were four stories high in the party place, but we couldn't afford them.

And you can see me insisting on a Gothic architecture door! [laughs]

That shot of the sliding feet that is described there is in the movie. It's in the fight on the scaffolding.

And the gold artificial spinal cord is in the movie in the House of Pain.

The figure on the ground was an idea for how I could introduce one of the Bloodpack. I wanted one of them to be really petulant. When Blade arrives, he's lying on the floor, and he gets up, which is directly stealing from *Mad Max*.

The suit on the right [*opposite*] didn't make it, but this is what I wanted the vampire guards to wear. You can see how I'm echoing the helmet I became obsessed with for Abe Sapien with the asymmetry thing.

To the left of the vampire guard suit, you can see the bomb that Blade attaches to the head of Reinhardt.

MSZ: And what's this guy making the muscles?

GDT: I wanted a guy that was shaped like that to be part of the Bloodpack, but I couldn't find him.

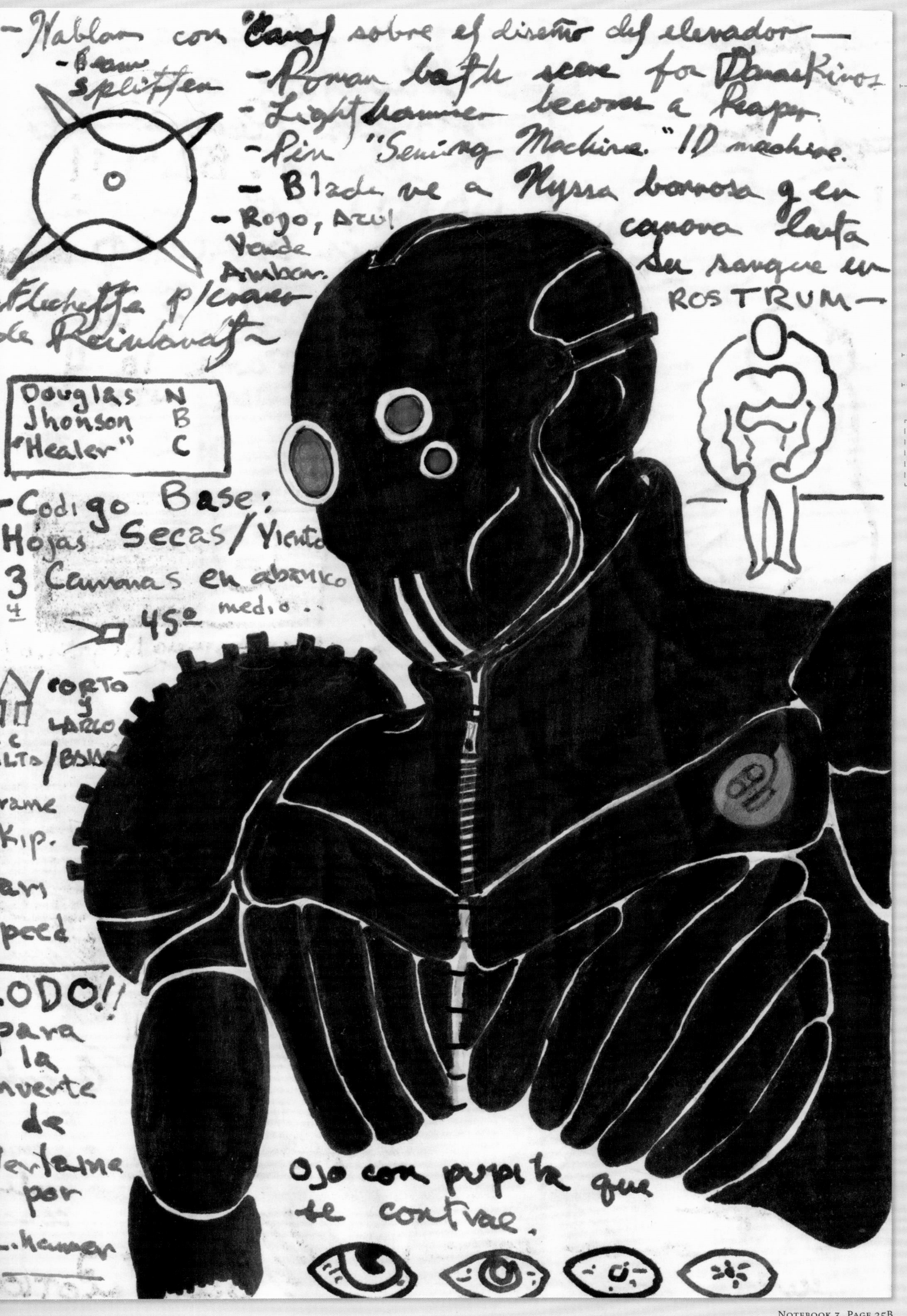

—Talk with Carol about the elevator's design—.

—Beam splitter

—Roman bath scene for Damaskinos

—Lighthammer becomes a Reaper.

—Pin "sewing machine." ID machine.

—Nyssa appears blurry and in slow motion to Blade, her blood in ROSTRUM—

—Red, Blue, Green, Amber.

—Flechette for Rheinhardt's head—

Douglas N
Jhonson B
"Healer" C

—Base code: Dry Leaves/ Wind

3 cameras on fan

R 4 45° medium.

Short and long

High/Low LC

Frame

skip.

Vam

Speed

MUD!! when Verlaine dies because of L.hammer

Eye with pupil that contracts.

–Is this closure? As close as its gonna get . . .

–Panicked crowd reveals Reaper latched on Priest. BAM!! BAM!! It turns around.

–Someone is DRAGGED away.

–Speak urgently with Carol about the possibility of a tunnel like this:

–For the 4 WAY INTERSECTION

–Large goggles, 22 FPS

TATTOO

Use negative space!!

Blood cascades out in SLOW MOTION *in the wind*

—Use the G CALVE [?] *in the scene* with Segura—.

Notebook 3, Page 26A

(ABOVE RIGHT, BOTTOM RIGHT) Del Toro originally wanted to have Nomak feast on the head of a helmeted guard as if it were a soft-boiled egg. While this particular scene didn't make it to the film, Nomak (Luke Goss) adopted a similar pose while finishing off Priest (Tony Curran) (ABOVE).

GDT: Some stuff here [*above*] made it into *Blade II*; some stuff didn't.

On the bottom of the page is a very brutal moment I wanted to put in the film—of Nomak with a broken helmet of a guard, eating him like a boiled egg. I couldn't quite get it, though.

And I just liked the pose of this figure [*on left*] for one of the Bloodpack.

I wanted one guy to have a crash test dummy tattoo because I thought it would be, like, really hardass.

The rest didn't make it. Little ideas about scares, or fight techniques. The little box there, with the face in it—that's a cheat that I like to do. I haven't done it much, but the idea is that if the audience sees negative space on the right, they expect something to come out on that side. The idea was to use a shadow because it makes it doubly intriguing—you know, the audience immediately says, "Oh, something's going to come out of the shadows there." So you get them scared that something is going to come out from the right, and then it comes from the left.

I did it in this movie, but I did it really, really badly. It doesn't work. You can see it in the House of Pain. When Nyssa enters and she hears a noise, Nomak comes from the other side. But I think we were, like, half a day late. Instead of doing a really great sequence, we had to do it in one shot. So I failed miserably. [laughs] But, you know, one day I'll do it right.

MSZ: And is that someone being decapitated by two swords?

GDT: Yeah, it's a move I wanted Blade to make, which was to do like a twist around a guy, and after he lands, the head comes off. We didn't do it.

The guy on the next page [*opposite*], I wanted him to be part of the Bloodpack, with that red tattoo, sort of tribal. And again, I drew the gold spinal cord, in case I forgot.

—Gold spinal column with ribs

Black fabric for Chupa

Light comes from above

–Slow motion with strobe lights (72) (48) (8)

–Very shallow focus, with things entering and exiting the visual field

Marble.

–Timing for the big fight that begins with the sound of an ice cube falling into a glass with liquid in it—.

–Sound is meant for *a* <u>*GRIPE*</u>

–Even I have now been infected by time . . .

–Chain link fences on both sides.

–220° to give a little "[?]" and at 12 or at 8 FPS (print at 8 FPS?).

–When you die you turn to dust

–Perhaps give Chupa a cowboy hat and make all his clothes black.

–Ultra slow motion *for the* <u>*bite*</u>

Notebook 3, Page 26B

–1/2 Dissolve spanking for Reapers.

–They go crazy with pain like B.R.P.

–Film some of the fights at 22 fps with variations in the shutter: 45°, 90°. Do some tests

–The Reapers should move on all fours like apes, but they need to make very high-pitched sounds, like squealing pig-people.

–The call of the Reapers should be like the trailing breath of a human laugh: cackle-cackle

–The Prague sewers are oval in shape, not round, and they're made of concrete. There are carvings on the bricks.

–The oldest vampire's lair should look much older than the rest of the building in which it is located.

–Look for a memorable detail for Scud and one for Whistler: perhaps he finds his wedding ring behind a moldy machine.

- 1/2 Dissolve spanking for Reapers.
- Se vuelven locos de dolor como B.R.P.
- Filmar algunas de las peleas a 22 fps y con variaciones en el obturador: 45°, 90°. Hacer pruebas
- Los Reapers se deben mover a cuatro patas como simios, pero deben de sonar muy agudos, como el chiflido de un cerdo-human
- El llamado de los Reapers debe de ser como la última parte de una risa humana: cackle-cackle
- Las alcantarillas de Praga son de forma ovoidal, no redondas y de concreto. La anteravía está en el ladrillo.
- La guarida de el vampiro más viejo debe de parecer mucho más antigua que el resto del edificio en el que está ubicada.
- Buscar un detalle para Scud y uno para Whistler: quizá encuentra su anillo de casado detrás de una máquina enmohecida

Notebook 3, Page 27A

(ABOVE) Nyssa (Leonor Varela) plays cat and mouse with a Reaper in the sewers. The Prague sewers, which served as the underground location for *Blade II*, were scouted extensively by del Toro and other members of the film crew.

GDT: This is the drawing [*opposite*] I did based on some photographs of the Prague sewers, which have a very vaginal feel. We scouted the sewers for the movie. It was a really unforgettable experience.

MSZ: What made it unforgettable?

GDT: I love urban exploration. I used to do it a lot as a kid in Guadalajara. And there's a thing that you find in sewers, a white mucus that is really, really thick, and it hangs in stalactites in sewers, and it is literally like huge cultures, bacteria cultures, like a living mucus.

So in Prague, when we went, it was the biggest amount of mucus I've ever seen. Mike Mignola and I entered, and it smelled like old yogurt, and it was like they had shot a porn film with Godzilla. It was incredible, complex. There were, like, traceries and alcoves of mucus. And just going through the sewers and seeing the domes, the big areas, the small areas, the narrow areas, it was fantastic. I asked a sewer worker in Prague, I said, "Do a lot of people scout?" And he said, "No, nobody comes in here that doesn't have to." There was an area where they opened it up and he said, "We'll wait for you outside."

GDT: This drawing [*opposite*] was made because we didn't want to give any drawings to anybody, so when we were budgeting, I would show this drawing, or I would do a new drawing on a piece of paper for each of the makeup guys that were budgeting. Finally, the guy that did it was Steve Johnson. He's one of the best. I think he did phenomenal work. Obviously my drawing is very similar to the final one, but very different. I think the final one is so much better.

MSZ: Why didn't you want to give the drawings to people?

GDT: Because we thought that it was a really unique idea. It's very hard to think of a unique vampire, and I felt that I had arrived at a really good idea with the Reapers. I didn't want it to end up showing up six months later in *Buffy*. Like, "Oh."

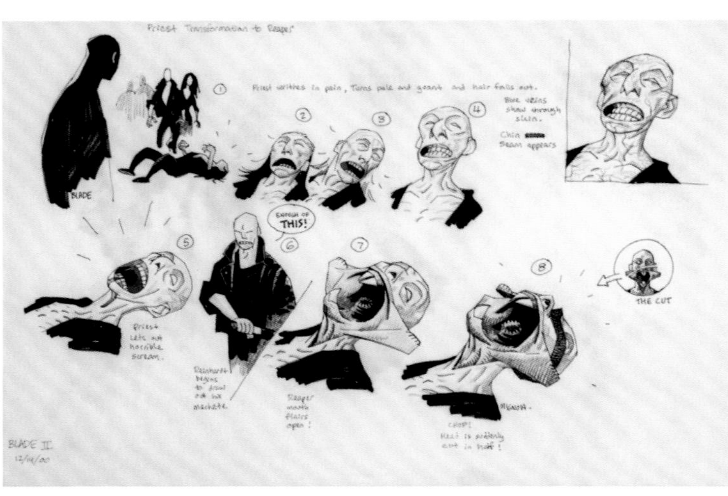

(OPPOSITE) Del Toro's concept for the Reapers, based in Eastern European vampire folklore, was carefully protected as the film moved toward production. (ABOVE) Makeup artist Steve Johnson created the final design, which revealed a nest of predatory organs accessible via a split in a Reaper's jaw, here visible on Nomak (Luke Goss) (RIGHT). (TOP) Concept of Priest's transformation into a Reaper by Mike Mignola.

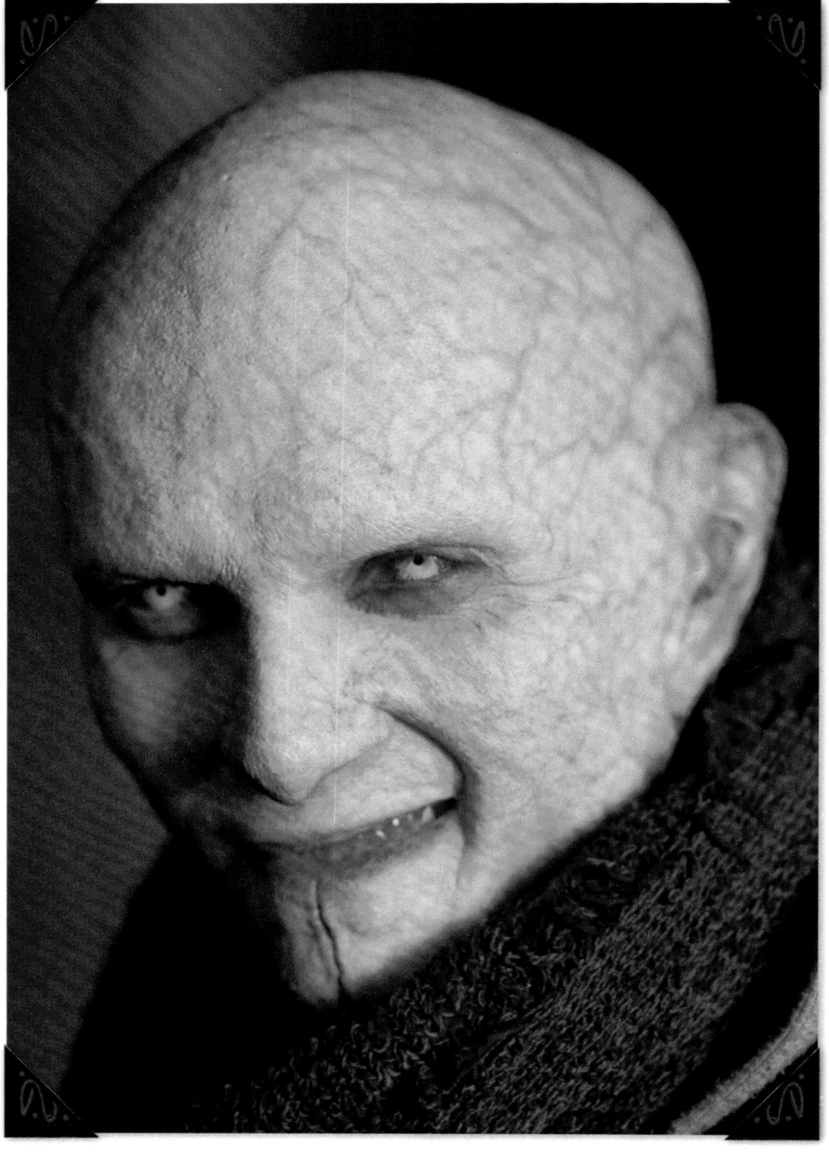

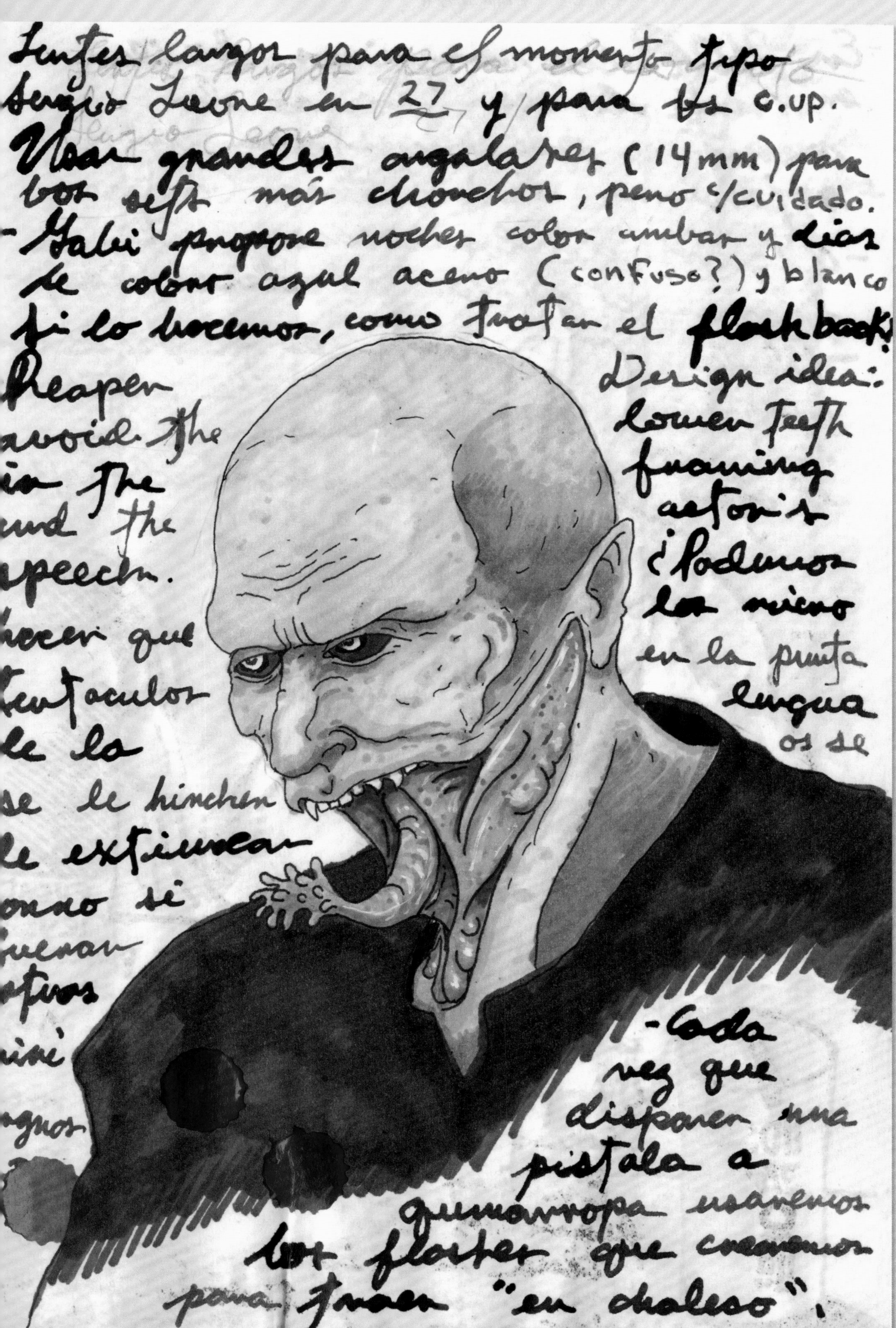

Lentes largos para el momento tipo Sergio Leone en 27 y para los c.up.
Usar grandes angulares (14mm) para los sets más chonchos, pero c/cuidado.
-Gabi propone noches color ambar y días de color azul acero (confuso?) y blanco si lo hacemos, como tratar el flashback.

Reaper
avoid the
the
and the
speech.
hacer que
tentaculos
de la
se le hinchen
se extiendan
como si
fueran
otras
mini
lenguas

Design idea:
lower teeth
framing
actor's
¿Podemos
los micro
en la punta
lengua
os se

-Cada vez que disparen una pistola a quemarropa usaremos los flashes que creamos para traer "en chaleco".

—Long lenses for the Sergio Leone–type moment in 27 *and for bs c.up.*

—Use wide-angle lenses (14 mm) for the deepest sets, but with caution.

—Gabi suggests that the nights be amber and the days steel blue (confused?) and white. If we go ahead with this, how do we handle the flashback

—Reaper Design idea: avoid the lower teeth in the framing and the actor's speech. *Could we make the same micro tentacles that are on the tip of their tongues swell up or extend outward as if they were additional little tongues?*

—Each time they shoot a pistol at point-blank range, we'll use the flashes we create for the actors to wear inside their "vests."

* Now that we have every reason to think otherwise, we hear a telephone conversation (only one side) and EVERYTHING has a double meaning (someone's listening).

* Somebody always THINKS badly about the NATIVES of a certain country and about those of his own country.

* Tumor or parasitic heart that works opposite a normal heart. It has a modular or "NODULAR" structure

* With a dirty plan, "foul play" in mind, they tell the "don": "It must be an error no doubt" and then after mulling it over for a long time, ". . . no doubt"

* Children playing in the waves, seen from behind.

* Somebody who knew ARTEAGA and made fun of him "REVEALS" to us his past.

* Object buried in his chest, when it's pulled, it pulls his chest.

* Ernie is "given" (he inherits) the "key" with which everything in the M/M runs

* Ernie: Kiss and faint.

92

* Ya teniendo todos los elementos p/ pensar lo contrario escuchamos una conversación telefónica (solo un lado) y TODO es doble sentido (alguien escucha)

* Alguien OPINA TODO el tiempo mal de los NATIVOS de algún país y de su país

* tumor o corazón parasitario que opera al lado opuesto del corazón normal. Su estructura es modular. o "NODULAR"

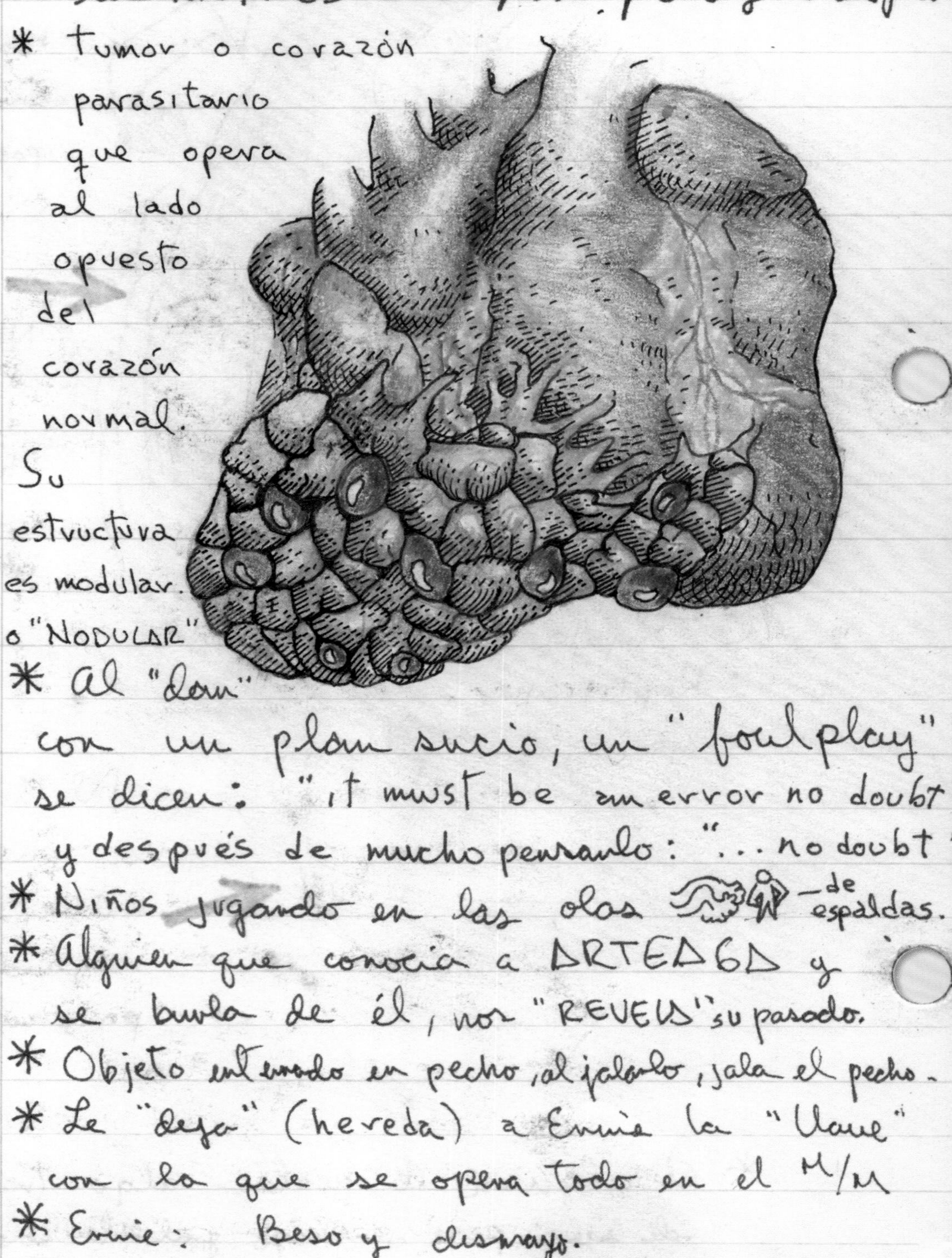

* Al "don" con un plan sucio, un "foulplay" se dicen: "it must be an error no doubt y después de mucho pensarlo: "...no doubt"

* Niños jugando en las olas — de espaldas.

* Alguien que conocía a ARTEAGA y se burla de él, nos "REVELA" su pasado.

* Objeto enterrado en pecho, al jalarlo, jala el pecho.

* Le "deja" (hereda) a Ernie la "llave" con la que se opera todo en el M/M

* Ernie: Beso y desmayo.

Blue Notebook, Page 92

* If you love "meee," make 'er bleed."

* *The A/B/C from the Quiroga plan.*

* *The needle's thread →CHRIST.*

* *Everybody talks about the Devil's evil, God's evil.*

* *He is: a man of God †/ Goat's leg and I'm the virgin devil, pure evil.*

* *She is the devil/of the devil.*

* CITY IN FIRE 1912.

* SAMURAI (police story)

* "How to MASTER U'R V. GOMES" *Finger exercises*

* PROOF: Move earlier

* I . . . you . . . I love your . . . the way you dress the way . . . your hubcaps . . .

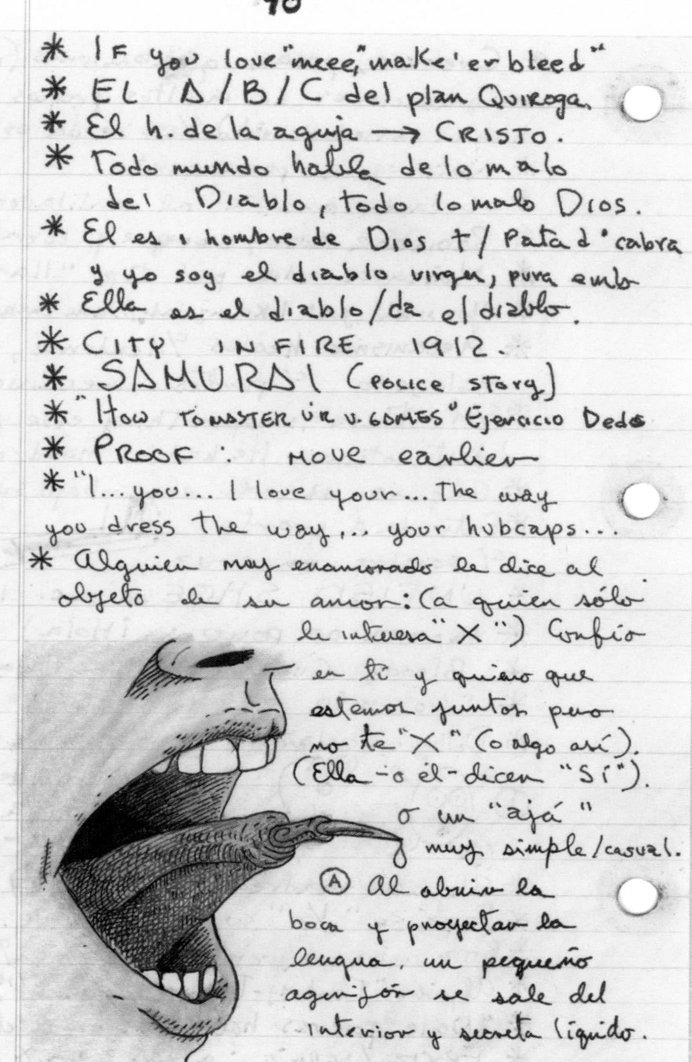

* *Somebody who's deeply in love tells his loved one: (who is interested only in "X") I trust you and I want us to be together but I don't "X" you (or something like that). (She—or he—says "Yes"). or "aha" very simply, casually.*

(A) When he opens his mouth and sticks out his tongue, a small thorn emerges from its tip and secretes a liquid.

Blue Notebook, Page 90

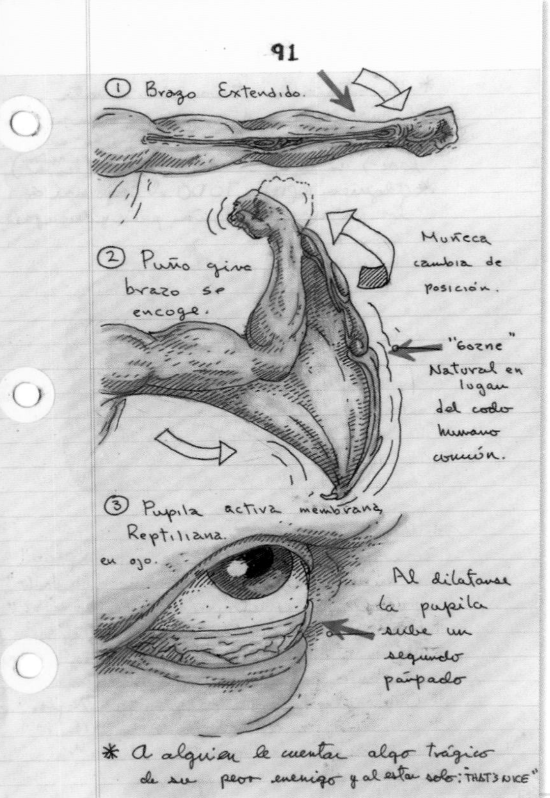

(1) Extended arm

(2) Fist turns, arm shrinks.

Wrist changes position.

Natural "hinge" instead of a common human elbow.

(3) Pupil activates reptilian membrane in his eye

When the pupil dilates, a second eyelid slides up over the eye.

* *Somebody tells him something tragic about his worst enemy and when he is alone:* "THAT'S NICE"

Blue Notebook, Page 91

● **GDT:** Now these pages [*above, left, and opposite*] are full of notes on vampirism that make it all the way to *Blade II* and *The Strain*. The stinger, the nictating membrane. It's funny. These were done in '93, years and years and years before. I write, "When he opens his mouth and sticks out his tongue, a small thorn emerges from its tip and secretes a liquid." When I was a kid, I had a fascination with the origins of vampirism, and in eastern Europe, the vampire, the *strigoi*, have a stinger under the tongue.

MSZ: So you were actually designing your vampires back in 1993 in these drawings?

GDT: Yeah, yeah. These were ideas I couldn't put in *Cronos*. I was making an inventory of vampiric stuff. Then this idea of the tumor, like a parasitic heart growing in the human heart, came to me at some point. My thought was, "Okay, how does it actually happen?" A vampire bites you, the virus spreads, parasitic organs grow next to your heart. They suffocate the heart. The patient dies, and then the vampiric heart starts beating and the vampire wakes up. That idea gave birth to *The Strain*.

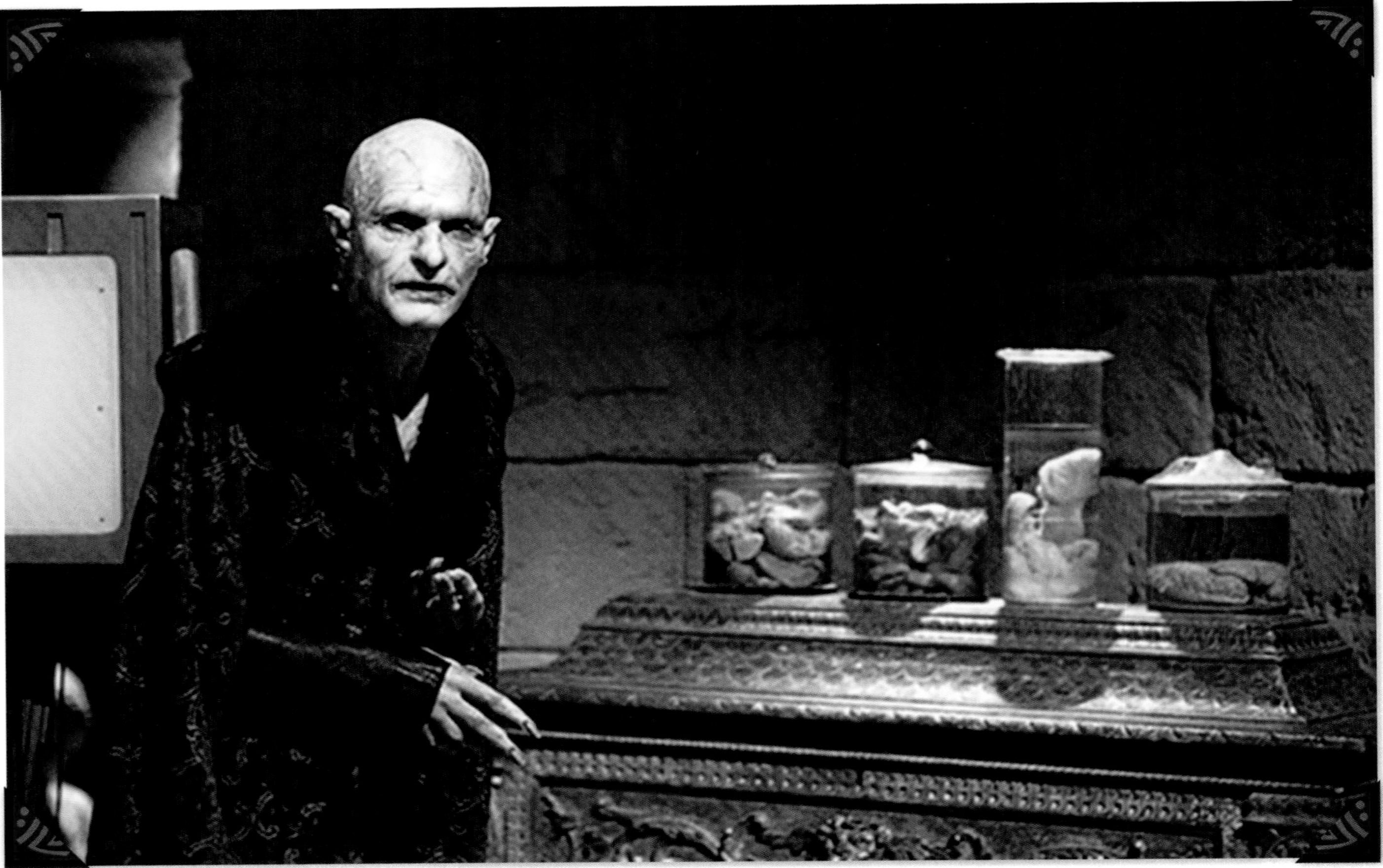

MSZ: So then we come to this illustration [*opposite*] of Damaskinos, the vampire king.

GDT: The idea here with Damaskinos was an exploration in color. Back then, I wanted to evoke a guy that looks like he's from a Bruegel painting—like an aristocrat from the Renaissance. And the idea of the skin being made of cracked white-blue marble? Like, see the striations of the marble? It's a demonstration of how old he is, and it comes from *Cronos*. I tried it first in *Cronos*, but the makeup was not good enough. And I tried it again here, and guess what? The makeup was not good enough again. I tried it yet again in *Hellboy II* with Prince Nuada. I think that came out decent. It was not marble by then; it was ivory. I'm bound to try it again.

MSZ: And then there's a halo, almost like a saint.

GDT: I was trying to evoke wall portraiture, so I wrote some fake Latin, too. Completely fake.

MSZ: And the notes you have along the periphery about 1930s motion detectors, a body that twitches and then appears to come alive, but that is really covered with squids. What was that for?

GDT: Well, that is all in *Mountains*. In a way. Not all of it, but some of it. The 1930s motion detectors are a good idea. [laughs]

(TOP & ABOVE) Del Toro wanted Damaskinos (Thomas Kretschmann), the vampire king, to have cracked, white-blue skin (OPPOSITE), an idea he had been toying with since *Cronos*.

–Cannibalistic squids in the whole torso of a victim. Animals are a part of a cave's texture (walls).

–They see the body twitch and the think: ALIVE!! . . . but when they turn it, it's covered with "squids"

–1930's motion detectors for the ice—

It is both sad, sad and very apparent that in this, the "age of communication" no one calls.

–Dead animals in a circle

–Under the ice chase w/ gun to take a breath

–In Hellboy, we'll use grays, blues, greens, etc., and except for Chinatown, things Nazi, and Hellboy himself, we won't use reds

–Diagonal beams "a la" Piranesi.

–A man is dismembering a corpse. Someone knocks at the door. He wants to speak with the man's wife to sell her a vacuum cleaner. NOT TODAY. NOT A GOOD DAY. *DAMASKINOS ON THE BLADE II POST 1/21/02.*

mas
-Ed
mos
SEPURA
DESGO ESS
MIGNOLA
FOR GUILLERMO -- My boy is in good hands -
MMII

HELLBOY

"AT ONE POINT, I was going to do *Mimic,* and Jim Cameron said, 'Aren't you afraid people will pigeonhole you as a horror director?'" Guillermo recalls. "I said, 'I'd *love* that!'"

Artist and writer Mike Mignola—the creator of the *Hellboy* comic book series—is a kindred spirit, someone who happily let his passion for horror tropes define his place in the world of comic books. "I've just always liked monsters," Mignola said in a 2012 podcast interview with *Geek's Guide to the Galaxy.* "Since I was a little kid, it was always the thing I found interesting. It's always what I wanted to draw. It's always what I wanted to read."

In the same interview, Mignola recalled how he came up with the comic's eponymous character. "I'd made some noise about creating my own comic. I'd been working for Marvel and DC for ten years, had done a little bit of everything. . . . The more I thought about it, the more I really wanted to draw just what *I* wanted to draw, and the only name I'd ever come up with was Hellboy."

Mignola added, "For whatever reason, the comic . . . appealed to a broader audience maybe than a lot of the regular comics I was doing. And then certainly you've got to give a lot of credit to the movie. I got really lucky that a very, very talented director happened to be a fan of the comic."

Harlan Ellison has said that everything a writer writes, whether fiction or nonfiction, is ultimately autobiography, and this is certainly true of Guillermo's approach to writing and filmmaking. The reason he was drawn to *Hellboy* was that he saw himself in this ungainly, unlikely superhero, this extraordinary outsider, this child-man striving to find a place for himself in a world ill-suited to his dimensions and diversions. Not for Guillermo were Batman or Superman, those oddballs who nevertheless so successfully imitate normal men. Hellboy, on the other hand, someone who lacks that ability, was a perfect fit.

From the start, Guillermo brought Mignola in to work closely with him on the movie's design and story elements, but nonetheless Guillermo felt free to deviate from Mignola's comic book to explore issues that were personally important. "Even though they both arrived on Earth in the forties, somehow del Toro's Hellboy is still a lovesick teenager," Mignola explains. "My Hellboy is modeled on my father in some way, a guy who's been in the Korean War, and he's traveled and he's done

(OPPOSITE, CLOCKWISE FROM TOP LEFT) Page from Rasputin's journal by Mike Mignola; storyboard panel of Sammael by Simeon Wilkins; drawing of Hellboy by Mike Mignola given to del Toro when wrapping *Hellboy* preproduction; sculpture depicting Hellboy's confrontation with the Behemoth; Rasputin (Karel Roden), flanked by Ilsa (Biddy Hodson) and Kroenen (Ladislav Beran); storyboard panel of Abe Sapien by Simeon Wilkins; concept of a young Hellboy by Wayne Barlowe; Sammael sculpture by Spectral Motion.

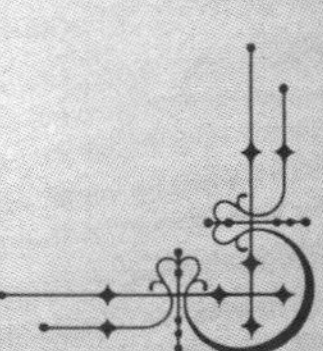

a lot of stuff, and he's kind of got a 'been there, done that' attitude. He's been in the world. And del Toro's change was to have Hellboy bottled up in a room and mooning over the girl he can't have. My Hellboy, there were just no girl problems. That element of the character was completely not in the comic."

As with *Blade II*, Guillermo realized that he wanted to craft a film that would appeal to a particular aspect of himself: the eight-year-old boy inside. That meant that *Hellboy* would be excessive, he explains, "in the way that a gold-leaf-covered Baroque church in Mexico is excessive. The whole statement is excess. And if you know me, and you know my life, and you know my house, I'm not exactly going for the Zen stuff. So the two *Hellboy*s are very excessive."

Hellboy's excessiveness extended in particular to the color palette, with no apologies. Visually, Guillermo notes, "the films I'm the proudest of are the *Hellboy*s, because I don't care if people like them or not, I just think they are absolutely beautiful to look at."

Not every bold idea planned for *Hellboy* made it into the final 2004 film. "Originally, the idea for *Hellboy* was that the whole movie was going to be told with *When Harry Met Sally*–type of interviews," Guillermo explains. "So people would be saying, 'I saw Hellboy over here. I saw him jump,' and a kid saying, 'I saw him on the rooftop.' Now everybody does it, but back then it was 1997, '98, and I thought that was a great idea. That was the first thing we cut out of the shooting schedule because [the studio executives] didn't understand it."

Even after being narratively domesticated, *Hellboy* provided fertile ground to plant seeds from earlier unmade projects. In the notebook pages, we see Guillermo drawing heavily on design elements from his unrealized film adaptations of *At the Mountains of Madness* (from the novel by H. P. Lovecraft), *Mephisto's Bridge* (from the novel *Spanky* by Christopher Fowler), and *The Left Hand of Darkness* (a version of *The Count of Monte Cristo* by Alexandre Dumas).

In *Hellboy*'s villain Kroenen (Ladislav Beran), the steampunk aesthetic of *The Left Hand of Darkness* was given a Third Reich twist. The studies Guillermo created for *Mephisto's Bridge* yielded Kroenen's face, devoid of eyelids and lips. And from the nightmarish Old Ones of *At the Mountains of Madness*, *Hellboy*'s demon Sammael (Brian Steele) was birthed.

Amid simulated blood splotches and arcane symbols reminiscent of Lovecraft's *Necronomicon*, Guillermo explored design elements for all *Hellboy*'s main characters. He was particularly intent on rendering both Hellboy (Ron Perlman) and his sidekick Abe Sapien (Doug Jones) vivid and—for all their peculiarities—human. Most notably, Guillermo strove to evolve Hellboy from the creature Mignola devised into something Ron Perlman could play, drawing him as a hundred-year-old Victorian, an elegant creation in long pants, or cloaking him in a U.S. Civil War–style leather coat. He wrote in the notebook's margin: "Hellboy has lots of cats running around everywhere." All these embellishments, Guillermo relates, were "my ways of finding Ron in there."

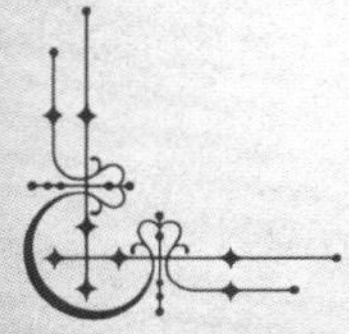

Many of the notebook's concepts made it into the film, while others were abandoned due to budgetary concerns, production logistics, or in the interest of gaining a PG-13 rating. In one case, though, Guillermo jettisoned a fish mouth intended for Abe Sapien because a horrified Mignola offered to give him any four original *Hellboy* comic panels if he would abandon the notion.

In the end, *Hellboy* shares the signature trait of all Guillermo's English-language, studio-sponsored films—Guillermo himself, who throws his entire self into every film wholeheartedly. "Everything about me is consistent," he observes. "People have a saying in Mexico, 'The way you eat is the way you dance, the way you dance is the way you fuck,' and you continue like that.

"I haven't made eight movies. I'm trying to make a *single* movie made of all those movies. To me, it's like Bleak House. I'm building room by room, and you have to take it as a whole in a way. Does that mean that maybe *Devil's Backbone* and *Pan's Labyrinth* make *Mimic* a little less terrible? I think so. Or the echoes of those may make *Blade II* more interesting? I think so.

"The one thing I can say is that, inarguably, I may go three, four years without shooting a movie here or there, but everything I've done I've done on my own terms. I've never had to stray from what I believe is right."

(ABOVE) The notebook containing del Toro's notes on *Hellboy* (Notebook 3), opened to pages 15A and 15B, which contain an early iteration of the demon Sammael with wings.

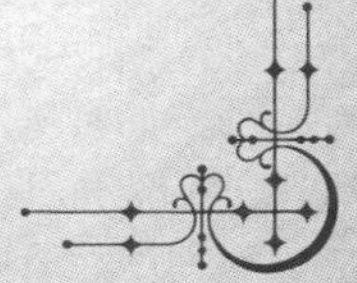

(RIGHT) Basil Gogos's portrait of Hellboy as a Victorian gentleman, commissioned by del Toro after his illustration of Hellboy at an advanced age (OPPOSITE).

● **MSZ:** And here [*opposite*], of course, we have this elderly Hellboy.

GDT: What is funny is that he is dressed like a nineteenth-century gentleman, and he is supposed to be a hundred years old. Mike plays with the universe of Hellboy, and I was fascinated by the fact that Hellboy can be in a samurai context, or he can be in a Victorian context, and there's no explanation given. I just like the idea that his sideburns are like Victorian sideburns. There's no explanation. I just wanted to do it. I also wanted to find a way to work with the stumps of the horns because Mike does them so quickly they are like goggles on top of his head. I was trying to figure out, "Are they jagged? Are they . . . ?" This was the first approach, where they are rolled, but that didn't work. We ended up grabbing a piece of ivory, breaking it, and doing those surfaces.

MSZ: In the notes on the page, you mention Basil Gogos—that you had hoped he would do a painting of this.

GDT: He did. It's upstairs at Bleak House. It's a funny story. I had not met Basil or contacted him. It was the early days of the Internet, so I went through the white pages, and I just found, like, four Gogoses in New York. There was a "Gogos, B.," and I called, and he picked up, and I said, "Are you Basil Gogos?" He said, "Yes." And I commissioned the painting. At the time it was so expensive for me. I don't know how I paid him.

–During the [?] they disconnect the phone, but she has the cell phone so he hears her whole plea. They cut the power off. They lock the windows and the doors, and open a window to blow out a candle.

–The tape is about the adults' failure and absence

–Someone discovers one of them trapped in one of the mousetraps. It's bleeding!!

When I made this portrait of Hellboy, I thought it would be used as the basis for an oil painting by Basil Gogos, but it looks as though this isn't going to happen. Yesterday I thought that Mignola might be able to do the Monte Cristo comic because his style lends itself very well to the Gothic. I think the mechanical hand might be very interesting visually. What would happen if I proposed to do Mephisto with Ted McKeever. I think it might be a good idea.

Señor HB at age of 101 yrs.

(OPPOSITE) To help ensure an actor could play Hellboy, del Toro thought to cloak the character in a duster that would hide the dissimilarity of square human shoulders to the sloping, ape-like ones of Mike Mignola's original character. (ABOVE LEFT) A classic Mignola depiction of Hellboy shows a more human look. Del Toro's idea was implemented in the costuming for the final film (ABOVE).

● **GDT:** This drawing [*opposite*] is a variation on Mignola, because Mignola does the sloping gorilla shoulders [*above*]. The reason I drew this was I was already thinking of Ron Perlman in the role, which meant the shoulders needed to be human. I wanted to see how he would look. Some of the stuff that ends up in the movie is already there. You can see he's wearing pants, whereas Mignola's Hellboy wears shorts. This is already my way of finding Ron in there.

This drawing is also important in the sense that it was right at the time where I felt, "It's going to happen." So I drew Hellboy because I felt, "Well, I gotta learn to draw him before I make the movie or I won't be able to understand him." So this was an attempt.

Notebook 3, Page 30B

Another version of Hellboy drawn just to kill time or so I don't forget.

Agoura Hills on 25/11/2001

—Domu, he's mugged in the subway and kills every one of them there.

—She and him are able to do the fastest reading of books and files.

—It takes 1 blackout to go back to the Middle Ages in any city anyplace.

—"Fuck you. I have more taste on my dick."

DAOD —Dad please get me out of here. I'm so, so tired. Get me out.

—You have a choice: You can believe her or simply think that she's having a total nervous breakdown. Either way her mother will help her calm down.

5/06/99 14.00 De Luca Pena Rojo.

H.B. running

—Climbing the rose trellis.

You're telling me that something reached out through that fireplace and pulled them through the hole?

—I only know what I've been able to piece together over the years. He opened the fireplace. But it was already there . . .

Smoke. Dissipated with wings

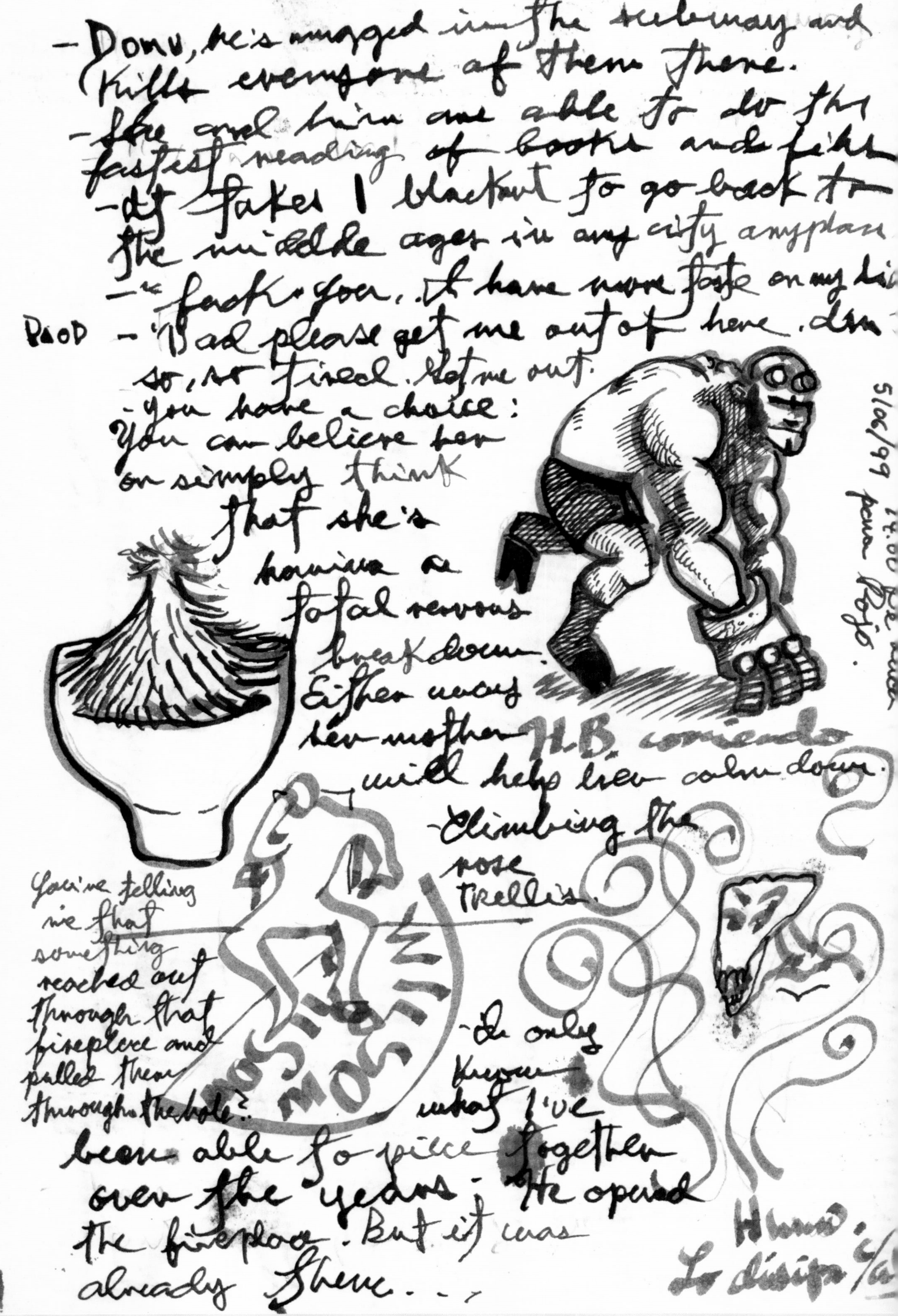

Notebook 3, Page 18A

One of the challenges del Toro faced on *Hellboy* was minimizing the ape-like qualities of his protagonist (OPPOSITE) and making the character more human, so that the love story between Hellboy (Ron Perlman) and Liz (Selma Blair) would be believable (LEFT). An important part of this process was finding star Ron Perlman in Hellboy's features (BELOW & BOTTOM).

MSZ: The evolution of how you approached Hellboy is interesting. I remember there's a note in this notebook where you say initially you were thinking of doing Hellboy as CG, and then maybe having close shots of a real person. But, of course, that evolved and that wasn't how you approached it.

GDT: Well, that shift came out of a conversation with Jim Cameron. I was saying to him, "I want to create a giant puppet like Mighty Joe Young," because I love gorillas, and I thought, "Hellboy could be kind of King Kong–ish—a big, ten-foot-tall brute."

I visited Rick Baker, and I saw the controls of Mighty Joe Young, and I said, "It's absolutely possible." I asked Jim, "What do you think?" And Jim said, "That's a great idea, except there's one thing you won't be able to do." And I said, "What?" "The love story. Because you can make the girl kind of like the monster, but the really human love story, that's not going to play." I said, "That's absolutely right."

So I went back and talked to Rick. He said, "Well, there are these two guys, Chad [Waters] and Matt [Rose], that are obsessed with Hellboy, and they want to do a test for you where he's Ron Perlman." And I always wanted him to be voiced by Ron regardless—I always wanted Ron to be the face of the character. So they did that bust on the stairs at Bleak House [*above right*], Matt did, and it was clear to me it was going to be a prosthetic job.

One-year embryo

Sammael as a fetus

Reversible arms for Sammael.

"Reversible" legs for Sammael

Fingers can turn in any direction

Mouth with outside tongue.

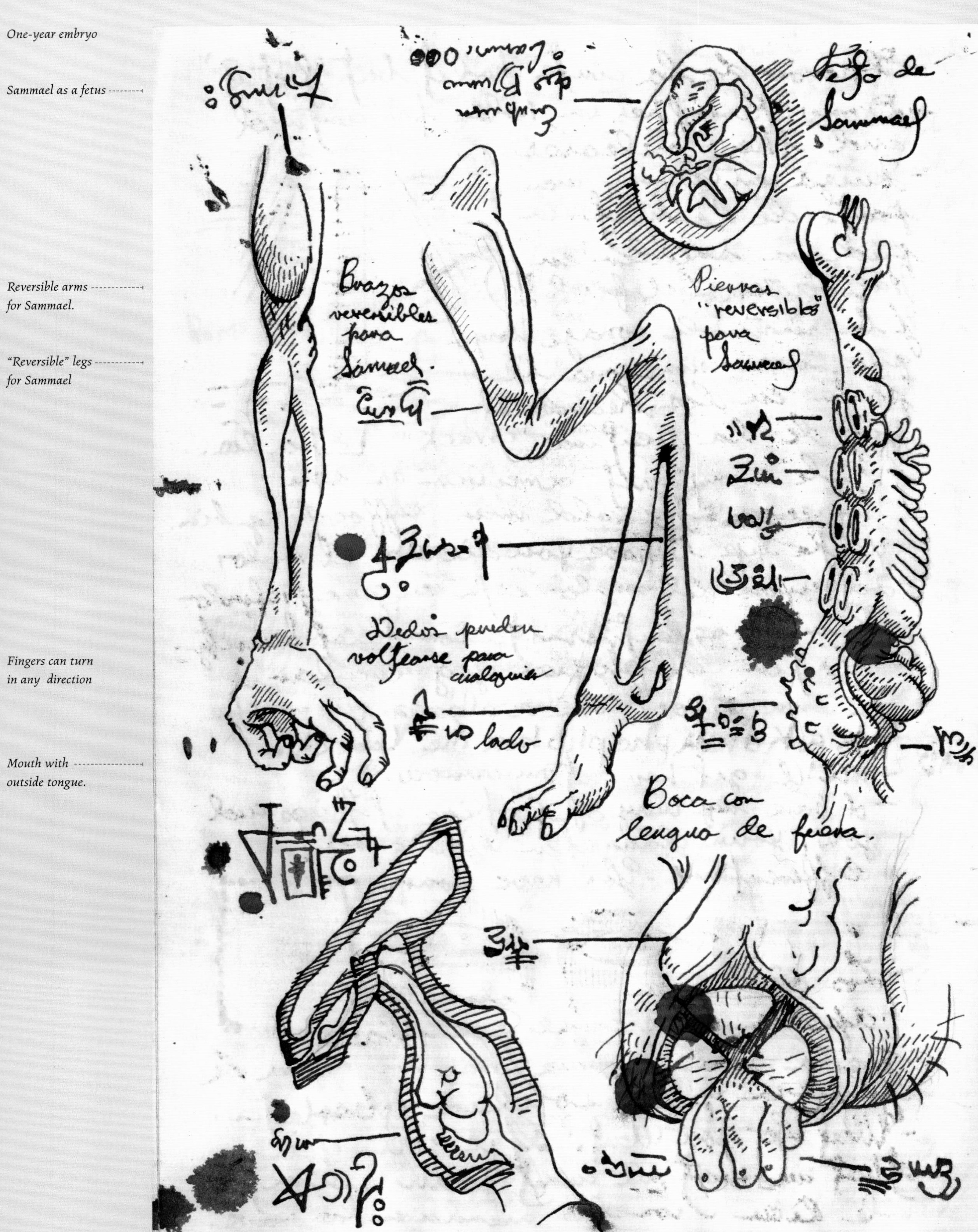

Notebook 3, Page 19A

GDT: The two creatures that have taken the longest to figure out in my films are Sammael and the plant guy on *Hellboy II*. They took the longest. Sammael went through—I'm not exaggerating—probably thirty or forty iterations, at the very least. Full on, "Let's go this way . . . No, no, let's go that way."

The elements I wanted were always there: bone, limbs that can change, a really long tongue. And here [*opposite*] I was just doing some anatomical sketches. The thing on the bottom right is the tongue. I was playing with the idea of limbs that could switchblade out of themselves. It's not very clear in the rendering, but the bone is in the middle of the forearm, so you can extend the forearm. And I was trying to figure out how he would roll the tongue inside of the thorax. Like, how much space the tongue would occupy, if I could put human fingers at the end of the tongue. Silly stuff, but I was trying to figure it out.

MSZ: It's great. And then are these little nonsensical annotations mixed in with Spanish?

GDT: Yeah, yeah, I liked them because I've always been in love with the idea of the *Necronomicon*.

MSZ: So, where does this fit into the design phase? Does it start with you doing something like this and then bringing it to your design team?

GDT: Yeah. This was done before I had Wayne Barlowe, or Mignola, or anyone.

MSZ: So this represents the beginning of the process.

GDT: Yes. In general, the more notes in the notebook, the less of a team I had.

One of del Toro's main concerns with the design of Sammael (ABOVE) was figuring out how to make the creature's limbs changeable (OPPOSITE). Wayne Barlowe created the first successful concept that addressed this need by incorporating a hidden bone spur into the demon's forearm (TOP LEFT), which Mike Mignola then depicted in his signature style (TOP RIGHT).

–Kroenen's room. A dirty mosaic. Filled with pipes and black hoses

MOUTH on his "hand"

Structures made of bars on every street and in all the cavities of the buildings.

HB.

TWO OR THREE NIPPLES ON ONE SIDE

Sammael must be asymmetric like a crab or a malformed foetus. He has 2 eyes on one side and a big ass on the other one. A small claw on one arm

He should be an ornate creature much like H.B markings. Call him "brother"

He has double-jointed legs if Mike Elizalde thinks so.

Bigger claw with a Hai-alai basket of boney tissue.

ROWS OF NODULES

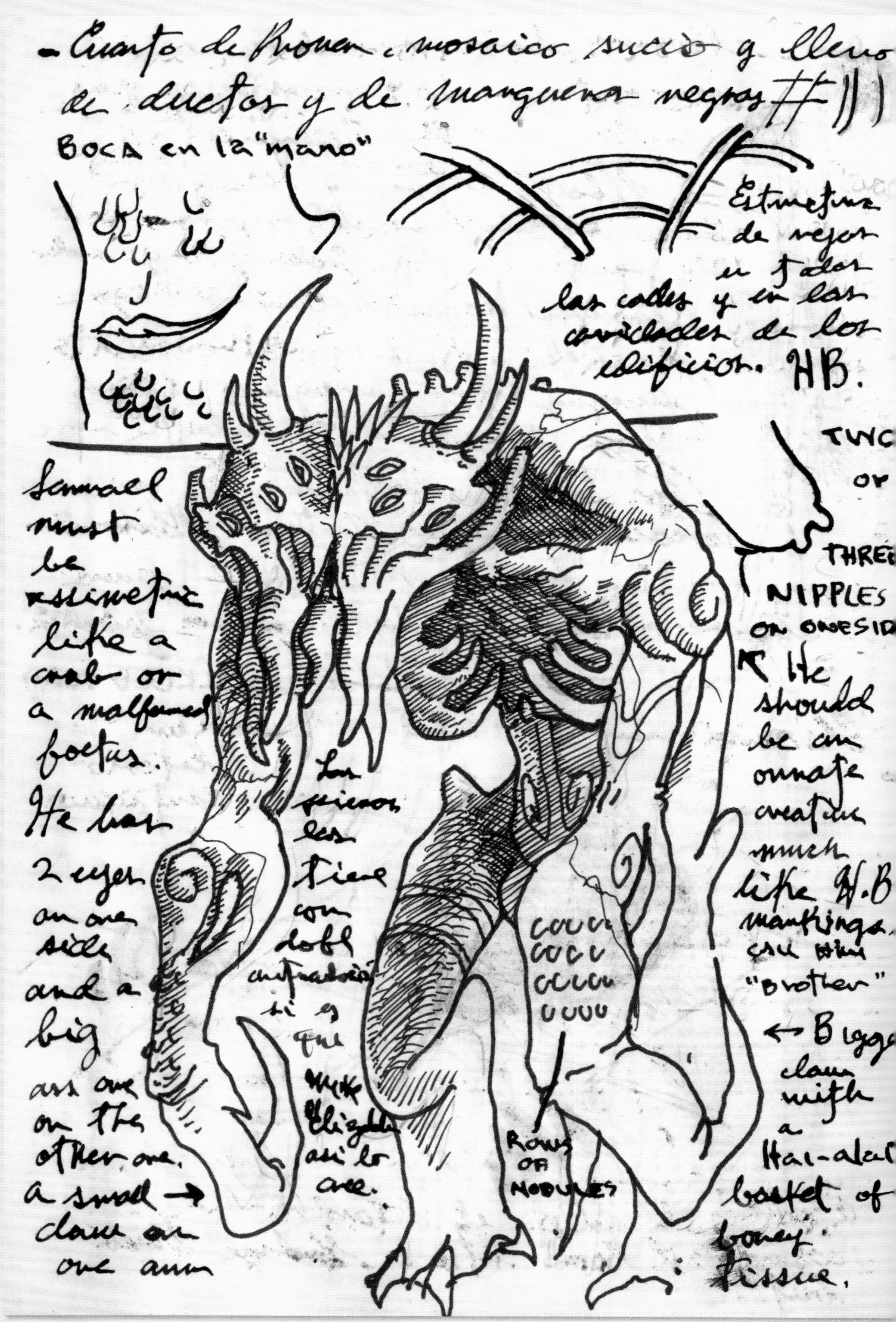

Notebook 3, Page 38A

GDT: Sammael again [*opposite*]. Now, the one thing that I am sad we lost on Sammael was the horns, because I really liked that demonic silhouette. But we preserved a lot of stuff. I love that double-jointedness for the pincers, but, again, it was very hard to keep. And, as you can see, he was always asymmetric. But the elements are all there—the circles, the spirals, the bones extruding from the skin, the tentacles, the eyes, the many rows of warts, the protruding pelvis, and the double-jointed legs. Those were things that were important, and you see them repeated again and again in the drawings.

The problem is, when you see a drawing like this, I find the silhouette interesting, but it doesn't feel like a creature. It feels like a bunch of notions put together.

MSZ: You said you were sorry to lose the horns. Why was that?

GDT: I liked the horns because they were designed to come out of the floating cheekbone, and then the floating cheekbone would echo the first row of horns, and then the second. I just liked that it had an African mask quality.

For a while during preproduction, Sammael had horns (OPPOSITE), which were abandoned in favor of tentacles (ABOVE). The creature's double-jointedness, seen in action in these storyboards by Simeon Wilkins (RIGHT) remained a defining characteristic throughout the creature design process.

—100,000 dollars you can visualize. A 1,000,000 fits in 2–3 cubic feet. Buys you a house. A really, really big, nice house. Then you start going into abstraction. Well is the same thing with years.

TANOSHI WILLOW TOWN—Boken Shonen Shadar, Ogon Bat, Toriton (OSAMU, T Nekome, Dororo, Marine and the patrol. oceanica, Okami Shonen Ken (pepito) Fushigina Melmo, Skyers-5 (s-5

–The interesting thing about Junji Ito is that he rarely offers explanations in his horror stories. He was a dental assistant and in a certain way his brand of horror shares the same precise attention to biological detail and exerts the same morbid fascination as his old job. Show, don't tell.

–The Sammaels move in unison like a "chorus line" a la Harryhausen in Jason.

–The world's greatest paranormal detective. I must say he can't detect much can he—?

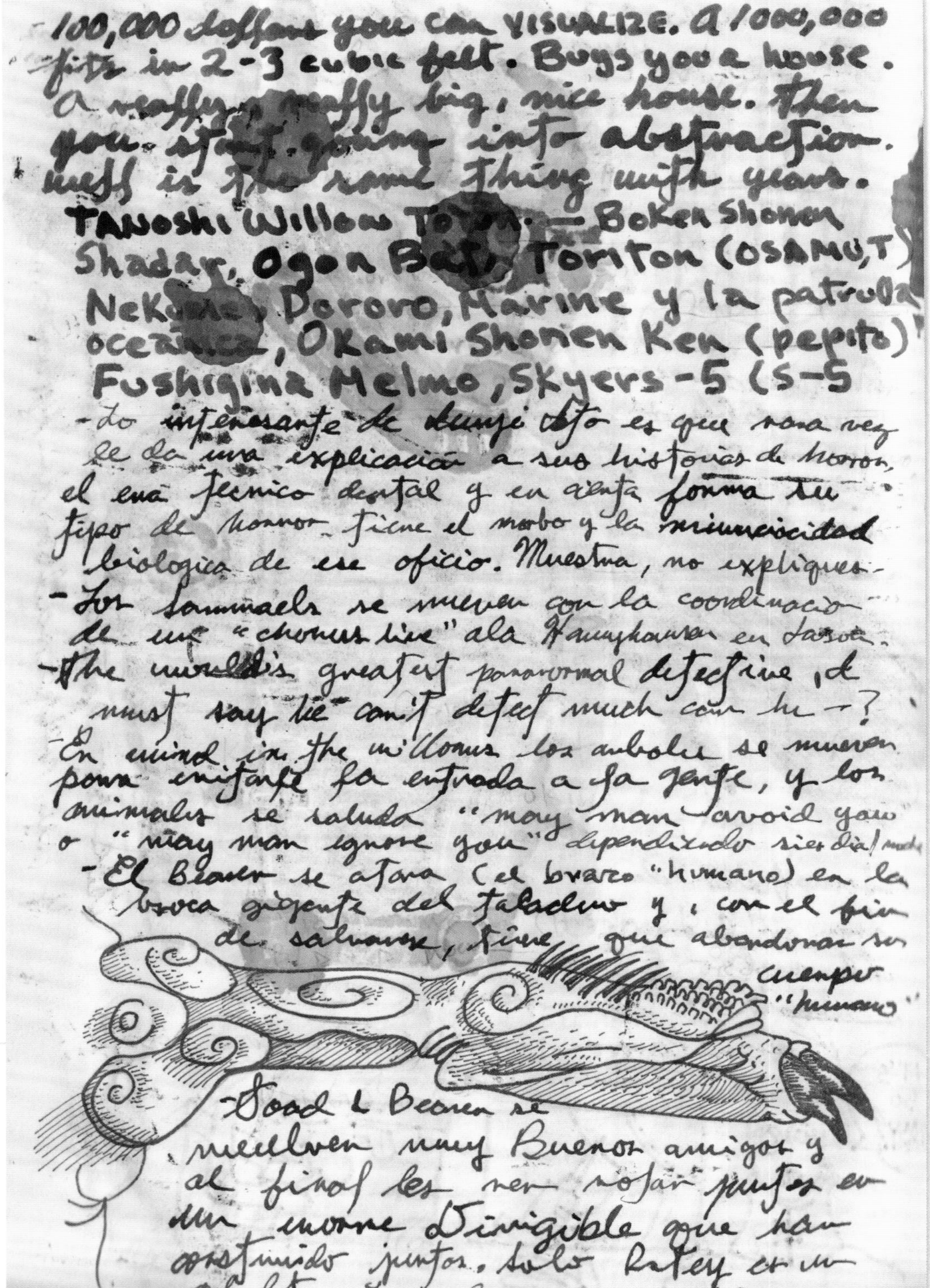

100,000 dollars you can VISUALIZE. A 1,000,000
fits in 2-3 cubic feet. Buys you a house.
A really really big, nice house. Then
you start going into abstraction.
Well is the same thing with years.
TANOSHI WILLOW TOWN.—Boken Shonen
Shadar, Ogon Bat, Toriton (OSAMU, T
Nekome, Dororo, Marine y la patrulla
oceanica, Okami Shonen Ken (pepito)
Fushigina Melmo, Skyers-5 (S-5
-Lo interesante de Junji Ito es que rara vez
le da una explicación a sus historias de horror,
el era tecnico dental y en cierta forma su
tipo de horror tiene el morbo y la minuciosidad
biologica de ese oficio. Muestra, no expliques.
-Los Sammaels se mueven con la coordinación
de una "chorus line" a la Harryhausen en Jason.
-The world's greatest paranormal detective, I
must say he can't detect much can he—?
-En wind in the willows los arboles se mueven
para impedir la entrada a la gente, y los
animales se saludan "may man avoid you
o "may man ignore you" dependiendo si es dia/noche
-El Beaver se atora (el brazo "humano) en la
broca gigante del taladro y, con el fin
de salvarse, tiene que abandonar su
cuerpo "humano"
-Toad & Beaver se
vuelven muy buenos amigos y
al final les ven volar juntos en
un enorme Dirigible que han
construido juntos. Solo Ratty es un
adulto. Los demas son chicos.

–In Wind in the Willows, the trees move so that people can't get in, and the animals greet one another with "may man avoid you" or "may man ignore you" whether it's day or night.

–The Beaver [?] (the human "boat") in the gigantic [?] and, in order to save himself, he must abandon his "human" body.

–Toad and Beaver become very good friends, and at the end they're seen flying together in an enormous dirigible that they both built together. Only Ratty is an adult. The others are children.

NOTEBOOK 3, PAGE 40A

GDT: What's great about this page [*above*] is the mechanism in Sammael's arm is almost exactly how it came out. The unfolding blade is there, and on the facing page [*opposite*] you can see me again trying asymmetric eyes. The wart rolls, the tentacles. And this element of the protruding bone again. But that didn't make it.

And there's a little note to have Hellboy grabbing the mosaic or the tile as he is being dragged backward, which made it into the subway scene [*opposite, top*]. In a different way, but I did it. I originally wanted it for a fight with Kroenen, but, you know. One does what one can.

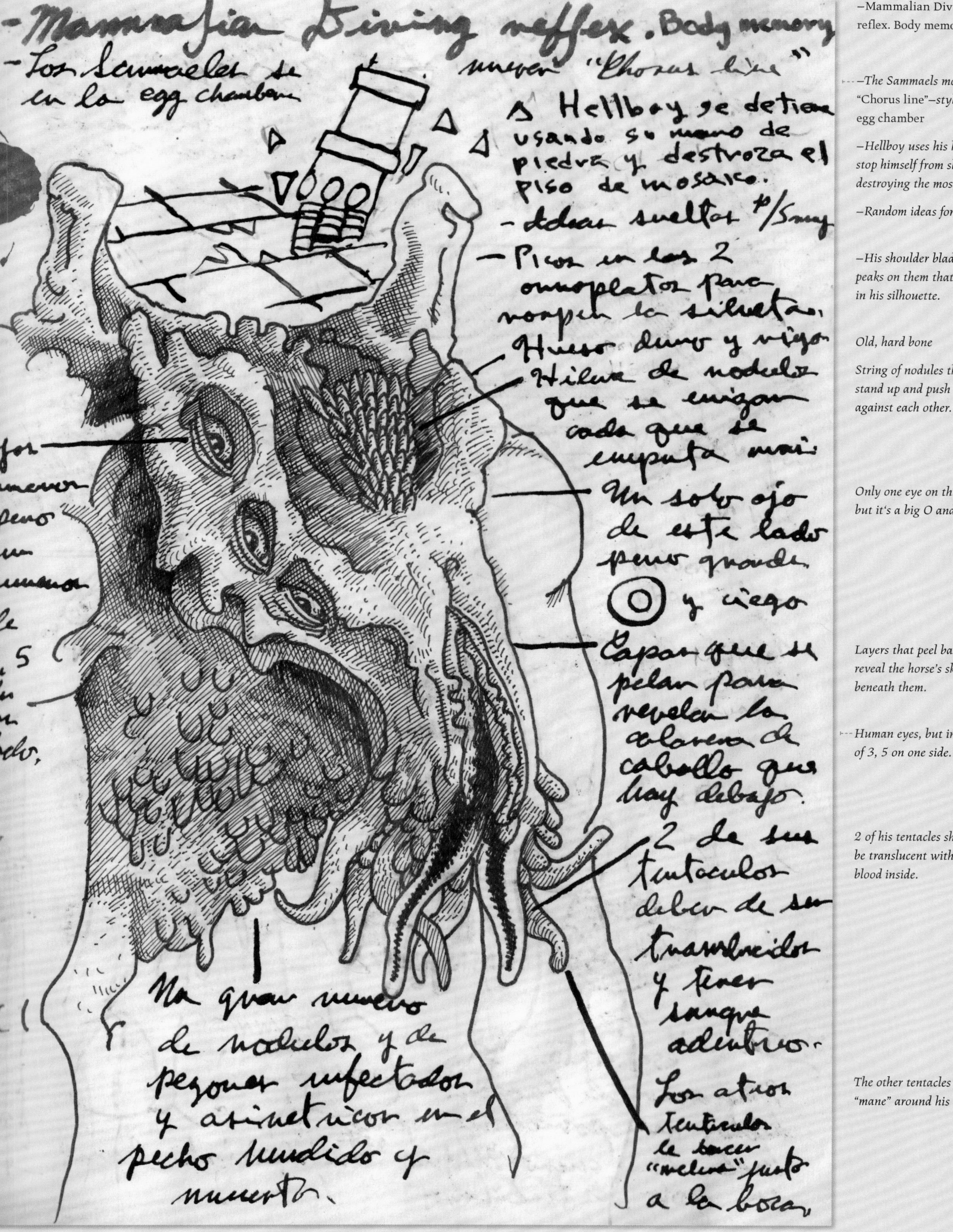
Hellboy se detiene
usando su mano de
piedra y destroza el
piso de mosaico.
Un solo ojo
de este lado
pero grande
y ciego
2 de sus
tentaculos
deben de ser
translucidos
y tener
sangre
adentro.

—Mammalian Diving reflex. Body memory.

—*The Sammaels move in* "Chorus line"—*style in the* egg chamber

—*Hellboy uses his hand to stop himself from sliding, destroying the mosaic floor.*

—*Random ideas for Sammy*

—*His shoulder blades have peaks on them that stick out in his silhouette.*

Old, hard bone

String of nodules that stand up and push against each other.

Only one eye on this side, but it's a big O and blind

Layers that peel back to reveal the horse's skull beneath them.

Human eyes, but in groups of 3, 5 on one side.

2 of his tentacles should be translucent with blood inside.

The other tentacles form a "mane" around his mouth.

A large number of nodules and infected, asymmetrical nipples on his sunken, dead chest.

Notebook 3, Page 40B

–Olivier is a tiger, Javier is a mammoth.

–Episode with a brigade soldier with a rifle in a tree. There he removes the ring he gives to Conchita. In the middle of a sandstorm.

–Look for the ghost's torso. It could be "splattered" with blue paint "blue screen." Irregular patterns. CGI

–Just a mistake, that's all, I thought I was human.

Hellboy has lots of cats running around everywhere.

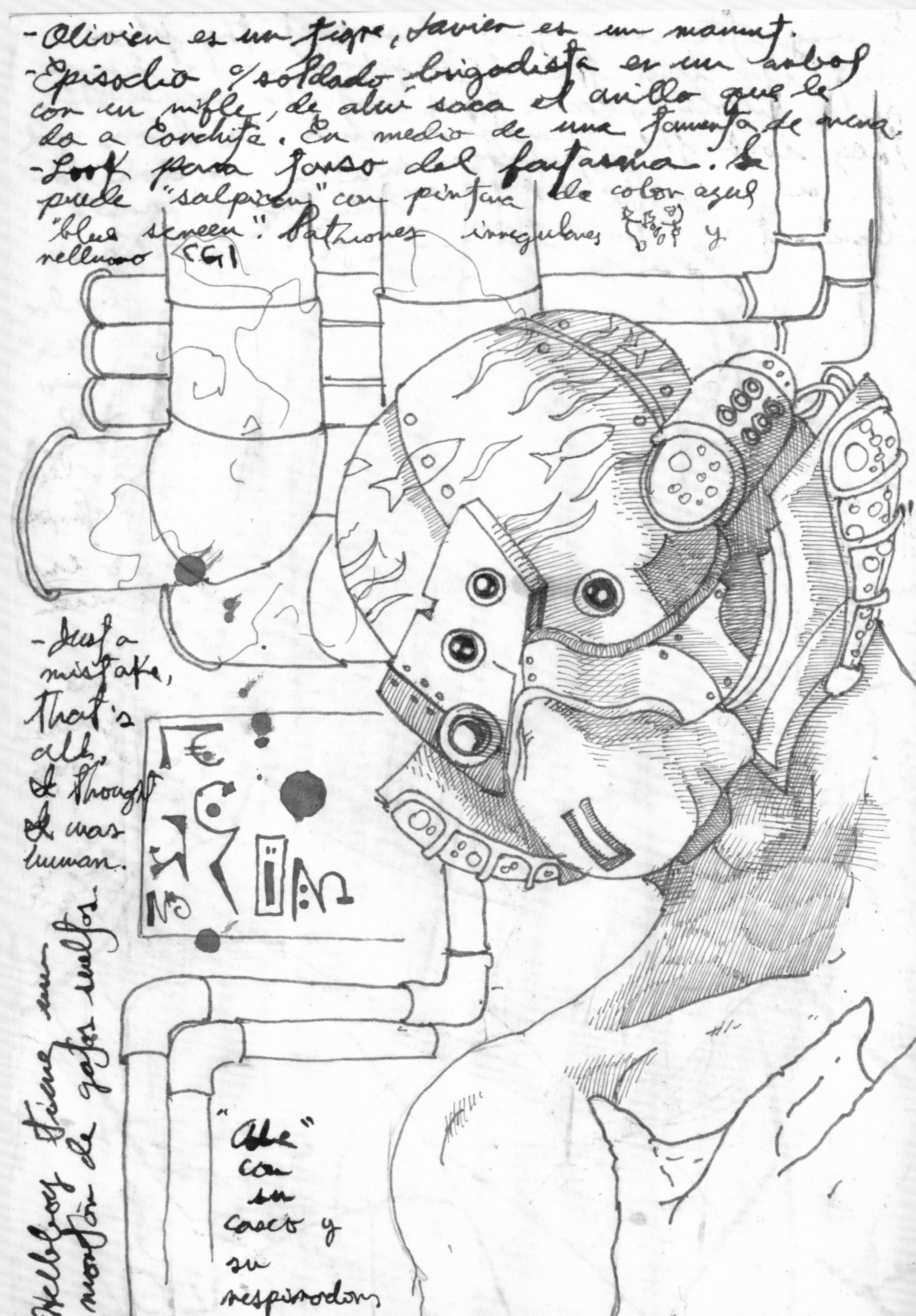

Notebook 3, Page 20A

"Abe" with a helmet and his respirator

GDT: The idea I was exploring here [*opposite*] was how to make Abe Sapien blink. Because back then it was so expensive to make him blink. I knew I needed to make him blink digitally because there was no way I could hide a mechanism in the face. So I said, well, if his breathing apparatus is very elaborate but cool-looking enough, I can have the bubbles in the water, and the eyes lit, and people will find him entertaining, and I don't have to spend all that money on making him blink. So I designed that, and I added little fishes in the way that you would draw a cheesecake girl as nose art on a World War II bombardier. Or the way that Joker puts "Born to Kill" on his helmet in *Full Metal Jacket*.

MSZ: So these aren't real fish. They're intended to be a motif?

GDT: Yeah. Like, he was drawing on his helmet. And the respirator on the side was sort of like a bellows. Those ended up being Johann's in *Hellboy II*.

MZ: Why did you move away from this design? Because it's a very fun design.

GDT: Well, I got away from it because, when we finally went to make the movie, José [Fernandez] at Spectral Motion took a long time to get to Abe. We fucked around for a long time. Then Wayne Barlowe did a beautiful drawing, and Mignola refined it, and then José sculpted it, and it was so gorgeous that I said, "I'm not going to fucking hide the face." So I just gave him goggles, goggles with water. Because the face, it was so harmonious. The worst thing you can do—and this is really useful advice—in any design, the worst thing you can do is make a big-headed design. The head has to be the smallest part of the creature.

MSZ: Why is that?

GDT: It's just aesthetically more pleasing. It's also the worst thing you can do with statuary. I mean, a lot of statuary is done like that because you are meant to look at it from below, so a lot of the sculptures have big heads and big shoulders because you're looking at them on a pedestal. But the sign of a really bad sculptor is that they do big-headed designs. And a bad draftsman, a lot of the time, has a tendency for big-headed designs.

The design of the breathing apparatus Abe Sapien (Doug Jones) wears when he is out of water went through a number of iterations, from an asymmetrical helmet (OPPOSITE) to a more elegant combination of goggles (BELOW) and neck-wrap. Underwater scenes, such as the one where Abe dives into the cistern to retrieve the reliquary (ABOVE) reveal his true, more expressive face. Storyboards by Simeon Wilkins.

GDT: At the top [*opposite*] here, on the left, I very much wanted Hellboy to be talking to someone who was trying to soothe him. You know, "Don't do that." But then Hellboy just punches him through the door. But I didn't do that until *Hellboy II*, when he punches Johann in the locker room. I like him losing his temper abruptly.

Then I'm gonna keep doing this drawing until I get a helmet with two lenses on one side and one in the other. First on Abe Sapien, then on Blade, and then here.

MSZ: What was this particular version intended for?

GDT: Well, I love Russian technology, and I thought of the idea of a leather cap for when they go to Rasputin's tomb in Moscow in the winter. I wanted to create a leather helmet like an aviator cap with a set of goggles for Hellboy. The idea was that he would use it to detect the talking corpse. Of course, that didn't happen.

(OPPOSITE) Throughout the notebooks, del Toro persistently draws variations of an asymmetrical helmet, which he has tried to incorporate into several films. This particular iteration was supposed to allow Hellboy to locate the talking corpse in *Hellboy*. Although the idea was abandoned for that film, del Toro was able to create something similar with the Schufftein glasses in *Hellboy II* (TOP & ABOVE).

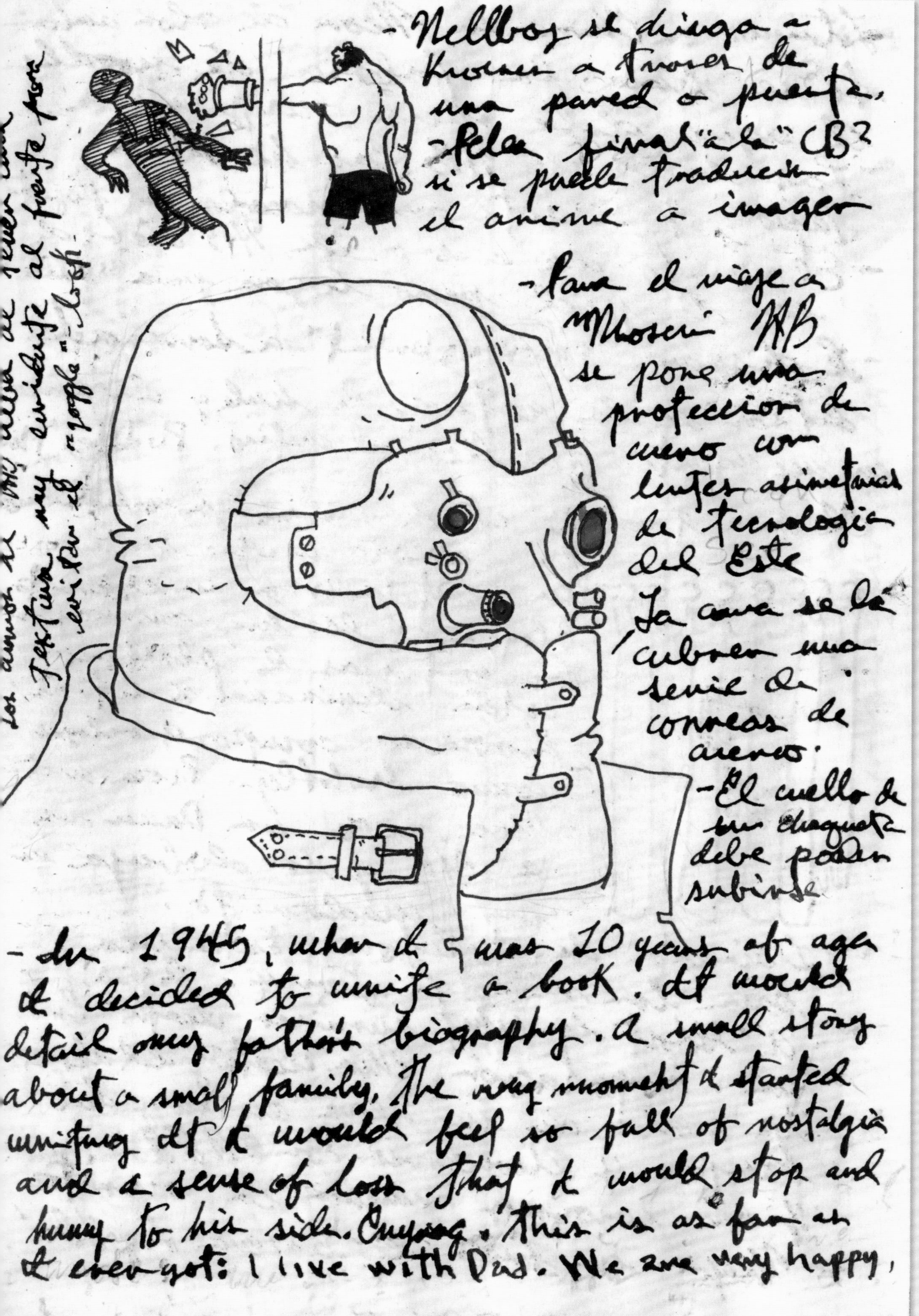

–Hellboy fucks Kroenen up through a wall or door.

–Final battle "a la" CB? If anime can be translated into an image

–HB wears leather protection with asymmetrical goggles of eastern European design for his trip to Moscow

The texture of HB's horns should be plainly visible so that they don't look like goggles

–His face is covered with a series of steel belts.

–The jacket needs to have a collar that can be turned up

–In 1945, when I was 10 years of age I decided to write a book. It would detail my father's biography. A small story about a small family. The very moment I started writing it, I would feel so full of nostalgia and a sense of loss that I would stop and hurry to his side. Crying. This is as far as I ever got: I live with Dad. We are very happy.

Notebook 3, Page 38B

- Letreros en Chino in Neon de color ambar
Si se hace la fabrica de noodles
el agua debe verse asquerosa.
- Las balas de HB las hacen en
Japón y se activan al sacarlas del paquete.
- El abrigo de cuero de HB debe de
ser de piel pero ligera para "vuelo"
- Se dispara "TRACKING bullet" a Sammael.
detras de la cortina de hule y desaparece
en una "grota" que lleva al metro. Puddles slow.
- El que trabaja en el metro ya lo habíamos
visto en otra secuencia
- Un ventilador o un extractor
bloquea la luz con vapor
Las cortinas de plastico
están iluminadas x detrás.
- Kroenen compone relojes
como hobby. Piezas sueltas
- Una niña con Down ve
a HB y lo dibuja en
un cuadernito.
- Llamada de telefono. Estatica.
para la niña de Down's. RISA.
- A Ghost is what survives death. Es
una amputación. Una cicatriz del alma.
Los restos de un alma destrozada.
- Rampas y elevadores con
- y con enormes numeros en concreto
- Viajan en truck de basura A y HB

–Amber-colored Chinese neon signs. If we make the noodle factory, the water needs to look disgusting.

–HB's bullets are made in Japan and are activated when they are pulled out of their package.

–HB's leather jacket should be made of leather but it should be lightweight enough to blow in the wind

–A "tracking bullet" is shot at Sammael from behind an oilskin window. It vanishes in a "grotto" leading to the subway. Puddles slow.

–We've already seen the man who works in the subway in another sequence

–An exhaust fan blocks the light with steam. The plastic curtains are lit from behind.

–Kroenen puts together watches as a hobby. Loose parts

–A girl with Down's syndrome sees HB and draws a picture of him in a little notebook.

–Telephone call. Static. For the girl with Down's. Laughter.

–A ghost is what survives death. *As an amputation. A scar on the soul. The remains of a destroyed soul.*

–Ramps and elevators with [image of lines] and with enormous concrete numbers on them

–They travel in garbage truck. A and HB

Notebook 3, Page 39A

● **GDT:** Well, the page above is mostly notes, with this image of a shower curtain with a symbol. I like the idea of things behind plastic. You can see it in *Mimic*, you can see it in *Cronos*. On *Hellboy*, I really liked the idea of finding a series of plastic curtains and seeing Kroenen moving behind them. The idea being that the symbol was painted in blood.

This ended up in the morgue when Kroenen resurrects. The DDT guys were covering the Kroenen puppet with a very light plastic sheet because they didn't want crap to deposit on the silicone. When I saw that, I said, "Give it to me for real." What I did is, he wakes up with the sheet attached to him, and as he takes a few steps, he steps on the plastic sheet, it pulls down, and it reveals his face. Then we go behind the screen, and instead of him, you just see the screen, and his silhouette in plastic, and then he comes out. So that made it into the movie somehow.

On the facing page is Abe Sapien and his two lenses on one side, and one lens on the other. One day, one day, it'll happen. I have faith. The respirator is not exactly like it is in the movie, but it's pretty close.

And you can see the lock in the safety deposit door that is the entrance to the BPRD.

On the bottom [*opposite*]: I originally had the idea for a mechanical collar on Kroenen that injected through clockwork—injected a substance into his brain to keep the corpse alive. But then I came up with this notion of a ridiculous wind-up. I said, "It makes as much sense as a syringe." I liked the idea of a really elaborate wind-up that is massaging his organs as he moves. It's an oblique reference to a guy in a James Bond movie that I saw when I was a kid—the clock that massages a little mechanism that awakens him from the dead.

MSZ: Then you have him saying, "It's so easy!"

GDT: Just a ridiculous statement. Like, "It's so easy to stay alive after you're a corpse. Boys and girls, order your injection today!"

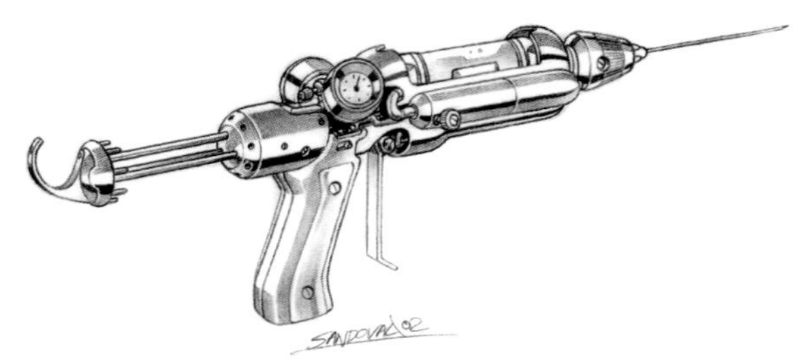

HELLBOY: Syringe 04

(OPPOSITE) Originally, Kroenen was to be kept alive through regular injections administered by a clockwork mechanism. (ABOVE) DDT created a number of concepts for the syringe that would hold the mysterious, life-giving substance before the idea was abandoned in favor of the wind-up mechanism seen in the final film.

—The "bad guys" emerge from mirrors or shadows.

—Post-cognitive. He knows what already happened

—Stainless steel pistons move in unison.

Abe with his water goggles and external respirator

—Railroad signals on the train or subway tracks.

—Shot of Kroenen's syringe. Camera turns 360° and then cuts!!

–Huge [images of bullet cartridges] from the Samaritan

–There are idyllic photographs of Nazi youths in Kroenen's room.

–Kroenen's hand with flesh interface.

The hand is heavily adorned.

–Skull-faced mask. Room with asbestos modules.

–1920 industrial Gothic.

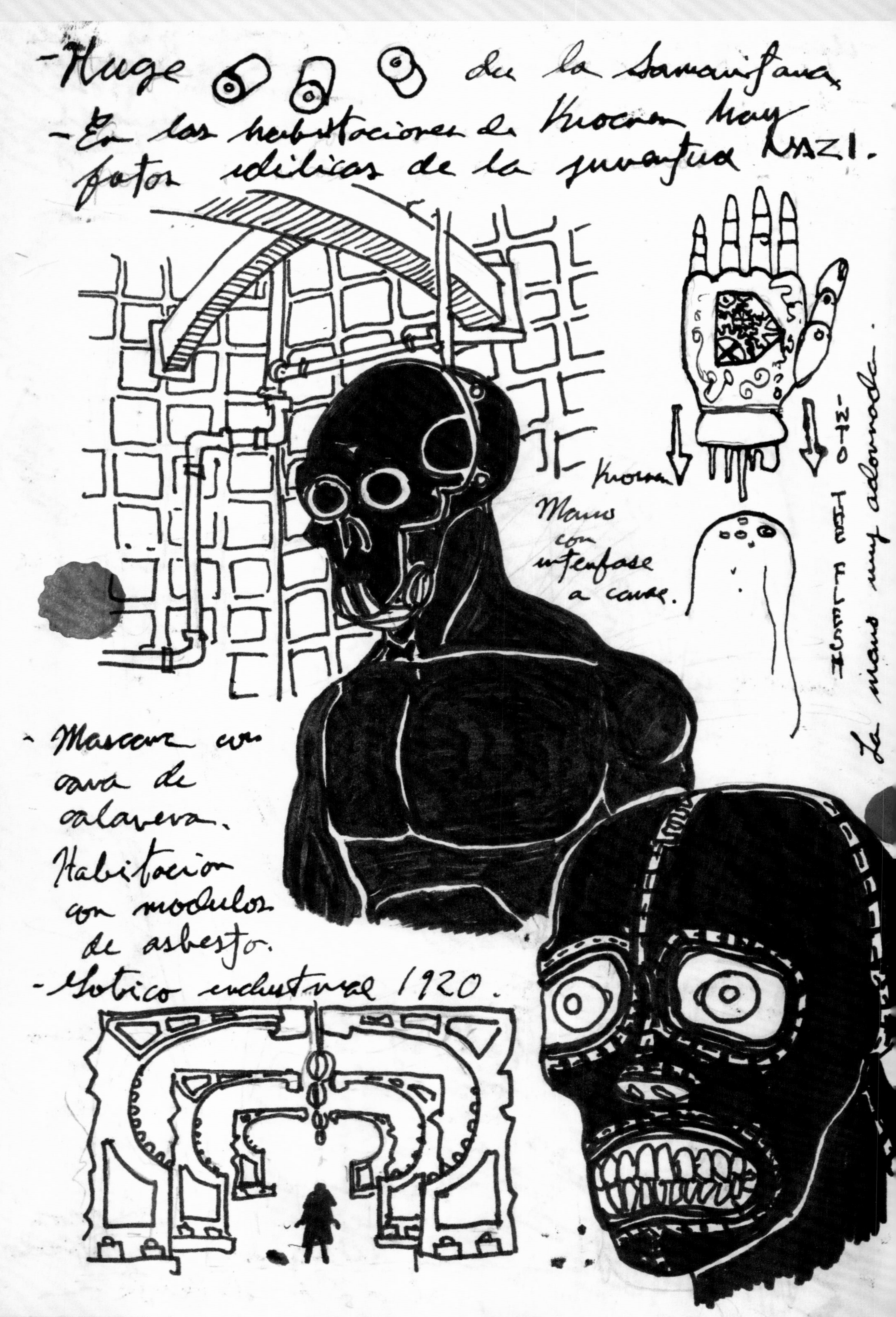

Notebook 3, Page 37A

GDT: Well, first of all, as you can read on the top left [*opposite*], one of the things that I wanted to do with the Samaritan was to create huge ammo for the revolver. Huge bullets. But originally I wanted it to be an automatic weapon that would eject the shells. And we couldn't do it. I couldn't find a way to design it properly. But we kept the idea of the shells being huge.

Ron is a big guy. He has a huge head and huge hands, so the gun looks normal, almost, in his hands. So I had to create the Big Baby in the second movie for it to look like a big gun, and the bullets of the Big Baby are the size of a baby's bottle, and they have a baby bottle inside.

Then there is a Kroenen hand on this page, which is literally, if you go back to the earlier drawings of *The Left Hand of Darkness*, the *Monte Cristo* hand [*see page 258*]. And, again, it's a matter of "I want that image. I don't care where it comes from." [laughs]

Then several designs for the mask, and the idea of him having no eyelids and no lips. I wanted him to be like the embodiment of S&M.

Then I wanted something that looked 1920s but high-tech, sort of like the *Nautilus* in *20,000 Leagues Under the Sea*. I couldn't do it. I didn't do it.

(TOP LEFT) Ron Perlman posing as Hellboy with Big Baby in a publicity photo for *Hellboy II*. (LEFT) Kroenen's lair was designed to have a 1920s high-tech, Gothic feel, reminiscent of the *Nautilus* in *20,000 Leagues Under the Sea* (ABOVE).

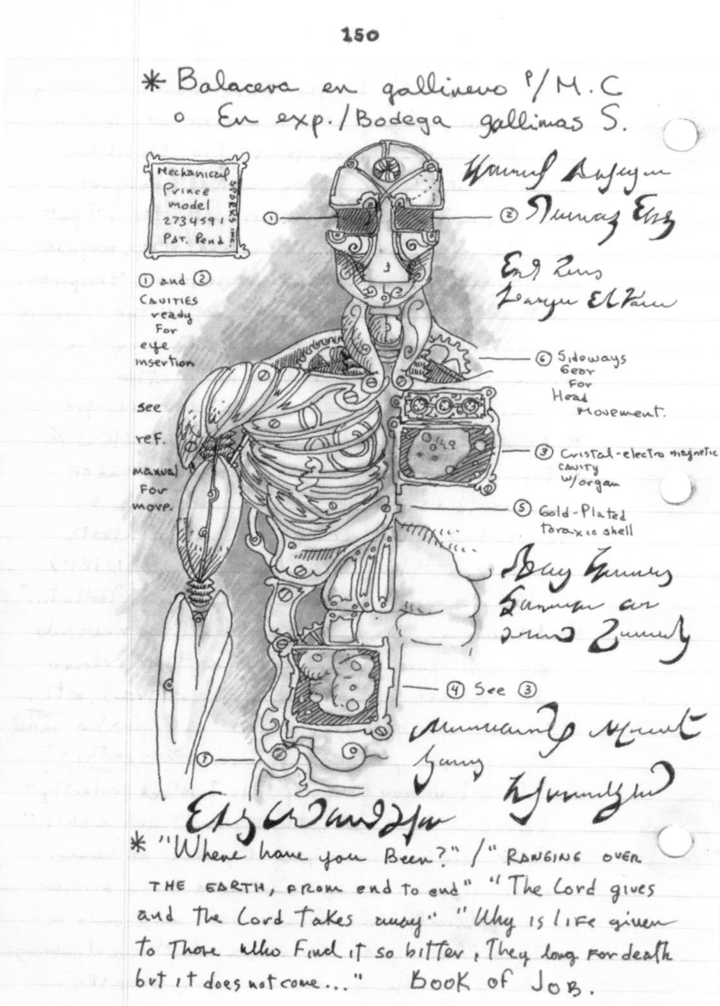
150
* Balacera en gallinero p/ M.C
o En exp./Bodega gallinas S.
* "Where have you Been?" / "Ranging over THE EARTH, from end to end" "The Lord gives and The Lord Takes away" "Why is life given to Those who Find it so bitter, They long for death but it does not come..." Book of JOB.

Blue Notebook, Page 150

* *Shootout in a henhouse for M.C.*

° *In exp./storeroom hens S.*

Mechanical Prince
model 2714591
Pat. Pend

(1) and (2) cavities ready for eye insertion.

See ref. manual for more.

(6) Sideways gear for head movement.

(3) Crystal electro-magnetic cavity w/organ

(5) Gold-Plated thoraxic shell

* "Where have you Been?" / "Ranging over THE EARTH, from end to end. "The Lord give and the Lord takes away" "Why is life given to those who find it so bitter, they long for death but it does not come . . . " Book of JOB.

The design of Kroenen (ABOVE) hearkens back to ideas del Toro explored for his semi-mechanical, lethal protagonist in an early, unmade project called *The Left Hand of Darkness*, an adaptation of *The Count of Monte Cristo* (ABOVE LEFT, *and see page 258*).

● **GDT:** Over here [*opposite*] is Kroenen coming out of the floor like a ghost. That was a very nice idea, but we couldn't do it. Couldn't do it, because he became physical. Originally I had this idea that he and Rasputin were able to come out of the shadows. And Rasputin does. If you watch the movie, in the mental asylum, the guard uses a flashlight, closes the door, and Rasputin comes out of the shadows.

MSZ: That's very, very cool. And, again, you're using very interesting palettes with the blacks punctuated by whites and reds.

GDT: Yeah. What is interesting with the pages in this notebook is that I started trying to do little compositions on each page. The blood helps now and then, as well as the little Lovecraftian symbols here and there.

MSZ: What's this detail in the margin, underneath the blood splatter?

GDT: Those are little bells—glass bells that I saw in *National Geographic* or something. They are used to shoo away spirits. I thought the shape was beautiful. I drew them because I don't like photographing stuff. That's one thing that is very curious—I hate photographing. For many years my wife said, "Why don't you take any family photos?" And I said to her—I know this sounds like an affectation, but it isn't—I said, "I can't just photograph something. I need to say what is in the frame, what is the color." You know, contrary to Stanley Kubrick. Kubrick was such a great photographer, and he found everything. I can't. I have to fabricate everything in the image. So whenever I see a drawing, or I'm in a museum, and I see something I like, I could take a photograph, but I do a sketch in the notebook instead.

Glass bells for evil spirits.

-Podemos abrir con sequencia en un mini-mart con 3 o 4 monstruos que rodean a la dependienta y Hellboy entra y los torea Luego se enciende un cigarro o se lo apaga con los dedos y lo guarda Pequeñas dagas rellenas de agua bendita. Malasyan Revenants hungry for virgin's blood

-You should date a little more.

-Los bosques Gallegos son muy cercanos a los de Arthur Machen

-Un hombre es llamado para reconstruir un laberinto de piedra.

-Para Wind in the Willows: PICKLED TOAD

-El mini-mart fue construido sobre un cementerio antiguo.

-A Hellboy le molesta el desorden en el camión: I know it's a Garbage truck but...

malos espíritus

—We could open with a sequence in a "mini-mart" in which 3 or 4 monsters surround the cashier and Hellboy comes in and taunts them. Then he lights or puts out a cigarette with his fingers and saves it for later. Little daggers filled with holy water. Malaysan Revenants hungry for virgin's blood

—You should date a little more.

—Galician forests are very much like those found in Arthur Machen

—A man is called upon to rebuild a stone labyrinth.

—For Wind in the Willows: PICKLED TOAD

—The mini-mart was built on an ancient cemetery.

—The disorder inside the truck bothers Hellboy: I know it's a Garbage truck, but . . .

Page 22

–Butchered cattle for sale on M street. Blood flows down the sidewalk. Steam pours out of the coffee-roasting machines. Very hot, wet streets

–Small gas lamp used at street stalls during the eighteenth–nineteenth centuries

–Rasputin (1872–1916). His name means "crossroads." In 1909, he becomes a member of the royal court. He travels in 1911 and sometime in 1912

Alias "Guisha." Letter to Ilsa. Beforehand

–Ride the body of a dead man so that he tells you his secrets

–Key for H's glove.

–Ilsa is given a small diary In it is written everything that will happen in the years to come. "The book of sand."

Photo of R. (6-1916)

–Facts are far more damaging than lies. Sometimes truth is the tool to use to bring a man down.

–Jackets *for Monte Cristo.*

Pagina 22

- Cadaveres de vaca p/venta en calle M sangre escurre a la banqueta. Vapor sale de maquinas asando o vendiendo café. Calles humedas y muy calientes
- Pequeña lampara de gas usada en "puestos" callejeros en Siglo XVIII-XX
- Rasputin (1872-1916) su nombre significa "Encrucijada" 1909 entra en la corte imperial. viaja en el año de 1911 o alrededor del 1912

Alias "Guisha". Letter to Ilsa. Beforehand

- Cabalgar el cuerpo de un muerto p/que te diga sus secretos
- Llave p/el Guante de H
- Le entrega a Ilsa un pequeño diario en el que esta anotado todo lo que ha de suceder en los años por venir. "El libro de arena".

Fotografia de R (6-1916)

1910

- Facts are far more damaging than lies sometimes truth is the tool to use to bring a man down.
- Para Montecristo Jackets

Notebook 3, Page 13A

The Rasputin character in *Hellboy* drawn by Simeon Wilkins (ABOVE LEFT) and played by Karel Roden (ABOVE), differed markedly from the historic image of the man—a long-haired, bearded, almost ascetic monk—with which del Toro began the character design process (OPPOSITE).

MSZ: So Rasputin, of course, had the long, black hair, but he's bald in *Hellboy*.

GDT: Well, that comes from the comic. I think Mike did it because he wanted to purposely imply more of a reborn magician.

You know, I read every book on him. I found fascinating theories of how he resisted death. There's one theory that says that Prince Yusupov, who was supposed to kill him, and supposedly tried to kill him for twenty minutes, was actually giving him a blowjob. So he came out and said, "I cannot kill him!" [laughs] Well, he was trying, but it was a very slow method. [laughs] It would take a long time. Another theory was that the cyanide in the food was a small dose. There was one book that literally explained, step-by-step, how it was just a really botched attempt at both a blowjob and an assassination.

But among the facts I found that were interesting was the fact that the explosion in Tunguska Forest, the famous explosion of an object that was never recovered, was like the equivalent of an X-File in tsarist Russia. I put that in the movie, in the director's cut. The storm came from that explosion. I tried to come up with a great backstory for Rasputin, which is not in the movie. He's a convert, and he really believes he's bringing about the end of the world for good, because this world is too corrupt, and so on, and so forth.

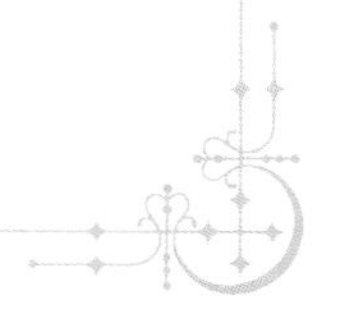

–*Room in which Kroenen opens the trap in the floor, leaving HB hanging from a rope. Abe, or a rucksack, falls on the spikes below*

–*A hospital for children of the war.* "Thousands of children came through these doors in the 1930s. Bad vibe"

–Some of us are like this cylinder of wax. We can replay whatever happened.

–*Open-air Chinese pharmacy with an anatomic model*

–*Patterns on the floors for the* TOP-SHOT

–*In HB's room, the pick-up "bed" is where he saw Liz for the first time.*

–*Cartoons and movies are playing on HB's televisions.*

–*The Baby Behemoth's birth*

–*Tentacles emerge from his eye whenever anyone says "Hellboy" to him!* "Child . . ." "Look what you have done"

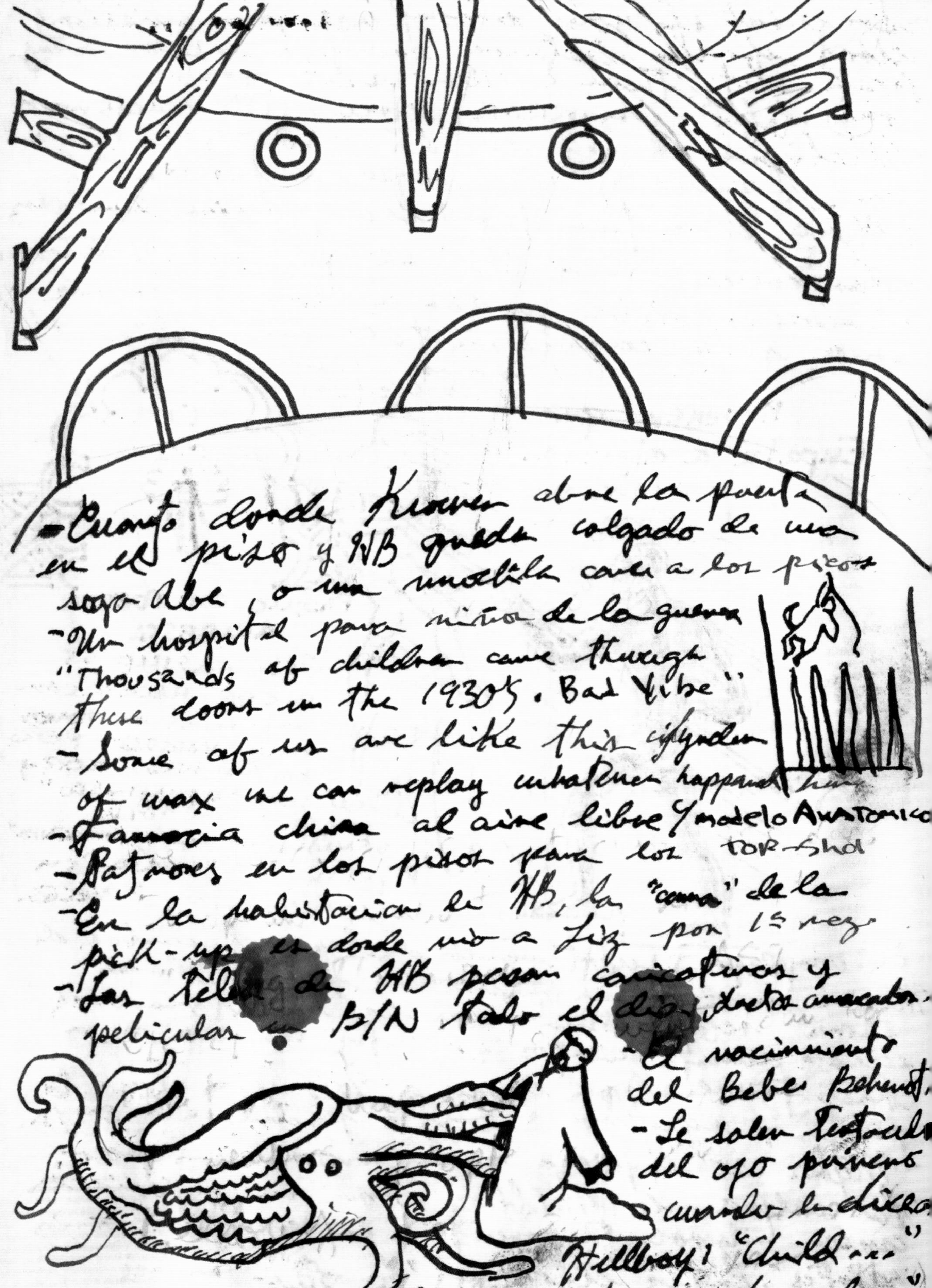

Notebook 3, Page 36A

Del Toro knew he wanted to include a spiked pit trap in *Hellboy* (OPPOSITE, RIGHT), which ended up claiming Kroenen (Ladislav Beran) as a victim (ABOVE). Likewise, *Hellboy* provided an opportunity to deploy a tentacled, Cthulhu-like creature (OPPOSITE, BOTTOM LEFT), the likes of which del Toro has been drawing for years (BELOW).

GDT: There's a piece of architecture on the top here [*opposite*] that I thought would be intriguing. We never made it on *Hellboy*.

On the right is the sort of trap door with spikes that ended up in Kroenen's lair. I just wanted to have that really pulpish feel. I love Sax Rohmer's Fu Manchu. The great thing about the Fu Manchu novels is how inventive the traps are. To this day, my favorite trap in a Fu Manchu novel is, there is one where they say, "This is his deadliest weapon." And they go, "Oh, my God," and then they prepare the revolvers, and they go, "At the count of three, open the door," and they open the door. They enter, and it's an empty room. There's nothing. And they go, "Nothing happened." And then all of a sudden, a giant mushroom blooms from the mouth of one of them, and the other one starts screaming, and a mushroom blooms from their noses, mouths, eyes, and they realize the room is full of spores. I love that. Anyway, that's the spikes.

And then at the bottom, you can see a thing that is ultimately in the movie, which is like a Cthulhu creature being birthed out of the midsection of Rasputin. [laughs]

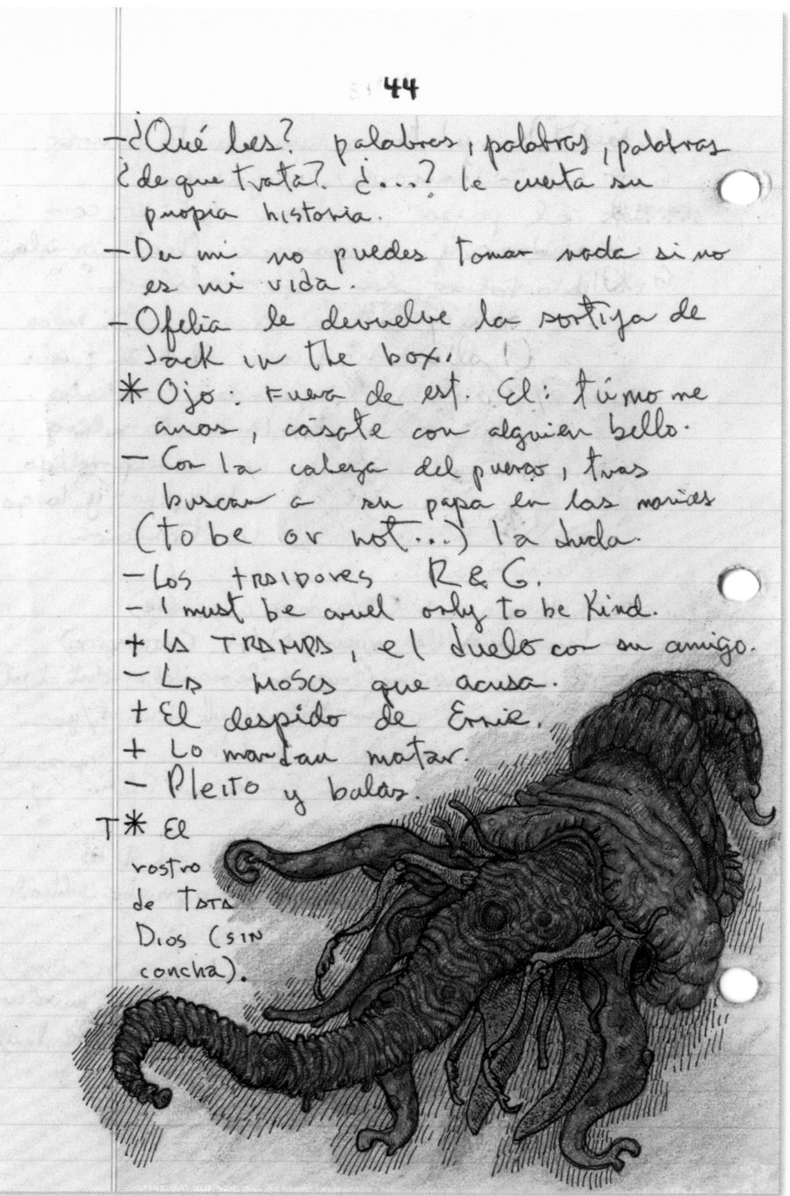

44

-¿Qué lees? palabras, palabras, palabras
¿de que trata? ¿...? le cuenta su propia historia.
-De mi no puedes tomar nada sino es mi vida.
-Ofelia le devuelve la sortija de Jack in the box.
* Ojo: Fuera de est. El: tú no me amas, cásate con alguien bello.
- Con la cabeza del puerco, tras buscar a su papa en las narices (to be or not...) la duda.
- Los traidores R & G.
- I must be cruel only to be Kind.
+ LA TRAMPA, el duelo con su amigo.
- La mosca que acusa.
+ El despido de Ernie.
+ Lo mandan matar.
- Pleito y balas.
T* El rostro de Tata Dios (sin concha).

–What are you reading? Words, words, words. What's it about? . . . ? He tells him his own story.

–You can't take anything from me but my life.

–Ofelia returns the jack-in-the-box engagement ring to him.

** Careful: beyond this. He: You don't love me. Marry someone handsome.*

–With the pig's head, after looking for him in its nostrils (to be or not . . .) *the doubt*

–The traitors R & G.

–I must be cruel only to be Kind.

+THE TRAP, the duel with his friend.

–The fly that accuses.

+Ernie's farewell.

–Fight and bullets.

T The face of daddy-God (without the shell.)*

Blue Notebook, Page 44

(OPPOSITE) As *Hellboy* moved closer to production, del Toro began to record ideas for specific scenes, including images of Hellboy silhouetted against the moon (ABOVE). Storyboards by Simeon Wilkins.

GDT: These illustrations [*opposite*] were done closer to production, but not yet in production. And, again, I knew that Mignola drew the shoulders more sloping, and I knew that there was no way to do that to a human silhouette, because the thing that determines how you do the architecture of monsters is the articulation points. That's the only thing you cannot change in a human body. You have a joint, or you don't have a joint. I didn't know how to make the shoulders more like the drawing, so I came up with the idea of a Civil War–type of coat, with the little cape on the shoulders. And I was praying that it would work in leather, and it came out very well, I think. I was trying to see if it was still Hellboy with big boots and pants, because in the comic, again, he doesn't wear boots—he has hooves—and he has short pants.

Then on the top right I knew I wanted him to rip off a sword, a sword from a statue, and use it to battle a tentacled monster. And that's in the movie.

There's some other stuff that didn't make it into the movie, though. Some compositions—him silhouetted by the moon, certain roofs, and stuff like that.

MSZ: There's these little arches again, these pointed arches.

GDT: Well, I always like architecture that frames the characters, if I can do it.

MSZ: Also, there are references to *Wind in the Willows* throughout these notes. Was that a project that you were working on?

GDT: Well, it's a project that I wrote with Matthew Robbins for Disney, and I think it's a really good screenplay. We tried to make it really, really as true to the book as possible, and then we went to Disney and they said, "Could you make Toad skateboard?" And I left the project.

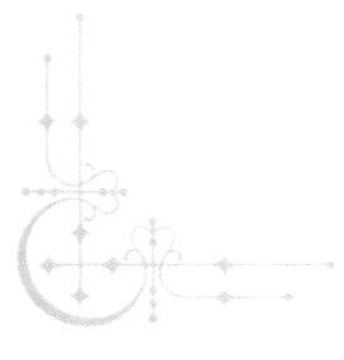

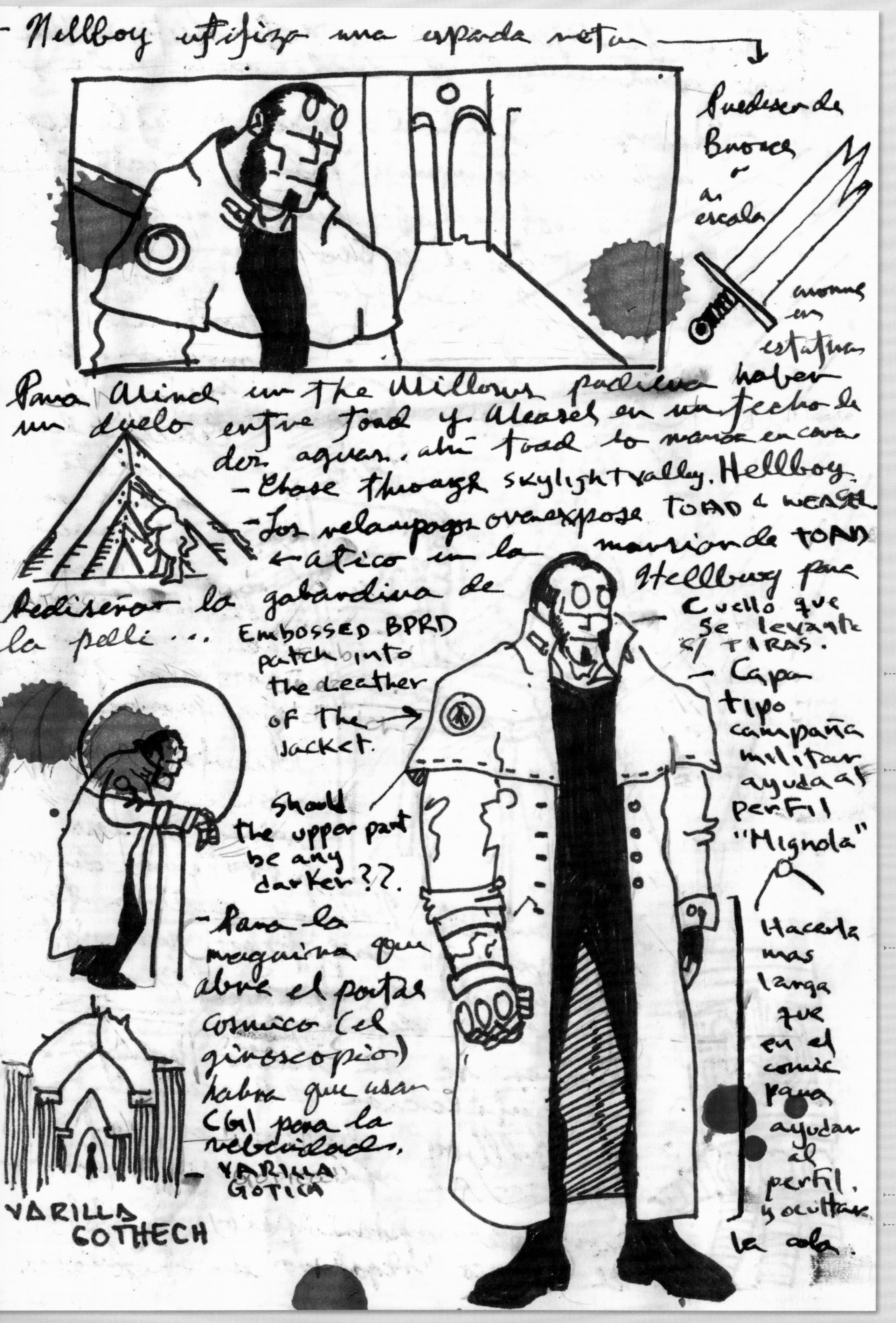

– Hellboy uses a broken sword. It could be made of bronze and enormous enough for a statue

–In Wind in the Willows there could a duel between Toad and Weasel on the gable roof. There Toad [?] him in the face

–Chase through skylight valley. Hellboy.

–The lightning overexposes *TOAD & WEASEL.*

Attic in Toad's mansion

Redesign Hellboy's overcoat for the movie . . .

Embossed BPRD patch into the leather of the jacket.

Should the upper part be any darker??

–Collar kept standing up with TAPE.

–Military campaign–style cape helps give him a "Mignola" outline

–For the machine that opens the cosmic portal (the gyroscope), CGI needs to be used for realism.

Make it longer than in the comic to help the outline and hide the tail.

GOTHIC LINES

GOTHIC LINES

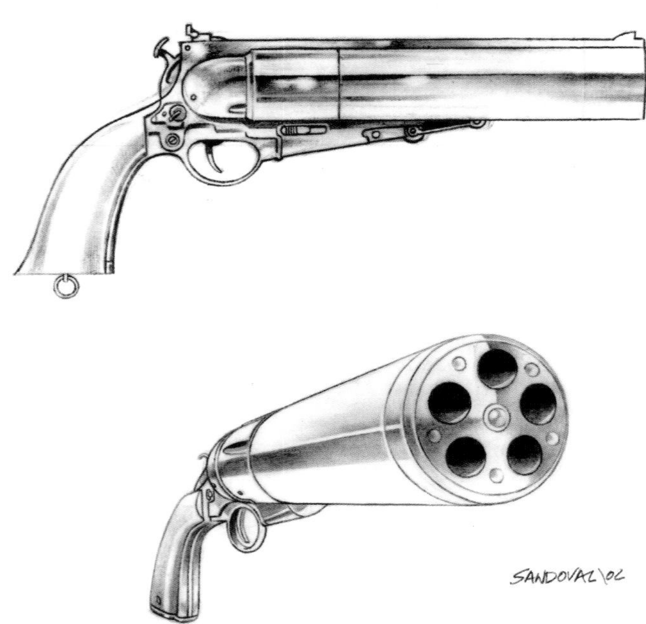

GDT: Well, one of the gags here [*opposite*] is in the movie, which is Hellboy sliding. I wanted him sliding and shooting backward.

Above him is a really early design of the Samaritan, and this is the page where I came up with the name "The Good Samaritan" for the gun. People think it's in the comic. It's never been.

The bottom was something that I wanted to do that is not there. It was like a Jacques Tourneur moment in which you see Sammael's shadow in the foreground.

Then in the middle, I like to play with the flashlights. We did some of that, but not to that degree.

Del Toro named Hellboy's gun "The Good Samaritan" and asked his art team to develop a series of studies, including those by Sergio Sandoval at DDT (ABOVE) and TyRuben Ellingson, who came up with the final design (BELOW & RIGHT). (LEFT) Here, del Toro instructs Ron Perlman (Hellboy) on how to point the massive gun, which somehow looked the right size in Perlman's large hands.

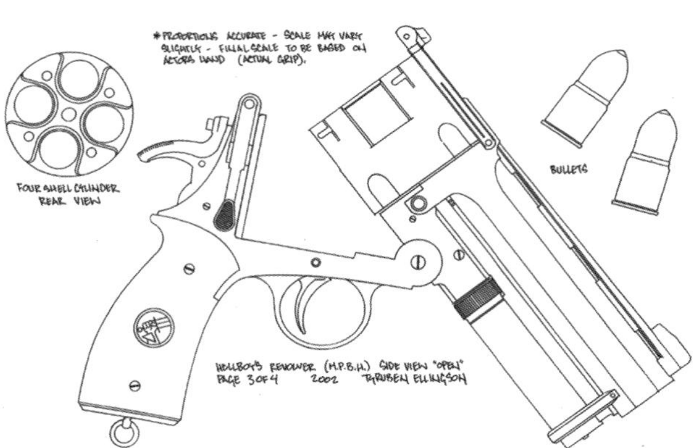

—He grinds his teeth so hard when he smiles that one of his front teeth breaks. With push in.

—We need to give the pistol a name

—Ellipses with fluttering of moth wings.

—Hellboy falls down a ventilation shaft while fighting with Sammy

—Even though it's a revolver, the pistol should eject cartridges like an automatic. The silencer might retract

The Good Samaritan.

—When the underground dwellers are killed, hobos *warn them about Sammael and his enormous appetite.*

F L A S H L I G H T S

Shadow and bone noises in the museum.

—Hellboy gets punched but manages to land well. He breaks the tiles in a straight line as he slides across them.

—Kroenen should listen to his Wagner records with a refined, absolute delight.

–Kodo drum ensemble, but without techno elements.

–Trip to Japan with Lorenza, Marianne, and in-laws courtesy of Blade II. I hope the movie is a hit in this country. I want to take my girls to Ghibli Museum to see Miyazaki's stuff.

Hellboy sets a booby trap filled with barbs. He's the one who sets it off: "Trigger" in the floor

Yellow light.

–Concrete tunnel in Tokyo.

–Dessert: NATAREKOKO.

LANDMINE sends barbs flying when it explodes.

NATAREKOKO

Scarlet

Kroenen's mask. Made of white porcelain or black leather with a bright red device that fits over his mouth

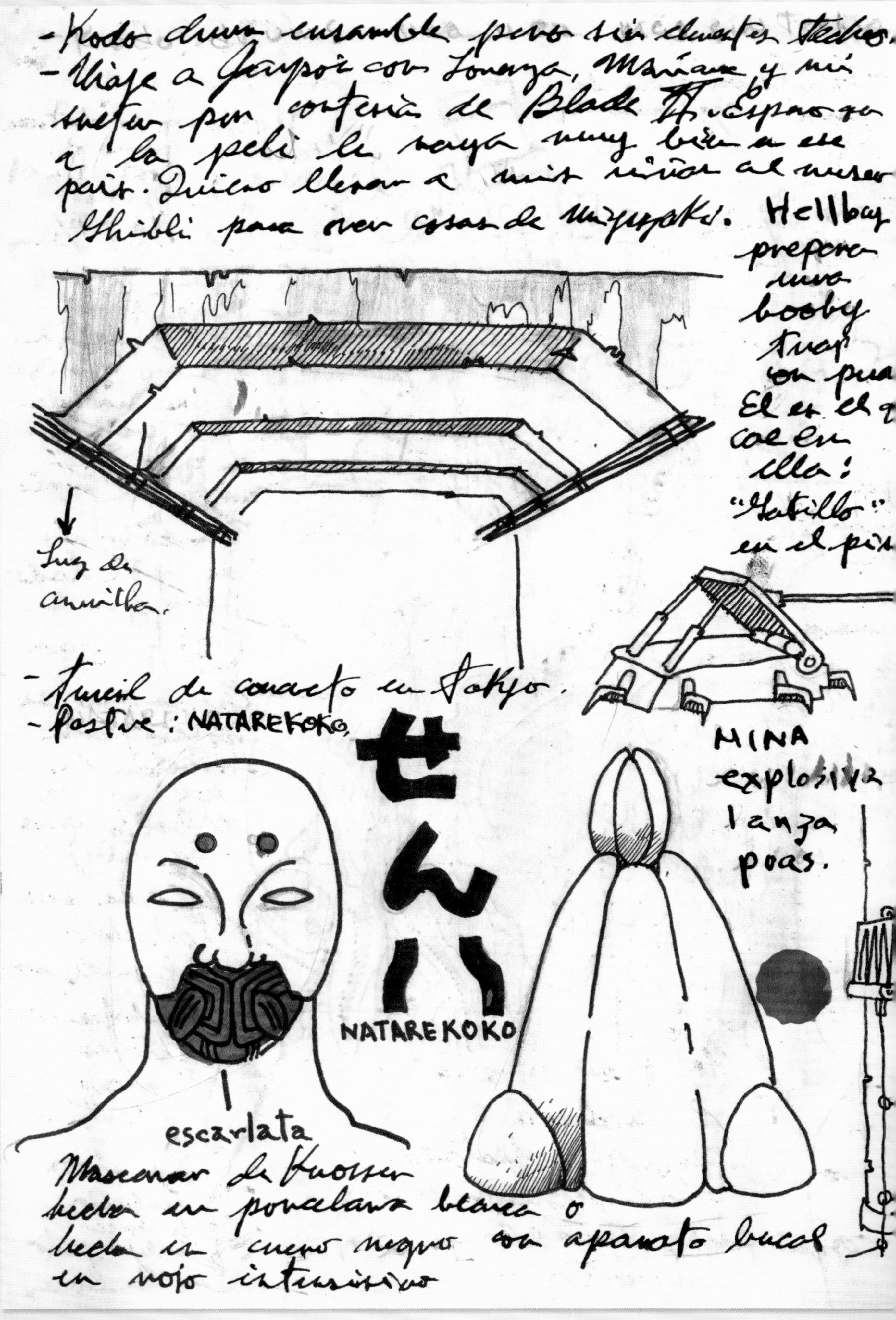

Notebook 3, Page 41A

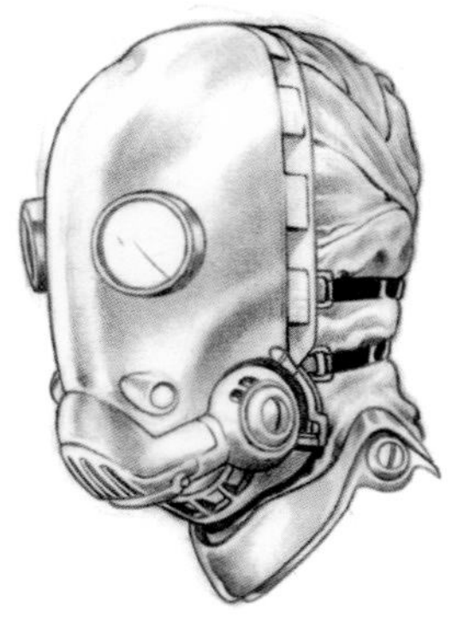

—We left the hotel early and ate sushi in the street—a disaster.

Amber light illuminates Sammael as he eats a guard.

The smoke from a blackout heightens the backlight.

—Paint job *a la Z II on his face.*

—The world's greatest paranormal detective. He doesn't really detect that much. He's a bit of supernatural bouncer.

—For the set's metallic finish refer to Chichone.

—Sammael attacks Left-Right *and then vice-versa, in serious ass-kicking mode.*

—He stabs his arm.

—Push in and follow HB as he backs away.

—There should be some Oriental influence on the design of Kroenen's Nazi uniform. Flags with [swastika]

—Amaniga moves his creatures really quickly despite the fact that they're so large.

—Sammael's voice should be made by fusing three voices played backward that alternate pronouncing letters:

NOTEBOOK 3, PAGE 41B

Sergio Sandoval at DDT did numerous conceptual iterations of Kroenen's face and mask (TOP). The final design (ABOVE) was inspired by a Japanese mask del Toro recorded in his notebook (OPPOSITE).

● **GDT:** This page [*opposite*] is from a visit to Japan to promote *Blade II*, with my daughter and my wife. I love those concrete shapes in the tunnel. They ended up being in the BPRD in *Hellboy*.

Then I saw a Japanese mask that had no bottom, and I thought, "Wouldn't it be great to give Kroenen a mask like that, but full of tubes that are red in the bottom, maybe kind of gory?" And he basically has the mask.

On the right is a sculptural detail, and in the middle is a Japanese sign that says "natarekoko," which is a dessert that I was eating at the time.

Then on the right-hand page [*above*], in the middle, I wanted Sammael to stab Hellboy, and I didn't do it—PG-13.

On the top, I wanted Sammael to be eating a corpse, backlit against the steam of the intestines of the corpse. But at the end of the day, two things prevented that: PG-13 and the fact that the horns and the protruding bones in the shoulder blades had to go. Backlighting the silhouette we ended up with would have been very boring, so I hung him upside down instead.

Dust rearrange

–The device HB uses to find the corpse. GEIGER.

They move up and down like switchblades

Long snout, skull with no skin on it

His snout pulls back like a lion's mane revealing the bone below

Bladder

Ear or not?

Abe's mouth hyperextends like a fish's mouth.

Fish mouth at rest.

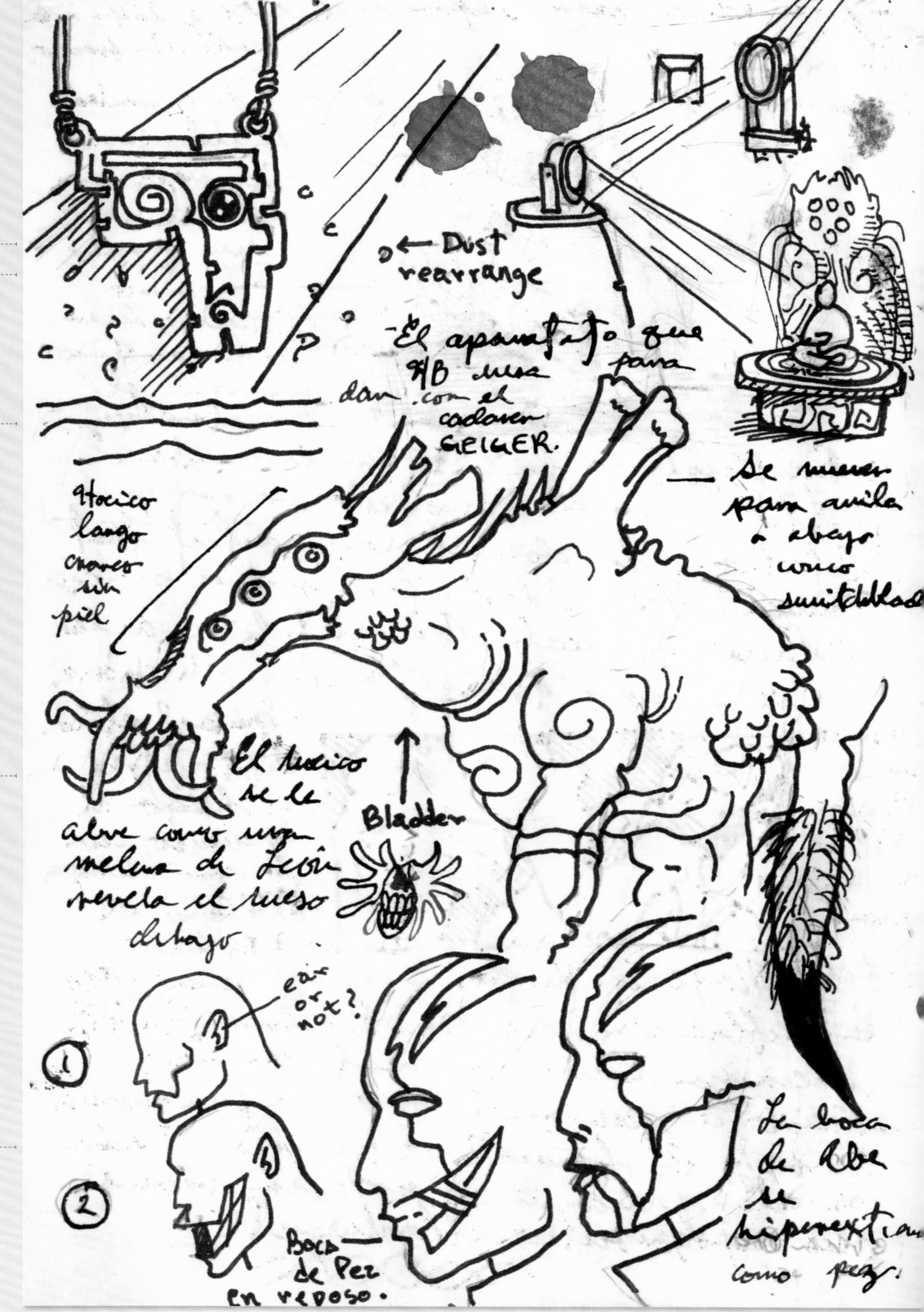

GDT: These pages [*opposite*] are from the same visit to Japan. While I was there, I tried to meet with my heroes: Katsuya Terada and Yasushi Nirasawa. I love their work, so we went to dinner at a sushi place that Nirasawa's father owns, and he drew the three of us on a chopstick cover, and I glued it to the notebook [*right*].

MSZ: So this is his drawing of you?

GDT: Yeah. It's really good! I look like a Miyazaki character.

MSZ: This is the only time I've seen a page where your writing goes in this direction.

GDT: That's probably because I put in the chopstick-cover illustration. I didn't start writing until after I put it there. And what I tried to do, in this particular notebook, was to finish all my thoughts at one time on a single page. I didn't want anything continuing on the next page. I knew that if I did it vertically, I would run out of space, so I did it like that.

MSZ: So each page is self-contained?

GDT: Yeah, I'm pretty sure. I mean, there may be an exception. That's why facing pages have their own subjects. On the left [*opposite*], for example, there are multiple ideas for *Hellboy*, but none of them bleed over to the next page.

Here, I was thinking of an amulet that Hellboy could have to awaken the corpse, which affects the dust particles in the air.

Then I came up with an idea that was too expensive, which was to have Rasputin frozen in a statue like in the comic, and then to have a series of mirrors that were clockwork-operated, which would beam the light into him.

Then, at the bottom, I wanted Abe to have an articulated mouth like a fish. You can still see the old Abe, which is a bit like Moebius's Silver Surfer. The mouth was going to project out like a fish mouth. And Mignola was so horrified by this idea. He said, "That's the worst idea!" He was so horrified by the idea of the mouth that he said to me, "If you don't do that, I'll give you four pages of any of my stories you like." And I have the four pages upstairs. I'm a cheap man.

Then you see Sammael, again, attempting the same thing. This drawing is a little more similar to what we ended up with. And the claw—I wanted it to look like a lobster claw in the air. That didn't make it.

MSZ: Now, as we're going through these pages and seeing the designs of Sammael, it's becoming refined. Were you working with your design team at this point?

GDT: I was already talking to Mike at this point. I think Wayne Barlowe was already on board, and I started to send him these things, but these were still my own musings.

MSZ: What's this bladder?

GDT: The idea was that the neck would inflate like a bladder, and the tentacles around his mouth would do a "Brrrr!" and expand to reveal his teeth.

–*Floor and murals on the walls*

–[?] *digital lines for punch*

–*Vibrating shine in the eye a la ANIME*

–Medieval architecture mixed with industrial

–*Blue set, blue character, blue days*

–*The eggs shine, acrylic nest*

–*The* [?] *for the tentacle BW.*

–*Build the outside space (eye).*

–*Dry leaves* around him (a la O).

–*Cloud from above, see tentacles*

–*Nest with eggs made from acrylic.*

–*Theatrical effects for water* [?].

–No baby [?] to No Abe injured.

–Tongue design should be bigger than the mouthspace visible outside (7 feet).

–Steadicam guy should be Varomia. Tell Patrick ASAP.

Notebook 3, Page 42B

Triumvirate
Katsuya Terada
© Terada San
© chopsticks for sushi.

Drawing of Terada, Nirazawa, and Hellboy with me below them. 5/29/02 Tokyo

I Budget w/ FANTASY II

MASTERPIECE

SOLD OUT

Ton of pus!

Masterpiece!! *Dinner with two Japanese buddies, both very friendly and talkative.*

–clak clacks clikty-clack, clack clack, then grows silent. The mouth smiles.

Try to keep Sammael changing his *silhouette whenever possible.*

His bones dislocate. This helps

–Broom's autopsy: "a piece of nail split his spine in two, the impact pulverized two vertebrae.

–The idol on the altar should be a highly stylized Behemoth

octopus's pupil

–When we film Sammael, we should vary the speed and perhaps use a long lens for detail.

Lower teeth are bigger than upper.

Backlit Fog

–Hair implants for one of the agents.

–[?]

–The "little hand" establishes the episode CBL.

–The "Marita" establishes the episode CBL.

–Wax cylinder for the recordings of memories in a journal, *in AMOM.*

–Use ribbons or climbing ropes to come and go in the areas of temporal distortion. Movement sensors.

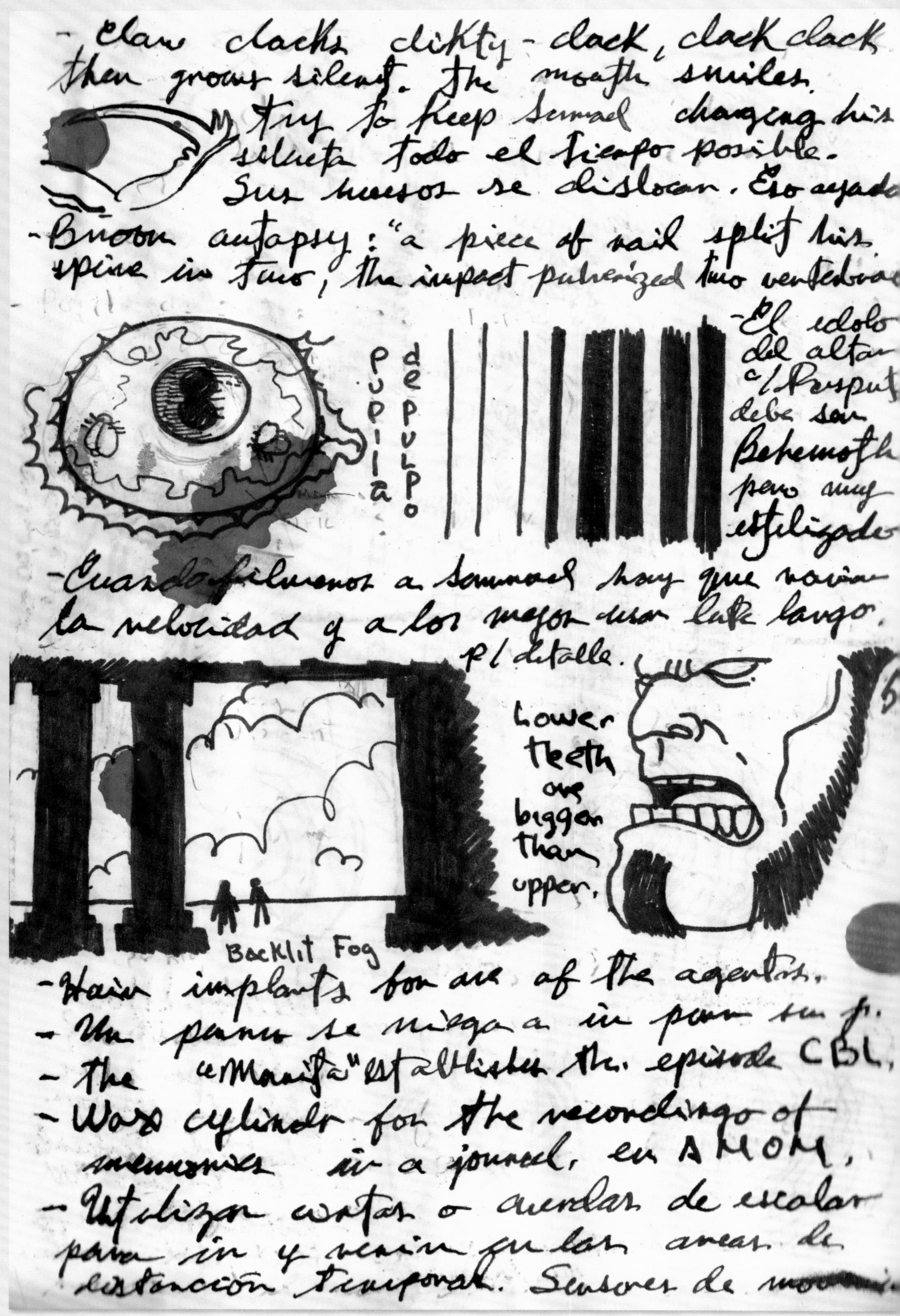

Notebook 3, Page 44A

● **GDT:** The eye here [*opposite, top*] is me exploring the idea that Sammael would have an egg-shaped pupil that would dilate. And I thought, "One of the eyes could have flies on it," which is very disgusting.

At the bottom of the page is me reflecting on how to fit vertical information in a 1:85 frame.

The next idea was to give Ron Perlman longer lower teeth than upper teeth, which ended up in the movie. He has huge fake teeth in the movie, but the lower ones are bigger than the top ones. Now, why did I want the lower teeth bigger? Hellboy has a really extreme lantern jaw in the comics [*above left*], and one of the ways Mike does it is by doing the lower teeth the way Jack Kirby did. Kirby used to have his bottom teeth come up above the lip in a straight line.

Hellboy's jaw, with its distinct under bite, was a mixture of Mike Mignola's original character (TOP) and Ron Perlman's bone structure (ABOVE).

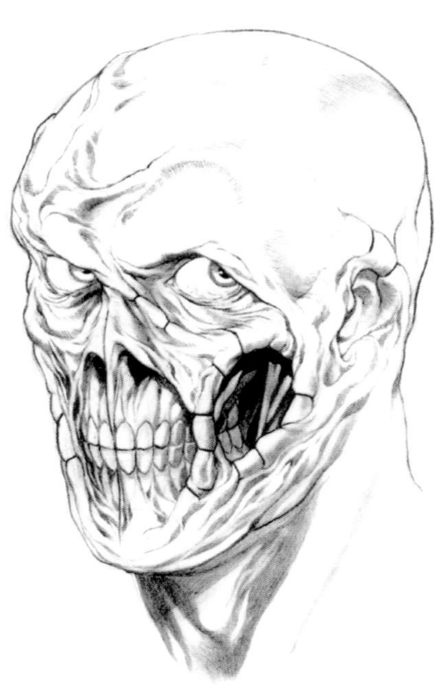

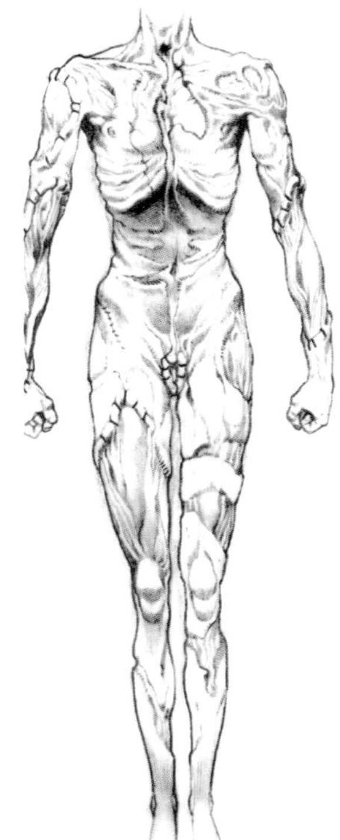

GDT: You can see [*opposite*], as strange as it is, I'm already trying to draw Hellboy like Ron Perlman. I'm trying to find a way. And there is a nick in the flesh of his cheek, which I wanted to be very, very deep. I couldn't do it. But it's the nick that Kroenen gives him in the final fight.

And I wanted Hellboy jumping between buildings with the moon silhouetting him. I didn't do that.

This is pretty accurate to the way he looks in the Apocalypse, though—at the top of a mountain of debris, with the horns.

Then, in the center are Kroenen's skin grafts. DDT was using these sketches, and they were becoming a little extreme. I was thinking, strangely enough, that Kroenen needed to be sexy. And I know an eyeless, lipless guy is not sexy, but I thought, "There needs to exist some kind of really, really, really twisted girl that is going to get off on Kroenen." So I said, "For that, my minuscule audience, we have to make him sexy."

Then there is the lock on the safe that needed a triangular key. It ended up being different in the movie, but it's similar, and the key is triangular.

Then Mignola has Hellboy with sort of a ponytail. And in 2001, ponytails were, like, really for porn producers. So I gave Hellboy a Japanese sumo wrestler haircut that kind of indicated he had some fighter training. And, also, Mike has Hellboy with male pattern baldness, and I felt that was not very sexy, so I gave him the scalp shaving of a Japanese warrior. He shaves his head. So, all in all, I wanted Hellboy to keep to the comic but to be a little sexier.

MSZ: You're dealing with so many design elements from the film right here in this one little compact area. As well as different parts of the film.

GDT: And there's things from *Mountains of Madness*, too. Now, in *Mountains of Madness*, they wake up and time has been altered. A potato has sprouted. That's in the movie. Cthulhu in the fog. It's always more than two projects.

MSZ: That's something you've alluded to—that when you're working on a multitude of projects, if anything falls through on one, you're, in a way, somewhat insulated because you're working on multiple things.

GDT: When I concentrate on a single thing, that's when I get blocked. What I find—and I'm not saying this works for everyone—is that the promiscuity of having four or five things online actually makes them feed each other. And you go, "Aha! That idea is great for *Madness*. That idea is great for . . ." And you keep them alive. It's a dialogue.

(TOP) Sergio Sandoval at DDT elaborated on del Toro's idea of a stitched-together, cadaverous being (OPPOSITE, CENTER). Del Toro tried to place Hellboy's ponytail in a warrior tradition by giving the character a sumo wrestler haircut (OPPOSITE, RIGHT & ABOVE).

–IN AMOM, they wake up to find time altered. Potato, etc. without realizing it

WOUND CAUSED BY KROENEN

Follows Liz.

Hellboy door lock

Apocalypse

Kroenen

Toshiro hairstyle

–Cthulhu in the mist. Above it, rising like an Everest of pale, corrupt flesh.

–How long has it been? Hours—days.

–Pulsating vein CGI *in HB's neck.*

–She is dead, her power depleted.

–Your love for the girl. How could we have foreseen that??

PAN'S LABYRINTH

PAN'S LABYRINTH REPRESENTS Guillermo at the crossroads, "trying to redefine my life, creatively," and choosing the right path—one of his own devising that led to a movie he *needed* to make. At this point in his career, he was turning down many top Hollywood offers, films that would have netted him millions of dollars. Instead, he chose financial struggle and artistic triumph.

In *Pan's Labyrinth* (2006), everything Guillermo had been working toward came together in a grand panoply that is by turns brutal, gentle, intimate, and majestic. The notebooks he kept during this period reveal his consuming passion for the project. As he evolved the storyline and visual world of *Pan's Labyrinth* in the notebooks, he laid bare all the specifics of the film, like a photograph emerging in a developing tray. He reflected on casting, historical background, specific shots, dialogue, sets, characters, costumes, and creatures. In these pages, *Pan's Labyrinth* comes alive in glorious detail.

As Guillermo notes, paraphrasing and building on Heraclitus, "One never bathes in the same river or sees the same film twice." He considered possible variations of every element of *Pan's Labyrinth* and struggled to determine "which would the public understand more readily?" In this, Guillermo clearly grasps the difference between presenting mysteries that intrigue and beguile and simply failing to communicate one's intent and confounding an audience.

"It's only through art that you're able to glimpse otherness," Guillermo wrote, and everything we see in these detailed sketches and notations serves the goal of helping us see the alien as personal, familiar, and meaningful. In our daily lives we often insulate ourselves from what is unlike us, viewing otherness as threatening and ultimately rejecting it. But safe in our homes and theater seats, Guillermo's art encourages us to consider the repulsive and the rejected with compassion and empathy—to expand our definitions of ourselves by encompassing the range of human (and even inhuman) experience.

In the case of *Pan's Labyrinth*, Guillermo ruminated on plot motifs drawn from folk and fairy tales and classic children's literature—enduring rites of passage that help children make sense of strange and unfamiliar things. Some of the imagery this evoked, such as the mandrake root that comes alive, remained virtually unchanged from notebook to film. On the other hand, the loathsome, terrifying

(OPPOSITE, CLOCKWISE FROM TOP LEFT) Vidal (Sergi López) threatens Ofelia (Ivana Baquero); an illuminated drawing depicting the Faun, the princess, and the labyrinth; concept of the Pale Man by Raúl Monge; concept of the main monolith by Monge; Ofelia (Baquero) in the forest; study for one of the frescoes in the Pale Man's lair by Carlos Jimenez; concept of the subterranean city where Ofelia's parents reign by Raúl Villares.

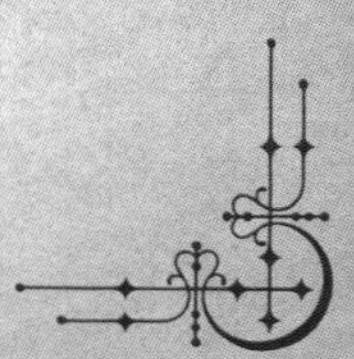

Pale Man morphed from a wooden doll in a tree to an old man with eyes floating queasily in liquefied flesh, to the figure's final, unforgettable state as a visionless face with eyeballs snatched off a plate and inserted into stigmata wounds in its palms.

Lost along the way, but captured in these pages, are such tidbits as children "that the well swallowed up," a changeling brought by elves to replace the baby they've stolen, gold rather than food arrayed on a tabletop to lure Ofelia, and perhaps most disturbing of all, "the dead children who eat fairies." Any of these items might have worked individually, but the totality would have presented a storyline that was "ungainly," as Guillermo puts it. His goal was to craft a film of elegance and inevitability.

Even in his marginalia we see his concern over making "the other" intelligible, as Guillermo grappled with translating the title of the film into English. He strove for more recognizable and compelling wording for an American audience and eventually settled on *Pan's Labyrinth*—although Pan is nowhere to be found in the film.

Everything in *Pan's Labyrinth* is rich with multiple shades and layers of meaning, including the main character's name, Ofelia (Ivana Baquero), which hearkens back both to Hamlet's dreamy, doomed lover and to the daughter of Roald Dahl, one of Guillermo's favorite writers. Taking shape in these pages are such iconic images as the ominous dead tree with its "fallopian nature"; Ofelia's dress, like Alice's "but with different colors"; and the Faun, who at first looks like a muscular, goatish variation on Hellboy before becoming the lean and lyrical being in the film. Indeed, throughout these pages, Guillermo was also hashing out *Hellboy II: The Golden Army*, which he was writing at the same time, while "working on deadlines, juggling projects."

When jotting these notes, Guillermo continually reminded himself to take courage, to stand for *exactly* what he wanted in all things. This included selecting American actor Doug Jones, previously Abe Sapien in *Hellboy*, as "the only guy to play the Faun" (Jones also played the Pale Man in *Pan's Labyrinth* with equal brilliance). Only their collaboration could have created the Faun, but that decision meant paying more than a Spanish actor would have cost and dubbing all Jones's lines in Spanish with another performer's voice. When Jones was offered and turned down films in the *X-Men* and *Men in Black* franchises, choosing instead to complete *Pan's Labyrinth*, Guillermo triumphantly wrote: "2007 . . . It's my year: Guillermo del Toro."

Even the briefest notations in these pages lends a deeper insight into the finished work, as in the passage, "Faun has a flute made from a thigh bone." Again, here is the beautiful and the grotesque in a *danse macabre*, blurring together, becoming one and the same. Elsewhere he jotted one of his finest epigrams: "I believe in two things: God and time. Both are infinite, both reign supreme. Both crush mankind."

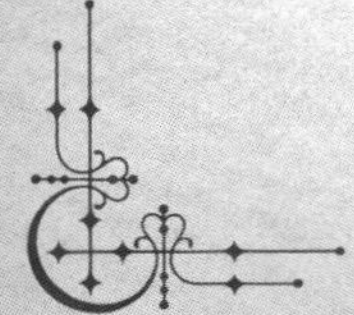

Guillermo's obsessions and grand themes are rendered in his notebook with masterful control and consideration. As in *Cronos* and later in *Hellboy II: The Golden Army,* clockwork mechanisms figure prominently, in this case the workings of a pocket watch mirrored in the oversize gears of a mill. "We ended up using them in the mill to represent the captain being trapped in his father's watch," Guillermo observes of this man obsessed with remembrance. "But I find gears really fascinating," he adds. "They represent, I think, the mechanism of the universe, cyclical nature, the inexorable."

In *Pan's Labyrinth*, as everywhere in his oeuvre, Guillermo's villains appear in vivid detail—evil, real, dreadful. No detail is too small to escape his scrutiny, including a description of what the villainous captain wears: "coat on his shoulders, gloves, glasses . . . hair parted in the center, patent leather shoes." Finally, the watch, the glass of which he shatters to preserve his time of death so that he can be remembered by his son—an action that ultimately proves futile. Taking pains to show us his villains' longings and their scars, both emotional and physical, Guillermo does not mean to excuse their terrible actions, but rather to reveal the human in the monster and the monstrous in the human.

Disrupting expectations, juxtaposing opposites, contrasting the fantastical with taken-for-granted reality: This effort to illuminate both what we refuse to see and what we blindly look past drives Guillermo's work. The most profound juxtaposition in *Pan's Labyrinth* is between the very notions of fantasy and reality. Guillermo took great pains to design visual metaphors that differentiate these two worlds. He noted in his journal: "The real world is made of straight lines, and the world of fantasy is curved. Reality is cold. Fantasy is warm. The fantasy world should feel UTERINE, INTERIOR, like the subconscious of the girl. . . ." Guillermo's film gives audiences intimate contact with an interior life—the world that must be believed to be seen.

The *Pan's Labyrinth* journal entries also include another startling juxtaposition—the presence of someone else's handwriting in these most personal pages. This guest contributor provided Guillermo with the film's first review, letting him know how the great gamble of *Pan's Labyrinth* had turned out. Written when the film was completed, on the day Guillermo screened *Pan's Labyrinth* for his favorite living writer and that man's son (another writer of note), the note says simply: "WE HAD A BLAST!! Steve King."

Mr. King and his son were not alone. *Pan's Labyrinth* was lauded far and wide, both within the industry and among audiences. The film won Oscars for art direction, cinematography, and makeup, netted an Oscar nomination for Best Foreign Language Film, and became the highest-grossing Spanish-language film ever released in the United States. Most satisfying of all, this acclaim rewarded Guillermo's fidelity to his own values and aesthetic, or as he concludes: "I didn't have to do a serious piece about Edwardian drama to be nominated for an Oscar."

–"Don't get me wound up, animal . . . don't push me"

–They use the binoculars to spy on the police officers who arrest the fighter from the train. They can make them out perfectly.

* Julio Vélez, a good actor to play a civil guard. Thin.

–Hellboy calls the new agent "Lil' fella" or "squirt."

–Abe has "insight" that they are very weird "Kidney."

–When I was a boy, I could feel them in my bones. My hand.

–The spotlight doesn't work. Would there be electricity?? In the middle of the countryside??

–High Relief, Portico, LEDGE, CORNICE, Pillar, Post

—Chimneys in the Pyrenees.

–One never bathes in the same river or sees the same film twice. Memorable TRUEBISMO #1

–Ofelia has: a very slight hunchback DDT or a lame leg (?)

–Take your hat off when you speak to me you goddamn son of a bitch!!

–Production Designer: Martin Childs for HB/MoM.

–Maria Portalez Cerezuela is the name of B.'s mother.

–What Vidal keeps in his safe must be SEEN (dry sausages).

–Crown/how much, sleeps, fire in the window, the house awakens, labyrinth. enter (stable-ish dynamite). It's you. It's you. Here we go.

–The wooden man instead of the ghosts

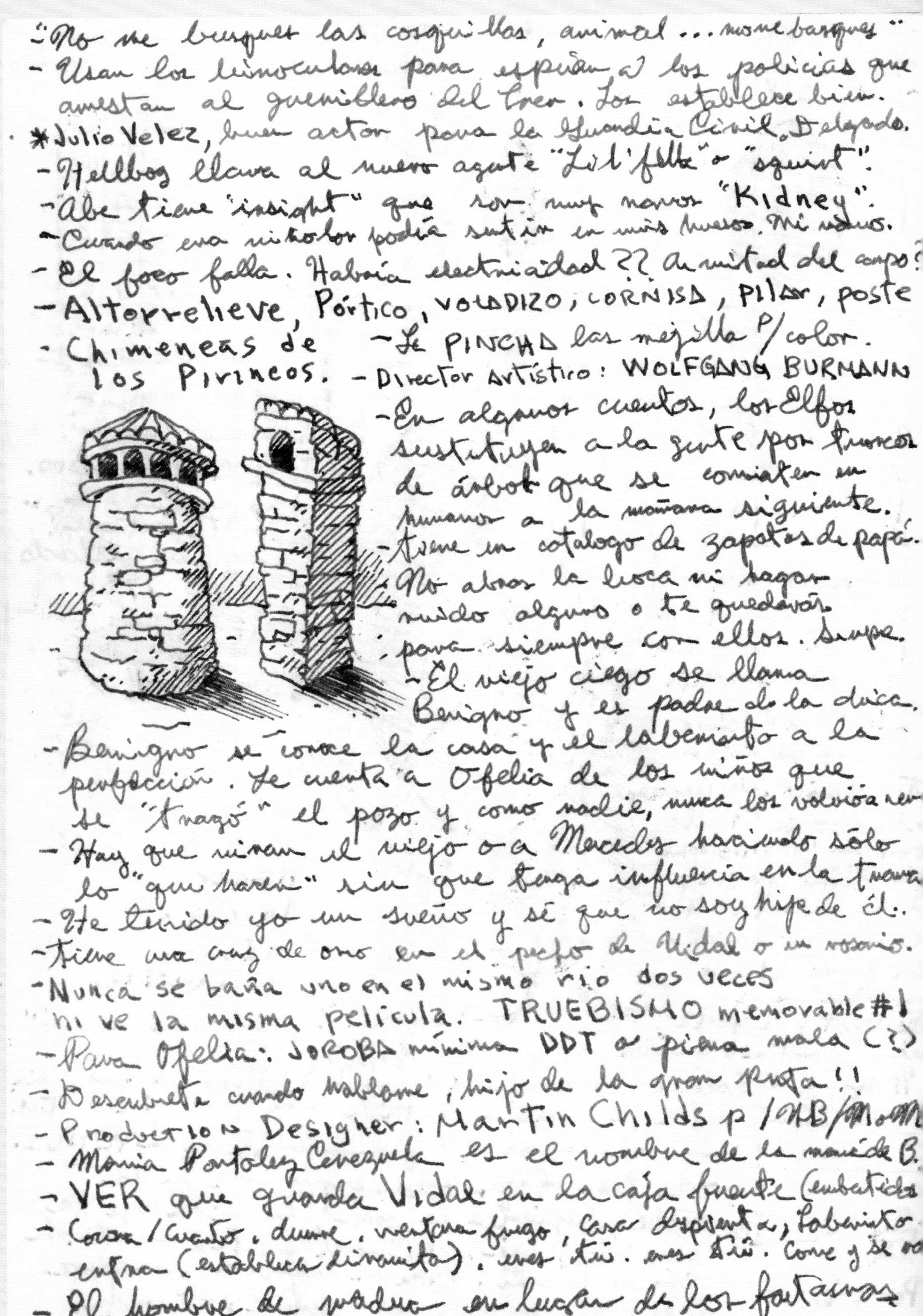

"No me busques las cosquillas, animal ... no me busques"
- Usan los binoculares para espiar a los policías que arrestan al guerrillero del tren. Los establece bien.
*Julio Velez, buen actor para la Guardia Civil. Delgado.
- Hellboy llama al nuevo agente "Lil' fella" o "squirt".
- Abe tiene "insight" que son muy raros "Kidney".
- Cuando era niño podía sentir en mis huesos. Mi mano.
- El foco falla. Habría electricidad?? A mitad del campo??
- Altorrelieve, Pórtico, VOLADIZO, CORNISA, Pilar, poste
- Chimeneas de los Pirineos.
- Le PINCHA las mejilla p/color.
- Director Artístico: WOLFGANG BURMANN
- En algunos cuentos, los Elfos sustituyen a la gente por troncos de árbol que se convierten en humanos a la mañana siguiente.
- Tiene un catálogo de zapatos de papá.
- No abras la boca ni hagas ruido alguno o te quedarás para siempre con ellos. Siempre.
- El viejo ciego se llama Benigno y es padre de la [illegible].
- Benigno se conoce la casa y el laberinto a la perfección. Le cuenta a Ofelia de los niños que se "tragó" el pozo y como nadie, nunca los volvió a ver.
- Hay que mirar al viejo o a Mercedes haciendo sólo lo "que hacen" sin que tenga influencia en la trama.
- He tenido yo un sueño y sé que no soy hija de él.
- Tiene una cruz de oro en el pecho de Vidal o un rosario.
- Nunca se baña uno en el mismo río dos veces ni ve la misma película. TRUEBISMO memorable #1
- Para Ofelia: JOROBA mínima DDT o pierna mala (?)
- Descubrete cuando hablame, hijo de la gran puta!!
- Production Designer: Martin Childs p/HB/MoM
- María Portalez Cerezuela es el nombre de la mamá de B.
- VER que guarda Vidal en la caja fuerte (embutidos)
- Corona/Cuanto, duerme, ventana fuego, casa despierta, laberinto entra (establece dinamita). eres tú. eres tú. Come y se va
- El hombre de madera en lugar de los fantasmas

Notebook 4, Page 5A

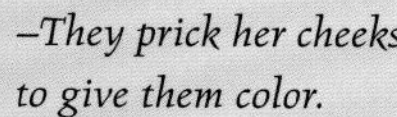

—They prick her cheeks to give them color.

—Art Director: WOLFGANG BURMANN

—In some stories, elves replace people with wooden logs that turn into human beings the next morning.

—She has a shoe catalog that belongs to her father.

—Don't open your mouth or make a sound or you'll remain there with them forever. Forever.

—The old, blind man's name is Benigno and he's the girl's father.

—Benigno knows the house and labyrinth inside out. He tells Ofelia about the children that the well "swallowed up" and about how nobody ever saw them again.

—Mercedes and the old man need to be seen doing "what they do" without it having anything to do with the plot.

—I had a dream and I know I'm not his daughter.

—Vidal has a gold cross or a rosary hanging from his neck.

GDT: I did a lot of research on the architecture of northern Spain while working on *Pan's Labyrinth* because the north of Spain is very peculiar. It has sort of a fairy-tale feel, both the northeast and the northwest. Whether you're in Galicia or on the border with France, either way you get these lush, cold forests.

And I just made the house they lived in out of the chimneys of the Pyrenees because I thought it needed to feel crooked, or needed to feel like straight lines going wrong, like a motion detector.

Then [*opposite*] it says, "In some stories, the elves replace people with wooden logs that turn into human beings the next morning." That is the changelings. I thought, at some point while creating *Pan's Labyrinth*, that there would be elves who would take the baby into the labyrinth. I obviously changed that.

"One never bathes in the same river or sees the same film twice." This is a reference to Heraclitus, a Greek philosopher, who said that about rivers, but it's also true about film. You never see the same film twice.

Then it talks about Ofelia having a limp leg. I wanted her to not be completely normal, but then I thought what is great is making her physically normal, but making her different in other ways.

(OPPOSITE) Del Toro drew inspiration for the main building in the film from the chimneys characteristic of the historical architecture of the Pyrenees. (ABOVE & LEFT) This reference was carried through in the design of the mill seen in this production artwork by Carlos Jimenez.

GDT: There are some notes here [*opposite*], like I'm playing with what the movie would be called in English because I knew that "The Faun's Labyrinth" would be bad.

And then it says, "Coat on his shoulders, gloves, glasses, and silver cane." Everything but the silver cane is the captain. And it says, "Hair parted in the center, patent leather shoes, beige scarf." No scarf, but the shoes and the gloves were very important for me with the captain because I needed him to creak.

(ABOVE) Del Toro gave Vidal (Sergi López) stiff leather boots so that he would creak when he walked. (OPPOSITE) Del Toro sketched the house where Luis Buñuel grew up in his notebook, using it as an inspiration for the film's main building, conceptualized by Carlos Jimenez (BELOW).

MSZ: What is this house? Is it something you invented or remembered, or did you come across it?

GDT: It's actually the house where Luis Buñuel lived as a kid. I thought it would be great to use it as the model for the house in *Pan's*, but I abandoned it because I thought the mill was a better thing.

I went to the cinemathéque in Spain and read a lot about Buñuel for *Pan's Labyrinth*. He's one of my two favorite filmmakers of all time, along with Hitchcock. Formally, they're polar opposites. But, content-wise, they are very similar, and there are traits of their personalities that are interesting. As a friend of mine put it very brutally, "The only difference between Buñuel and Hitchcock is that Buñuel was handsome." Which is a big difference. But they were both guys that lived very bourgeois, very middle-class lives. They lived like gentlemen. You went to Buñuel's house, and he was very rigid. He was very much a male, a very macho guy with his wife. It was like old-school gentlemen, but in their imaginations, they were anarchists. Buñuel was a huge fan of the Marquis de Sade, and he was obviously a man with many, many twisted ideas and an iconoclast. Hitchcock was the same. The curious thing is that they lived these guarded lives and had completely unguarded imaginations.

So for *Pan's*, I was very attracted to the idea of making some kind of reference to Buñuel.

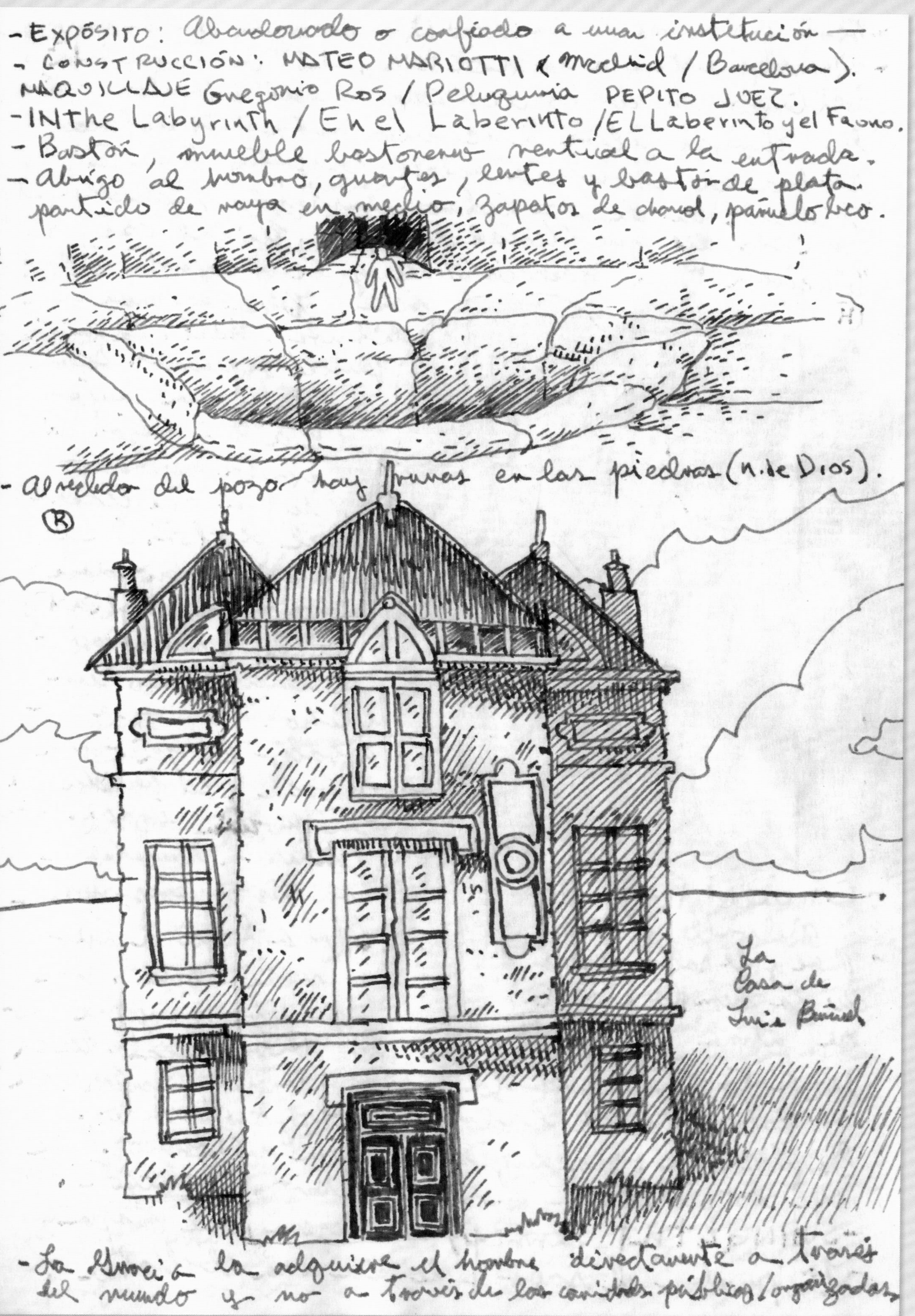

-EXPÓSITO: Abandonado o confiado a una institución —
- CONSTRUCCIÓN: MATEO MARIOTTI (Madrid / Barcelona).
MAQUILLAJE Gregorio Ros / Peluquería PEPITO JUEZ.
-IN the Labyrinth / En el Laberinto / El Laberinto y el Fauno.
- Bastón, mueble bastonero vertical a la entrada.
- Abrigo al hombro, guantes, lentes y bastón de plata.
partido de raya en medio, zapatos de charol, pañuelo bco.
- Alrededor del pozo hay runas en las piedras (n. de Dios).
La Casa de Luis Buñuel
- La Gracia la adquiere el hombre directamente a través del mundo y no a través de las caridades públicas / organizadas

–FOUNDLING: Abandoned or consigned to an institution

–CONSTRUCTION: MATEO MARIOTTI (Madrid/Barcelona).

MAKEUP: Gregorio Ros/ Hair Stylist: PEPITO JUEZ.

–In the Labyrinth/ In the Labyrinth/ The Faun's Labyrinth.

–Boston, Bostonian furniture, vertical in the entrance.

–Coat on his shoulder, gloves, glasses, and silver cane. Hair parted in the center, patent leather shoes, beige scarf.

–There are runes on the stones around the well (name of God).

Luis Buñuel's house

–Man may acquire grace directly from the world and not through public/ charitable organizations

–A watch instead of liquor. He/she tells them the story—

–I believe in two things: God and time. Both are infinite, both reign supreme. Both crush mankind—

–For the coffin with blurred "edges."

–My mother taught me how to live. My father taught me how to die. To die with courage. The only decent way to die. That's where the broken watch comes in.

–The doctor is going to help him "DIE WELL."

–Why do you smile when you say it . . . this? You call this a smile?

–Ramon Fontserè for the role of the priest in P.L.

–Kate Corrigan drums her fingers incessantly on the table

–We have gained arrogance instead of Wisdom, gained cruelty instead of intelligence and made the world a cruel, cold place.

–Abe, you look like a woman when you laugh like that.

–Devane's Speech in Marathon Man *to explain the BPRD.*

–Abe to HB: You should have a "blurb" a one-liner, a signature piece that people remember you by, like: Crime is a disease and I am the cure. *Later HB tells him,* Aw, crap.

–Use Abe Sapien in the programs with the Hannusen model

–Hellboy versus the GIANT PIG MAN/flaming skeletons.

–Good punch, HB!! *K.C. says,* "Somehow I think it'll take more than that, *Red responds.* Abe makes his "AOL" impersonation.

–Manning explains his "BALL OF GAS" theory to the press.

–1/23/05 Carmen gives clothes to my daughter./Better life/She believes in weddings.

–You cannot deny that your soul has been touched by fire.

–You don't Diddly-squat about us.

–For the ghost VFX it would be worth it not to use a conventional [?] but instead to use a CH [?].

–STOP MOTION instead of CGI.

–Hellboy flicks away a fairy with his finger.

Notebook 4, Page 13A

–She puts the mandrake root under the bed. Explosions. Pitched battle. A wounded man. Theft of the antibiotics. They've captured one of them. Mercedes and the doctor speak to one another. The antibiotics are the same. Torture, the deaf-mute's suicide.

● **GDT:** At the top [*opposite*], I have the captain's watch, broken. This came, actually, from a Fascist movie. There's a Fascist movie called *Balarrasa*, which is a movie that was done during the Franco years, so the heroes are Fascists. And one of them hits his watch right before he thinks he's going to die, and he says, "I want people to know the time of my death."

And I thought that was a really arrogant gesture, and I took it for the captain's father, who says, "Let my son, like his father, die like a true man." And he's ready to do that at the end. He pulls out the watch and he's ready to say, "Tell my son—" And they say, "We won't tell him shit. You're gonna be forgotten." And then he says something I feel very much about the Old World right now, and it's very much the theme of *Hellboy II*: "We have gained arrogance instead of wisdom, we have gained cruelty instead of intelligence, and made the world a cruel, cold place."

And then it says, "She puts the mandrake root under the bed. Explosions. Pitched battle. A wounded man." This is pretty much the way the movie is. "Theft of the antibiotics. They've captured one of them. Mercedes and the doctor speak to one another. The antibiotics

The tunnel full of roots below the tree began in del Toro's notebook (OPPOSITE, LEFT) and was developed by Raúl Monge (TOP RIGHT), eventually becoming the site for the scene in the final film where Ofelia (Ivana Baquero) confronts the frog to retrieve the gold key in its stomach (ABOVE).

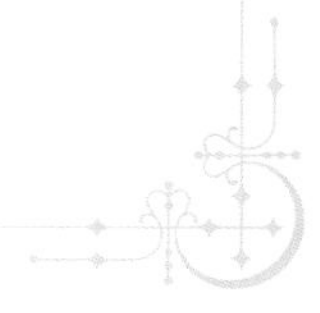

are the same. Torture, the deaf-mute's suicide." And I made him a stutterer instead of a deaf mute. But at one point I thought, "Well, what if the guy survives, and they find he's a deaf mute? And they have to interrogate him, but he can't speak. So he starts writing, and as he is writing, he commits suicide." I thought he would grab a pen and stab himself rather than talk. But, as it is, they tortured this stuttering guy.

Then, on the right hand side [*below*], we have almost exactly the shot that I have in the movie, in which Mercedes turns around and her umbrella covers the frame. And then, when she turns back, the captain is there.

–*IN HB II, Abe:* You've been listening to Barry Manilow. —No, I most certainly am not *(and he hides the CD) The book Remains*

–*Later you'll both listen to him together and you'll break into tears*

–*Abe is delighted by all the jokes Kate Corrigan tells*

–FACE REPLACEMENT *in the case of the faun.*

–Do you haunt this bridge?

–*How much does it cost to support HB?/annual.*

–*The Spanky method to disappear in the river, use it in HB II*

–*Cloak of invisibility/ring.*

–*Prison Break/MAXIMUM SECURITY area.*

–*The inside of the mill is RED.*

–I'll need something small in return: your seed.

–*Stuart Baxter:* LOCATION SCOUT *and professional* PHOTOGRAPHER.

–*The guests are DRY and DEAD:* A SOUL SUCKING PIG.

–*Use a* THORN FOREST *for HB with a sword.*

–*Sequence in the rain in which Liz or RC is kidnapped.*

–Anything you want to tell us about your foes: Well they have great fancy-pants names "Lord of this-that" and they smell.

–*How much do they owe? Don't worry about it— a hand gesture would be better*

–*Look at me you,* BASTARD. *The captain in the cantina.*

–*There are a thousand ways to kill a man, only one way to give him life.*

–*He who has nothing but feet will contribute his feet.*

He who has nothing but eyes will contribute his eyes.

For this great spiritual project. "The finger and the moon" A. J.

–*You can SEE the forest from the valley, but not from the forest.*

–*As soon as the self ceases to exist. The world exists.*

–*Criticism gives one the illusion of participating in the act of creation by way of an autopsy. The act is there and it exists and moves and challenges you while criticism fights to approve and validate.*

–*EVERYBODY TALKS ABOUT HIMSELF.*

IT'S ONLY THROUGH ART THAT YOU'RE ABLE TO GLIMPSE OTHERNESS.

–*One door is made of gold, another silver, another wood.*

–*Signed by the lawyers at* GUILFOYLE & GUILFOYLE.

–*SCARLET dress for the girl during the episode with the toad.*

–*Story of the fox and the [?] pigeons.*

Notebook 4, Page 13B

THE MAGICIAN

CORNELIA FUNKE

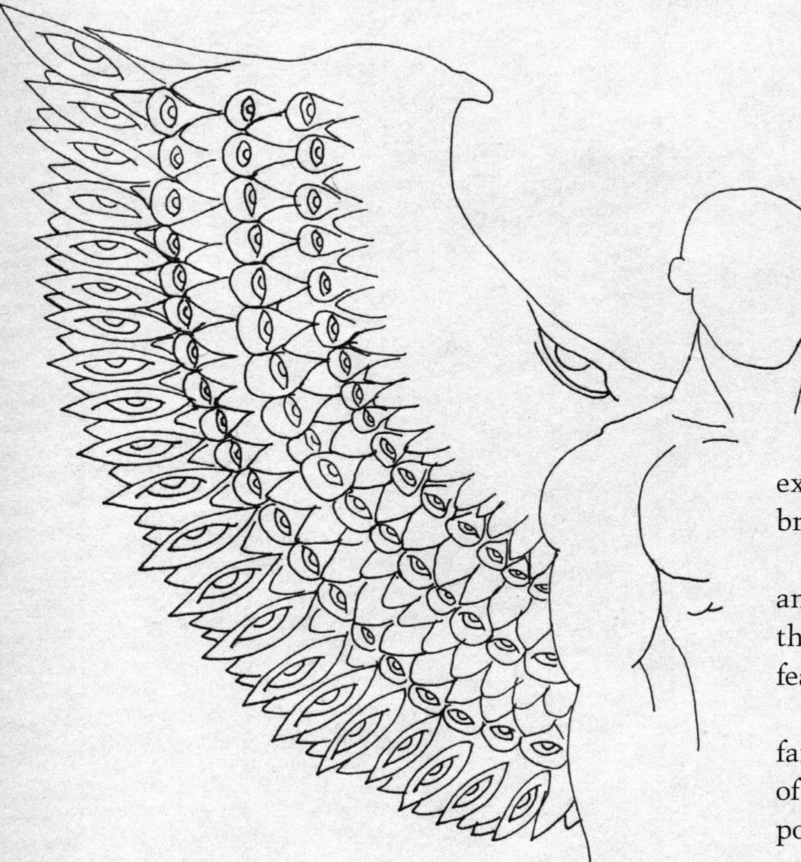

HOW DOES ONE WRITE about a true magician? It is quite a dangerous task, as a true magician can't be summoned or captured by words. And Guillermo del Toro is one of the greatest magicians of our time. Under his spell, words whisper and spread burning sparks over the silver screen to explode in a thousand archetypal images, so old and so new at the same time.

Guillermo del Toro takes "Once upon a time" and wraps it into black and golden yarns. He weaves the truth about the world from images and words until the shimmering fabric tells us all about the darkness and the light—the shadows that haunt us and our most secret wishes and dreams.

The labyrinth of the human heart . . . Guillermo knows all about it. And like every true magician, he dares to lose himself on its winding paths. He explores even its most frightening corners, just to bring back the truth.

He hunts for creatures and tales between its hedges, ancient remnants that have guarded our secrets since the very first story was told around a fire to fight the fear of what hides in the dark.

Guillermo brings back the treasures of myth and fairy tale and feeds them with the fears and hopes of our time. That's what makes his storytelling so powerful and unique—he deciphers our modern age with tools from the past. He uses the oldest language to reveal what we try to hide—all the desires of the human heart, all its weakness, fear, anger, and cruelty. Fairy tales never lie about human nature, and neither does Guillermo del Toro. His art proves that nothing is more realistic than fantasy. He paints the political reality of our world and times on the screen using the colors of our subconscious.

But he doesn't just reveal the demons. Guillermo also knows about the angels. And maybe it is that quality that makes all his work so unforgettable and profound—he looks at us with such tenderness although he knows about our dark side. Guillermo's haunting screen landscapes are deeply humane, and even his most nightmarish horrors know about love. That's something only a true magician can do—summon all the demons and, despite their growls and screams, still let us hear the angels' footsteps in the dark.

(ABOVE) For the unrealized *Mephisto's Bridge*, del Toro drew on the iconography of archangels to design the demon called Spanky [*see page 254*].

–Anno Domini: "In the year of our Lord" 2005 A.D.

–The Celts entered Hispania from the Northwest at almost the same moment they entered Great Britain, circa 500 B.C.

The LA TENE period. Sophisticated sculptures

4/10/05 Yesterday F. Trueba, Cristina and David Trueba had dinner with Lorenza and me: a couple of names were suggested: ZAY Nuba and Joaquín NOTARIO from S. of G. for E. L. d. F.

–This group was the most feared of all since their words confirmed the prophecies.

–VISIT the R. Dahl Museum in Buckinghamshire.

–Her last name was "STREGA," from the Italian for witch

–Patricia [?] and Gerardo [?] on Eve's list.

–DEVICE to flood and demolish the entire temple and make the army disappear.

–I've heard about you. You're one of us.

–The grandmother in The Witches was inspired by R.D.'s grandmother, whose name was Sophie.

–He loved the bull's tail soup.

–Galicia, the cave of the cathedrals, looks like a landscape in the north of U.K.

Ofelia's bed.

–Manolito at the cave's entrance.

–Try to use a little animal that falls in love with Liz Sherman and that H.B. despises

–H.B. to Manning: "It's time to pimp ma' ride."

–4/22/05 After the [drawing] we're having dinner with L.D.

–IN CONSILIIS NOSTRIS FATUM NOSTRUM EST.

–Sunshades for the mill. Bread in little bags, suitcases, soldiers with measurements they use for rationing. If anyone asks for more, bring him to me.

–Abe tells HB that there's a lot of annoying things about him

–The legacy of a gone era. Handed down through time.

NOTEBOOK 4, PAGE 16A

Iñigo
Carlos
Raul M.
Raul [?]

–In the Spanish village of Tronchon, there is a relic of a mutilated hand that once belonged to one of the Innocent Saints and that prevents the rain from falling.

–A king with only one eye and one leg whom we recognize when he appears, now much older.

(OPPOSITE) Del Toro wanted to embellish Ofelia's bed with carvings of owls, an idea developed further by Raúl Monge (ABOVE & RIGHT) and Carlos Jimenez (ABOVE RIGHT) and carried out in the film's production design.

MSZ: Let's talk about the images on this page [*opposite*]—the mask and the owl.

GDT: If you watch the movie closely, the owl is carved in the bed of Ofelia. And owls, in occult lore, they are birds that represent many, many things—among them awareness and awakening. I thought it would be really nice to have those in the bed, ironically. Her awakening comes at that moment.

And then I wanted to carve the face of the Faun everywhere we could. If you watch the movie again, that face is in the banister, and that face is in every doorframe in the whole movie, but it's very, very subtle.

● **GDT:** At the top of this page [*opposite*], it says, "In the labyrinth, gigantic gears grind someone to pieces." We abandoned that idea, with good reason. But we ended up using them in the mill to represent the captain being trapped in his father's watch. We made it more pertinent.

You can see the fallopian nature of the tree and the reference to the Alice dress for Ofelia, but with different colors. And a note for the eye of the Pale Man, which we ultimately didn't follow.

There's a note that says the Faun has a flute made of thigh bone, which he does. You don't see him use it, though.

The ruined tree and the *Alice in Wonderland*-like dress Ofelia (Ivana Baquero) wears were other strong images that originated in del Toro's notebook (OPPOSITE) and were developed by Raúl Monge (BELOW) before making it to the final film (ABOVE).

- Engranajes gigantes TRITURAN a alguien en el laberinto.
- "Please forgive me" le dice la princesa a Abe Sapien.
- Puede volver la piel dura a voluntad, como acero.
- Johann es un "gizmo guy" HB le odia por ser Alemán.
- Estos se consiguen en el mercado negro IIIrd century tooth fairies, illegal, very hungry and not very nice.
- Liz an HB go to Brooklyn, Abe & Kate go X.
- HB le arranca la cabeza a un ídolo de piedra
- Fauno con flauta hecha con un fémur.
- Abe rescata a la princesa de los sabuesos del príncipe y la ama mientras ella está convaleciente en coma

- La primera vez que Abe ve a la princesa es tan solo un avistamiento y no hay contacto alguno.
- Pelean por poseer la tercera pieza de la corona y los ayudan los duendecillos que son diletantes.
- El príncipe puede transformarse en animales.
- Obtienen la corona y pierden a la princesa. Abe mismo se roba la corona para rescatarla de su prisión. Manning quiere arrestarlo.
- teñir el vestido de Ofelia p/funeral.
- Ojo hombre Pálido: - Rojo
- Después de hallar una campa para construir nuestros principales decorados en Navarra el humilde viejecillo que nos la mostró, llama a su sobrino, un pijo de Donosti que nos pide un cuarto de millón (€250,000) por usar la campa 4 meses. Con esto nos retrasa 2 de 10 semanas de preparación.
- Silencio en la banda sonora y luego una nota o dos.

–In the labyrinth, gigantic gears grind someone to pieces.

–"Please forgive me," *the princess says to Abe Sapien.*

–He/she can make his/her skin as hard as steel whenever he/she wants.

–Johann is a "gizmo guy." HB hates him because he's German.

–You get these in the third-century black market. Tooth fairies, illegal, very hungry and not very nice.

–Liz and HB go to Brooklyn, Abe & Kate go X.

–HB pulls the head off a stone idol.

–Faun has a flute made from a thigh bone.

–Abe rescues the princess from the prince's bloodhounds and falls in love with her while she's in a coma

–The first time that Abe sees the princess it's nothing more than a look, there's no physical contact between them.

–They fight to obtain the third piece of the crown and the fairies, who are nothing more than dilettantes, help them.

–The prince can turn into different animals.

–They obtain the crown and lose the princess. Abe steals the crown by himself to free the princess from her prison. Manning wants to arrest him.

–Dye Ofelia's dress for the funeral.

–Pale Man's eye: Red

–After finding an empty lot where we could build our main sets in Navarra, the humble old man who told us about it calls his nephew, a rich jerk from Donosti, who charges us a quarter million (250,000) to use the lot for four months. This sets our preps back 2 out of 10 weeks

–Silence for the soundtrack. Then one or two notes.

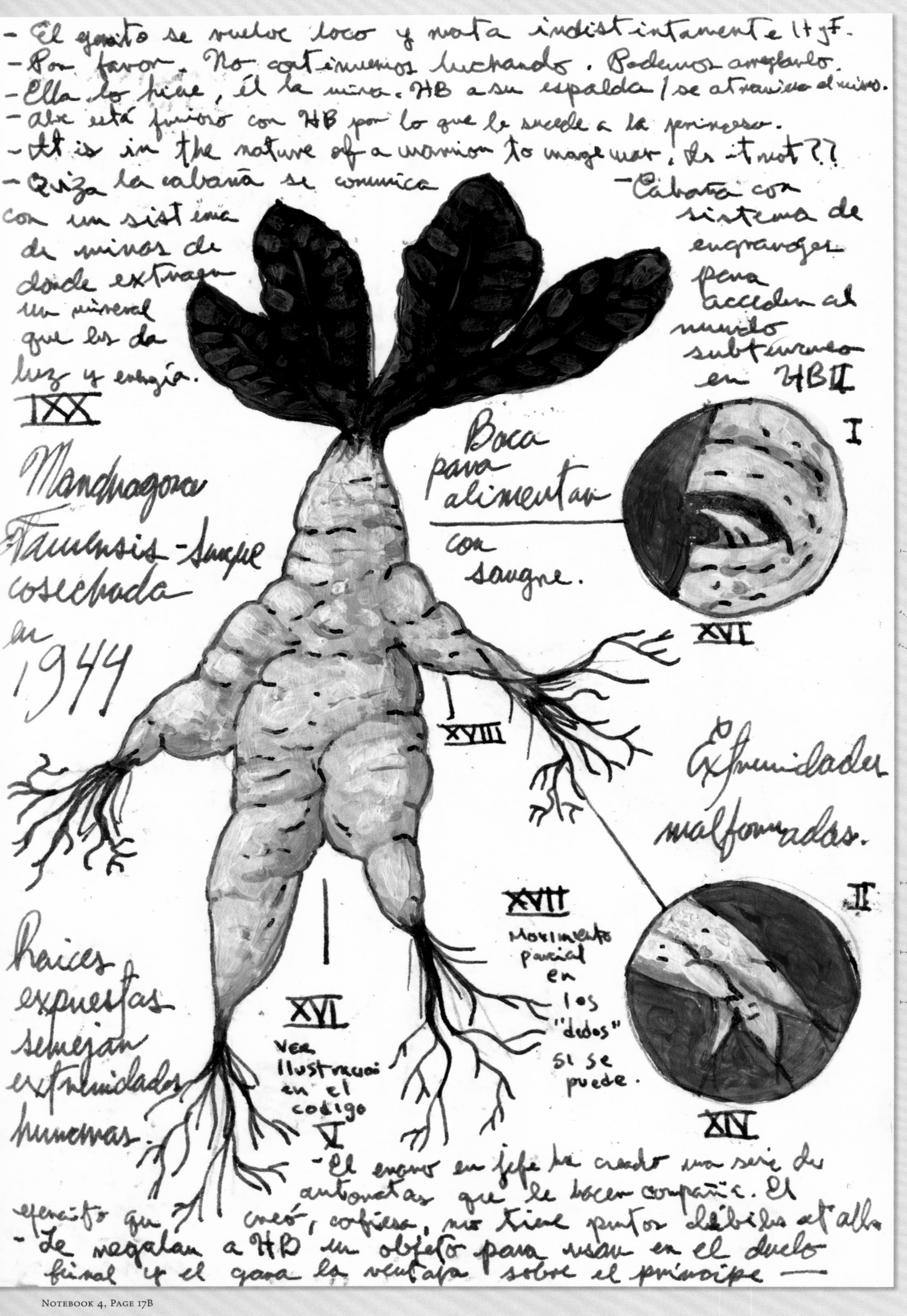

–The army goes crazy and indiscriminately kills [?].

–Please. Let's stop fighting. We can work it out.

–She has him. He looks at her. HB at his back/it goes right through him.

–Abe is furious with HB because of what happens to the princess.

–It is in the nature of a warrior to wage war. Is it not??

–The cabin could be connected to a system of mines in which a mineral that gives them light and energy is extracted.

–Hut with gear system that needs to be passed through to reach the underground world in HB II

IXX Mandrake root [?] harvested in 1944

Mouth for food

with blood.

Deformed limbs.

XVII
Partial movement in the "fingers" if possible.

Exposed roots resemble human limbs.

XVI See illustration in code V

–The dwarf in charge has created a series of automatons to keep him company. The army he created, he admits, has no Achilles heel at all.

–HB is given an object as a gift to use in the final duel. It gives him the advantage over the prince—

Notebook 4, Page 17B

MSZ: Tell me a little more about the image of the mandrake [*opposite*], which seems to bring together a couple of themes that run through your work—fetuses, artificial life.

GDT: The mandrake root is something that I've been obsessed with since I was a kid. I don't know where I read about it, or where I heard about it, but before I was seven years old, I was asking for a mandrake root for Christmas. There is a tape recording of me asking in a tiny child voice, "Can I get a mandrake for Christmas?" Because I wanted to turn it into a living being.

It's one of the legends: that you can nourish the mandrake into becoming a baby, like a living, small person, like a homunculus. I really obsessed about the mandrake. I obsessed about the fetal, baby-like quality of it. I thought it would be really disturbing for it to have a tongue.

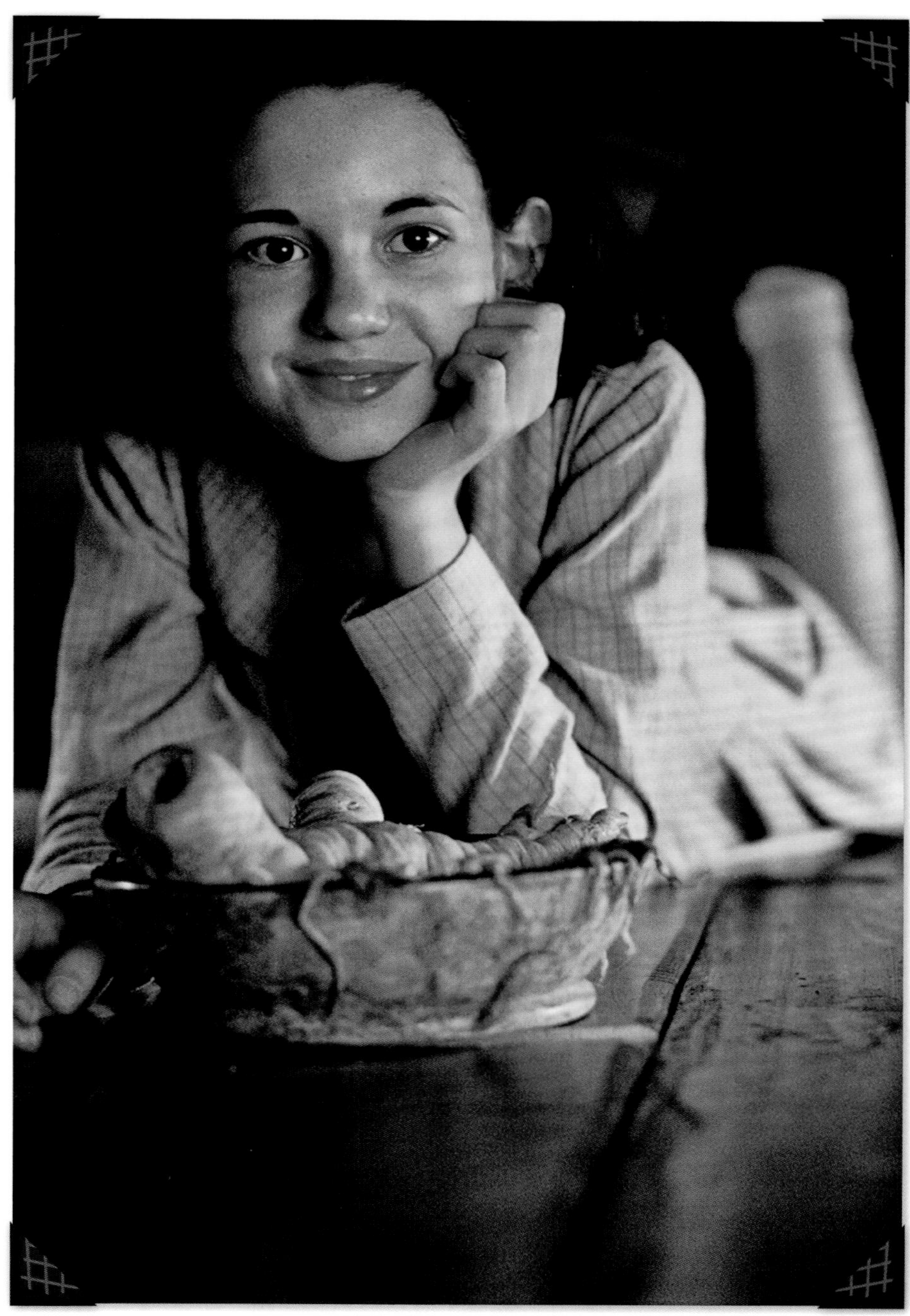

(OPPOSITE) From an early age, del Toro has been obsessed with mandrakes, a mythological creature he was finally able to bring to screen in *Pan's Labyrinth*. (ABOVE) Storyboards of Ofelia nurturing the mandrake by Raúl Monge. (RIGHT) Ivana Baquero (Ofelia) posing with the mandrake root prop in a publicity photo for the film.

Cuentan que hace mucho mucho tiempo en el mundo subterraneo donde no existe la mentira ni el dolor vivia una princesa que soñaba con el mundo de los humanos Soñaba con el cielo azul la brisa suave y el brillante sol Un dia burlando toda la vigilancia la princesa escapo Una vez en el exterior la luz del sol la cego y borro de su memoria cualquier indicio del pasado La princesa olvido quien era de donde venia Su cuerpo sufrio frio enfermedad y dolor Y al

(LEFT) A page from *The Book of Crossroads*, rendered in the style of a medieval manuscript and echoed by del Toro with an illuminated drop cap on a page in his notebook (OPPOSITE). This page also houses del Toro's first drawing of another important prop—Vidal's phonograph, which was developed by Raúl Villares in this concept of the captain's office (ABOVE).

MSZ: So this page [*opposite*] is from the beginning of the notebook that covers *Pan's Labyrinth* and *Hellboy II*. What was it like starting a new book?

GDT: I was starting a new notebook and I remember where I began. It was in a little hotel near the Gran Vía in Madrid. I remember exactly how full of hope and joy I was.

The movies would change rapidly through the notebooks. Some of the stuff survived—like the little phonograph at the bottom for the Fascist captain. But you see the elements that didn't, too. For example, this little "nerve ghost," which is what I call this little ghost with all the nerves exposed. They ate the fairies, which eventually the Pale Man does. I had this idea, which is on the next page [*page 194*], about a wooden puppet that lives in the roots of the tree, which holds a chestnut that contains the key. Eventually that became two separate tasks for Ofelia, and he became the Pale Man instead of the wooden doll. I just thought it was really creepy to have a wooden doll coming to life.

MSZ: Here you say to use the stick bug instead of the fairies to guide Ofelia to the labyrinth at the beginning, and you mention a blind man. Blindness seems to be an issue that you deal with in a lot of your work, even with the Pale Man, for instance, where you're obliterating the eyes.

GDT: The idea was there was a blind man who can traverse the labyrinth by knowing it, but not by sight. It was sort of a silly metaphor about real knowledge or faith, like faith being blind, and the girl believing in herself. At the beginning of *Pan's Labyrinth* there were a lot of good ideas, but not necessarily in a shape that I found "gainly." It was very ungainly.

MSZ: These places where you seem to be struggling to get things to cohere, and seeing which things to retain and which things should be jettisoned, are very interesting. You also mention them hanging the grandfather instead of the granddaughter. There seems to be a grandfather character in this, as well, hearkening back to *Cronos* and *Mimic*.

GDT: I decided that the blind man was the grandfather to the housekeeper, and then I decided I liked the housekeeper better with a brother than a grandfather. I thought she needed to be more active and less passive.

In "The Labyrinth" use the stick bug instead of the fairies at the beginning. Use it as a "guide" to lead the girl to the labyrinth. The blind man tells her the story while putting out bird traps.

–They hang the grandfather instead of the granddaughter

–Create a man made of wood instead of a toad.

–In L.M.L. use a voice-over, as if it were an instrument.

–In H.B.2., the burly agent is the troll brother.

–The grandfather was left blind from gunshot wounds, but what side was he on?? Vidal, what does he make of him?

– The doll with the nut licks up a drop a blood

–The trials are: (1) The nut, the one found in the hollow tree at the edge of the labyrinth. (2) There is a key inside the nut that unlocks the secret room in the Library. It opens the door where the dead children who eat fairies appear to her. (3) Using the tools she has gathered up, she "harvests" the mandrake root and hides it under her mother's bed. (4) Kill the little one.

–If I switch 2 and 3 around, I achieve a bit more visual variety and can make use of the little phials filled with sleeping medicine

–Look at this drawing. The contrast between the blue and the intense reds is a bit risky.

–What key could be more interesting than the insect (??) and how could it be found?

–Will the wooden doll have a nut (??) Will his voice (the doll's) be heard through a gramophone?? If so, make it a cylinder gramophone.

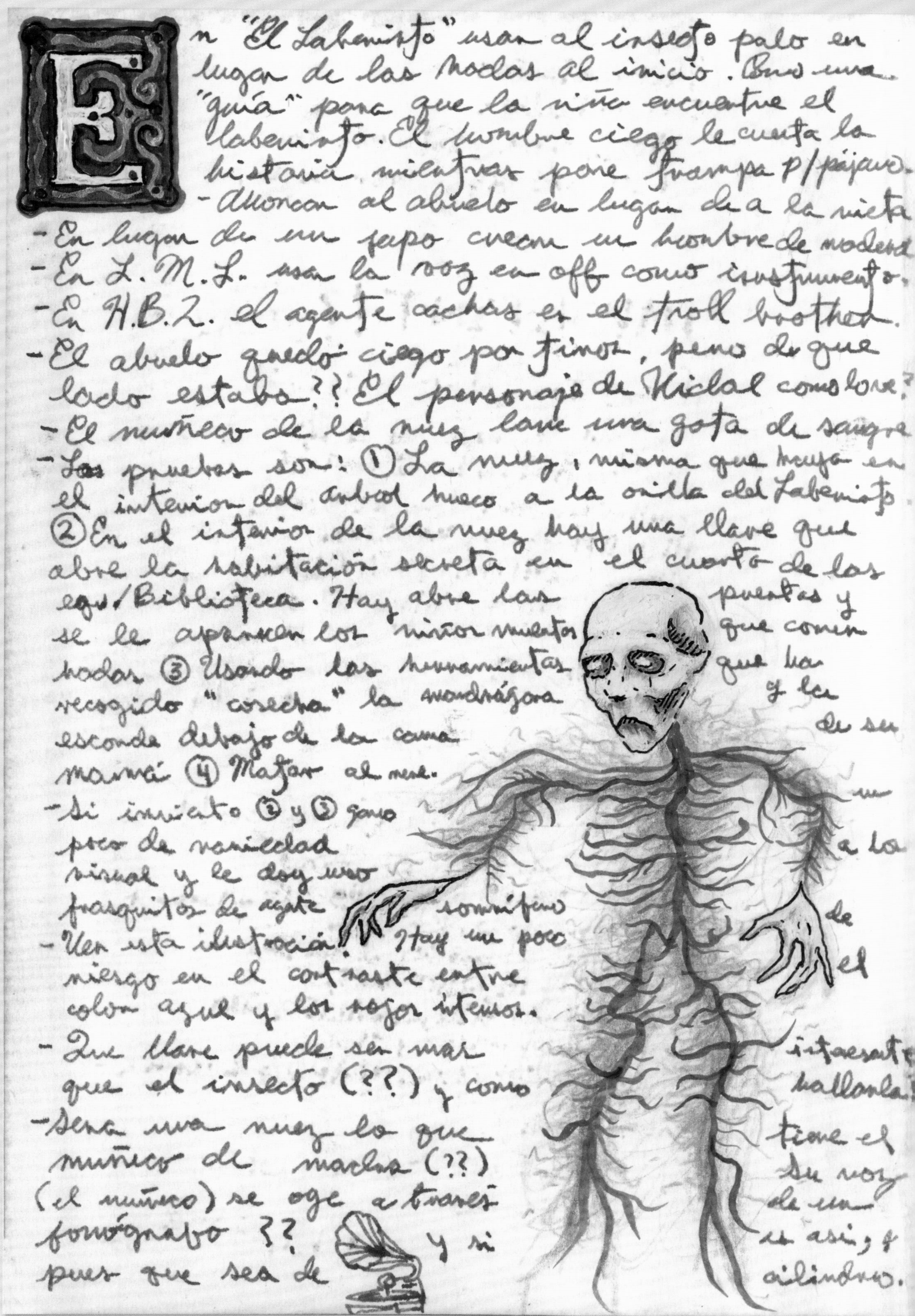

-Inicio libreta nueva. Conocí a Steven Spielberg y me dijo lo mucho que le gustaba "Hellboy" Alucinante.
-"La flexibilidad vence a la rigidez"
-Bulbos.
-Semillas.
Dentro de la castaña vienen 5 semillas que hay que sembrar justo debajo de las ramas del arbol viejo en luna llena.
El muñeco de madera con la llave secreta.
-8/9/04
Encontramos un piso al lado del Retiro en la calle J.J.
-El oro es parte muy pero muy vital de los cuentos de hadas Europeos. En el nuestro pondría oro y no comida en la mesa de la tentación. Que entendería el público más fácil de los dos (???)
-Revisar el regreso a Oz de Walter M. para sonidos

–Starting a new notebook. I met Steven Spielberg and he told me how much he liked "Hellboy." Unreal.

–Flexibility defeats rigidity

–Bulbs.

–Seeds.

Inside the chestnut are 5 seeds that need to be planted beneath the branches of the ancient tree when the moon is full. Gifts to [?] The wooden doll with the secret key.

–Gold plays an extremely vital role in European fairy tales. In our tale, I would put gold and not food on the table of temptations. Which of the two would the public understand more easily? (??)

–8/9/04

We found a flat near El Retiro on J.J. street

–Watch Walter Murch's Return to Oz again for its sound effects

MSZ: You have a note here [*opposite*] about gold playing an extremely vital role in European fairy tales, and you were playing with the notion of putting gold instead of food on the table as a temptation, which of course was an idea you abandoned.

GDT: Yeah, I abandoned it and, unfortunately for me, I cut a phrase in the editing room. That is the only phrase I regret cutting in *Pan's* where you are reminded that the girl, no matter how strong her convictions, has not eaten in more than a day because she was sent to bed without supper. Then her mother bleeds, she's horrified, she doesn't eat. The line I cut was where the maid tells her, "You haven't eaten all day."

But the way I brought together the two ideas of the food and the gold was to make everything in the banquet red. I thought, "If gold has a uniformity of color, then it would be great to give that uniformity to the food by making everything red—the gelatin, the grapes."

MSZ: Stylistically, in previous notebooks, it looks as if you were dealing with calligraphic elements, with typography. Here it looks more as if you're throwing stuff down. There's not as much of the tricks and musings. There's more of a sense of, not haste, but of definitely getting on with business.

GDT: Yeah, yeah. I think that more and more the books became more and more practical. So there was less of a sense of design. Curiously, I like these pages more than the old ones, because they're complete—they're not looking for anything. They're just me looking through myself, in a way.

(OPPOSITE) The Pale Man was originally associated with both the tree (where the frog dwells in the final film) and the color gold, representing temptation. Red food replaced gold, and the Pale Man (Doug Jones) was given a more disturbing lair for Ofelia (Ivana Baquero) to visit (ABOVE).

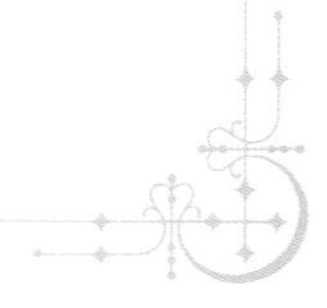

The comics, like the pulps before them, didn't speak for the social elite. Their point of view was that of the man in the street. Perhaps for that reason, their hatred of Nazis or "foreign enemies" foreshadows the U.S.'s posture toward WWII. The 30's and 40's see an explosion of heroes of all sorts: The Spider, The Shadow, Doc Savage, Captain America, Superman, The Avengers, etc. etc. Hellboy is a child of the pulps, Kirby and Sgt. Rock (1959, Kanigher).

–Charles Fort (1874–1932, New York) Blind, like J. L. Borges.

–From the moment we're born, we begin a long journey toward death. It's called life, and you catch on in the end.

–Go from the last piece of the crown to the auction.

–A piece of the sword breaks off inside H.B. It "moves" if they touch it and will kill him when the "bad guy" returns at the end

–One eye, One arm!!

–There's no hope left. There never was any. I know.

–Relic/Auction

–I pity the fool.

–It's like walking in on yourself.

6 wings for the fairies.

–Hellboy fights with "Iron Shoes" at some point in the film.

–The point of the spear reveals Hellboy's location

–Tim Curry for the role of one of the U.M. professors.

–Hellboy finds the Golem in Prague and Johan reanimates it with his ectoplasm.

Notebook 4, Page 11A

GDT: Here [*opposite*] we have a possibility for the Pale Man.

MSZ: This one still had eyes in its head.

GDT: The idea was that the eyes were in like a liquid space. Like, the flesh was moving, so the eyes would gently float in the sea of flesh, and they would never be at the same height.

MSZ: They're reminiscent of some of the portraits by symbolist painters.

GDT: Proto-symbolist, actually. It's older, but it's a very strong influence on that. Eyes are very important in fairy tales, and there's a great story called "One-Eye, Two-Eyes, Three-Eyes," about three sisters. One of them is born with one eye, one is born with two eyes, and one is born with three eyes. And they think that the one with the two eyes is the freak, the ugly-looking one. When you go back to Greek mythology, too, there are so many images of eyes being absent or singular—the cyclops, the gorgons, for example.

Here I wrote about comics for some reason. "The comics, like the pulps before them, didn't speak for the social elite. Their point of view was that of the man in the street. Perhaps for that reason, their hatred of Nazis or 'foreign enemies' foreshadows the U.S.'s posture toward World War II." These are notes about *Hellboy II*, or just notes to myself. I remember clearly that Marvel and the pulps and the comics were using Nazis as villains before it was a popular posture.

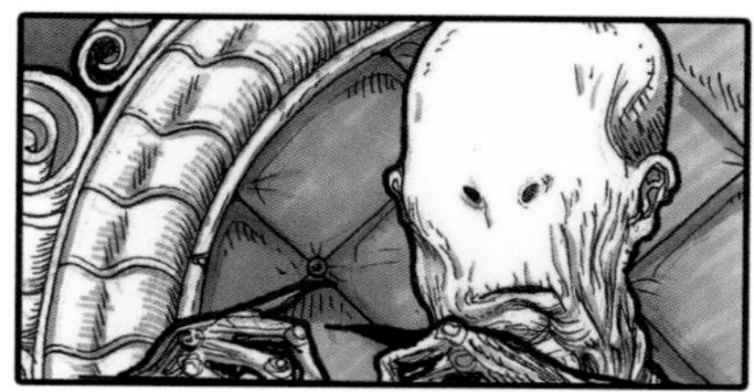
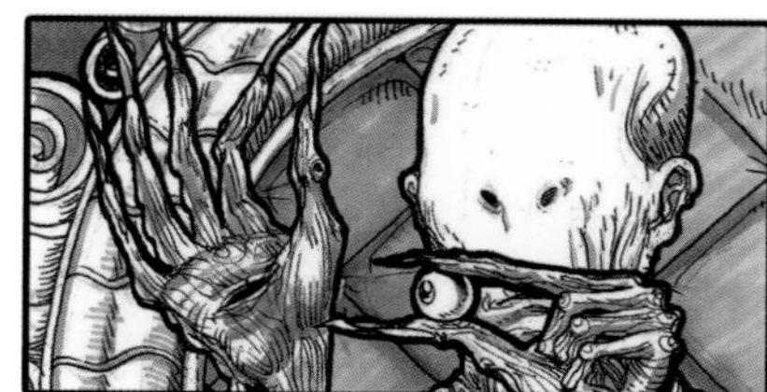
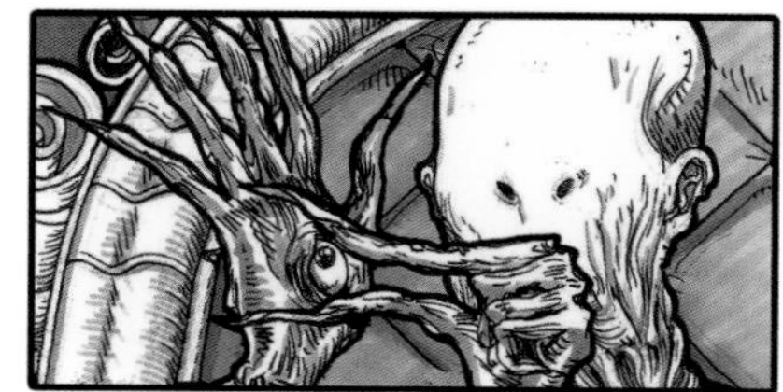
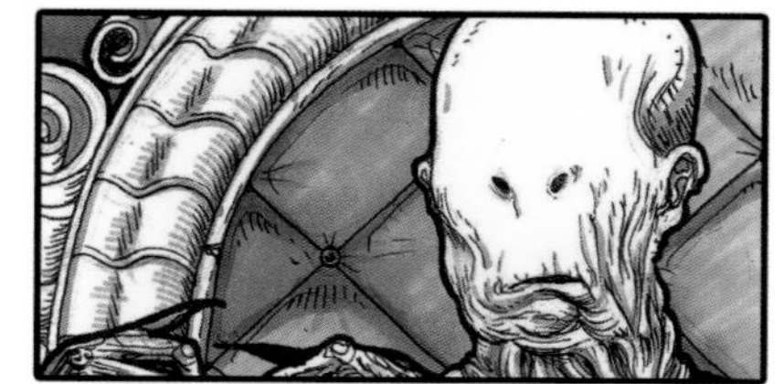

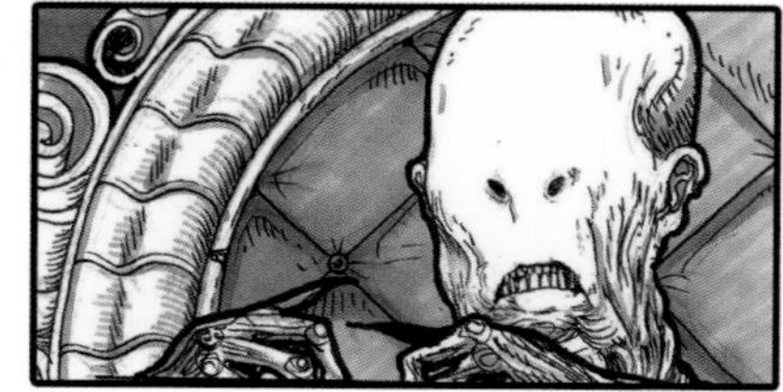
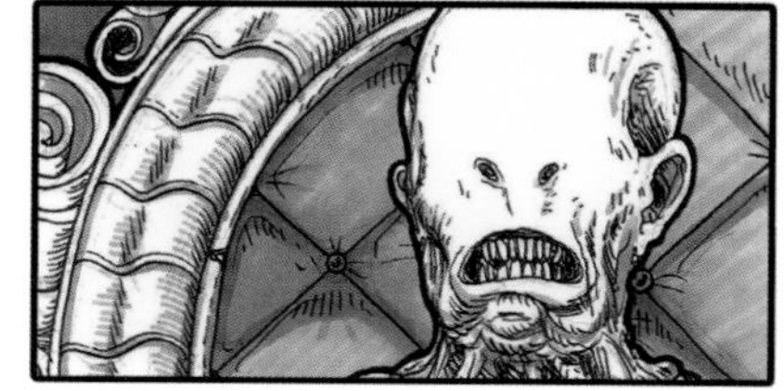

(OPPOSITE) An early drawing in del Toro's notebook depicted the Pale Man with eyes in his head. Displacing them to the creature's hands created a much more disturbing being, seen in these storyboards by Raúl Monge (RIGHT) and the final performance by Doug Jones (ABOVE).

–Blue dolphin to Big Red, Yes, Abe? Not Abe, Blue Dolphin, abide by the security code, Brother Red. Procedure comes first.

–These days, whenever people talk about a "good screenplay," they're thinking about plot. They assume that the actors are the ones who create the characters, who improve the action and dialogue.

–Does the prince have a double agent?

–When he's going to scold Hellboy, he asks everyone to step out of the room.

–<u>And</u> you stole a six-pack!!

–6/1/05 Today I'm getting the email from AA offering me XB, along with HPB and MIB and C of N, decisions that will follow me for the rest of my life.

5/30/05 Based on DDT sculpture.

Read: Connor McPherson.

–I'll create a sword for you.

–SMOKE for light columns.

On the plate: eyes that fit in his palm.

Ofelia puts her hands on her head and walks BACKWARD, talking with Mercedes.

2007/41 It's my year: <u>Guillermo del Toro</u>.

–Broken mirror. Created by a tiny demon. When it was shattered, it launched shards into the air that got lodged in the eyes and hearts of human beings

–Why does the BPRD airplane crash? Because dozens of harpies attack it

–Double Load bullets. DRILL

–An enormous library at BPRD to which only Abe has access

–The book contains every possible destiny, every possible future, which your decisions could create. It was made just for you, written in your father's blood, and will reveal its secrets to your eyes alone. Infinite and limited

–Your role in this story will be determined tonight.

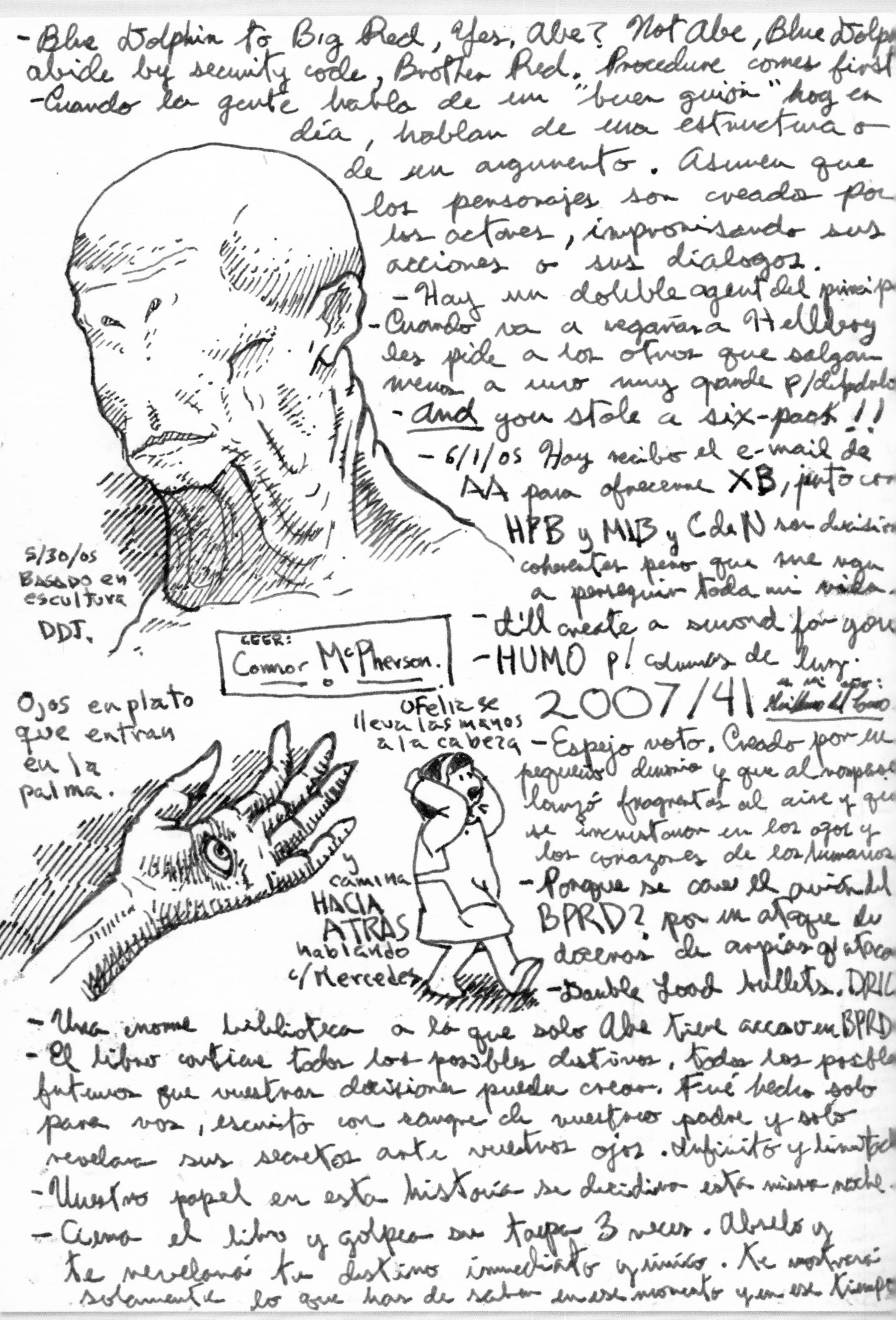

Notebook 4, Page 17A

–He closes the book and taps on the cover 3 times. Open it and your fate, and yours alone, will be revealed to you. It will show you only what you need to know at that particular moment, that time.

(ABOVE) Concepts by Raúl Monge show that, up until very close to production, the Pale Man was more of an elderly figure with eyes in a humanoid face. The final concept (LEFT) first came to del Toro while working in the notebooks (OPPOSITE) and occasioned a change of course with DDT while it was in the middle of sculpting the creature according to an approved concept that included more of a human visage.

GDT: This [*opposite*] is a very important page for me. This is where the movie starts to take more shape. On the left, there is a drawing of the Pale Man, and what I did is, originally that figure had a human face, and it was sculpted by DDT. This was my drawing of that sculpture with the face removed. I did a rougher drawing of this and I mailed it, faxed it, to DDT.

It's one of the two times we've had a disagreement, because they had worked so hard doing that sculpture. It was an old man sculpture. And they loved it, and they said to me, "Oh, this is really ruthless. We were doing this." I said, "Listen, trust me, it's going to be worth it."

The reason I insisted on changing it was because I was having dinner with my wife, and I had seen the sculpture, and it was great. It was a great sculpture of an old man. I had a picture with me, which was more or less the picture as it is in the drawing here but with a face. I was looking at the picture and I was telling my wife, "I have two options. One of them is you have this old man with stumps for a hand, and then in front of him there's a plate with two wooden hands that he puts on and they move. Or, I take off the face and I put two eyes on the plate, and he puts the eyes on the face." And she said, "I like the plate with the eyes better." Then I thought, why don't we do the stigmata, since he's supposed to be the church. And it just all fit together.

MSZ: Removing the eyes of the Pale Man and doing exactly what you did, it took guts. There's the challenge of coming up with something new, something fresh that will resonate with an audience, but also the challenge of sticking to your guns.

GDT: I was very sensitive about telling the guys at DDT because I was a sculptor, and I know what it takes, and I know they'd done a fantastic job, and there's no way of rejecting it and not sounding glib. "Take it off," you know? It's like, "Let them eat cake." But it was necessary. Sometimes, as a director, you have to be an asshole. Even if you're trying not to be, you're going to come out as one in the short term. But if the movie is worth it, it's worth that.

MSZ: And then there is this drawing [*page 198*] and note about Ofelia talking and walking backward. Where does that come from?

GDT: It's just something I saw my daughter do. I didn't do it in the movie. Then it goes, "Today, I'm getting the email from AA offering me XB." I got an email, yes, I got an email from Avi Arad at Marvel, and he was offering me some big, big, big movies. I was very broke at that moment because the money for *Pan's Labyrinth* hadn't materialized. They were offering me *X-Men 3*, and they were offering me *Fantastic Four*, I think. He offered me *Thor*. Anyway, it was a moment where money-wise, I was tight, and I thought, "Should I leave *Pan's* to do that, and then come back?" And I chose to stay. So, again, this is an important page for me.

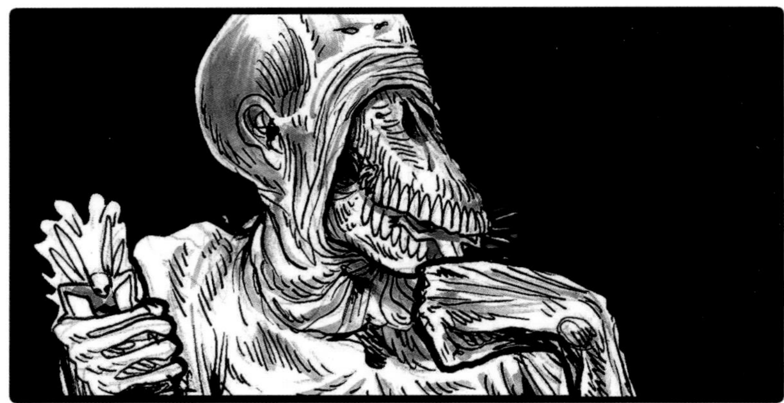

(RIGHT) The storyboard panels by Raúl Monge show how the design for the Pale Man returned to a much older concept that had been haunting del Toro for years—a figure he calls the "Shadow Man" (OPPOSITE).

● **GDT:** Funny enough, here [*opposite*] is an early version of the Pale Man, in a way. This time without the eyes. At the time, I was calling him the Shadow Man, which was a soul eater. But if you look at his teeth, they are larger, but they are exactly the same shape of the teeth of the Pale Man, which are very thin and blunt.

66

S.M. **** Montaje de humo en disolvencias que crearan la apariencia de Espíritus

*S.M.**** Montage with smoke in dissolves which create Spirit images*

S.M. **** Shadow-man, el que se come las almas.

M/M 6 * Is he dead? pregunta alguien BAM! BAM! BAM! Now, he is...

S.M. **** El duelo entre Q y Carl empieza de manera física y se vuelve mental, Q lo atosiga y se le encima en el pecho a madrearlo hasta que Carl estalla.

S.M. **** Q es así por algo en su niñez (Flash back)

* La sesión c/Dorian es telemetrica

S.M. **** Derrame en los ojos cuando Q o Carl usan sus poderes al máximo.

* Los antepasados de Ernie eran unos chingones, héroes de guerra.

S.M.**** Shadow-man, *the one who eats souls.*

*M/M G** Is he dead? *someone asks*

BAM! BAM! BAM! Now, he is . . .

*S.M. **** The duel between Q and Carl begins in a physical way and then it becomes mental. Q poisons him, climbing onto his chest and fucking him up until Carl bursts.*

*S.M.**** Q is the way he is because of something that happened to him during his childhood* (Flash back)

** Dorian's session is telemetric*

*S.M.**** Hemorrhage in their eyes when Q or Carl use their powers to the maximum.*

** Ernie's ancestors were big shots, war heroes.*

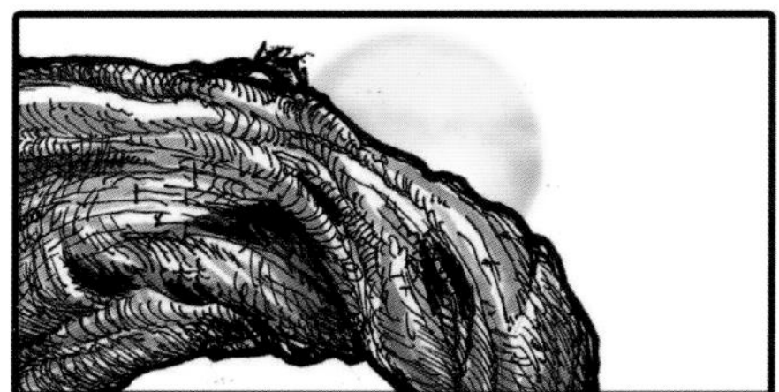

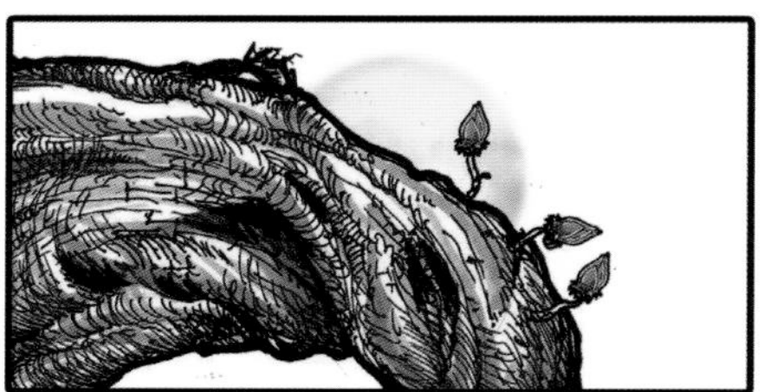

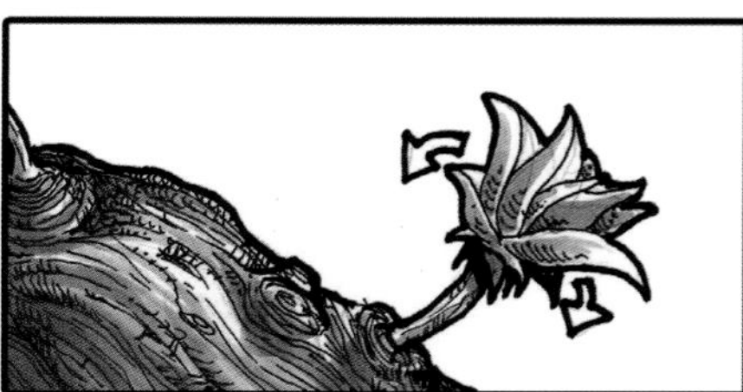

GDT: Here [*opposite*] it says, "My life is halfway over. Forty years and I barely have a thing of my own to leave behind. I made captain, imagine that. But my name, the only thing I have left to pass on is my name." This was part of the speech the captain gives in *Pan's*, musing about age.

On *Pan's Labyrinth*, frankly, I was thinking about these things. I don't write the bad guys in my movies without knowing what they feel, and I understand the captain. I don't like him—I wouldn't want to hang out with him—but I understand him.

I thought it would be interesting if posterity will remember the girl through little details, but no one will remember the captain because he's so obsessed with being remembered.

In that sense, I was also writing for Ofelia. I always go back to this quote by Kierkegaard that says, "The reign of the martyr starts with his death. The reign of the tyrant ends with it." And I thought that was the clash at the center of the movie: a guy that is obsessed with his name being remembered, and a girl that doesn't care. But she makes the right choices.

(ABOVE) Del Toro, here on set with Sergi López (Vidal) and Maribel Verdú (Carmen), was able to understand Vidal, having created him. (LEFT) While Vidal is obsessed with being remembered, the film and these storyboards by Raúl Monge underscore that Ofelia is the one who makes the difference that matters to the world.

- Con balas no, que cuestan mucho. Vamos a dejar una señal muy clara de lo que vamos a hacer aquí.
- El padre fuma puros mientras escucha el radio.
- Ya estoy a mitad de mi vida. 40 años y muy poco tengo para dejar detrás mío. Llegue a capitán aquí fíjate. Pero mi nombre, solo me queda el nombre para darlo.

Charlan mientras prepara el conejo para la cena. Ella le dice que eran familia 5 de 3 hermanas 2 hermanos padres y ... Su hermano murió en el frente (PAUSA) Y el otro? también — Nota el titubeo.

- Hay 3 puertas en la biblio.
- Dejar los platos sucios el viernes y los encuentras el lunes con toda la mierda pegada. Para eso estoy aquí.
- MARIA BOTTO. MARIA.
- Te vi en la ventana. Que piensas de mi? El señor no necesita saber lo que yo opino. Al señor no le interesa lo que yo piense. Ese hombre no era culpable. Pero yo no estoy aquí para hacer justicia. Estoy aquí para traer la paz. Y a la paz le da lo mismo un muerto que otro. La mejor ofrenda para la paz es la que está colgando de ese arbol. Todo mundo la entiende. tarde o temprano voy a colgar a alguien que los

–Not with bullets, which cost too much. We're going to make a very clear statement about what we're doing here.

–The father smokes cigars while listening to the radio.

–My life is halfway over. Forty years and I barely have a thing of my own to leave behind. I made captain, imagine that. But my name, the only thing I have left to pass on is my name.

–They talk while she cooks rabbit for dinner. She tells him that she comes from a family of 5. 2 brothers, 3 sisters, and her parents. Her brother died at the front (PAUSE). And the other brother? Him, too. He hears the hesitation in her voice.

–There are 3 doors in the library.

–You leave the dirty plates in the sink on Friday and find all the crap stuck to them on Monday. That's what I'm here for.

–MARIA BOTTO. MARIA.

–I saw you in the window. What do you think of me? Sir, you don't need to know what I think. You aren't interested in what I think, I'm sure. That man wasn't guilty. But I'm not here to dispense justice. I'm here to bring peace. When it comes to peace, one dead man is as good as any other. The best offering for peace is what's hanging from that tree. everyone understands that. sooner or later I'm going to hang someone that they're

As the idea for the Faun evolved into a more delicate creature (OPPOSITE), del Toro recruited Doug Jones for the part, here seen performing with Ivana Baquero (Ofelia) (ABOVE).

● **GDT:** This [*opposite*] is the restaurant bill for an Indian lunch with Joe Hill and Stephen King on the day I showed them *Pan's Labyrinth*. It was one of those cheap thermal papers, so it faded, but I glued it on my notebook with the little note that Stephen King did, "We had a blast!! Steve King," and a smiley. Because I think he is my favorite living writer. I think he is one of my favorite writers of all time. And that day I still didn't know if he was going to like it or not, but I had just shown my movie to Stephen King, you know? So I drew the Faun on the empty paper of the faded receipt. And then beneath is a sketch for Abe Sapien's new glasses.

MSZ: This also speaks to the design evolution of the Faun. Earlier, it was almost like a *Hellboy* kind of thing—muscular with big horns.

GDT: Definitely. And it evolved a lot even after this. DDT made an exquisite creation. I was making it bigger to hide the mechanics, and they said, "We think we can really sculpt it so that it can be the actor's mouth. We can do that delicate a sculpture." And I must say, without them, the Faun would not be what it is. They are masters of their art. I knew Doug Jones was the only guy to play the Faun, because his sensibility in playing Abe Sapien is amazing.

—Screenings P.L. WB, FD, M.P. & S.S. they need to clean it!!

Feeling a little afraid is normal when facing something new, in a place or in a way you've never experienced before. But to learn something it's necessary to surpass that fear completely.

—Luke Goss for the role of the prince, but will need to work his eyes, forehead

—We need Johann for something that is not the final gag?? And I know that it would be Abe who would appear before the B.P.R.D. and is loved by everyone and makes Hellboy jealous? If it was so, then Johann could be introduced in the Eurospec portion of the movie.

—I have an irrational fear. A superstition. I fear that a terrorist act will take the world one more time. As was the case on 9/11 during Backbone.

—Bring me BIG BABY, but Manning said—he said, to be discreet!! HB: And the silver please—and B.B. (watch out!) it's enormous.

—Sometimes (Abe says) with feeling an extraordinary desire to cry.

—I know—yes??!!— Yes!! Oh God!! Oh God!! Silence—give me another beer.

—Perhaps in the place of Goggles. Abe with new Goggles. Abe uses CONTACTS or glasses.

–It's impossible to find the beautiful without first exploring everything that is terrible. 2/14/05 Madrid.

–They CHANGE the princess into a

–The nano-robots *are called* CELLBOTS.

–I GUESS I'M OUT.

–He's just about to step outside when they insult him. He closes the door quietly and turns around with a smile on his face. The camera makes a push . . .

–We are—you see?—the fallen. HB II

–The point of the sword moves toward his heart

–For how long? Until you can stand on your own two feet.

–I know what I am but I didn't know the name others have for it. What to call it.

–You can go up and see her. She's resting right now.

–A biography's lucidity is the result of the man, the journey he takes in his final days as he unknowingly approaches his own death.

– Thin. in front.

–Or the proportions could be even more extreme:

–The prince slices off Johann's hand/arm. Protoplasm escapes out.

–IRON SHOES.

–Wheelchair Ghost.

–HB imitates static while talking with Myers over the radio.

Well.

–Keep the mushrooms for the Toad's lair (fig tree).

–The real world is made of straight lines, and the world of fantasy is curved. Reality is cold. Fantasy is warm.

–The fantasy world should feel UTERINE, INTERIOR, *like the subconscious—of the girl/photo.*

Notebook 4, Page 14A

GDT: Here [*opposite*] it says, "It's impossible to find the beautiful without first exploring everything that is terrible." I think this is true. I mean, this is probably a conclusion I reached there. But it's true.

"The real world is made of straight lines, and the world of fantasy is curved. Reality is cold. Fantasy is warm." These are *Pan's Labyrinth* ideas for the initiation pit in Portugal.

The pit is still pretty much the same in the movie—the composition is almost the same; the labyrinth corridor in front of a pit. There are these pits in Portugal that have great alchemical and occultist symbolism, and we reproduced that shadow in the pit where the Faun lives. These are little things—details that are important for me or for my designers.

MSZ: And what are all these little doodles? One of the figures looks like Abe Sapien smoking a cigarette. And the pig?

GDT: Some of those are for *Hellboy II*—ideas that were abandoned. The guy with the cigarette is the captain, lifting weights in his undershirt with dark glasses. And the pig? They make those pigs in Mexico. They come with a little tape that you put a fly on. You put it inside, and as the fly dies, it animates the pig.

To design the labyrinth in the film, del Toro's drawing (OPPOSITE) and Raúl Monge's illustration (BELOW) made reference to prehistoric monuments in Portugal.

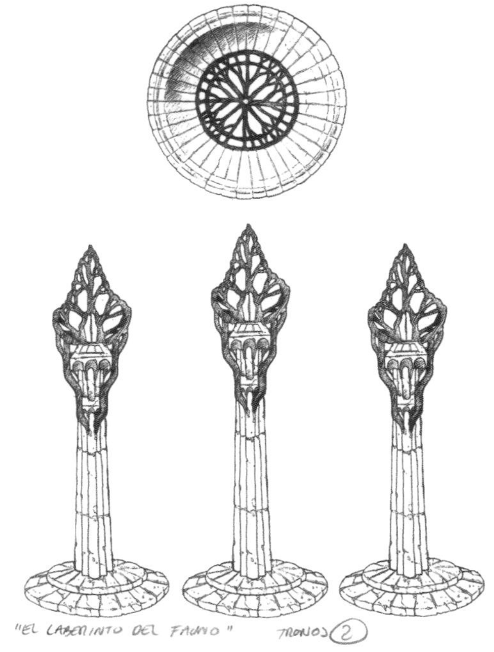

MSZ: This [*opposite*] is the underground city Ofelia goes to at the end of *Pan's Labyrinth*. I have a question about that, because at the last moment, when she returns, it seems so cold and so austere. Was that your thinking?

GDT: When she comes back, I wanted her not to embrace anyone because then it would become very sappy. So I put her father and her mother in these super-high thrones, because if we made her embrace them and then you cut to her dying, it is melodramatic in the wrong way. There is melodrama that is a little more austere, and melodrama that is a lot more syrupy, and I thought if we had them all dancing around her and embracing her, and then you cut and she's dying, it's really cheap. But if you hear them applaud, and she's there but she's alone, still alone, it's an easier transition to her dying. So I made them sort of very high and mighty, literally.

For *Pan's Labyrinth*, del Toro envisioned an underground city (OPPOSITE) where Ofelia (Ivana Baquero) would meet her parents in a throne room and be declared Princess Moanna (ABOVE). Raúl Monge's sketches (TOP LEFT & TOP RIGHT) and storyboards (RIGHT) of the high thrones that kept Ofelia at a distance from her parents, helping to avoid an overly melodramatic ending.

Walk with him for the reaction shot

—Open with the TITLE PAGE/CLOSE.

—The exterior world is blue/Hades: Gold

—The sky was truly blue in those days and the grass was greener—And now—Now look at what it has all become. What the world is today.

—USE THE MIRROR—to escape/Ofelia needs to react in front of the mirrors—

—Cages with hens in them—

—SUNlight/Ed/CGI.

—The Mouros live in underground cities. They're beings related to the giants. In Galicia, it is believed that the mountains are hollow and contain underground palaces. Kingdoms.

—The girl is <u>THIRSTY</u>.

—We had dinner with Belen, Paolo Basili, Manuel Villanueva, and Alvaro at Viridiana Tuesday/2/05

—Commemorates the 600th anniversary of the TREUCE

—The prince is irritated by what people say to him at the auction and he gets very angry

—They will eat the souls of all of you, infidels.

—Manning walks through the hall with Abe Sapien/explo.

—The prince gets his arm cut off in the story. Perhaps the BPRD keeps the arm in its museum of FREAKS. "No wonder he is pissed off." HB.

—There goes a pissed off fish, *HB says to Abe.*

—The film begins at Christmas with PC in the snow. The demons have lost HB.

F Porto 3/5/05 Use the sketch of Gaudí's "Sagrada Familia" cathedral as a model.

–In the face.

Pillars for the duel. Travels in order:

(1)Lilliput, (2)Brobdingnag

(3) Laputa, Balnibarbi, Glubbdubdrib, Luggnagg, and Japan.

(4) Houyhnhnms.

–The key to the crown. Change the beginning and make it a flashback to the scene with the stack of pancakes. Return and find the book again in the library/storeroom of BPRD.

–Abe and the princess use the "magic" escape route to reach the other side of the planet. The BPRD uses the $ media buys.

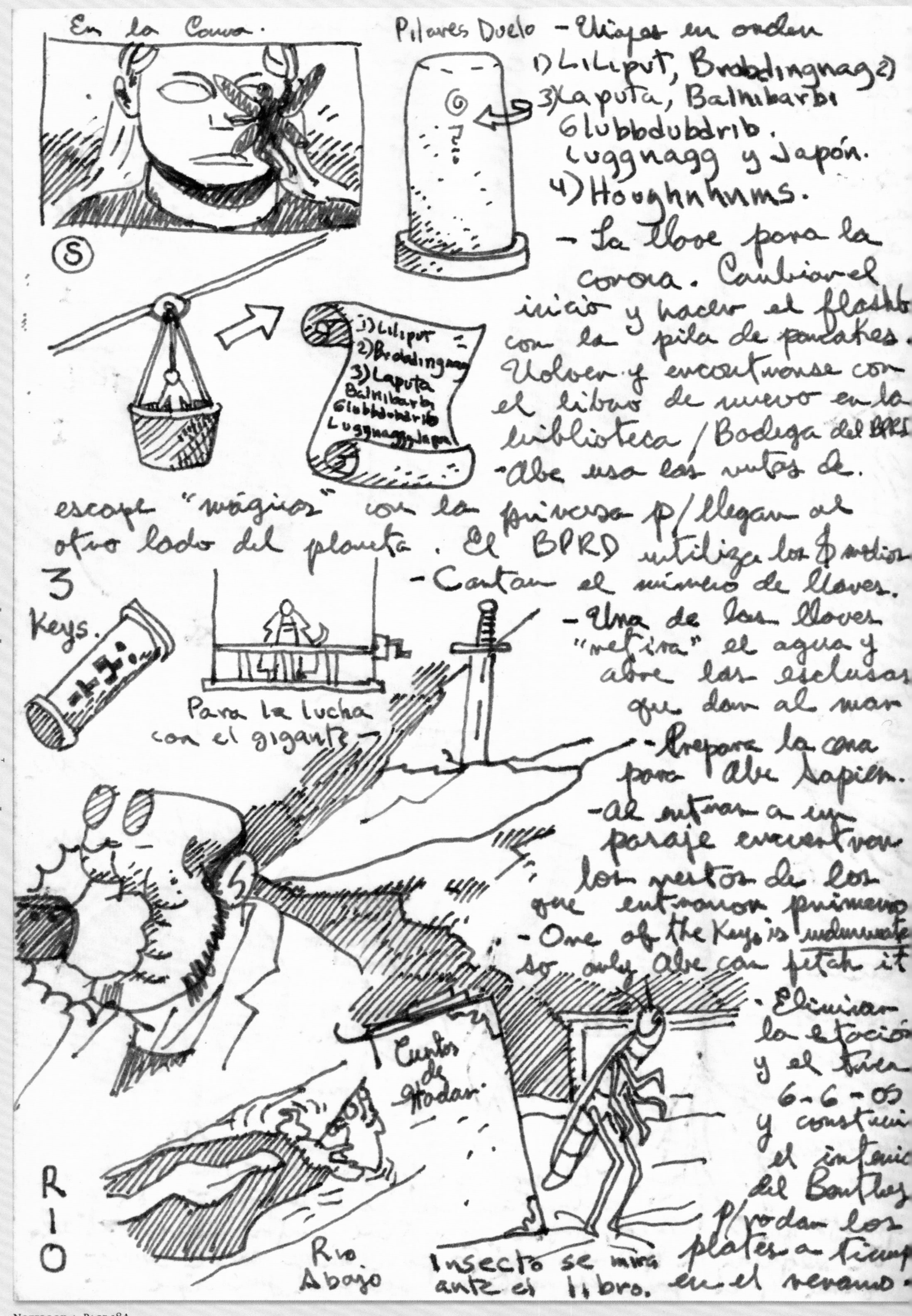

3 keys

–Count the number of keys.

–One of the keys makes the water level drop and opens the locks to the ocean.

For the battle with the giant.

–He/she cooks dinner for Abe Sapien.

–Upon entering a certain place, they find the remains of others who entered first.

–One of the keys is <u>underwater</u>, so only Abe can fetch it.

–Eliminate the station and trains 6-6-05 and build the interior of the Bentley to fill the plates in time for summer.

RIVER

Notebook 4, Page 18A

Downriver. Fairy tales. Insect looks at itself in front of the book.

GDT: This frame here [*opposite, top*] is the moment in *Pan's Labyrinth* where Ofelia shows the insect the illustration in the fairy tale book and it becomes a fairy. The act of magic I believe in is if you tell the world what you want out of it, the world conforms. Not if I hold a picture of a Porsche against my forehead, a Porsche's going to come to me. Nothing as base as that. But the world is like a torrent of impressions, I think. Spiritual, physical, all of them. And we're like a sieve. If you adjust the size of your sieve, and you declare something, you declare the size of the sieve, you start seeing reality, and interacting with reality, in a different way. I love the idea that this girl tells the bug, "Are you a fairy?" And the bug transforms for her. It's a moment in which magic occurs, and it becomes objective.

Pan's, for me, responds to an original principle: that, at the end of the day, in the geological time scale, we are all insignificant. In other words, at one time or another, long after we are gone, the worst-worn pocketbook is going to mean the same as the entire oeuvre of Dickens or Shakespeare. In geological time, in five million years, we will be a stratum in the geological plate that is going to be found by no one, perhaps. All we can do is change the world in small ways. No work of art is so big that it's going to change the world, to make a difference, geologically. That's why the Faun says Ofelia changed the world in very, very, very small ways. Like, there are people that will remember her, and there's one little flower blooming in the fig tree because of her, because she killed the frog. It's a tiny, tiny change, but it says she left traces of her time in the world for those who know where to look. I think that's all of us.

The artist only changes the world in tiny ways. To think, "Oh, my work is so important," is misguided. Really? In what perspective? Seriously. I mean, who remembers the great poet Triceratops?

(TOP) While reading *The Book of Crossroads*, Ofelia (Ivana Baquero) inspires the insect to become a fairy. Del Toro's notebook (OPPOSITE, TOP), Raúl Monge's storyboards (LEFT), and the film itself persistently refuse to declare whether this transformation is real or imagined.

Christian Bailly
independientes.
One for Mankind
Two for the
Sons of the Earth

HELLBOY II: THE GOLDEN ARMY

"I HAVE CERTAIN PROCLIVITIES," Guillermo del Toro commented while being interviewed on the show *Hollywood Shootout*, just after completing *Hellboy II: The Golden Army* (2008). "I have some fetishes for certain objects and certain things, and I like to explore them again and again."

Hot on the heels of the critical and financial success of *Pan's Labyrinth*, Guillermo dove into his sequel to *Hellboy*. In truth, the film might have been called *Guillermo del Toro's Greatest Hits*, as Guillermo reexamined and revisited virtually every one of his major character, story, design, and thematic elements, from *Cronos* on. Audiences and critics responded with widespread (if not universal) enthusiasm. *Hellboy II* is an undeniably delightful ride, a wild rush of moments and details burnished to a high sheen by a writer-director drawing on everything he loves and delivering it to his audience with creative relish.

Guillermo says, "I think that *Hellboy II* is a sister movie to *Pan's Labyrinth* in many, many ways, texturally, spiritually." This occurred as much out of practical necessity as artistic choice, for Guillermo was working on both projects simultaneously. On both, he says, it was "me jamming ideas. Mind you, I'm writing *Hellboy II* as I'm writing *Pan's Labyrinth*. As always, I was multitasking: (a) in order to meet deadlines and (b) because *Pan's Labyrinth* had no deadline. I was not making a living on *Pan's Labyrinth*, so *Hellboy II* was sort of sustaining me through *Pan's Labyrinth*. The way you're paid on a script is commencement, delivery of first draft, revisions, and production money. So I essentially lived on the commencement money for a year and a half or more, and I needed to deliver in order to pay quickly mounting debts."

Immediately upon finishing *Pan's Labyrinth*, Guillermo leapt into preproduction on *Hellboy II*. Although he and his family were living in a suburb of Los Angeles at the time, he found himself shooting everywhere from Spain with *Pan's Labyrinth* to Budapest for *Hellboy II*, and then moving to New Zealand for two years to work on *The Hobbit*, which he was originally slated to direct. As Guillermo said at the time, "I live like a ventriloquist's dummy. I fold in a suitcase and I go."

One thing *Hellboy II* exudes is confidence, for by now Guillermo felt assured in his instincts and choices, his interests and predilections. As with the first *Hellboy*, Guillermo brought *Hellboy* creator Mike Mignola aboard to work on designs and

(OPPOSITE, CLOCKWISE FROM TOP LEFT) Notebook 4, Page 40A, depicting the origins of the root creature; puppets of Prince Nuada and Princess Nuala from the film's opening sequence; tooth fairy concept by Wayne Barlowe; Hellboy (Ron Perlman) and Abe Sapien (Doug Jones) drink Tecate; a page from the book Professor Broom (John Hurt) reads to young Hellboy (Montse Ribé), illustrated by Raúl Villares; a drawing of Hellboy overshadowed by a member of the Golden Army by Mike Mignola.

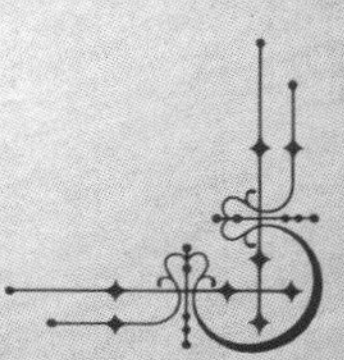

story ideas. Mignola found it a very different experience from the first time around. "The second film was much more a del Toro picture, so a lot of my influence, it's there but it's buried under layers of other people's stuff," Mignola revealed to *Geek's Guide to the Galaxy.* "The Hellboy character in that second picture is so far away from *my* version of Hellboy. . . . In fact, there was a moment in one of the meetings where I said, 'Well, Hellboy wouldn't do that.' And del Toro said, 'Your Hellboy wouldn't. Mine would.'"

Despite such boldness, Guillermo had concerns about the logistics for *Hellboy II.* "It was not a gigantic-budget movie," he notes. "*Hellboy II* was eighty-five million bucks. But we tried to make it luxurious and luscious."

He also had to make it *fresh*—a daunting challenge, since every fantasy film of the decade, from *Harry Potter* to *Lord of the Rings*, was exploring similar terrain. But Guillermo was not intimidated. He searched far and wide for unusual designs that could bring a new inflection to the Celtic-dominated visual language of contemporary fantasy. "We did a very careful study," he explains. "If you look at Balinese architecture, and then you look at really Nordic, Slavic architecture, if you migrate, you find shapes that echo one another, like curved ceilings, curved rooftops with pointy edges. With *Hellboy II*, what was fascinating was that, when you start twisting the Celtic knot, and you toy with it, it becomes a Chinese symbol. And if you tweak it a little more, it becomes a Hindu symbol. It is extremely easy to manipulate. There is a very fluid, universal language in the Celtic design that is fascinating, and you can find it in Slavic design. So we tried to explore it and move it away from any sort of rigidity."

Guillermo adds that in *Hellboy II*, "I wanted to have a quality that is sensual," especially in the case of the giant elemental forest god Hellboy kills. "It has the moss on the chest, a lot of leaf foliage, but then, if the tentacle moves, you see the substrata. It feels like a juicy vegetable, translucent. It was like celery. And we went to great lengths. I think that everything needs to be painterly and sensual, and you need to be aware of the texture. For example, in the corridors of the BPRD [Bureau for Paranormal Research and Defense], even then the concrete surface needs to really feel like concrete."

In the notebook, Guillermo developed a variety of the striking images found in the film, adding layers and lushness to visions that echo his earlier works. The cracked blue-white marble skin of the vampiric Jesús Gris in *Cronos* (where, Guillermo admits, "the makeup was not good enough") morphed into the cracked porcelain head of the ghost-child Santi in *Devil's Backbone* and the tombstone-white face of the overlord Damaskinos in *Blade II*, until finally becoming the delicate, pale visages of Prince Nuada and his sister, Nuala, in *Hellboy II*. "It was not marble by then," Guillermo points out. "It was ivory." *Hellboy II*'s eyeless Angel of Death, eyes scattered across its wings like stars in the night, recalls not only the Pale Man of *Pan's Labyrinth*, but Guillermo's work on *Mephisto's Bridge* and tropes from his beloved symbolist painters, too.

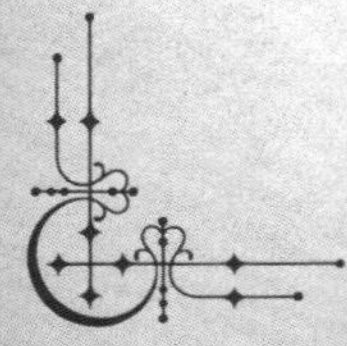

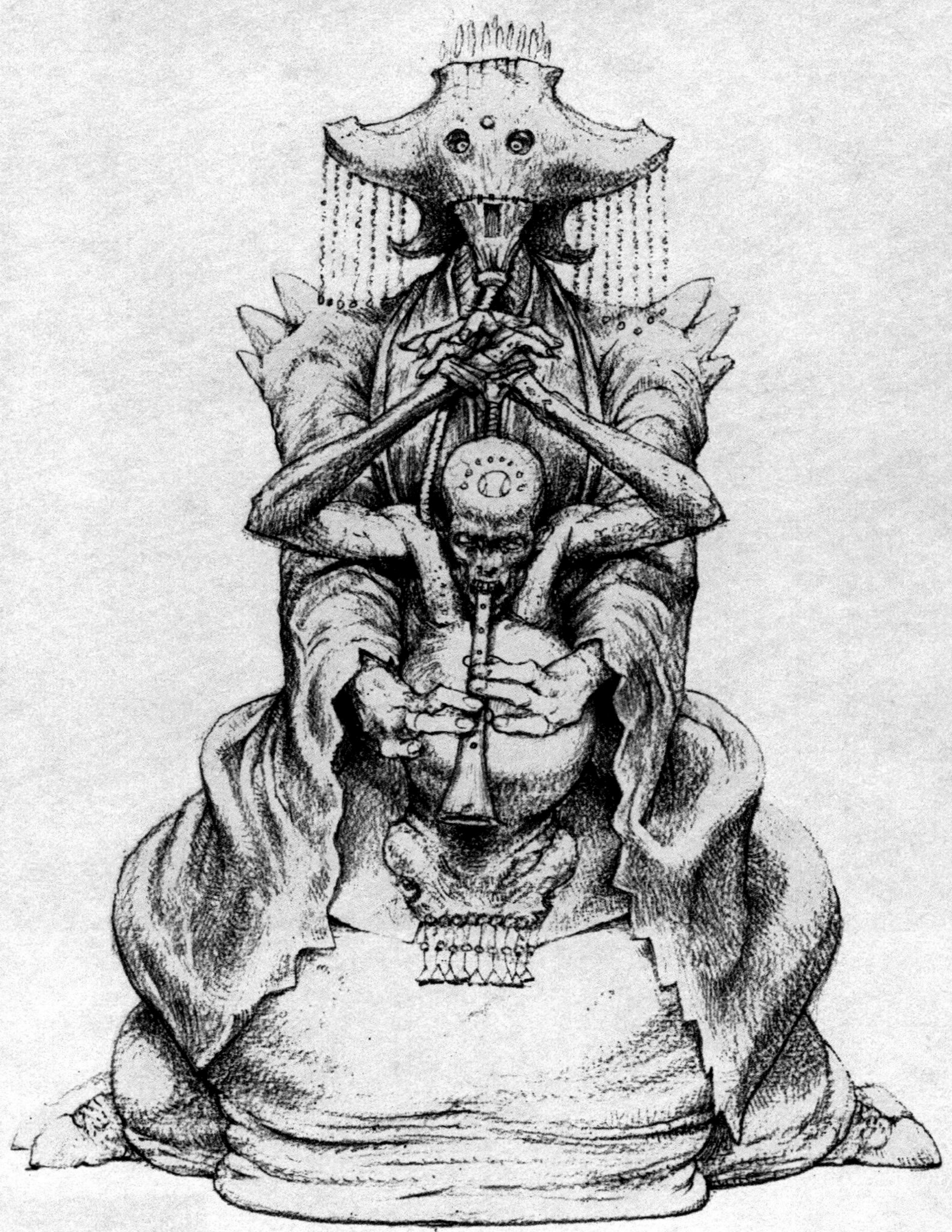

(ABOVE) Troll Market street musician concept by Wayne Barlowe.

Johann's helmet, Liz's cross, the bestial Mr. Wink, Cathedral Head, the vast gears that fill the elfin throne room, the Golden Army—golems opening like gigantic *Cronos* devices—are all lovingly rendered in these pages. Most detailed of all is the bustling Troll Market, full of wonders at every turn.

Initially, Guillermo envisioned a trilogy of *Hellboy* films, but now he thinks a third *Hellboy* movie won't happen. If *Hellboy II: The Golden Army* is Guillermo's swan song to the franchise, he feels well satisfied. No film is ever perfect, or could ever fully transmit every notion or realize every detail, but with *Hellboy II* Guillermo is unconcerned, he says, "because I like it so much. I'm in love with what we got. I cannot be objective. I don't want everybody to agree. I'm just declaring that, for me, it's one of the most beautiful things I've done."

GDT: This [*opposite*] is a test of the Prince Nuada makeup. Curiously enough, this is me drawing it over an actor. That is Charlie Hunnam, who was one of the two guys I had in mind for the part; the other was Luke Goss. But I tried it on Charlie, and it looked to me like it was too extreme and made the prince too hard. Blood makes the prince exquisite and kind of delicate in a good way.

With Prince Nuada (Luke Goss) (ABOVE) and Princess Nuala (Anna Walton) (BELOW), del Toro wanted to create a race of elves with pale, porcelain-like skin, an idea he explored in the notebooks (OPPOSITE), and which resonates with figures from his other films.

MSZ: Again, the continuity of ideas from movie to movie is interesting. You start, with *The Devil's Backbone*, to use porcelain skin that cracks, and then you go do this. How did that play into your ideas about how to push elves and fantasy away from the Celtic tradition?

GDT: Well, I think elves should be kick-ass. I love Michael Moorcock's Elric, and I think elves are really savage warriors. I love the idea of an elf being white, completely white, almost ivory-like. And being creatures of such perfection that they almost shouldn't be flesh-like.

I'm very proud of Nuada and Nuala, his sister. They're very beautiful creations, and the idea that when elves die, they turn to stone? I love that idea because I thought then entire fields—battlefields—of elves are now stones, fallen stones. And when they go to Bethmora and the Giant's Causeway, they see a lot of stones, and I'm just thinking, "Those are fallen elves that fell defending the city."

Notebook 4, Page 28B

ARABIC!!

Signs indicating the names of the zones in the Troll Market, made of bronze or a similar material and posted on the columns in the tunnel.

—Lights made by sources in the floor and wall

—Why is A.S. so driven to speak with the princess so fast?

—A story that reunites the best moments of M.R., one by one.

—Perhaps the prince's chamber could be in the TROLL MKT, *which would be why the organ grinder's monkey finds it so easily.*

—Sufism is infinite and therefore it's everywhere and nowhere. It's inside us but eludes us. It doesn't exist but it's always present. It consumes us each day, as if we were petty nourishment for its fires, which are our own.

—Everything that happens strengthens us. Pain, loss (which is nothing but exchange),and death which is but another transformation of our energy.

—C.C. of the rest of the film

• Map Shop *in Gold/Greens*

• Army Base 1955. *Earth tones, military green, and blue and yellow Christmas lights.*

• *Flashback in shades of Scarlet and gold that don't regain their intensity until the end of the film.*

Nuada Silverlance

—The magic world's color code.

• *The T.M. GREENS BLUES GOLD* RUST RED.

• *Throne Room: GOLD and BLACK*

• *Bethmora: Ochre/Gray/Amber*

• *G.A.C. Golds/Scarlets*

• *Little hallway Ipepe: Greens/Gold.*

11/8/06 13 Goyas and I'll throw out the A. Shave. *I hope everything turns out well.*

11/24/06 War, murder, people killing people they don't know, those are facts. The barrier between us, that one we can't break, you and I, that is tragedy. Pure and simple.

–If I move the prologue so that it contains the legend of G.Q., it will make the TROLL MARKET *section lighter.*

–It's important for the "Elemental" sequence to feature a large-scale scene and show us "NATURE VS. M"

–They show the king the Elemental grenade and call it "the Bad"

–Placing our faith in organized religion makes beggars of us, starving people pleading for something that they carry, and have always carried, within

–You disgusting–meat sacks of GARBAGE.

HB [?] set.

—THE WORLD—etc. "Keep up the good work"

The prince does his "cleansing," little by little the graphics mix together with the graffiti.

Royal markings

–Angel of Death.

plays with lives.

–What is evil if not the work of the virtuous man?

–Perhaps it would be a good idea if Abe "read" the state of Liz's pregnancy.

–"the immoral and impious straight line" Hunderwasser.

–Solitude and silence are the greatest gifts or the worst punishments.

–"Fairy cottage" *or* "Storybook architecture popular *during the* 20's/30's

Notebook 4, Page 24A

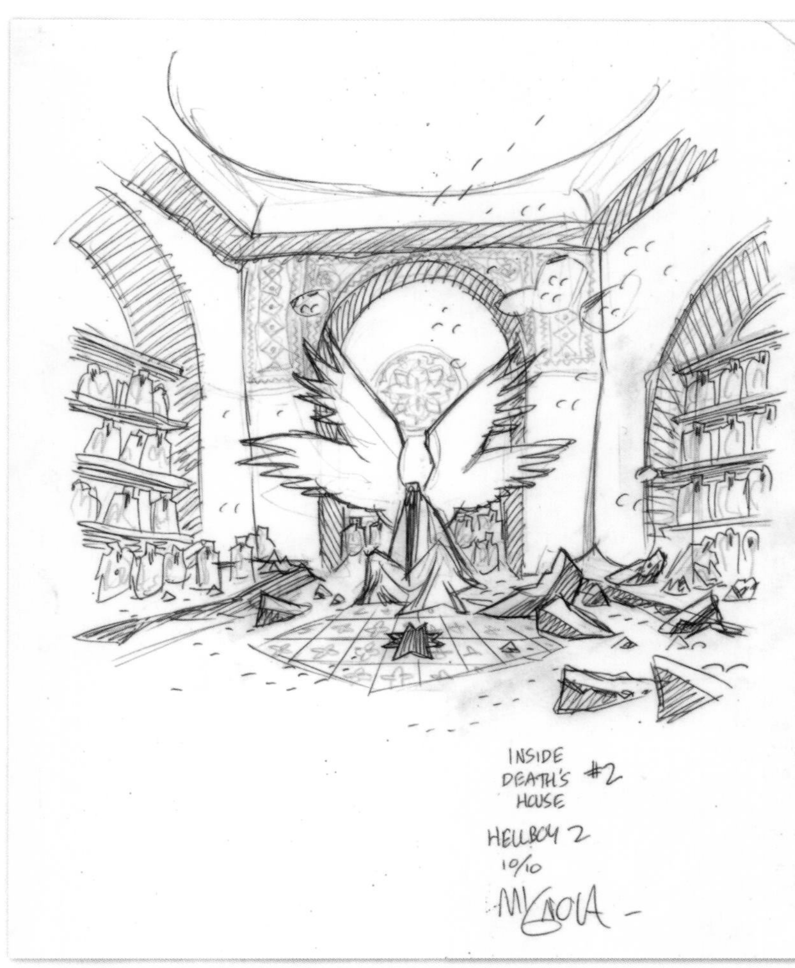

MSZ: Here we have the Angel of Death, which is such an important figure in *Hellboy II*, but which can also be traced back to some of your ideas for earlier, unmade projects.

GDT: Yeah, the first time I designed the wings of the Angel of Death was for a project called *Mephisto's Bridge*, but they were much more elaborate. Every feather had an eye, and each of the eyes in the feathers represented a soul. But the Angel is really rooted in medieval illustrations, which show angels with four wings and eyes in the wings. I just love that image, and I keep it in my head.

And I wanted him to be blind in the sense that he doesn't care if you choose one path or the other. That gives him a distance. There's something really, really sinister about the angel that is blind to human suffering, if you will. And we took a long time sculpting the faceplate because I wanted it to feel like a helmet, like a crown, but to give it the texture of real bone. And then we added the asymmetry of the crack—in a character that is all about symmetry, you put in an asymmetrical detail.

MSZ: The faceplate in the final design isn't something I see reflected in the early drawings.

GDT: No, it literally came out when we were sculpting. I went to visit the makeup effects department, and when we started there was no faceplate. So I took a bunch of Plasticine and I started expanding it into a faceplate. And then Norman Cabrera found the half-moon shape. And we started saying, "Let's make it bigger," and it just happened. Sometimes I like "sketching" with clay. I used to sculpt, and am an okay sculptor, so I can get away with it, although not all of the makeup guys like it when I do it.

MSZ: And then the Angel's teeth remind me of the Pale Man's.

GDT: That's exactly right. I like really narrow, small teeth that are long. I think they are very threatening. If the only makeup you use on an actor is just changing the teeth, it's already super creepy. And it's very subtle. People don't read it at first.

Del Toro's original idea for the Angel of Death (OPPOSITE) was given a lair by Mike Mignola (TOP). The angel's faceplate (ABOVE), absent in the original design, was developed during the sculpting process.

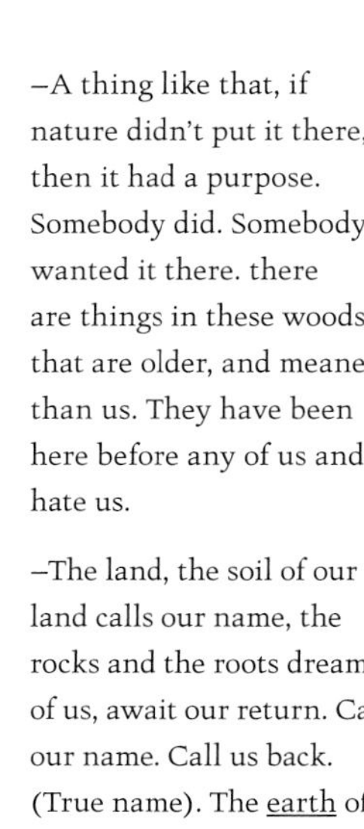

–A thing like that, if nature didn't put it there, then it had a purpose. Somebody did. Somebody wanted it there. there are things in these woods that are older, and meaner than us. They have been here before any of us and hate us.

–The land, the soil of our land calls our name, the rocks and the roots dream of us, await our return. Call our name. Call us back. (True name). The <u>earth</u> of our land dream of us.

–Mirror Helmet for J. TO AVOID REFLECTION/SET. Plus <u>TORSO</u> J *to establish it at the start of the film*

–That's a long sword, your highness, overcompenseting?

Arno [?]

4:35 28/11/06

–The prince needs to show his sister ONE room just like things were in their splendor.

"The worst"

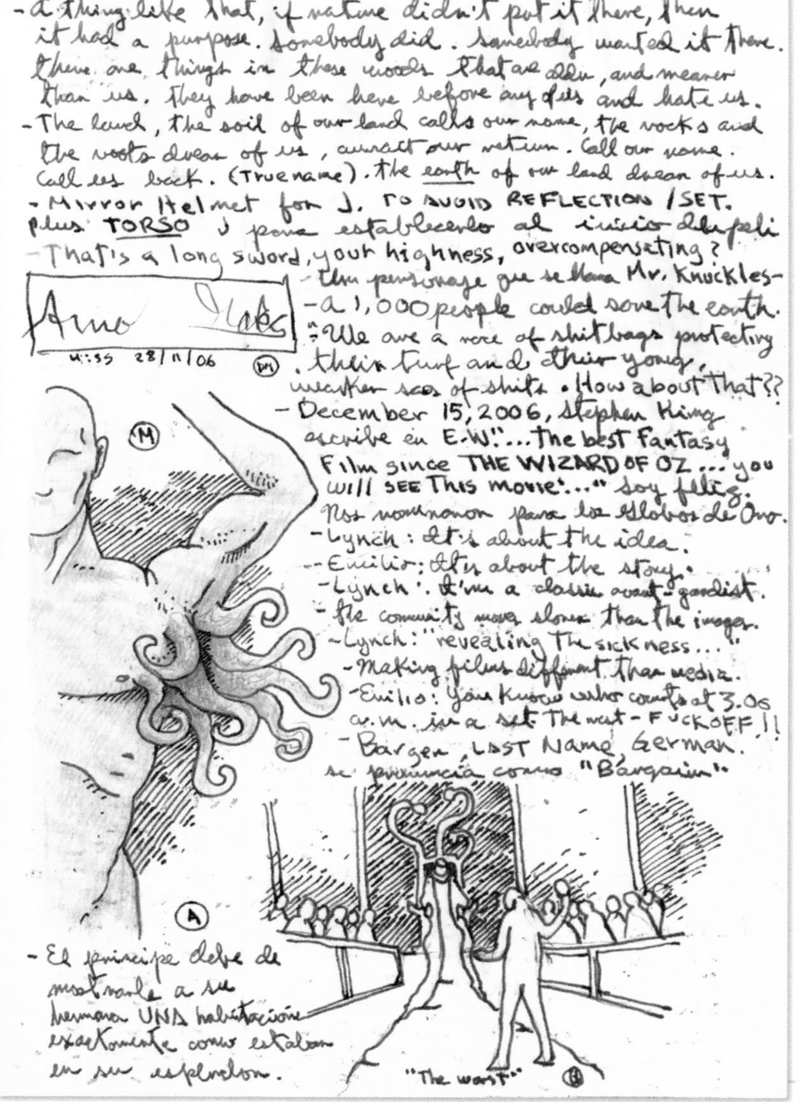

–A character called Mr. Knuckles–

–A 1,000 people could save the earth.

–We are a race of shitbags protecting their turf and this young, [?] of shits. How about that??

–December 15, 2006, Stephen King *writes in* E.W. " . . . the best Fantasy Film since THE WIZARD OF OZ . . . you will SEE This movie . . . " *I am happy. They nominated us for the Golden Globes.*

–Lynch: It's about the idea.

–Emilio: It's about the story.

–Lynch: I'm a classic avant-gardist.

–The community moves slower than the images.

–Lynch: "revealing the sickness . . . "

–Making films different than media.

–Emilio: You know who counts at 3.06 a.m. in a set. The west—FUCK OFF!!

–Bargen, LAST Name, German. *Pronounced like* "Bargain"

Notebook 4, Page 24B

MSZ: What is this tentacled armpit for?

GDT: I just found it disturbing—the idea that in a Lovecraftian movie a character could raise their arm and you would see a bunch of tentacles moving. It's an image I would like to use one day.

Below it is a sketch I did of the council of the elves on both sides of the throne, which ended up in *Hellboy II* in a different way. It says "The worst" because the prince says, "And for that I will call upon the help of all my people and they will answer. The good, the bad, and the worst." He's including "the worst" in his oath, which is the Golden Army. And I was playing with the idea that the train of the king's robe was also the carpet leading up to the throne. But I didn't use that either.

MSZ: Let's talk about this portrait of the king [*opposite*].

GDT: I like the idea of a creature having ornamental elements that grow out of their body—of ornaments that are biological. You know, when you see a stick insect, it looks like a design. Or if you look at a flower or a vegetable, there is a symmetry and an elegance to the inside that is completely natural, organic. For example, when you slice a tomato, the veining is beautiful.

And this was especially important for the king of the underworld because he is related to trees and all the stuff they don't have anymore. The idea is that the culture that was given the forests is now living in an abandoned, rusty train station, next to a boiler room. And yet, in their nature, they're still wood. They're still the evocation of nature. The elves in *Hellboy II* are really a displaced tribe. Mignola and I always talked about the prince being like Geronimo, and the elves having received the shittiest reservation thanks to their deal with mankind.

–URIA HEEP, CHEVY SLYME, Mr SPPITLETOE, NICKELBY, Mr PECKSNIFF, TOM PINCH, Scrooge, PIP, FAVISHAM, PICKWICK, SMIKE, Newman, Maggi GNOTI SEAUTON–

Bouderby.

GHOST

Liz's invasion of H.B.'s space is reflected by an overwhelming increase in shoes and clothes that he'll never wear.

–She confronts the public in order to save him.

King Balor.

–The clothes worn by royalty should be full of fabric, with several layers and shapes, too.

-URIA HEEP, CHEVY SLYME, Mr SPPITLETOE, NICKLEBY,
Mr PECKSNIFF, TOM PINCH, Scrooge, PIP, FAVISHAM,
PICKWICK, SMIKE, Newman Maggi GNOTI SEAUTON-
Bouderby.
FANTASMA
-Su invasión del espacio de H.B. por Liz se refleja en un aumento desmesurado de zapatos y de ropa que nunca habrá de ponerse.
-Ella se enfrenta al público por salvarlo.
H
El Rey Balor.
-La ropa que lleva la realeza debe ser muy llena de tela y muchas formas con capas y demás.

A gnome, seen behind the expo of H.

—Jane Eyre has arrived at Sharpe's mansion without [?], calm. Blessings and congratulations and good fortune for your future.

—The Crimson Peak mansion "breathes" for the children.

—The Alchemical principle of "dissolve and coagulate" as part of the supreme creation can be applied to the processes of the soul/body.

—Wink's fight is restricted by the space between the columns of the T.M. and I need to use the vertical space above. The problem is that the roof is made of solid stone too. I'll ask Steve to build a machine that grinds the flesh and bone of the cats in the T.M./ without blood

—THE NUMINOUS

—Leather cowl.

Angel in Castle in Budapest

—King Balor's visual "motif" should be a circle of Light in the past and in the present.

—By what mythology do we live by? I believe that TAO, HOMEOPATHY, ALCHEMY and JUNG are the 4 pillars.

"The Bone Crusher."

HELLBOY II: THE GOLDEN ARMY. BUDAPEST, 2007.

Mignola left me this card on the tiny desk in the Hotel Sofitel in Budapest after we finished the storyboards for the Golden Army sequence for the film HBII April 8, 2007. This week Dona, Scott, Mike and David came to discuss the proposal and he took 2 weeks. 3 million dollars in key departments. Ydig was lost and we must kill my beloved Wink in the middle of the film instead of doing it at the end.

NUMINOUS, INSCRUTIBLE, INDIFFERENT, MYSTERIOUS, RECONCILIATION, TRANSMUTATION.

—It is the power of art to reconcile us with life and to seduce us with mistery. Or perhaps the other way 'round

—"The decisive question for man is this: Is he related to something infinite or not?" *Jung asked himself this in his writings and man combats the void and Cosmic indifference looking for the answer.*

GOOD LUCK!

MIGNOLA

FROM ME! (MAGNUS)

NOTEBOOK 4, PAGE 32B

(OPPOSITE, RIGHT) The initial concept for the massive grinding machine in the Troll Market. (ABOVE) Ron Perlman (Hellboy) and del Toro in front of the final machine on the Troll Market set.

GDT: Here [*opposite*] I sketched an angel I saw in one of the castles in Budapest, where we shot a lot of *Hellboy II*. I came up with the idea of a circle behind the king like the halo of a saint, and I came up with this design for the grinding machine in the Troll Market, which I just love.

Above is Mike Mignola's drawing from when he departed *Hellboy II* in preproduction. He left me this little illustration saying, "Good luck!"

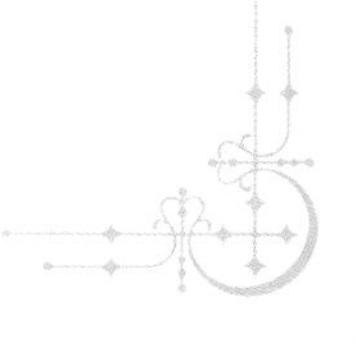

General view of the Troll Market

Notebook 4, Page 29A

GDT: Here [*left*] I'm trying to portray the Troll Market. I originally thought it would be these crooked places, and you could see small doorways next to giant doorways next to normal doorways, with little staircases next to normal staircases. I wanted to do it all in greens and golds.

MSZ: The market and the elemental [*opposite*] share the same palette. Originally, was there supposed to be a strong visual link between the two?

GDT: The original idea was that the other world was life, so I wanted to make it green, like nature, or red, like blood. But this is a very early idea. We still have a lot of green, but we eventually made it very lively with a lot of colors. What I did is I started evolving the movie toward a more controlled palette in the human world and an incredibly colorful palette in the fantasy world.

So Hellboy lives in the BPRD, which is essentially steel and concrete, straight lines. When you're out on the street, everything is blue, greenish but with really cold lines. Then he sees the Troll Market and he goes, "Holy shit, you should see this." He starts to understand where he belongs. Hellboy's real life and his true nature are in these places.

(LEFT) Initially green like the elemental (OPPOSITE), the Troll Market took on more diverse colors in this keyframe by Francisco Ruiz Velasco (ABOVE), eventually becoming a riot of saturated colors in the final film.

Soft Xenon spotlights at half power, sweeping past the stone columns in the T.M. the whole time.

–ETCHED plaques inscribed with "TROLL" letters on the walls in the T.M. tunnel for the FACELESS CAVE BERSERKER *with a lantern.*

–A scene in which the victim wakes up with the vampire sucking at his arm, suddenly, without prior warning, like a bald, blind leech.

–Window from Polanski's The Tenant *in the T.M.*

–Scene in which the corpse is identified: When you look at it—him, Please forgive me but—have you ever assembled a J. Puzzle? You concentrate on a piece. A finger, lip, brow, beauty mark, Anything you can. Avoid looking at anything else. Concentrate in the particular things, ignore the rest.

–King Balor has a crown of antlers coming out of his own skin.

–The prosthesis should be limited to the upper part.

What are you? No, better yet—What am I NOT??

Elemental

Blind

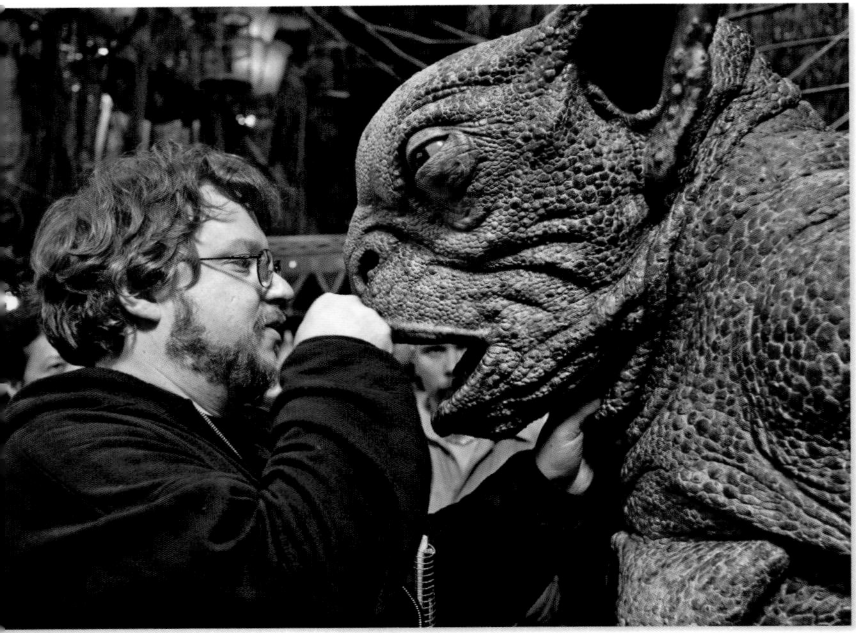

who designed him. When he was drawing political cartoons, where he didn't have to do it that well, he would really put thought and effort into it because he loved it. And George Lucas saw his illustrations and said, "Okay, I want to work with him." I think there are kindred spirits within the arts—both behind the scenes and in the audience. The moment you connect, you just get it instantly.

GDT: Yes, there's an imprint.

(OPPOSITE, TOP RIGHT) Del Toro's early idea for King Balor's royal guards gave them owl-like helmets. This idea was developed by Francisco Ruiz Velasco (ABOVE) but eventually discarded in favor of the "butcher" design seen in the final film. (TOP) Del Toro, like many other filmmakers before him obsessed with their creatures, has a deep affection for his monsters.

MSZ: What project was this imperial owl guard for?

GDT: We ended up discarding it [*opposite page, top right*]. But it was actually a great design for the guards who were guarding the king in *Hellboy II.*

And then here [*opposite, bottom left*] is an idea for layering the helmet for Johann to be invisible. Both Michael Elizalde, who was makeup designer on the film, and I are amateur magicians. I'm a terrible amateur magician. He is a great amateur magician. We were talking about creating the helmet as an optical illusion, so we slanted the helmet, creating a lid, raising the shoulders. It's a really great illusion. It really is a very nice design.

MSZ: It's amazing how much care you put into these things.

GDT: As you are making a movie, the easiest thing to forget is that it's going to be viewed at a different speed. Like, the thing that you've labored on for months, which you've designed and constructed, is in the movie for two seconds. But sometimes an understanding develops, like with *Star Wars.* For a generation of kids, it takes Greedo nothing but a few minutes to live, enter, and die. Or my favorite creature, Hammerhead. He's in one shot.

People talk about fantasy movies, and they say, "Well, this movie of yours was not loved by the critics," or "It didn't make money." And I go, "It doesn't matter." It doesn't matter. I assure you, there will be an eight-year-old kid in Milan, or Peru, or Mexico, who cherishes it as his favorite movie in the world because he saw it at age eight. Our generation worships movies that were critically savaged when they came out, and we enthrone people from Lucio Fulci to Mario Bava who were critically not well received or regarded at all.

MSZ: As you said, this appreciation all stems from love. Because, when you're talking about Hammerhead, that was Ron Cobb

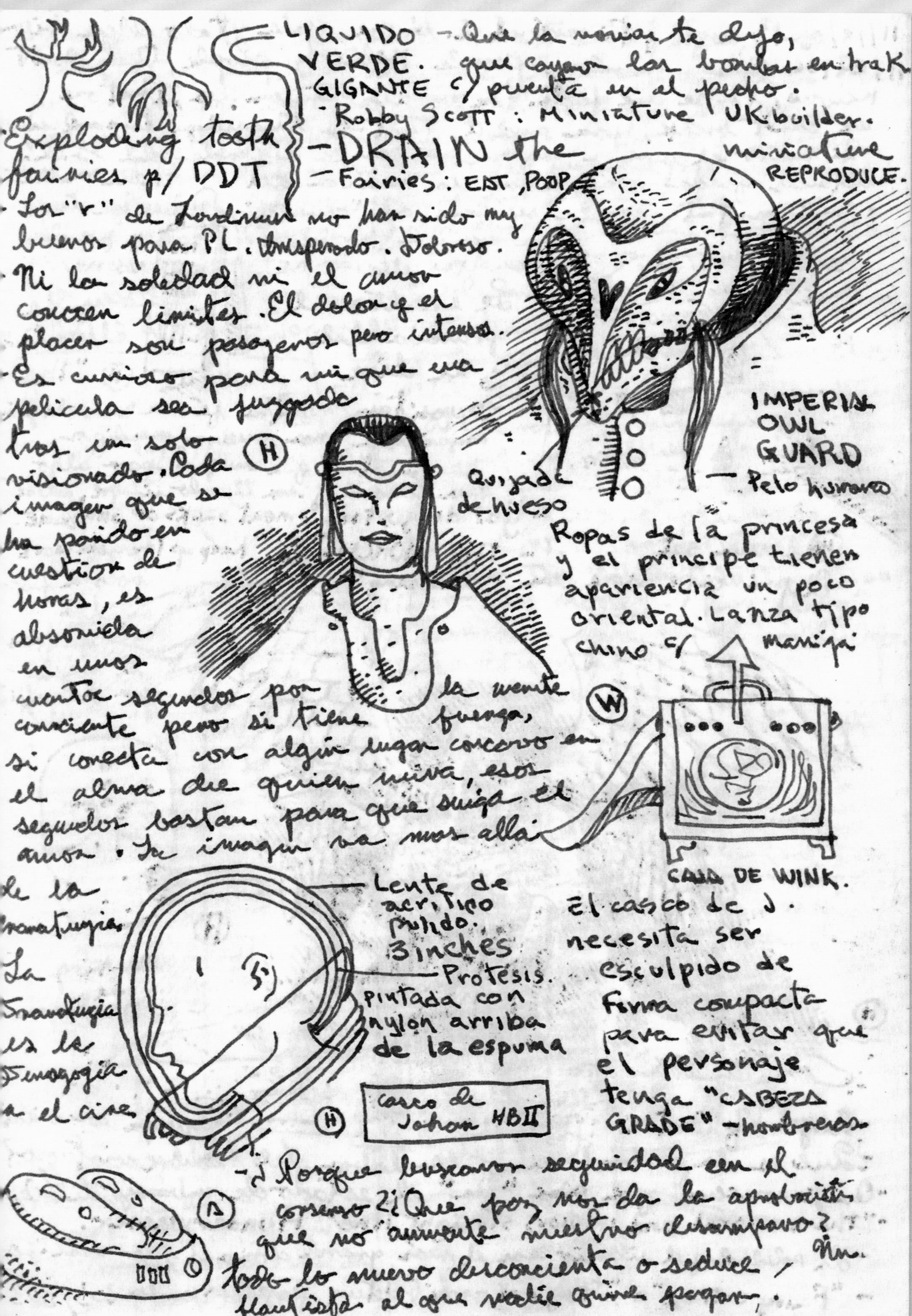

GREEN LIQUID. GIANT

That your girlfriend left you, that bombs fell in Iraq, with a door in his/her/ my chest.

–Robby Scott: Miniature UK builder.

–Exploding tooth fairies *for DDT*

–DRAIN the miniature

–Fairies: EAT, POOP, REPRODUCE.

–Lordimar's "r's" have not been very good for PL. Unexpected. Painful.

–Neither loneliness nor love knows any bounds. Pain and pleasure are fleeting but intense.

–Judging a movie after only one viewing seems strange to me. The conscious mind absorbs every image, which took hours of work to create, in a matter of seconds. But if the image is powerful, if it speaks to the viewer's soul in some deep way, then those few seconds are enough for love to take shape. Image transcends dramaturgy. Dramaturgy is Demagogy in the cinema

Jaw made of bone

IMPERIAL OWL GUARD.

–Human hair

The prince's and princess's clothes have a slightly oriental look to them. Chinese-style spear w/ shaft

WINK'S BOX.

Polished acrylic glass lens. 3 inches

Painted prosthesis with nylon over the foam

J's helmet needs to be sculpted small so that the character doesn't have a "BIG HEAD"— shoulder pads

Johan's helmet HB II

NOTEBOOK 4, PAGE 23B

–Why do we look for peace in consensus? Is there any peace to be found in the approval of others that doesn't leave us feeling more helpless? Anything that is new either unsettles or seduces, a flautist nobody wants to pay.

–Video Feed in the truck—

–"Heavy, heavy load" Tadpole V.

–Reverse the dialogue in a pair of scenes. Give Liz dialogue and share the "FOCUS"—H.B. and Johann.

Water Kick
USE the <u>*CHI*</u>

–The water and the fire flow freely. They're not any one type and they're shapeless

Wink hits Abe.

–Wink uses the magic/hand to "bring" H.B. and Abe to him and then push them.

–Little bits of glass are scattered when Wink crushes him. They're scattered around his head like little pieces of TEXAray.

–Corkscrew turn around the same shot and break a 3-D patch on the Butcher Guard??

–I will kill everyone in this room.

Abe Sapien

and then lifts him off the ground, smacks him against the floor, the column, and the <u>*wall*</u>.

–Bolero in Wink's hand.

"Abe vs Wink"

Vent.

If possible, the smoke should come out here.

Angle to hide his head.

Black metal.
Blue steel type

Design of Liz's necklace

Johann

–I LOVE YOU SQUIRREL, you and my GIRLS.

Notebook 4, Page 38A

GDT: Here [*opposite, bottom*] I designed the cross that Selma Blair wears in *Hellboy II*. I'm very proud of that design. I almost think it would sell. I mean, it's a great piece of jewelry.

The idea of putting steel around columns is for the Troll Market, because we found this abandoned quarry, and that's where we shot the Troll Market. I didn't like how flat the columns were, so I said, "Let's put iron clamps around them and have the iron bleed outside so that they look a little more textural."

Then you see the final proportions of the helmet of Johann. We came up with the idea of a funnel so that the actor would have a little more leeway. Still, it was a killer. The first or second day, John Alexander, the actor, wore it; we removed the helmet, and it was like a crown of thorns. He had punctures with blood. He said, "I cannot wear it like this anymore." We had to create some padding. And we had to hire a second actor because John could only wear it for so long.

Then, in the middle of the page, Wink is hitting Abe. I never filmed this particular moment. We tried to do it but couldn't. It was going to be a big fight between Abe and Wink, but part of our budgeting process was losing it. So Abe never fought, really. We had Wink putting his hand on top of Abe's head, when he says, "I'll take care of this," and then he goes, "Oh, dear," and we cut.

(OPPOSITE) Some of del Toro's notebook pages include a critical mass of near-final designs. This page features strong concepts for Mr. Wink (Brian Steele) (BOTTOM), Johann's helmet (John Alexander) (BELOW), and Liz's necklace (Selma Blair, with Ron Perlman as Hellboy) (LEFT).

(1) Closed *[?] the opening* (2) Open *The [?] below is the jaw*

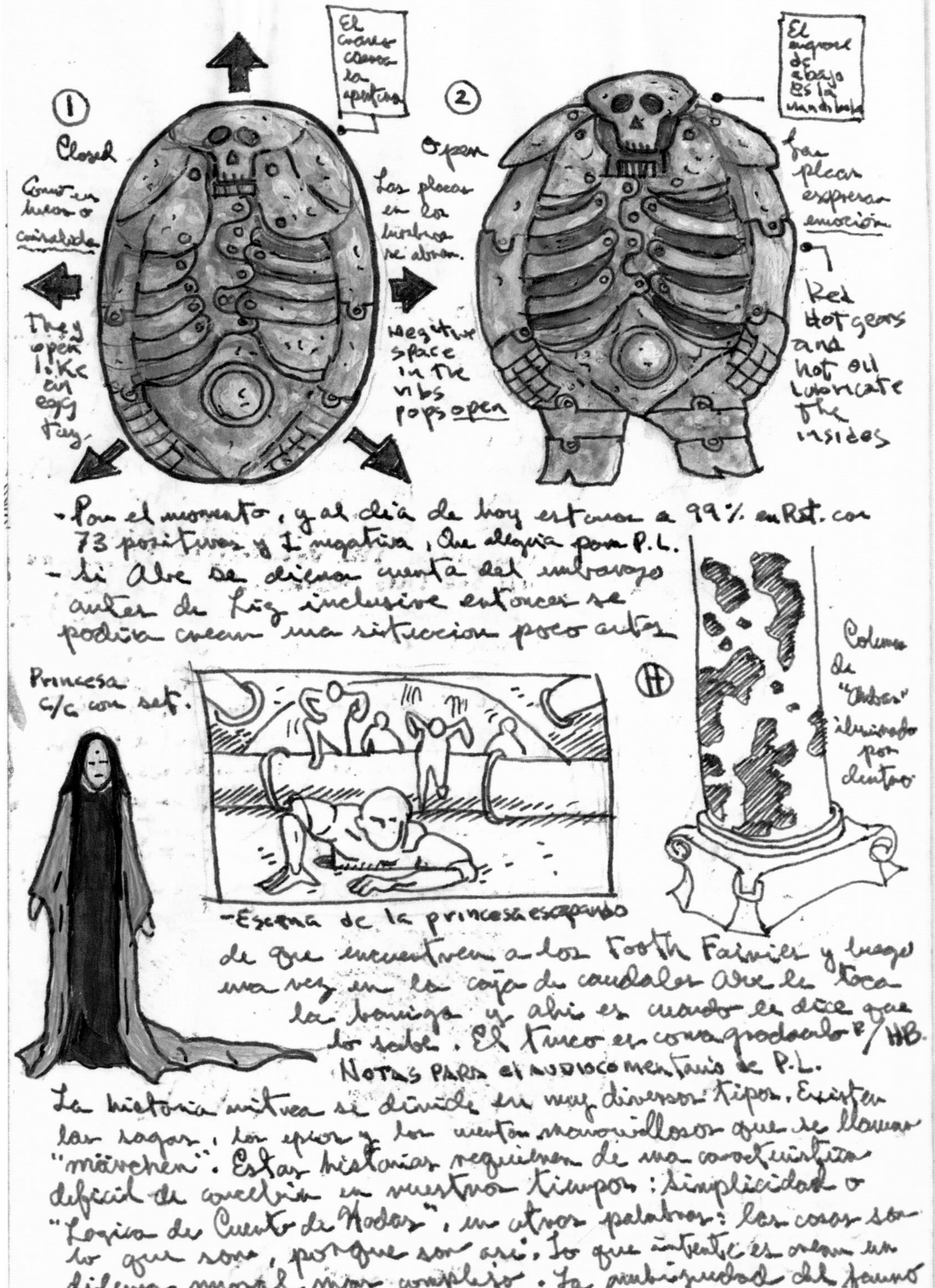

Contains eggs or a *<u>cocoon</u>*

The plates on its shoulders open.

They open like an egg toy.

—For the moment, as of today, we're 99% in Rot.com with 73 positives and 1 negative, what joy for P.L.

—If Abe realizes that Liz is pregnant before even she does, then it would create a situation a little earlier

Princess c/c with set.

Mythic stories fall into several categories. There are sagas, epics, and fantasy stories called "märchen." These stories depend on something difficult for us to conceive these days: Simplicity or the "Logic of the Fairy Tale." In other words: things are just what they are, because that's just the way they are. What I'm trying to do is create a more complex moral dilemma. The faun's ambiguity [continued page 231]

The plates express *<u>emotion</u>*

Negative space in the ribs pops <u>open</u>

Red Hot gears and hot oil lubricate the insides

"Amber" column with interior illumination.

—Scene of the princess escaping when they discover about the tooth fairies and then, once they're in the box, Abe touches her belly. That's when he says that he knows. The trick is how to [?] HB.

NOTES FOR P.L.'s AUDIO commentary.

Notebook 4, Page 25A

● **GDT:** This [*above*] is my first sketch of the Golden Army, which fortunately was highly improved. I wanted them to have these golem-like proportions. I wanted them to be cute, and I wanted them to all be eggs that transformed into the open figure here.

On the right [*opposite*] is one of my favorite designs, which is Cathedral Head. It says, "The man with the city in his mind." It was one of those designs that just came out fully formed in my head. I did a sketch, and it's very similar to the way it came out in the movie.

would be unusual in "marchen." These stories frequently examine or teach a moral lesson, exalting it or exposing a particular flaw. If the story is a parable or doctrinal, one of its goals is to delineate the characters as "types" in order to illustrate this basic lesson, characters which make the story whole and who are also contained by it. The lives of these "types" can and must have links with the past and the future but their role ends with the story

In a magic story, the flow is more important than the logic. Man invented monsters to explain the entire universe. Once man began to live in an organized way, with a "social contract," an abyss was opened up between his instincts and his thoughts, and monsters started to REPRESENT another universe altogether: man's inner universe. The pagan prefigures the social and offers us a glimpse of the deepest reaches of man's soul, articulating a primordial, savage universe, populated by fauns and ogres and fairies

"The man with the city in his mind." 11/1/06

MY DAYS WITH DEL TORO

MIKE MIGNOLA

I'M A LUCKY BOY. I first worked with del Toro on *Blade II*, sometime in late 2000. We'd met a few years earlier when he was first trying to get *Hellboy* up and running. We'd stayed in touch while he took all kinds of meetings—meetings he kept me out of because (as he told me later) I would not have survived them. He was almost certainly right. Anyway, when it became clear that this *Hellboy* thing was going to be a hard sell, he took on *Blade II* and brought me along. I'm pretty sure this was mostly to see if we could work together, on the off chance that *Hellboy* would actually happen. It certainly was *not* because I knew anything about being a preproduction artist. Though I served no real function (my title was "Visual Consultant"), he brought me with him to Prague to scout locations. It's that trip that I'll always remember: discovering the wilds of eastern Europe together for the first time; wandering through endless ruined (and yet somehow still functioning) factories; wondering if (or when) our very scary driver was going to pull over into the woods and shoot us; hunting for a really good Kafka puppet (I still maintain that he should be wearing a hat); descending into the Prague sewers (which we discovered are coated in semi-transparent living goo); and just laughing like crazy about a whole lot of stuff I can't repeat here.

The less said about the actual design work I did on that film, the better. Although del Toro and I like a lot of the same things (art, books, movies, etc.), when it comes to design I am sort of a minimalist, a "less is more" guy. He is very much a "more is not enough" guy. Often I would start a design and then he would hand it over to one of the other designers (usually my genius officemate, TyRuben Ellingson) to add a whole lot of stuff that would light up and spin around. The running joke was that if you could get steam to spurt out of the thing (whatever it might be), del Toro would *really* like it. The great artifact I have from that time (along with a bug-eyed, green vampire puppet) is a particularly terrible drawing I did of an autopsy table. It was so pathetically simple that del Toro was actually at a loss for words. He gently took my pencil from me and drew in Elmo and Big Bird standing behind the table. The look on their Muppet faces spoke volumes. That was *Blade II*.

Of course, we did go on to work together on both *Hellboy* films. On those I got to be there from the beginning (*Hellboy II* literally started with the two of us sitting in a room having no idea what we were going to do), through preproduction (I contributed a bit more on these films), filming, postproduction, and all the strangeness that comes after. I not only got to have Guillermo del Toro adapt my comic book character to film (which in my world is pretty much like winning the lottery) but I got to watch him do it. It was an amazing experience. And if I never set foot in another production office or sit on another film set, it will be okay, because I've done it—and I got to do it with him.

(LEFT) An early sketch of Rasputin from del Toro's third notebook, Page 108.

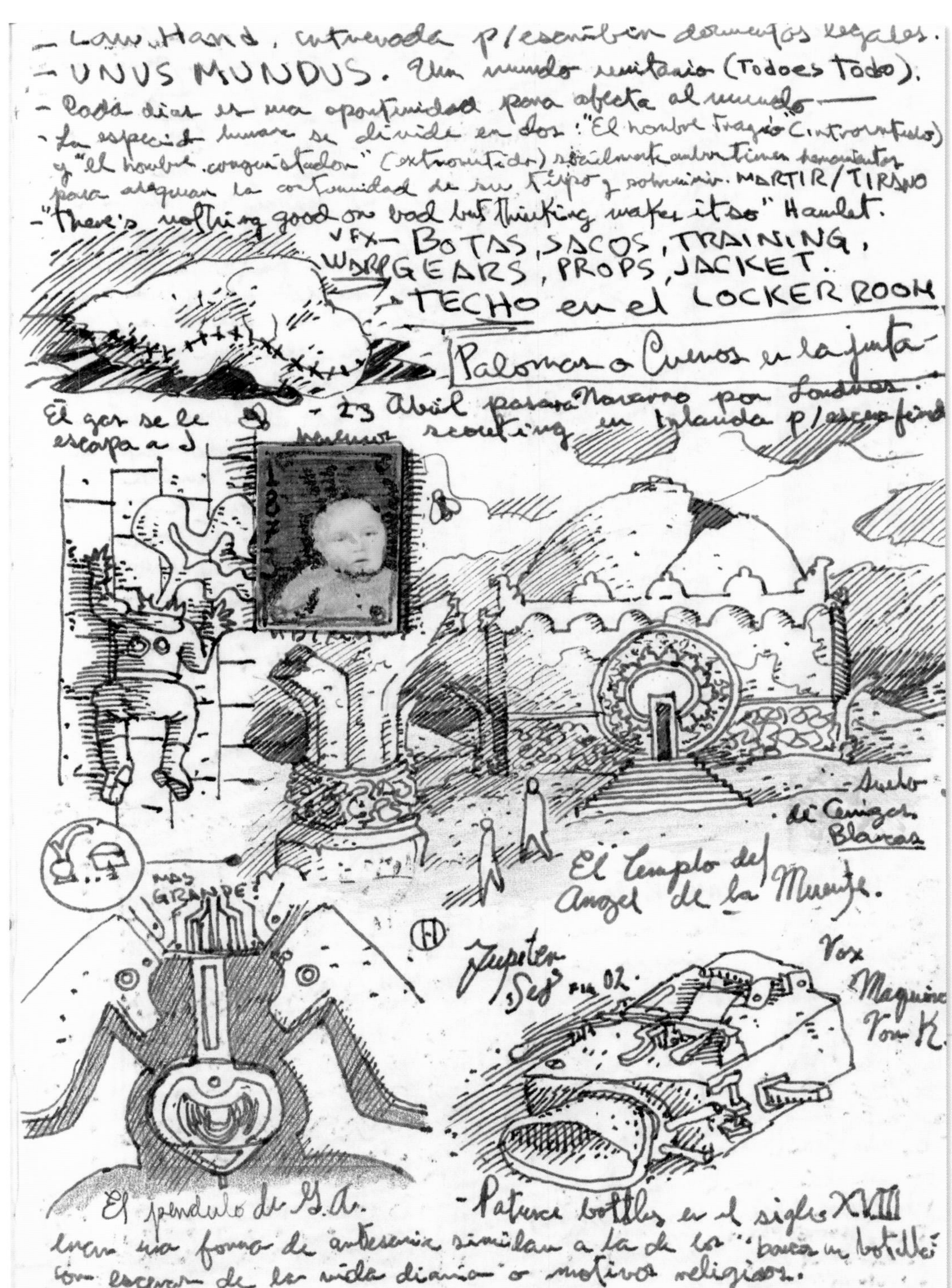

—Law Hand. *Trained to write legal documents.*

—UNUS MUNDUS. A unitary world (everything is everything).

—Every day is an opportunity to affect the world—

—The human species can be divided into two types: "the tragic man" (introverted) and "the conqueror man" (extroverted). Socially, each one has tools to ensure the continuity of his own type and survive. MARTYR/TYRANT

—"There's nothing good or bad but thinking makes it so" *Hamlet.*

VFX—BOOTS, BAGS, TRAINING, WARP GEARS, PROPS, JACKET. *ROOF in the* LOCKER ROOM

Pigeons or crows in the meeting—

—In April Navarro will pass through London. We talked about scouting in Ireland for the final scene

Gas comes out of J

Floor is <u>*white*</u> *ash*

The Temple of the Angel of Death.

BIGGER!

Jupiter. Machine Vox Von K.

The pendulum of G.A.

—[?] bottles in the eighteenth century

It was a handicraft similar to that of "ships in bottles" with scenes of daily life or religious motifs.

Notebook 4, Page 31B

● **GDT:** Here [*above*], you can see Johann emptying himself, literally, on the floor of the locker room, next to a photo I bought of a dead baby. I bought a bunch of old photos in Budapest, and one of them was a dead baby. And it was really, really disturbing.

Also on this page is the entrance to the Angel of Death's place, a detail of a mechanism of the Golden Army, and on the bottom right is a mechanical voice box created by Baron von Kempelen, who created the Turk, the mechanical chess player. There was an exhibition of his machines in Budapest, including a reproduction of the Turk.

The device was meant to reproduce the human larynx, and I just made a sketch of it. I don't take pictures. I don't think I've taken more than two dozen pictures in my entire life. I don't like still cameras. If something is very important, I'd rather sketch it.

V E R T I C A L

For the TROLL MARKET, vertical light sources in the middle, in 1:85 high resolution, for example with the Striders passing by there.

—I must make LHOD now. It's time. But with Bardem in Argentina.

—WORMS. In the excrement of certain urban pigeons there can be found a particularly pernicious type of worm. It deposits its larvae/eggs subcutaneously and has a special predilection for the tissues of the eye.

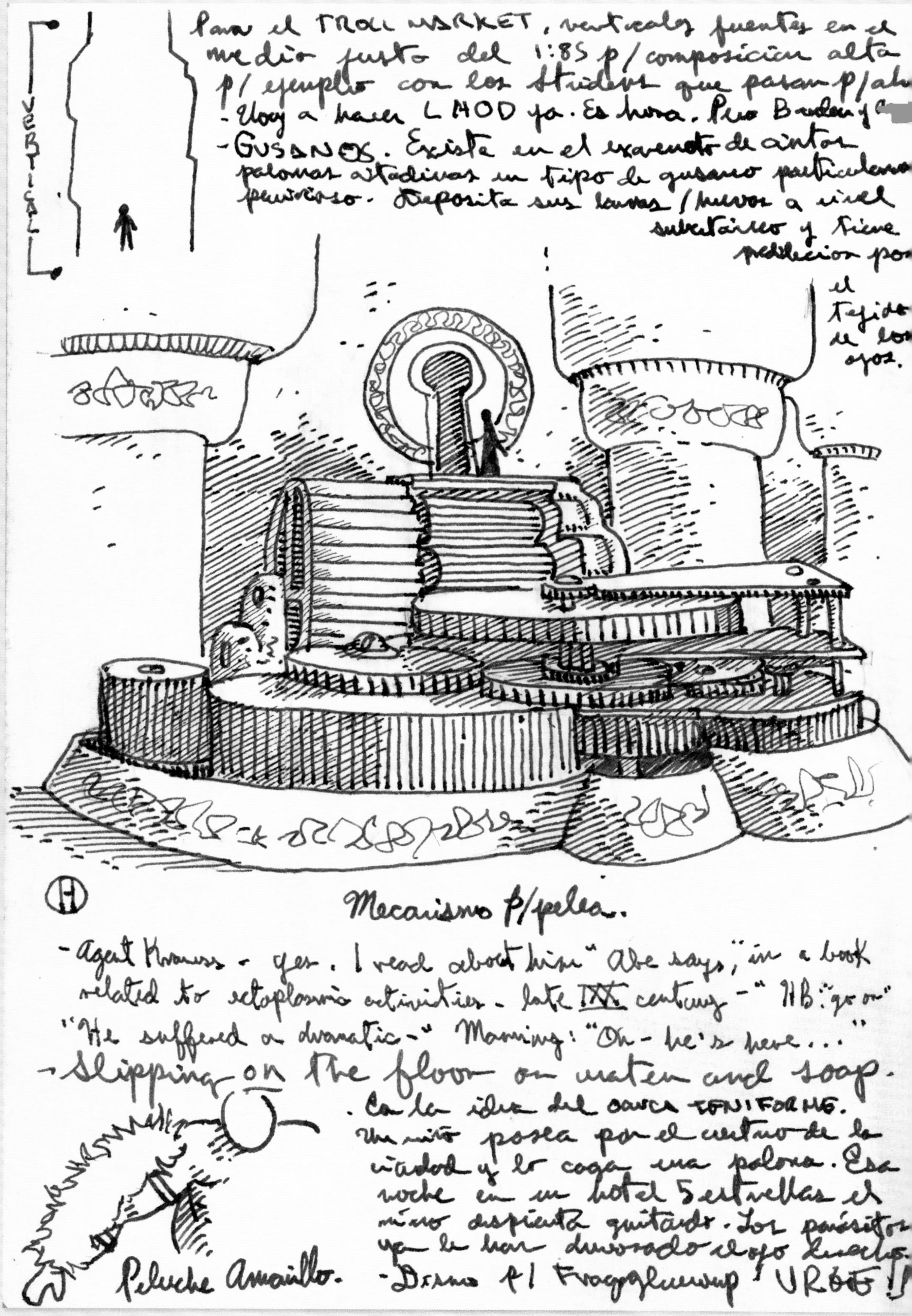

Mechanism for the fight.

—Agent Krauss—Yes, I read about him" Abe says, "in a book related to ectoplasmic activities—late nineteenth century—" HB: "go on" "He suffered a dramatic—" Manning: "Oh—he's here . . ."

—Slipping on the floor on water and soap.

—With the idea of the old-fashioned TAPEWORM. A boy is walking around downtown and a pigeon shits on him. That night, in a five star hotel, the boy wakes up screaming. The parasites have already devoured his right eye.

Yellow fuzz.

—Design for Fragglewump UROE!!

● **GDT:** It took us the longest time to come up with the design for the gears in the palace [*opposite*]. We fought with everyone, and finally I came up with this layout, which Francisco Ruiz Velasco made better, and which is the one that is in the movie. It was very difficult to design that set, the idea being that the whole chamber was like a windup mechanism for the armor. You started these big gears, and then they started more stuff.

(OPPOSITE) Del Toro's idea for the giant gears that set the Golden Army in motion was refined into the design for a real working mechanism before being built as a set, here pictured with Johann (John Alexander), Abe Sapien (Doug Jones), Hellboy (Ron Perlman), and Liz (Selma Blair) in the foreground (ABOVE).

–MUD and gauze for the "extras" in the J.M.—

–Mar/4/2007 A strange thought: the Academy ballots were turned in on the 20th (I went to television station) and were counted over the course of the next few days. In other words, the 20th is ahead. I, PC, W, and AW had already "lost" and it didn't matter at all. Once the statistics have been made manifest they do not matter. I'm surprised that I am so calm.

GIANT

–Chihuahua WITH COLLAR—*at the auction.*

–and then they find the bones that have been gnawed on.

BANNERS F/TH

Two headed shop owner. He hand puppets the 2nd head.

Rusty duct and lots of tubes in cement

Vapor type

Fluorescent Light Tubes which blink on and off in the T.M./steam.

Papers on the walls, put everything along the way.

Hellboy B.P.R.D.

–Blood on the floor of the entryway to the Troll Market

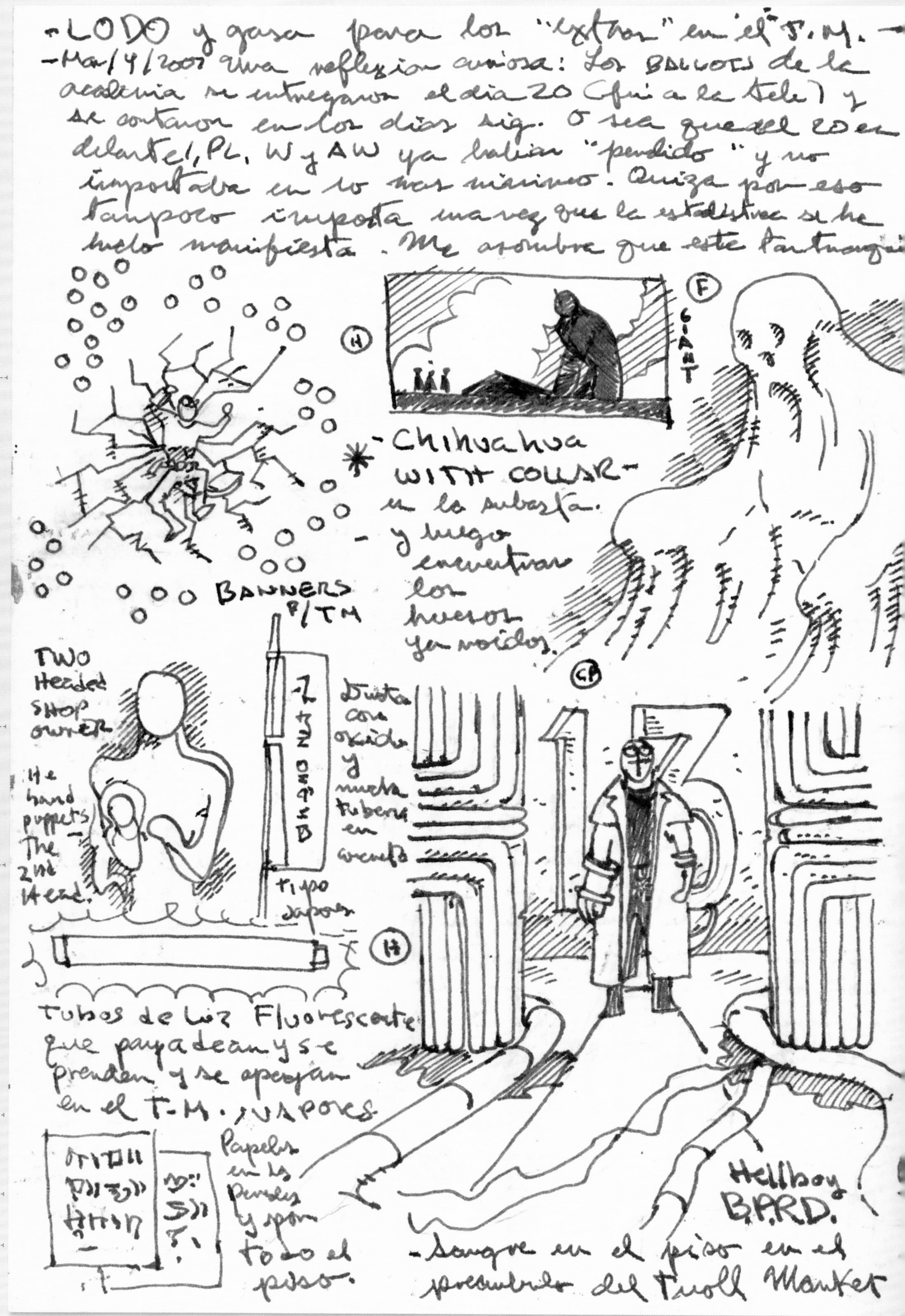

Notebook 4, Page 28A

MSZ: And on this page, are these sketches to the right initial concepts for the giant?

GDT: Only the one in the little vignette. Wayne Barlowe really created the design for the giant. I wanted very much the center of the door to look like a keyhole—I have a thing with keys and keyholes, visually. I'm sure Freud would have no problem explaining that, but it's something I go to a lot. It's in *Devil's Backbone*, and it's in *Pan's Labyrinth*, and it's in *Crimson Peak*. I just like the idea of portals, doors, and keyholes.

The image to the right of the giant is actually a ghost for *Crimson Peak*. See the two initials at the bottom—"CP?" I sometimes put little initials next to each image to remind me which film it is for. So the image of the giant has an "H" next to it, which is *Hellboy II*. And "F" means I wanted to find an alternative use for an idea if I didn't get to use it in a film. I drew the other "H" image—the pattern of pipes—here for the BPRD. But those actually show up in the Troll Market, in the scene where Wink beats up Hellboy.

MSZ: Next to it are some Lovecraftian symbols, kind of like the ones you drew in the first *Hellboy* notebook. Except here they're contained within a frame.

GDT: That is troll writing for the map shop. I think it's one of my favorite sets, because it had every sort of paper—all sorts of maps and atlases—covered in troll writing.

(OPPOSITE, CENTER) Del Toro's idea for the threshold giant was developed by Wayne Barlowe into a finished concept (ABOVE) that informed the final computer-generated creation (LEFT).

Napoleón inicia
la campaña
Los ejercitos
Inglaterra
Belgica
KNIFEHEAD
KNIFEHEAD 1
KNIFEHEAD 2 "Pharaoh"
SLATTERN Tokyo Flashback
KIMOTA
MEGADORAH Hong Kong Rumble
TRESSPASSER
Esta batalla sucede
encrucijada entre
Bruselas
Genappe
concretam
región

PACIFIC RIM

AS GUILLERMO GAINS GREATER FAME and scrutiny, and as security on the tentpole films he crafts becomes ever greater, the notebooks have become a two-edged sword. They are valued as works of art in themselves, but could also become liabilities by revealing great secrets if lost or stolen. In addition, these pages reflect not only the changing nature of Guillermo's life and art, but also the changing relationship between him and his audience. He is no longer a fledgling unknown clamoring for attention but a celebrity operating in public view.

Even today, Guillermo is reluctant to acknowledge his widespread popularity and vast influence. "I'm still not on the world stage. There are people who care for me. Still, the large majority of people don't know who I am. I'm not a household name; I'm an acquired taste."

Genuine modesty aside, Guillermo has learned the need for ever-greater caution regarding the notebooks. He must constantly be mindful of them. He became sharply aware of this on *The Hobbit* (2012); he was originally scheduled to direct the film series, and on the first film he shares cowriting credit. "The problem with the notebooks is, there was a very fractured relationship with them during *The Hobbit*. I kept a lot of notes, but I was very paranoid of them being lost because that was a supersecret project. To this day I'm very paranoid about that book, which is not finished; I'm still writing in it. So I pull it out less often because if it gets lost, if I reveal anything that's stayed in the movies, it's legally very, very binding."

Once Guillermo was on board as *The Hobbit*'s director, financial difficulties with MGM led to the film's delay. After two years cooling his heels in New Zealand waiting for production to begin, Guillermo ultimately left the project, intent on making up lost time and getting back to work.

Back in the United States, Guillermo met with James Cameron, who asked him if he was still interested in making a film of H. P. Lovecraft's novel *At the Mountains of Madness*—because, if so, Cameron wanted to produce it.

Guillermo had been making notes—and notebook entries—on *Mountains of Madness* for more than fifteen years, and with Cameron fresh off the billion-dollar-plus success of *Avatar*, it seemed at last the stars would align to bring Guillermo's most avidly desired project to fruition. Tom Cruise and Ron Perlman were cast in

(OPPOSITE, CLOCKWISE FROM TOP LEFT) Sketch of a door to a Jaeger Conn-pod from del Toro's fifth notebook, Page 4; concept of Gipsy Danger, the heroic American Jaeger, by Oscar Chichoni; storyboard of the Kaiju Knifehead attacking Gipsy Danger by Rob McCallum; concept of the Kaiju skull temple in *Pacific Rim*'s futuristic Hong Kong by Doug Williams; concept of Mako Mori on the Shatterdome ramparts by Keith Thompson.

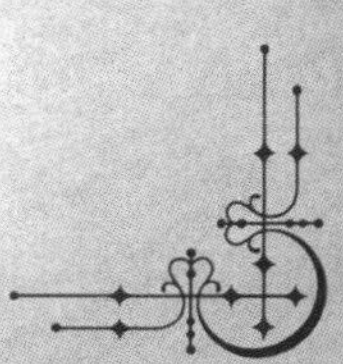

lead roles, and many months of intense preparation began, including astonishing creature designs, breathtaking production artwork, detailed storyboards of the entire film, location scouting, and more.

Then, at the last moment, the studio pulled the plug. No R-rated, two-hundred-million-dollar film had ever been greenlit to production, and the studio feared that the movie wouldn't turn a profit without the child and teen audience. Heartbroken, Guillermo leapt into another film he'd been developing with Legendary Pictures, *Pacific Rim*—the ultimate giant monster–versus–giant robot movie.

"I think I've been preparing for *Pacific Rim* all my life," Guillermo says. "When I was a kid, I saw *The War of the Gargantuas* in a shitty theater in Mexico, and I got a glass of pee thrown on my head from the balcony, and I stayed to finish the movie. That's how much I love *kaijus*, you know?"

Pacific Rim was the perfect remedy for all the emotional and psychic wounds Guillermo had suffered while trying to make *The Hobbit* and *At the Mountains of Madness*—then emerging without a picture to shoot after four years. As he puts it, "*Pacific Rim* has been the best experience for me in producing and directing a movie that I've ever had."

Best of all, this big summer movie embraces many of Guillermo's favorite themes and motifs: the balancing act between the forces of chaos and order, darkness and light, human and mechanism entwined, duking it out with gigantic weird creatures from another dimension—much like H. P. Lovecraft's Old Ones.

Filled with new creative fervor, Guillermo returned to working out designs and ideas in his notebooks. "*Pacific Rim* has a number of pages, which means a lot," he relates. "If I have more than two pages on a movie, that means I've been at it for a long time because I don't write that often in the book anymore."

He hasn't written in the notebook since completing *Pacific Rim*, but he adds, "Now that I'm doing [the TV version of] *The Strain* and *Crimson Peak*, I may restart. But I really want to finish this volume, so I can put it in a safe place, and I can start carrying a new notebook again. Once I'm not working on a supersecret project, I'll be relaxed."

What of the future? For a writer-director with such dark visions, Guillermo's outlook is enduringly hopeful. Paraphrasing science fiction legend Theodore Sturgeon, one of his favorite writers, Guillermo observes, "There's the famous Sturgeon's Law, which is, 'Ninety percent of everything is shit.' Now the way I live *my* life is the del Toro Law, which is, 'Ten percent of everything is *awesome*.' You know what I'm saying? I agree with Sturgeon, except I think that it's amazing that we get ten percent.

"All I know is that hatred makes life so much shorter and bitter. And every time you can give love, give love, if you can—and you can't all the time, I mean I'm not a candy-ass Teletubby, I'm a human being, you know. I hate people and I love people. But whenever you can, just fucking love. If you can choose, choose love."

(OPPOSITE, CLOCKWISE FROM TOP LEFT) Kaiju concept by Guy Davis; concept of Stacker Pentecost in his office in the Shatterdome by Vicki Pui; film teaser poster art by Hugo Martin; Mako Mori (Mana Ashida) is rescued by the Jaeger Coyote Tango; sketch of the Chinese Jaeger Crimson Typhoon by Francisco Ruiz Velasco; concept of a Precursor by Keith Thompson; concept of the Kaiju Knifehead by Wayne Barlowe; del Toro applying some more patina to the Alaskan wall set during shooting.

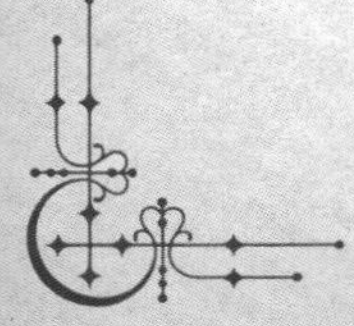

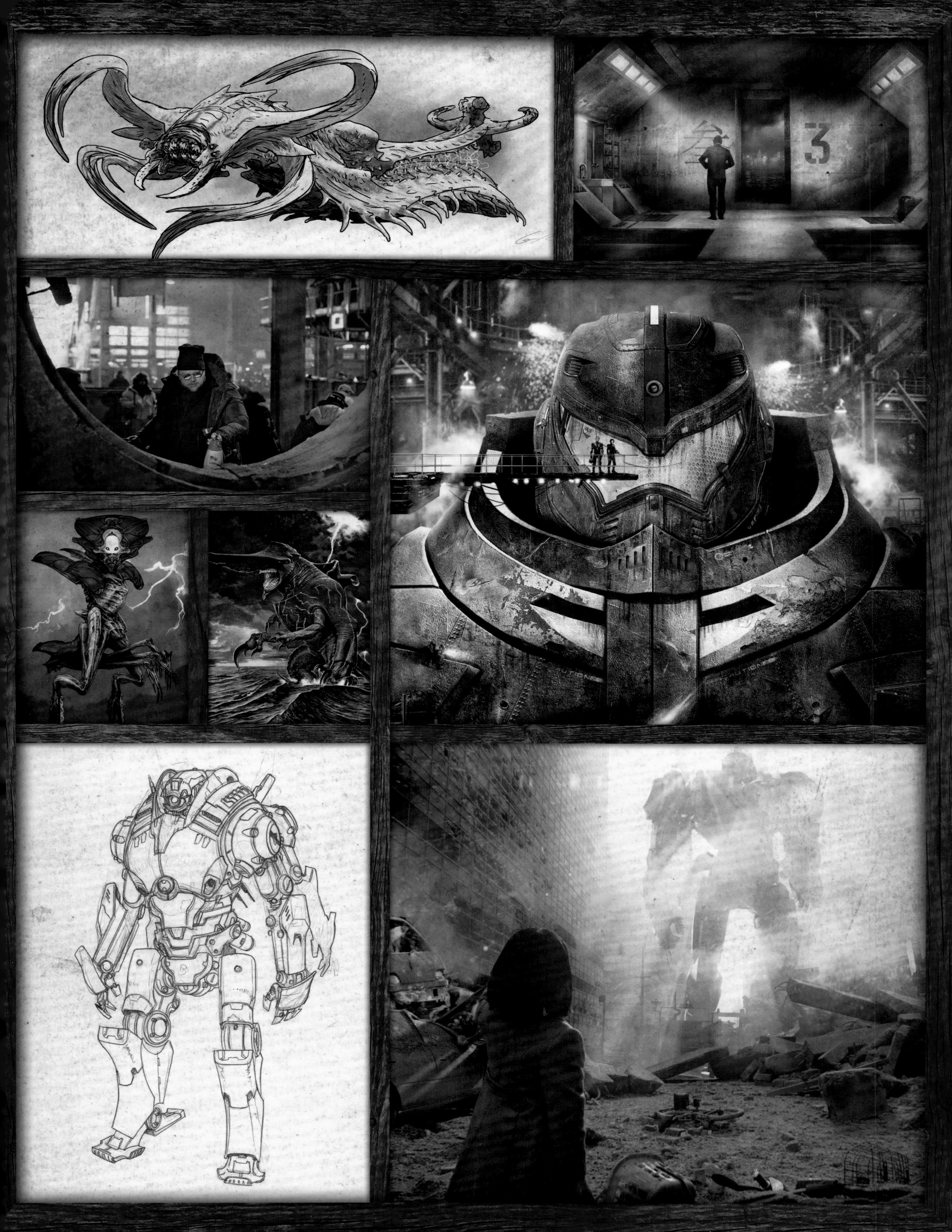
3

- Ultra Primes (T1.9) 14, 16, 20, 24
28, 32, 40, 50, 65, 85, 100, 135, 160 mm en ambas unidades
Macro Primes (T21) 16, 24, 40 mm, Variable Primes (T2.2)
16-30 mm 29-60 mm, 55-105 mm zooms 15-40 mm, 28-76 mm
17-80 mm 24, 290 mm ambas unid.

- En el FB Tokyo
el zapato
- Lluvia de
- En el campo
es lluvio
las líneas
las horizontales
y el castillo
potentes son
Los cañones
mando
infructuosamente
de las
- La confusión
batalla tendrá
en constante
y sensibles a

colores fríos salvo
en la mano de Mako.
cenizas grises y lentas.
de batalla todo
y sangre y lodo
más fuertes son
y a el bosque
las líneas más
las verticales.
destrozan el bosque
este intenta
detener el avance
tropas enemigas.
presa a la
a ambos ejércitos
estado de alerta
cualquier ruido
de cantera -

"Mako on the stairs"

- Usar el reloj de la guerra para marcar el tiempo con noticias en el último tercio de la película.
- "Don't let your feet touch the ground" de Ash Koley.
- La Bestia temía ser vulnerable y se aislaba del mundo buscándolo en sus libros y sus mapas,

—Ultra Primes (T1.9) 14, 16, 20, 24
28, 32, 40, 50, 65, 85, 100, 135, 160 mm for each unit Macro Primes (T21) 16, 24, 40 mm, Variable Primes (T2.2)
16–30 mm 29–60 mm, 55–105 mm zooms 15–40 mm, 28–76 mm
17–80 mm 24, 290 mm, each unit.

—Cold colors in the Tokyo FB except for the shoe in Mako's hand.

—Rain of slow, gray ash

—On the battlefield everything is blood and mud. The strongest lines are the horizontal ones and in the forest and the castle the most powerful lines are vertical. The cannons destroy the forest when they try unsuccessfully to halt the advance of the enemy troops.

—The confusion interrupts the battle, putting both armies in a constant state of alert, sensitive to the slightest sound.

"Mako on the stairs"

—Use the clock of war to mark time with news in last third of the film.

—"Don't let your feet touch the ground" by Ash Koley.

—The Beast was afraid of becoming vulnerable. He isolated himself from the world, poring over his books and maps.

–When is the right time to say good-bye? How can we know if we're unaware of the host's identity? How to know if we are midway through the meal or if it has already come to an end?

–I'm a father but I still feel like a son, I'm an adult but my fears are those of a child. I'm alone but I live among many, I feel like time is running out when everything is just getting started

–The dark fairy hated the prince because she loved him with a passion.

–Always say what you think, always do what you say, and know what makes you happy. Live or die abiding by firmly made decisions, doing what you think is the right thing.

Mako in the rain, sans helicopter

Notebook 5, Page 10

(FAR RIGHT) Del Toro's notebook sketch of Mako Mori's first appearance, alone in the rain, inspired costume designer Kate Hawley (RIGHT).

MSZ: So *Pacific Rim* is part of a new notebook, which includes notes you made while working on *The Hobbit*, correct?

GDT: Well, what happened is, I lost a lot of the rhythm of working in the notebooks during *The Hobbit*, because I was so afraid—I'm still afraid—of carrying that notebook. I used to grab my notebook and travel with it everywhere and make annotations, but with *The Hobbit*, secrecy was so paramount I was paranoid about leaving it behind in a coffee shop. So I stopped carrying it. And to this day, I have it at home, but until I finish that notebook, I cannot carry a notebook, because the three movies haven't come out yet.

MSZ: How did you get back into working in the notebooks for *Pacific Rim*?

GDT: I was really, really invested in this image of the girl with the red shoe [*opposite*]. Because it's something that I felt was very iconic, and it defined the entire palette of the movie for me. The movie is incredibly saturated with color, but I wanted Mako's flashback to have few colors and feel almost monochromatic. Blue is dominant in her memories and it permeates her in the present—her hair is streaked with that blue. She is marred by the past. I also wanted her introduction scene [*above*] to be monochromatic and we art directed that whole introductory sequence in the rain to be only concrete gray, cyan, and gold. So the two sequences are linked.

But once Mako and Raleigh connect, more colors begin to be associated with them. The first Drift they do is all in blue. After that, when they are fighting in Hong Kong, all these colors start coming in, and we end up with them immersed in a sea of red. And the red is the same red as the red of her shoe.

I think that if you're going to go crazy with colors in a movie like we do in *Pacific Rim*, you have to have peaks and valleys; you have to have places where the eye can rest. And so we have that regular red, for when Raleigh and Mako connect. And then when they are not connecting, or when they are alone, they each have another color. Mako's palette is cold, while Raleigh's color code for when he is by himself is rust and grime and amber.

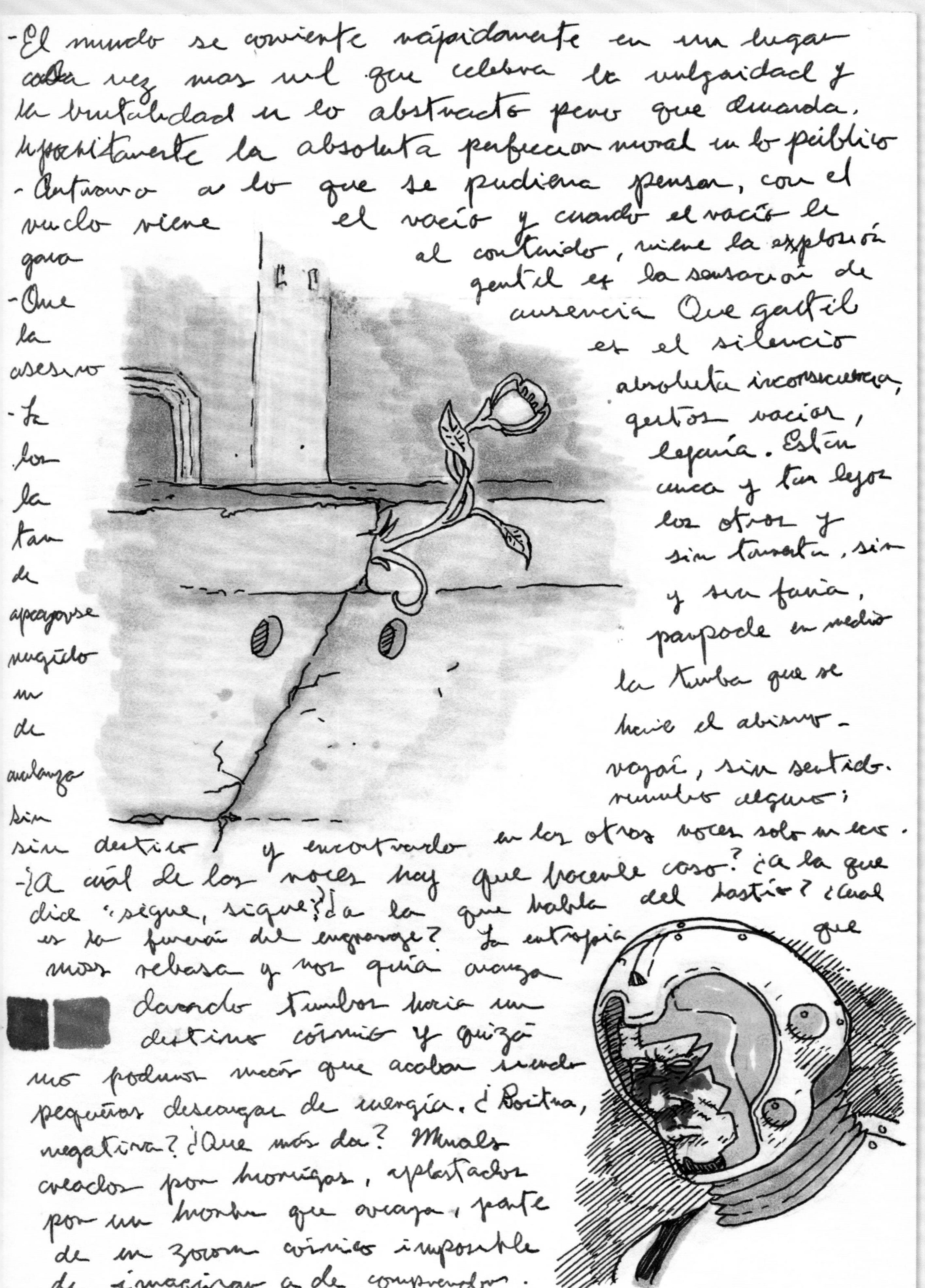

NOTEBOOK 5, PAGE 9

–The world is rapidly becoming a more and more vile place that celebrates vulgarity and brutality in the abstract but that hypocritically demands absolute moral perfection in public

–Sooner than you might think, with noise comes emptiness. The explosion occurs when emptiness trumps substance

–How pleasant is the sensation of absence. What a pleasing assassin is silence

–Absolute inconsequence, empty gestures, distance. To be so close and yet so distant from others; to fade away without thunder, without a roar and without fury. Without a vessel, without meaning, without a clear direction; without a destiny, finding nothing but echoes in the voices of other people.

–To which one of the voices should we pay attention? To the one that says "keep going, keep going"? To the one that speaks of tedium? What is the purpose of the gears? Entropy overcomes and guides us as we lurch along toward our cosmic destiny; perhaps, the most we can do is end our days as tiny discharges of energy. Positive, negative? What difference does it make? Murals made by ants, crushed under the feet of a man trudging along, part of an incomprehensible, indecipherable cosmic joke.

The code in the Kaiju's viscera should be fascinating. Blues, iridescence; translucent and opalescent. Bioluminescent blood should come from the glow sticks; this would help with the FX brain

–Before the written language in Cluva events were recorded by knotting cords or making notches on a stick (SINOGRAMS is what the symbols are called) 6 categories. XIANGXING, ZHISHI, HUIYI, XIESHENG, ZUANZAU, *and* JIAJIE —PICTOGRAMS.

–*Wide-angle lenses to capture the CHARACTER and the SURROUNDINGS in the same frame 18 mm*

–*For* Beauty and the Beast, *the* Age of Reason, *which is the period during the eighteenth century in which reason is enthroned above spirituality, which witnesses the birth of Diderot's Encyclopedia. It's in this spirit that the United States is born as a new country.*

–*Perhaps it might also be worthwhile to set it in the following period: during the Napoleonic Wars, when reason has been abandoned but spirituality has not been recovered or reclaimed.*

–BOXING FIST FIGHT *in the middle of a battlefield in F.*

–*Gathering pages from her encyclopedia Bella finds something ancient and magic.*

"Sprouting Boy"

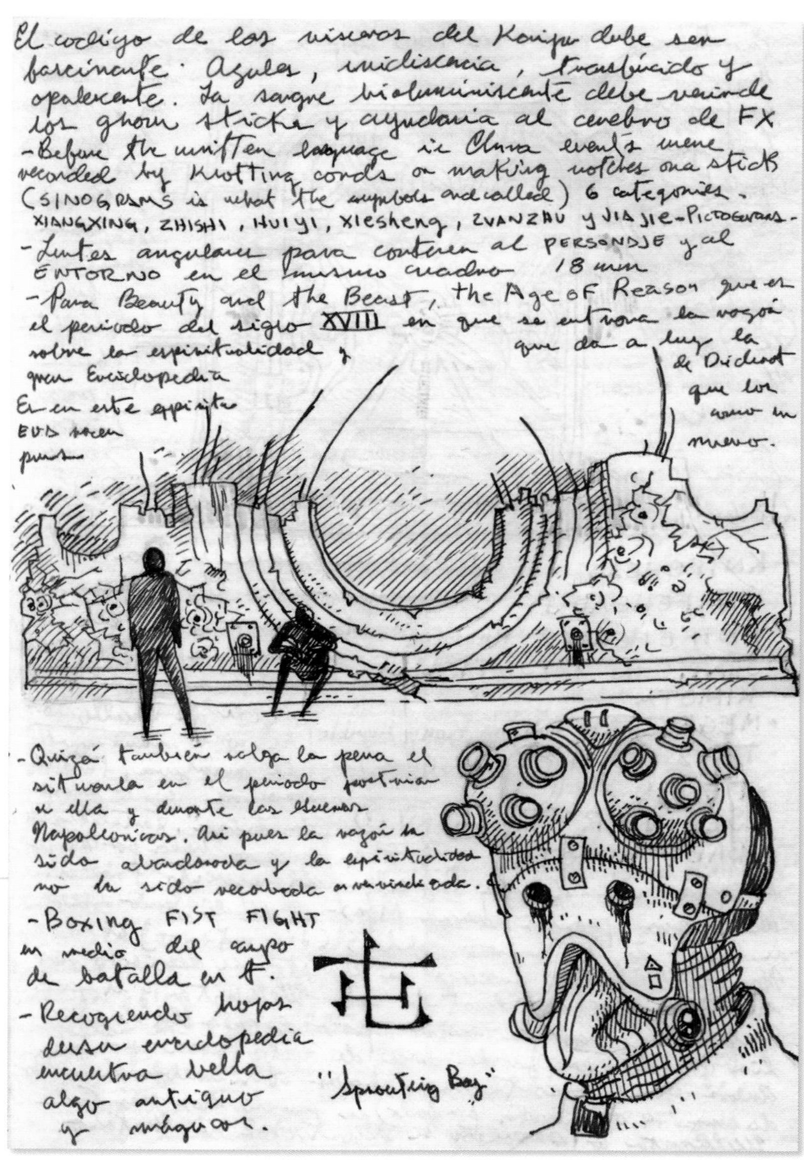

Notebook 5, Page 5

MSZ: What can you say about the flower here [*opposite*]? Does it resonate at all with the flower in *Pan's Labyrinth*?

GDT: The idea in both films is that the flower tells the story. But I abandoned the idea in the middle of shooting *Pacific Rim* because I thought we wouldn't have time. When we started shooting, the screenplay was about 130 pages long. That meant at least a 2-hour-and-45-minute movie for me.

But the idea was that the entire command center would be made of concrete and metal. And I wanted Raleigh and Mako to talk about themselves to one another, in the heart of the rubble. Originally, they were going to talk on a ledge outside, and she would notice a flower that was blooming in the concrete and she would say, "Oh, the poor thing, it won't live." And then, at the end of the movie, we would go back to the flower, and it would be blooming.

MSZ: It looks like there is an image of the rubble on the facing page. Can you say something about that?

GDT: I love finding beauty and symmetry in ruins, and I thought this crumbling half-pipe could look almost like a throne. I also used a circle for the throne in *Hellboy II*, which I think has a certain inherent magnificence. I wanted both scenes to feel operatic, if you will.

MSZ: And does the symbol on this page mean anything?

GDT: I wanted a symbol for the Kaiju organ harvester, Hannibal Chau, and I wanted it to look sort of like an Oriental character, even though it's just his initials. So that's an "H" and a "C."

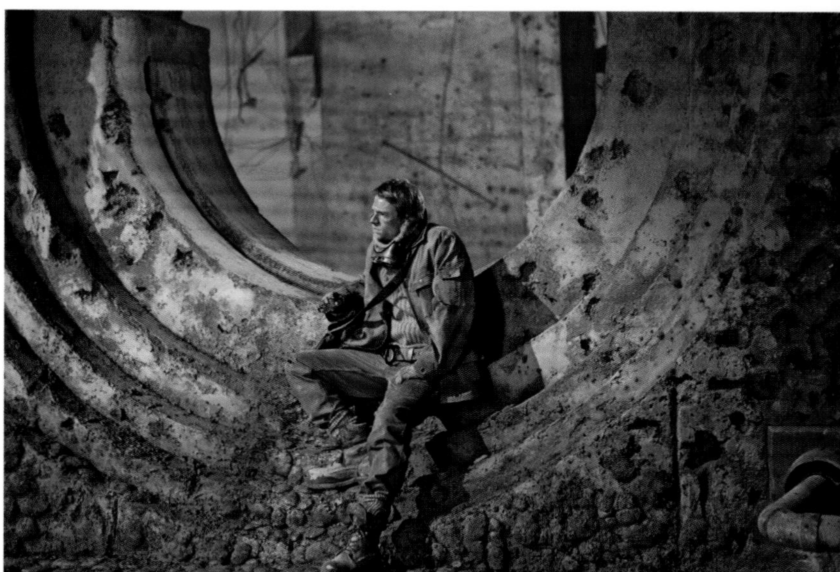

(TOP) Del Toro had a clear idea early on that a broken, massive circular opening could serve as a symbolic throne for his reluctant hero Raleigh Beckett (Charlie Hunnam) (ABOVE).

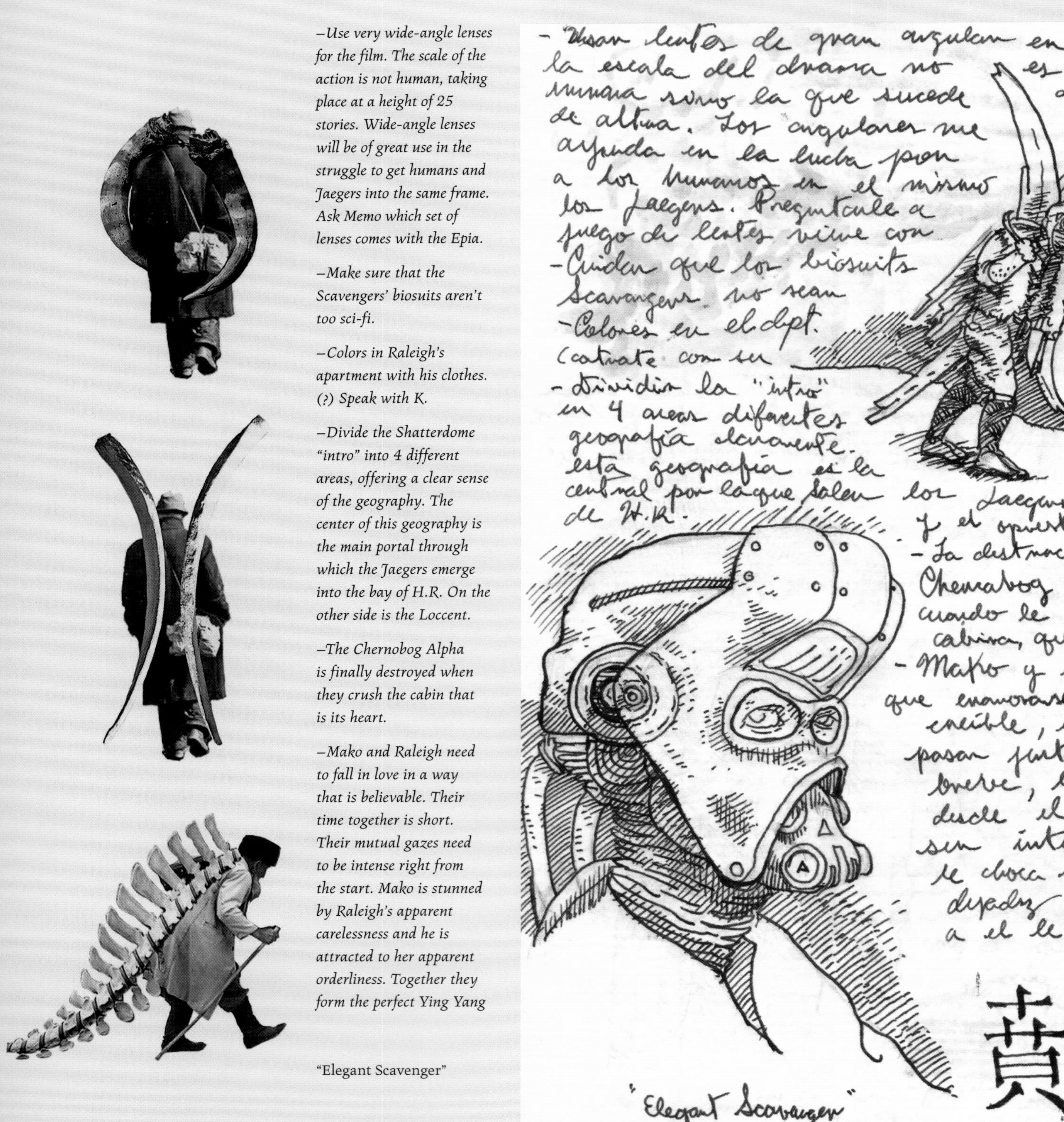

–Use very wide-angle lenses for the film. The scale of the action is not human, taking place at a height of 25 stories. Wide-angle lenses will be of great use in the struggle to get humans and Jaegers into the same frame. Ask Memo which set of lenses comes with the Epia.

–Make sure that the Scavengers' biosuits aren't too sci-fi.

–Colors in Raleigh's apartment with his clothes. (?) Speak with K.

–Divide the Shatterdome "intro" into 4 different areas, offering a clear sense of the geography. The center of this geography is the main portal through which the Jaegers emerge into the bay of H.R. On the other side is the Loccent.

–The Chernobog Alpha is finally destroyed when they crush the cabin that is its heart.

–Mako and Raleigh need to fall in love in a way that is believable. Their time together is short. Their mutual gazes need to be intense right from the start. Mako is stunned by Raleigh's apparent carelessness and he is attracted to her apparent orderliness. Together they form the perfect Ying Yang

"Elegant Scavenger"

Notebook 5, Page 4

MSZ: So you have a note here saying you didn't want the scavengers to be too high-tech.

GDT: I wanted them to be like seventeenth-century whalers. Their tools of the trade are blades and wicker baskets. Everything about them is a little funky—like steam-powered or clunky. So they are really, really low-tech. Even the robots and the control mechanisms in *Pacific Rim* have an analog component, which for me is very important.

MSZ: And the Kaiju here?

GDT: I wanted to evoke a whale. It was going to open and have another head inside. But it ended up looking like a crocodile—Francisco Ruiz Velasco took it in a completely different direction.

MSZ: And what about the note, "Kaiju cutie?" You've discussed the idea of giving monsters personalities, making them somehow sympathetic.

GDT: I just thought he looked cute, you know? But I love all the Kaiju in *Pacific Rim*. My favorite is Leatherback, the gorilla-like

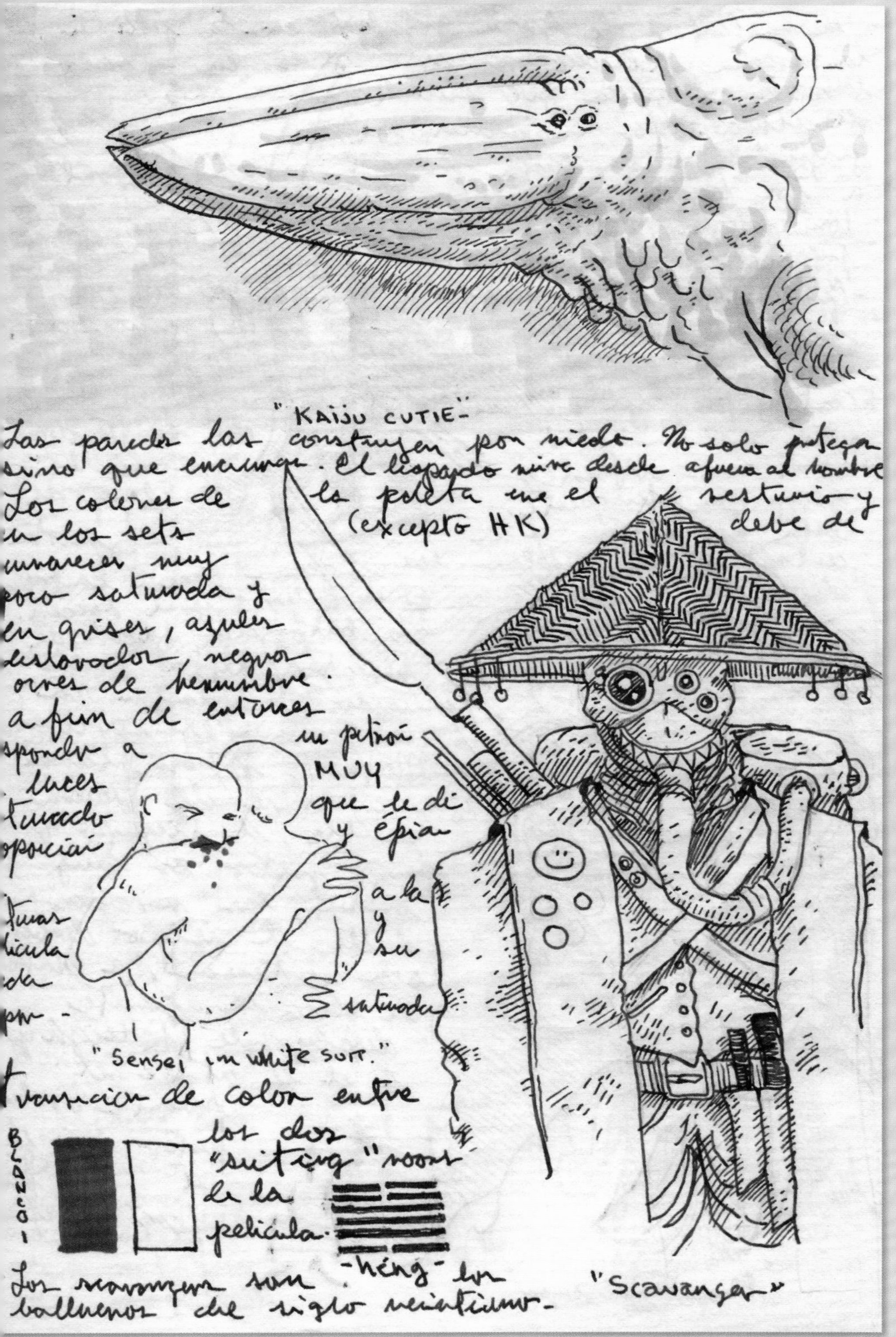

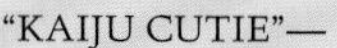

Notebook 5, Page 3

"KAIJU CUTIE"—

–Walls are built out of fear. They not only protect but also shut in. The leopard looks at the man from outside

–The color palette of the costumes and sets (except HK) should be very lightly saturated with grays, faded blues and shadowy blacks and ochres to respond to a pattern of VERY saturated lighting that can give the film epic stature and the feel of an adventure movie with super-saturated colors

"sensei in white suit."

–color transition between the two "suiting" *rooms in the film.*

RED/WHITE

–héng–

–The scavengers are the whalers of the twenty-first century—

"scavenger"

(OPPOSITE, RIGHT & LEFT) Del Toro drew on Renaissance dress codes and historic whaling gear to keep the Kaiju scavengers in the film low-tech. (OPPOSITE, LEFT & ABOVE) Concepts of the scavenger by Kate Hawley closely followed del Toro's direction.

one. I voiced three Kaijus in the movie, and Leatherback is the one I voiced most. Every time he moves, I'm complaining about weight. Like, I was actually saying the words, but then we distorted the sounds. I was going, "Oh, I've got to lose weight. Oh, I'm so heavy. I shouldn't have eaten that last pilot." I don't know how much of that is in the final mix, but when I was doing the sounds, I was complaining actively and thinking, *This guy really hates being out of the water*, because that happens to me when I get out of a pool. I go, "Shit, I'm heavy!"

MSZ: And what is the difference between the elegant scavenger and the regular scavenger you've drawn here?

GDT: Well the elegant scavenger is sort of like the head of the scavengers. In the Renaissance, you indicated your status by how much fabric you wore. The more fabric you wasted, the higher your status. So if you look at Tudor clothes, there's layer upon layer upon layer. And I like the idea of the elegant scavenger having four or five layers to his mask and his clothing using a lot of fabric.

Sept. 9, 2011 A TERRIBLE DAY *due to movement in the foot of the p.*

–"Is there anyone else here with us . . ." *she asks after having seen the prince in the palace garden in the moonlight. Eventually she finds the abandoned pelt.*

–"You may wish for whatever you want, and it will be yours." *There is no limit to Beauty's desires, the Beast has only one*

–"Love him who loves you" *the prince advises*

–Soldiers who are <u>RETURNING</u> *from war or* <u>GOING</u> *to war*

–She finds the painting of the prince as a human.

–The Beast carves puppets and automatons. He puts on a show for her.

–Birds and monkeys—

–Gargoyles and chimney—

–The furniture moves.

–Discuss the Beast's pelt.

–He gives her two magic rings.

–He gives her the entire key chain and warns her never to open the door to one room in particular which is locked every night and in which he leaves his abandoned pelt before going to the garden to speak with the fairy which cast a spell on him

–The specter of War needs to hover in the evil atmosphere of Beauty's village

–The castle exists in the center of a labyrinth of trees

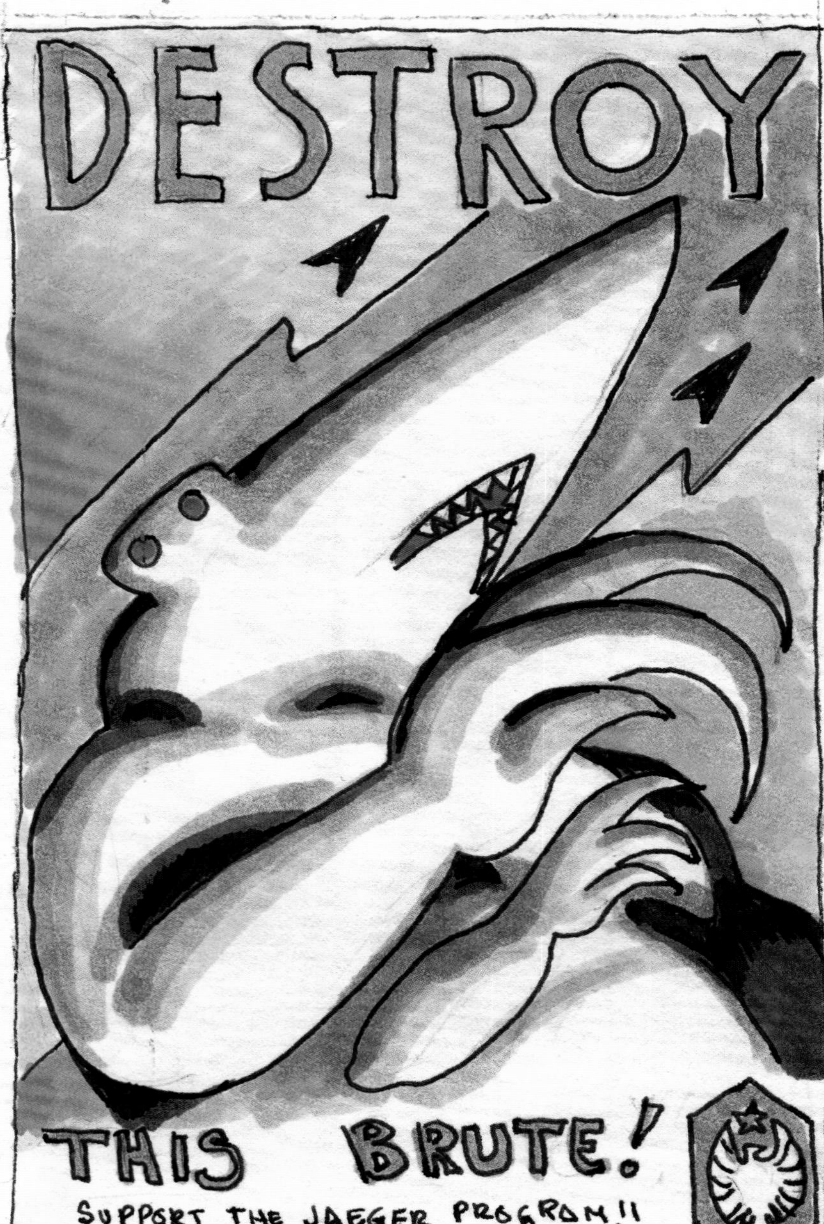

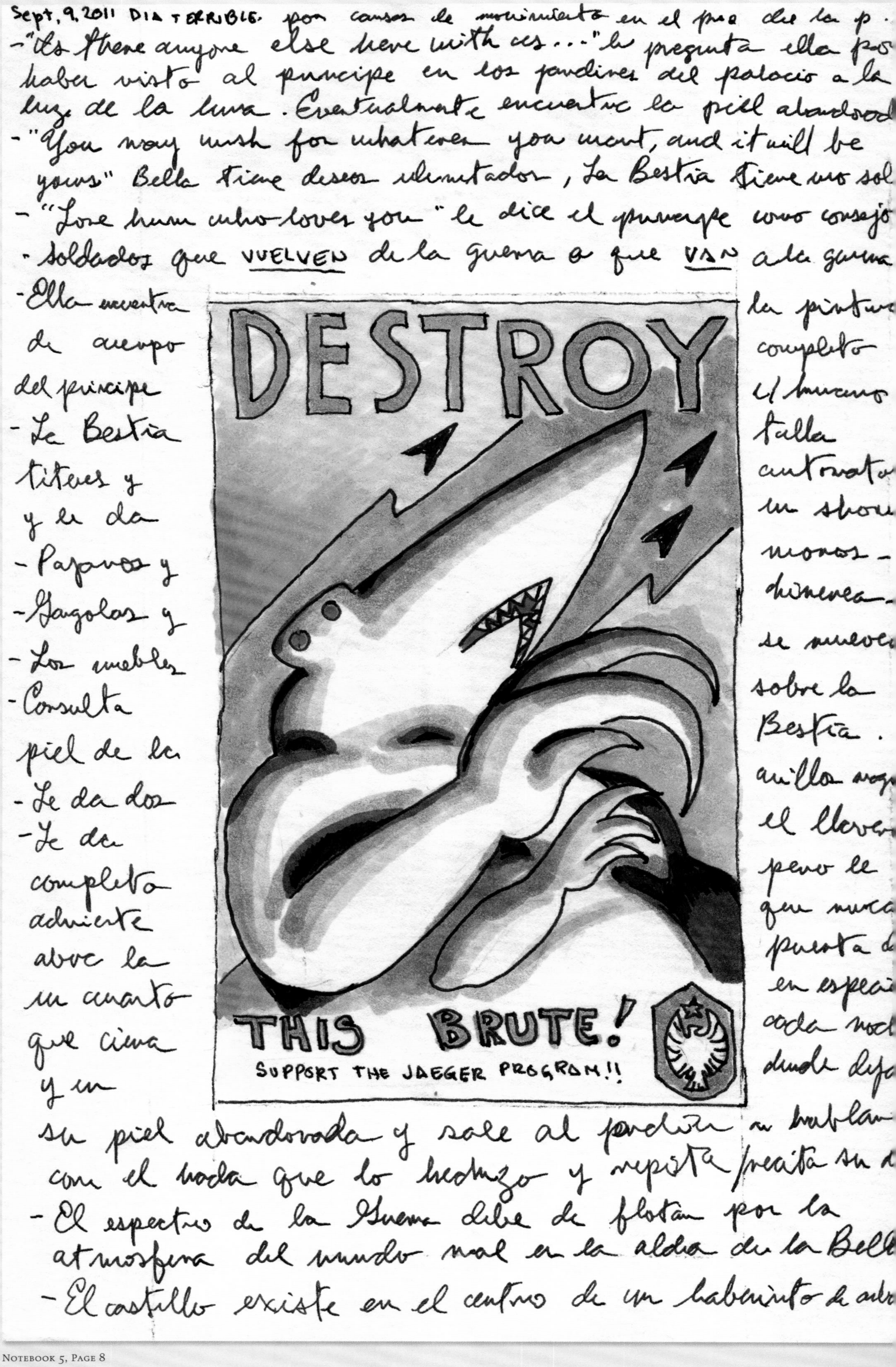

DESTROY
THIS MAD BRUTE!
YOUR COURAGE WILL BRING US VICTORY
THE SUCCESS OF THE PAN PACIFIC ALLIANCEAGAINST THE KAIJU DEPENDS ON YOU.
OUR ENEMIES ARE UNLIKE ANY WE'VE ENCOUNTERED BEFORE. HELP US BEAT THEM.

(OPPOSITE) Del Toro wanted to invent motivational propaganda for the film's war against alien invaders. (ABOVE) Keith Thompson's poster design, infused with Russian Futurist motifs, followed del Toro's original direction but was eventually abandoned in favor of a different approach.

MSZ: So this poster [*opposite*] is an odd blend of monster movies, Russian Futurism, wartime propaganda. What was your thinking here?

GDT: I like Soviet and Eastern European propaganda that is very graphic. And for *Pacific Rim*, we decided to explore a lot of World War II references since we wanted to convey the nobility of the wartime effort in the film. So we designed bomber nose art, uniforms, and propaganda posters, although we didn't use this one [*above*] in the end.

Guillermo

Cabinet of Curiosities

Unfinished Projects

Del Toro

* To . . . go OUTSIDE, WAIT IN WOULD . . . BE SUICIDE. Exactly . . .

* *Who is X . . . Why do you need to know? Bring us something for him . . . Ah, I am . . . BANG.*

* *Cell phones cause cancer.*

* *Massacre at the drive-in.*

* *Gynecologist who has no nose (an accident at work).*

* Who's on first *with foam rubber shit.*

* *Constant fire and smoke in the wind.*

* *Suicide on a conveyor belt.*

* *One of the child prisoners: Let me out, I won't say anything.*

* *A little girl wanders alone in a daze . . .*

* *Ernie does "weightlifting" with a hunk of meat.*

* *Ernie hides.*

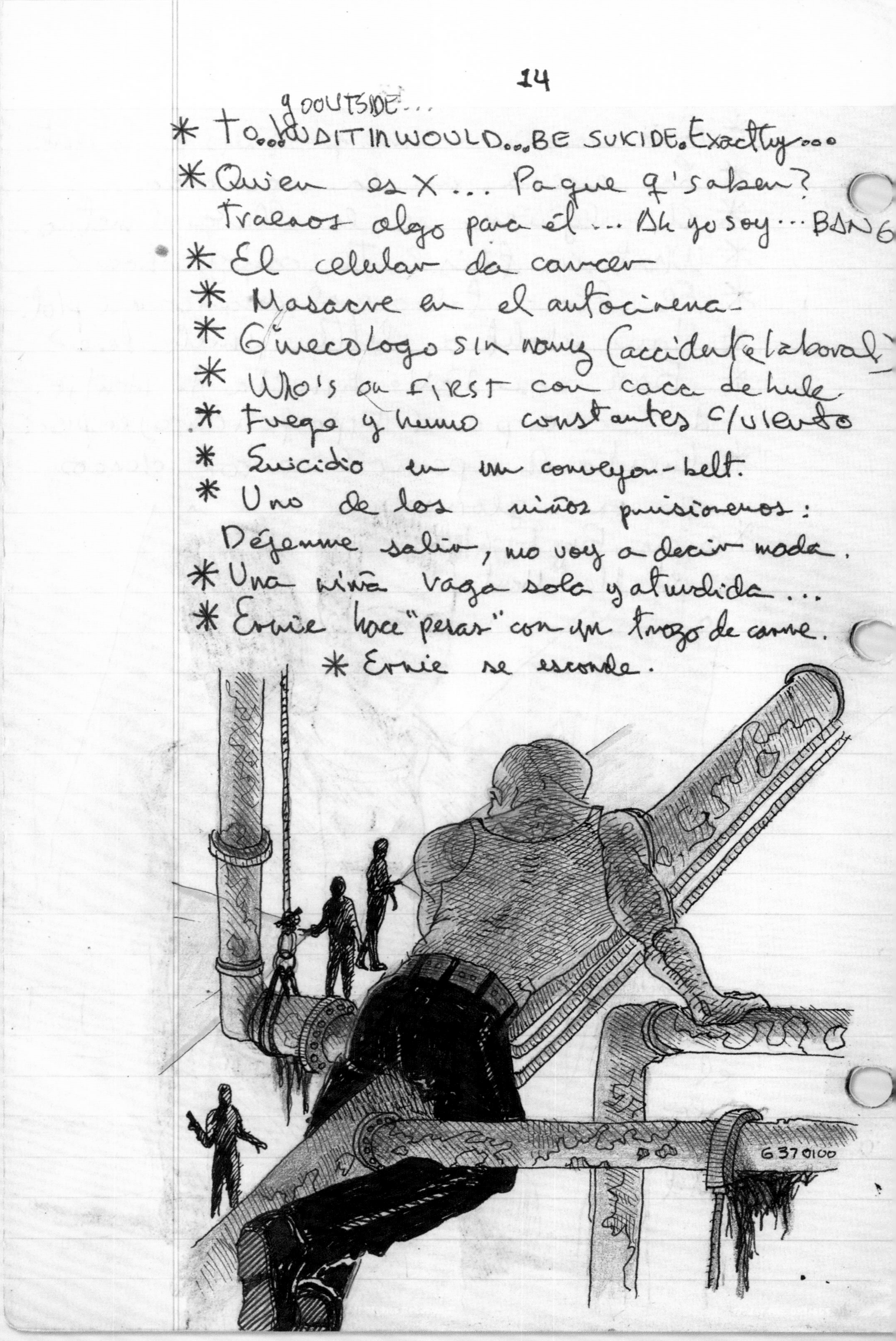

14

* To... go OUTSIDE... WAIT IN WOULD... BE SUKIDE. Exactly...

* Quien es X... Pa que q'saben? Traenos algo para él... Ah yo soy... BANG

* El celular da cancer

* Masacre en el autocinema.

* Ginecologo sin nariz (accidente laboral)

* Who's on FIRST con caca de hule.

* Fuego y humo constantes c/viento

* Suicidio en un conveyor-belt.

* Uno de los niños prisioneros: Déjenme salir, no voy a decir nada.

* Una niña vaga sola y aturdida...

* Ernie hace "pesas" con un trozo de carne.

* Ernie se esconde.

MEAT MARKET

* *The gynecologist alone with the lids of Campbell's soup (or sardine) cans.*

* *Cricket or soccer game with "goals" made of flesh.*

* *Cthulu "bottled" in a glass jar and "fed" by columns in the RUINS.*

* *The "birth of Venus" with the shell and all but also with monsters and Bactrian camels.*

HOC MOMENTUM ETIAM TRANSIBIT.

•• *Originally made at 12:44 on 3/3/93.*

* Fixed. Baby Ernie M/M *(according to IMCINE)*

DAY of NON-RIEL and NON-CRONOS commercial

Bertha spoke with Nacho Durán. Discouragement.

* Great Expectations. *MAGWITCH:* a convict, Miss Havisham (OF SATIS HOUSE), STELLA. PIP whose journey we follow to manhood. *The story begins one gray afternoon in a cemetery/* "I will give you a reason to fight" *to start a fight.*

•• *New version 2/5/95 How different!!*

Blue Notebook, Page 1

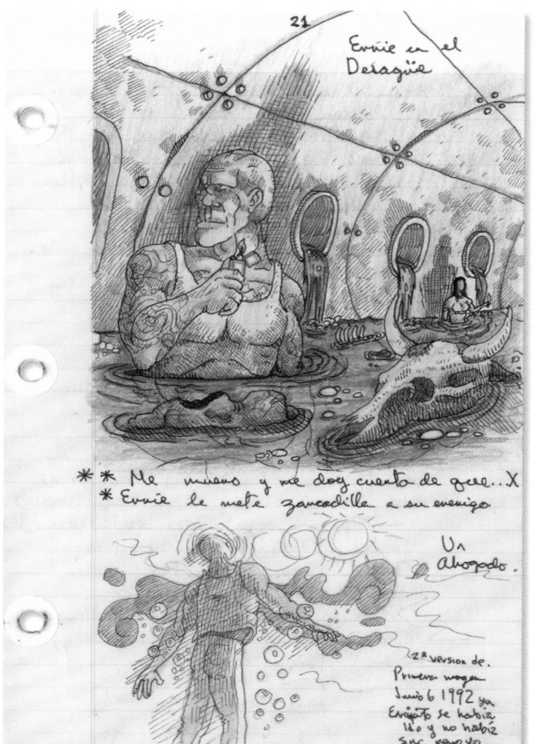

Blue Notebook, Page 21

Ernie in the Drainpipe.

** *I move and realize that . . . X*

* *Ernie causes his enemy to slip.*

A drowned man.

2nd version of. First image June 6, 1992 already Enriquito has already left and there was no Sinc. but I started editing.

● **GDT:** *Meat Market* is a story that is really close to my heart. At one point, it was called *Meat Market: A Love Story*. It was supposed to be like *Phantom of the Opera* set in a huge meat processing plant. The super-commercial pitch is: "*Hamlet* in a meat market, by way of *Phantom of the Opera*."

Ernie, our star and son of a meat-processing mogul, falls in love with Ofelia. And Ernie's uncle has killed his father to get the meat processing plant. But Ernie has been blamed for the murder and goes and hides in the sewers full of chunks of rotting meat. Eventually, he comes back to rescue Ofelia.

And I was going to have Ron Perlman play Ernie. So I tried to write it for him. And the idea was that Ernie was this baby who had been dropped and had his face broken on the concrete. They had to put him together the best they could, and he became sort of a mixture of the Phantom of the Opera and the Frankenstein monster. If I had Ron at age thirty-five, I would endeavor to find the money to actually make it.

(PREVIOUS PAGES) Notebook 3, Pages 28A and 28B.

MEPHISTO'S BRIDGE

GDT: *Mephisto's Bridge* was based on a novel called *Spanky* by Christopher Fowler. It was a Faustian tale about a guy who makes a deal with a devil, but the devil doesn't want his soul, he wants his body. He says, "You have no soul, but I can use your body to live for another hundred years."

The main character is this guy who thought he deserved everything but did nothing to get it, expecting that because he is a good guy, he should get the girl, the money, the car, the apartment. So this demon comes in and offers to help him get all that, and then he gets it and it's unsatisfactory because he didn't earn it. And the demon knows this, and he says, "You didn't want the car; you wanted the respect. You didn't want the girl; you wanted the love. You didn't want the apartment; you wanted the reward for your efforts."

Spanky, the demon, was this slender, almost beautiful creature that was kind of made of moving pieces when he was out of his host. It's one of my favorite designs I've ever made. I wanted him to be very ornate. Right here [*opposite*], pre-anything, are the roots of the Faun, and the *Hellboy* creatures, and Hellboy himself. This is where it all comes from, this basic form.

When Spanky is in his host, a transformation occurs. For that design, we started archangels, which are represented with a mouth on each feather, or with an eye on each feather. And the idea was that each of the demon's feathers would have an eye that represented a soul he had taken. So he was a walking epic. He was literally a lot of people together.

Mephisto's Bridge is one of my favorite things I've ever written and has some of my favorite designs, too.

** Spanky with wings (?) Based on Odilon Redon.*

The wings against the light, blocking the sun with "Flare"

** Someone scratches or breaks the glass in a window that they're going to open when they remember that it's the 9th floor!!!*

** Reinforce or change the* Billboard Fight *A III*

** Wings with layered colors or uniformly steel black, "blued" like a gun.*

** Rusty pendulum clocks hanging from a sheet on the roof.*

Step over a cross at the b.o/ritual.

Could be of Shadow/Light.

BLUE NOTEBOOK, PAGE 161

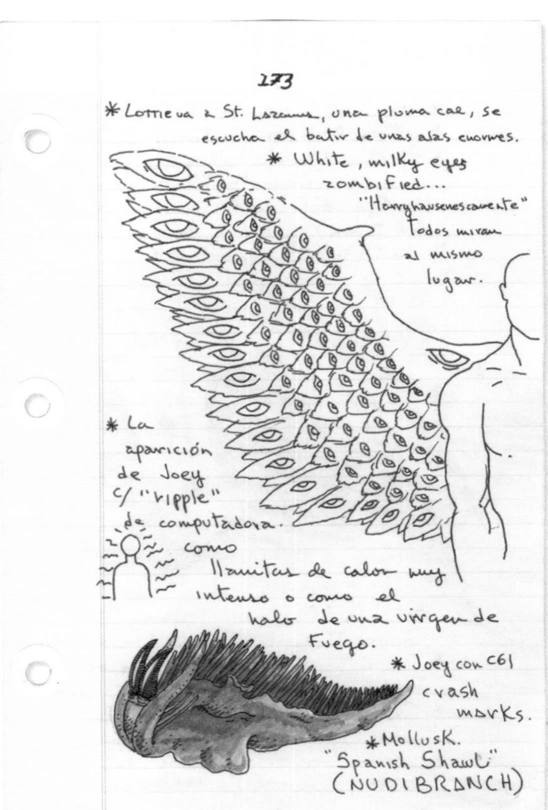

BLUE NOTEBOOK, PAGE 173

** Lottie goes to St. Lazarus, a feather falls out, the beating of enormous wings is heard.*

* White, milky eyes zombified . . . *"Harryhausenly" Everyone looks at the same place.*

** The apparition of Joey with computer "ripple" like intensely colored little flames and like the halo of a fire virgin.*

** Joey with* CGI crash marks.

* Mollusk. "Spanish Shawl" (NUDIBRANCH)

* *Voice-activated* light dimmer *in his APT*

113

* En su DEPA light dimmer c/voz activate
* "I'll race you little Faust..."
* Spanky tiene "patas" de tipo tentacular que se "abren" en dos partes c/u.
* 1 F/STOP mas para MONITOR c/un magazine dummy.
* Sometimes we trick people this way or the other but sometimes... truth is the tool to use, as simple as that"
* You're a couple of years 2 LATE.
* Whole new ball game pal.
* Y're like me You are ... X.

Spanky tiene "MOVIL" toda la textura en la piel..

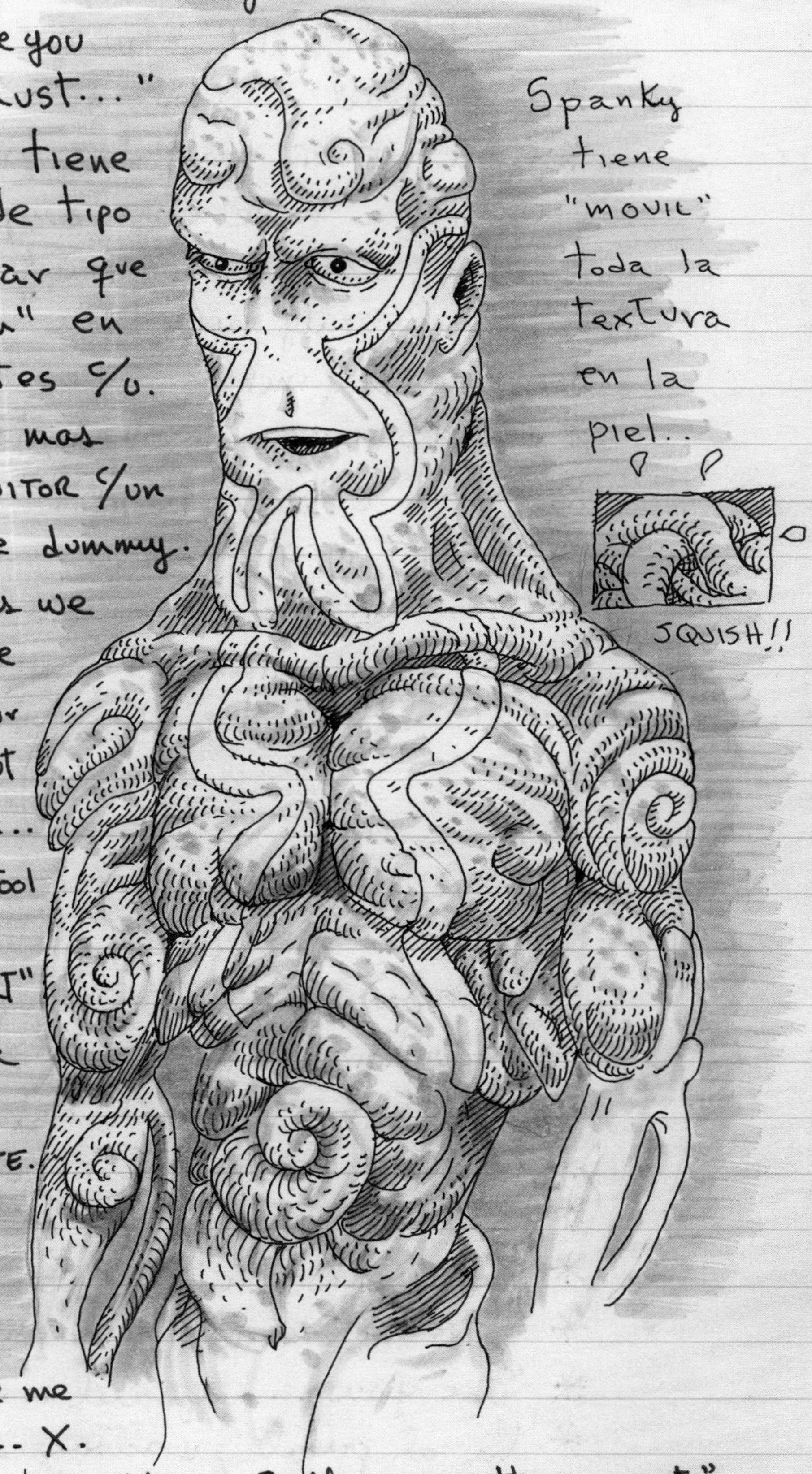

SQUISH!!

* Spanky: "Jus' Call me a therapist"
* "Martyn, I haven't been all bad 2 U have I?"

* "I'll race you little Faust . . ."

* *Spanky has tentacle-like "legs" that "open up" into two parts.*

* IF/STOP *but for a* MONITOR *with a* magazine dummy.

* Sometimes we trick people this way or the other but sometimes . . . truth is the tool to use, as simple as that"

* You're a couple of years 2 late.

* Whole new ball game pal.

* Y're like me, You are . . . X.

* Spanky: "Jus' Call me a therapist"

* "Martyn, I haven't been all bad 2 U have I?"

The texture of Spanky's skin is "in motion."

SQUISH!!

THE LIST OF SEVEN

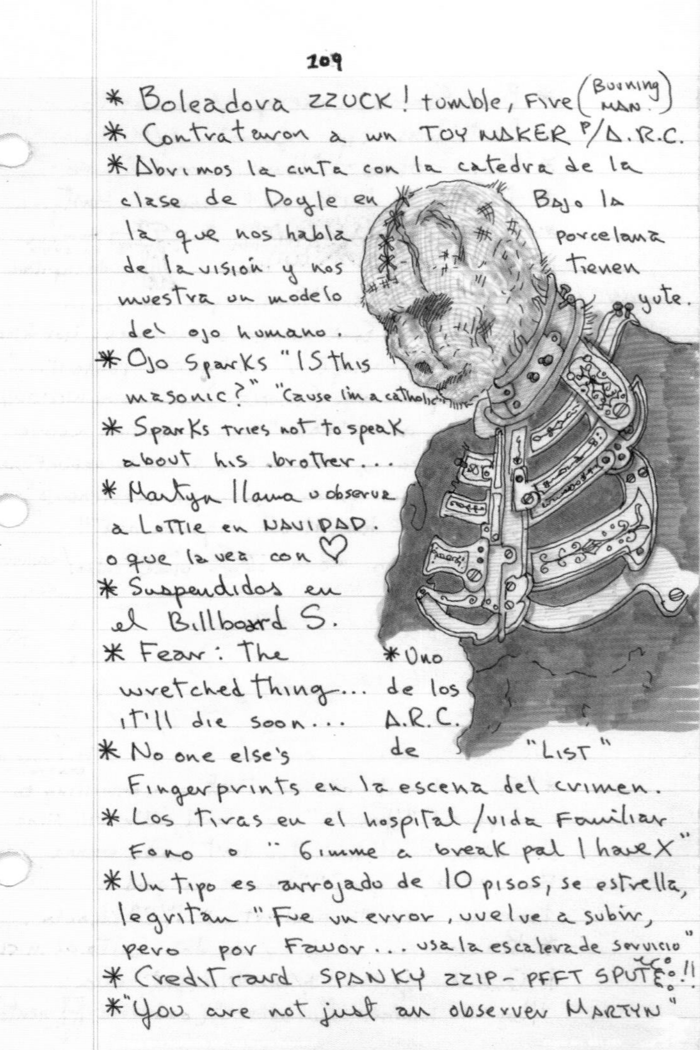

* *Bolas ZZUCK!* tumble, fire *(Burning Man)*

* *They hired a TOY MAKER for A.R.C.*

* *We open the tape with the Doyle-like professor on which he speaks to us of his vision and shows us a model of a human eye. They have jute beneath the porcelain.*

* *Take note, Sparks:* "IS this Masonic? "Cause I'm a Catholic."

* Sparks tries not to speak about his brother . . .

* *Martyn calls or observes Lottie on CHRISTMAS DAY or he sees her with a* ♥

* *Hanging from the* Billboard *S.*

Blue Notebook, Page 109

* Fear: the wretched thing . . . it'll die soon . . .

* *One of the A.R.C. from* "List"

* No one else's Fingerprints *at the crime scene.*

* *The cops in the hospital/family life or* "Gimme a break pal I have X'

* *The guy is thrown from the tenth story, he crashes, they scream at him "It was a mistake, go back upstairs, but please . . . use the service stairs"*

* Credit card *SPANKY ZZIP-PFFT SPUT!!*

* "You are not just an observer MARTYN"

● **GDT:** *The List of Seven* was based on the novel by Mark Frost. He also wrote the screenplay and produced a draft that I really like. It's a fantastic steampunk adventure.

The story is about Arthur Conan Doyle before he writes his first Sherlock Holmes story. He gets tangled up with an occult society in Victorian London that is planning to assassinate Queen Victoria and substitute an automaton for Prince Eddy. The society is building sort of a doomsday machine in a castle in the north of the United Kingdom. And I wanted to create these Caspar David Friedrich–type ruins and Piranesian spaces.

Mark is a very good writer of characters, so Conan Doyle was a really great personality in the screenplay. I love Conan Doyle and know his biography well, so I wanted to include details like the fact that he was an ophthalmologist. And the idea was that he succeeds in the movie only when he includes Holmes as a character, which is based on a secret agent for Queen Victoria named Jack Sparks, who is like a James Bond in Victorian times with all the accoutrements and the gadgets.

Guy Ritchie's *Sherlock Holmes* had a lot of the energy, which is similar to what I wanted to do with the Holmes character in *The List of Seven*. What I kept saying to Universal was that we didn't need to shoot Holmes boringly. We needed to shoot him to suit the adventure. We are so used to having a passive intellectual—a guy who lives a monastic life. But for me, Holmes is a guy who is pensive and immobile for long periods—like, literally, he could stay in the same pose on a sofa for days, not even eating—but then, when he says, "Come with me, old chap," he comes alive and it is an adventure.

123

*SIDE VIEW "List of 7 "Doomsday Machine""

*"You are going to regret This..." Se va

* "After all That I've done For you, you reFuse me a simple Favor" Spanky en biblioteca.

* La dueña de casa/cabeza cortada en paquete:
"No permitiré que me acerquen esa "COSA". Está en la despensa"

*"Holmes" examina el cordón y los diarios y papel q/envuelve el paquete c/cabeza.

* SIDE VIEW List of 7 "Doomsday Machine"

* "You are going to regret this . . ." *He leaves*

* "After all that I've done for you, you refuse me a simple favor" *Spanky in the library.*

* *The owner of the house/severed head in a package: "I won't allow anyone to bring that "thing" near me. It's in the cupboard."*

* *"Holmes" examines the cord, the newspapers, and the paper that's wrapped around the package with the head in it.*

THE LEFT HAND OF DARKNESS

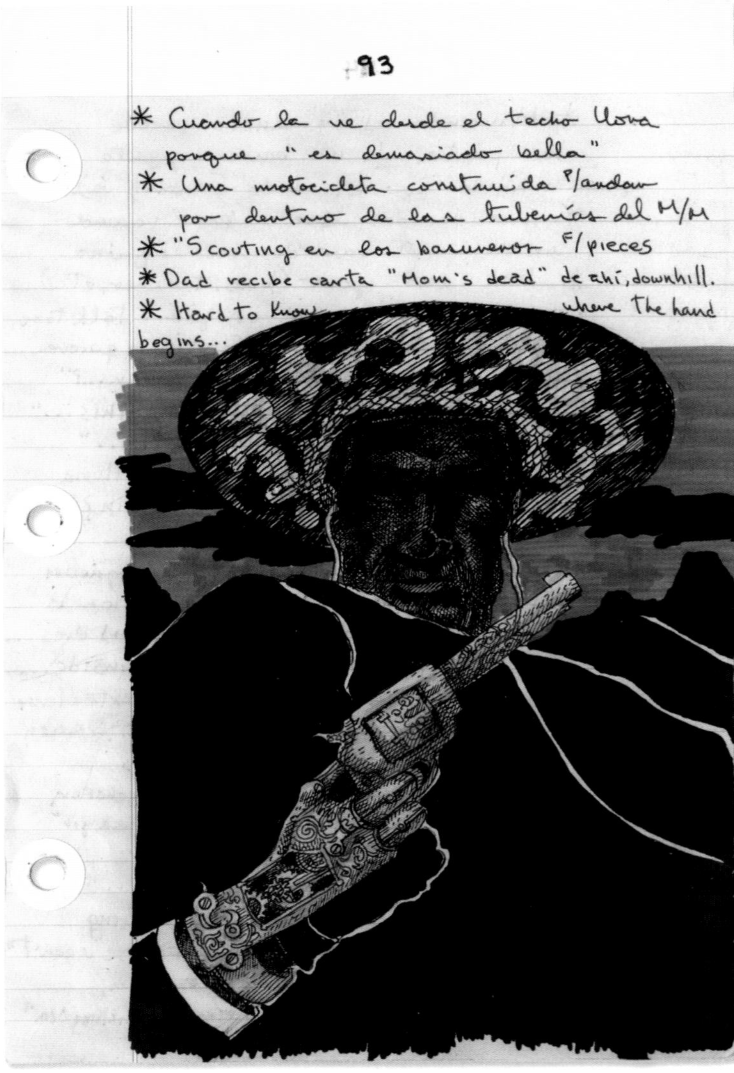

Blue Notebook, Page 93

* *When he sees her from the roof he cries because "she's too beautiful"*

* *A motorcycle built to be driven in the drainage pipes at the M/M.*

* "Scouting *in the trash dumpsters for* pieces.

* Dad *receives a letter* "Mom's dead" *from there,* downhill.

* Hard to know where the hand begins . . .

● **GDT:** *The Left Hand of Darkness* was an adaptation of *The Count of Monte Cristo* I did with Kit Carson. We started in '94, and it took us about two years to write the screenplay. And then when my dad was kidnapped in '97, I rewrote it. And all the anger I had about the kidnapping went into the Monte Cristo character. There's a great deal of personal grief in it, and I think it's the best screenplay I've ever written.

The Left Hand of Darkness is a story about vengeance, which I'm fascinated by because it is an empty act. There's this old saying, "When you seek revenge, dig two graves—one for your enemy, and one for yourself." I think revenge, when you enact it, ultimately leaves you empty. It makes you feel dirty afterward. And that was the choice we faced after the kidnapping. And we chose not to enact revenge.

But I thought an interesting way to personify vengeance would be to give the Count a mechanical hand that is not good for anything but killing. And he would say, "It's hard to know where the hand begins and the gun ends." They fuse. And the mechanical hand was solid gold and had a glass window in it so you could see the gears. This hand turned into the best part of Kroenen in *Hellboy*. There's a natural evolution.

And when the Count gets the mechanical hand, he becomes the fastest gunslinger in the West, because I had set it in Mexico, so the film became kind of a steampunk, Gothic Western. But there's a moment where the Count goes too far and becomes a monster. I wanted the audience to feel sickened at that moment by the fact that they'd been rooting for this guy for an hour and a half.

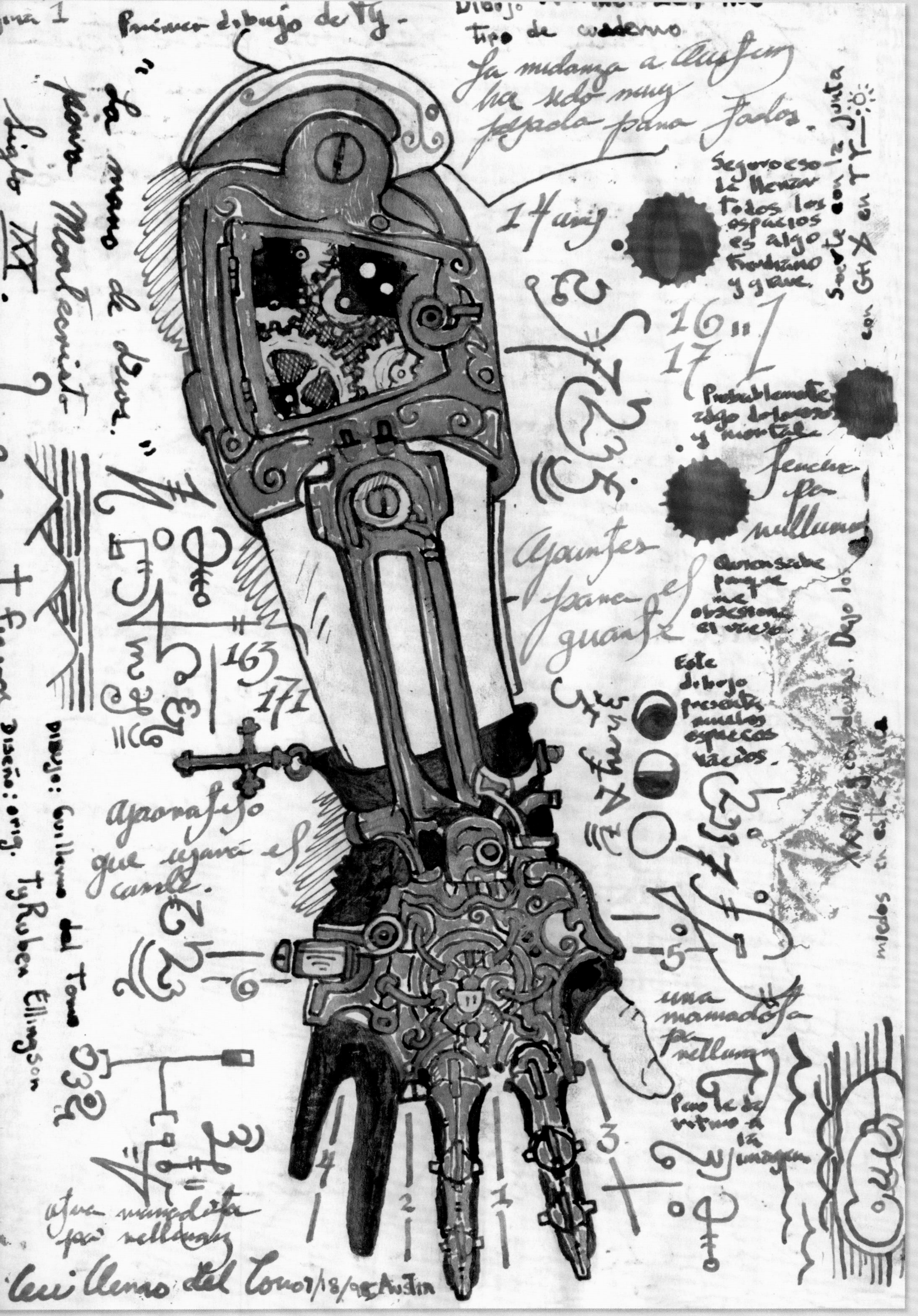

Ty's first drawing.

First drawing in new type of notebook

"The hand of God" for Montecristo

Nineteenth Century.

Drawing: Guillermo del Toro

Original Design: TyRuben Ellingson

The move to Austin was a bitch for everyone involved.

14 aug

No doubt the need to fill all available space is Freudian and very serious

Good luck in the meeting with GH in TT—O

16

17 " 1

Possibly painful and lethal

Date to fill

Who knows why I'm obsessed with the void.

Notes for the glove

This drawing presents new empty spaces.

Thirty-three and with debts. Leave your fears in this [?]

Bullshit to fill up space

But it gives rhythm to the image

Apparatus that the count will use

More bullshit to fill up space

Guillermo del Toro 7/18/98 Austin

AT THE MOUNTAINS OF MADNESS

● **GDT:** I've been trying to do *At the Mountains of Madness* for almost twenty years. Right after *Cronos*, I wrote a version of it set during the time of conquest of the New World with a bunch of conquistadors arriving at the Mayan ruins and finding another city beneath. It's never been far away for me. In terms of imagination and the creation of worlds, it's one of the most compelling projects. But I also think it's a very commercial horror film.

In the notebooks, I'm really thinking about *Mountains* more than drawing it. The funny thing is, Lovecraft excelled at being ambiguous about the way his creatures look. The creatures that he's very specific about, once you draw them, are kind of clunky. When you're drawing the flying cucumbers that are the Old Ones in *Mountains*, you have to go, "How are we going to make this work?" But the less Lovecraft describes, the more beautiful the creature. And I think the ambiguity provides the opportunity to make them shape-shifters.

What is funny, though, is that this sketch of a character in *Mountains* with tentacles over his mouth predates Davy Jones in *Pirates of the Caribbean* by about two years. When I saw *Pirates*, I was like, "OK, I'm screwed."

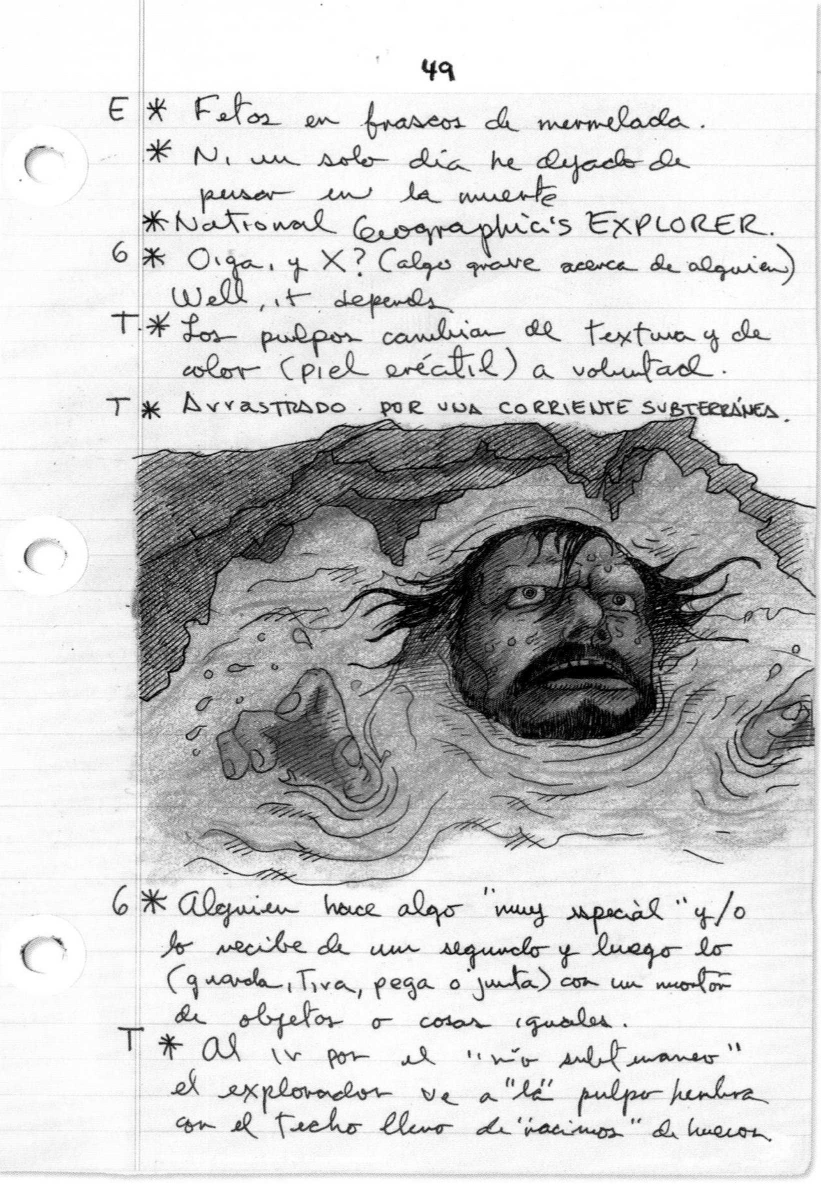

E Fetuses in jars of marmalade.*

** A day hasn't gone by in which I haven't thought about death.*

* National Geographic*'s EXPLORER.*

G Hey, what about X? (grave news about someone).* Well, it depends.

T DRAGGED UNDER BY A SUBTERRANEAN RIVER.*

G Someone does something "very special" and/or receives it at once and then (saves it with, throws it among, sticks it amid, or places it among) a pile of objects or things just like it.*

T As he goes down the "subterranean river," the explorer sees the female octopus and the ceiling littered with clusters of bones.*

Blue Notebook, Page 49

Entre la angustia y la esperanza la salida es el dolor.
Checar las locaciones p/ VOOI p/ Los M.M.
La ciudad ESCARLATA en medio de lo blanco.
- Green water / Paredes Escarlatas y corroidas
- Dietist: the key is to avoid eating large portions. Woman: ah,
yes that makes sense, D: tomatoes, lettuce, celery, non-fat
dairy products ... W: Well - that - that's good. But what about
lunch? D: Well at lunch you can give yourself a treat. W: Sure.
D: Or you'll go crazy. W: a treat! that's a good idea, thank you.
D: you are welcome. CORTE A: La tipa poniendose morada.
- a mass hallucination, suggestion or mass histeria.
- An empty shell, that is a ghost.

- Normalmente un
vivos una
El marido le
Una investigador
El fantasma
y alguien
es sólo
- Se graba en
para dar
imagenes y
catalogo
l marido
on
ondas
e una
adio
de
CB
como
le ruega
mún
ntido
mún.
Ella pide
una prueba
le dice:
Anna, I'm dead,
tell me why?"

fantasma trae a los
advertencia o presagio.
toma una fotografía.
es una monja.
aparece al borde de foto.
fenomeno ocurre que
visto por ella.
pequeñas NAGRA
fondo a las
dan un
a la U.
cree que

Un marinero del "Arkham.
- Quiza Pabodie tenga como hobby la construcción d'automatas

—Between anguish and hope, pain is the exit.

—Check out the locations for VOOI for the M.M.

—The SCARLET city in the middle of the white one.

—Green water / *Scarlet and corroded walls*

—Dietist: The key is to avoid eating large portions. Woman: Ah—yes that makes sense, D: Tomatoes, lettuce, celery, non-fat dairy products . . . W: Well-that-that's good. But what about lunch? D: Well at lunch you can give yourself a treat. W: Sure. D: Or you'll go crazy. W: A treat! That's a good idea, thank you. D: You are welcome. *CUT A: The woman pigging out.*

—A mass hallucination. Suggestion or mass hysteria.

—An empty shell that is a ghost.

—Normally ghosts bring the living warnings or premonitions.

—The husband takes a photograph of it.

—One of the researchers is a nun.

—A ghost is visible at the edge of the photo and a phenomenon occurs that she is the only one to see.

—Record it in small NAGRA recorders to give the images depth to give a catalog to the U.

—The husband thinks that they're radio waves or waves from a nearby CB and pleads with them to use their common sense.

—She asks for proof and it tells her: "Anna, I'm dead, tell me why?"

—An Arkham sailor

—Perhaps Pabodie, like Holly, knows how to build automatons

Notebook 4, Page 7B

AFTERWORD

AT THE MOUNTAINS OF MAGNIFICENCE

TOM CRUISE

I WOULDN'T SAY *AT THE MOUNTAINS OF MADNESS* didn't work out—I have worked on and postponed many films before they were finally made—it's just going to work out when it's supposed to.

While it was painful to watch Guillermo go through the experience of having to put on hold a project that was so close to his heart, I knew he would move on to extraordinary things, and he soon did with *Pacific Rim*. As I told him at the time, it's not over, it's just on pause for now. I'm still determined to work with him, and one day it will happen.

Over the years I've been fortunate to work with a lot of truly great filmmakers, and each and every one of them has their own unique tone and voice, which emanates from every frame of their films. This is particularly true of Guillermo's work. When you look at his movies, you know instantly that you're seeing a del Toro film, whether it's *Pan's Labyrinth* or *Hellboy*. His films are very much an extension of who he is and his ideas. It's in the design, it's in the lighting, it's in the composition. It's in every single creative decision. That's what makes him an artist. It's not analytical. It is instinctual; it permeates his work, his life. He has a vivid imagination that remains free against all odds.

Guillermo is a true artist, but he's also a hard worker. He's not someone who just talks the talk—he's actively going out and making things happen, constantly striving to be better at communicating with an audience. He's discovering what it is that interests people. He's smart about it, and I think that's why he's accumulated a very faithful audience.

He's very interested in people and hungry for life, he has no sense of self-importance or arrogance. You can always tell someone who's very competent, because they have an ease in talking about their craft and themselves; there's no defensiveness or overbearing confidence.

I've admired Guillermo's work since *Cronos*, and when we finally had

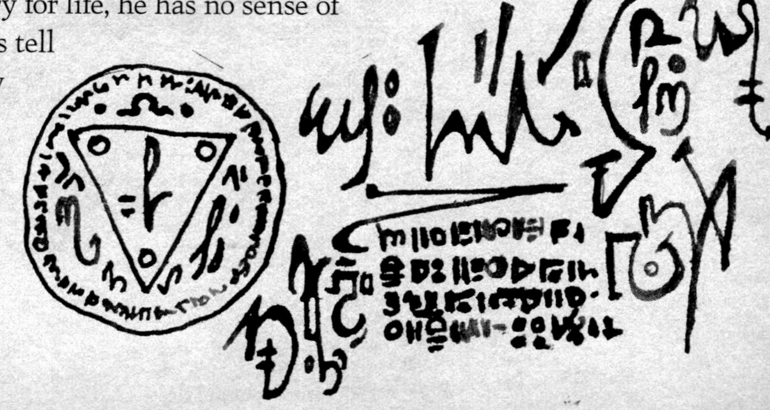

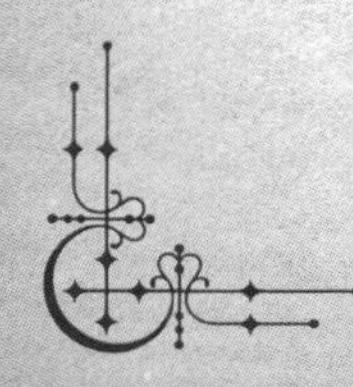

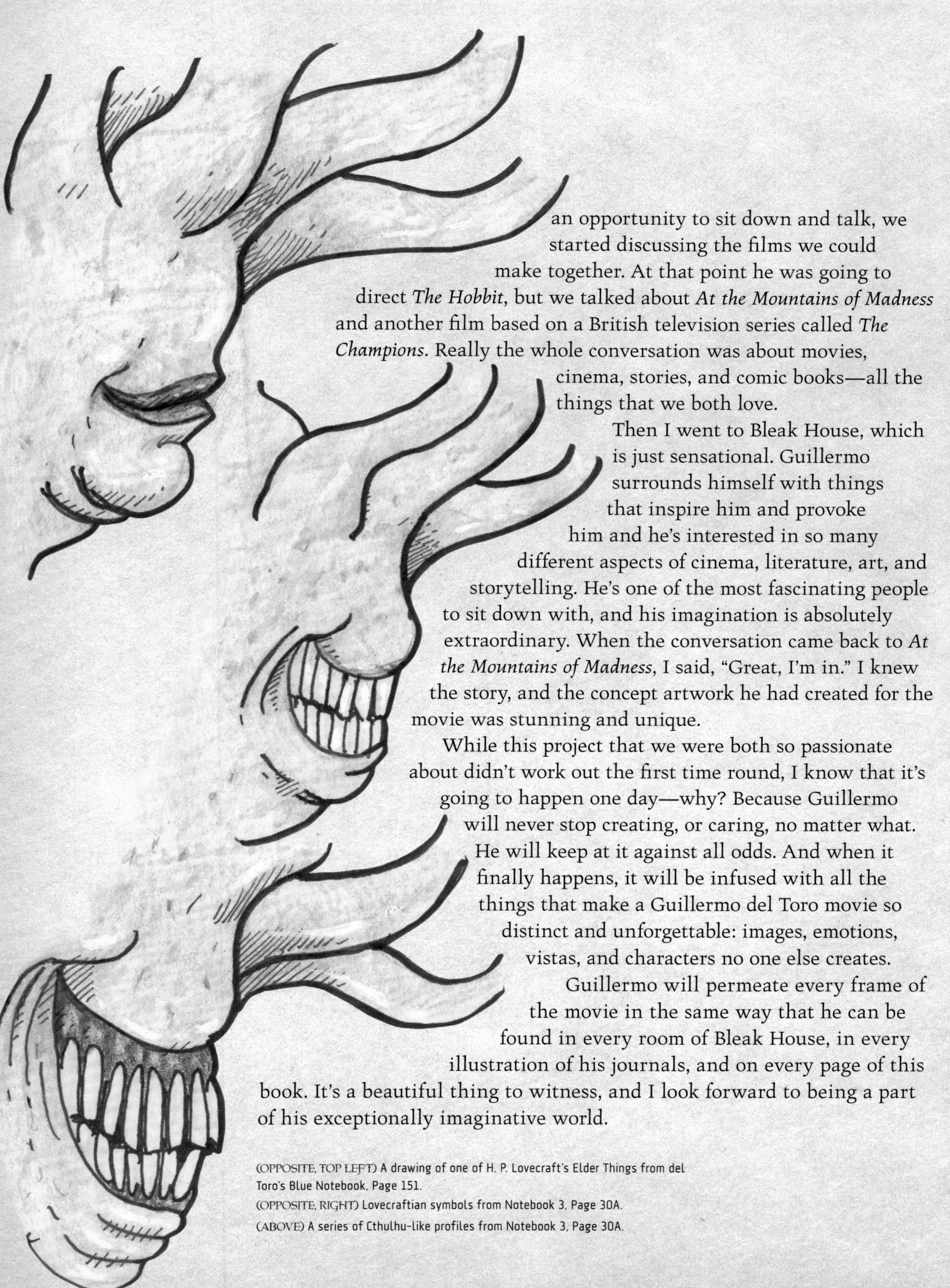

an opportunity to sit down and talk, we started discussing the films we could make together. At that point he was going to direct *The Hobbit*, but we talked about *At the Mountains of Madness* and another film based on a British television series called *The Champions*. Really the whole conversation was about movies, cinema, stories, and comic books—all the things that we both love.

Then I went to Bleak House, which is just sensational. Guillermo surrounds himself with things that inspire him and provoke him and he's interested in so many different aspects of cinema, literature, art, and storytelling. He's one of the most fascinating people to sit down with, and his imagination is absolutely extraordinary. When the conversation came back to *At the Mountains of Madness*, I said, "Great, I'm in." I knew the story, and the concept artwork he had created for the movie was stunning and unique.

While this project that we were both so passionate about didn't work out the first time round, I know that it's going to happen one day—why? Because Guillermo will never stop creating, or caring, no matter what. He will keep at it against all odds. And when it finally happens, it will be infused with all the things that make a Guillermo del Toro movie so distinct and unforgettable: images, emotions, vistas, and characters no one else creates.

Guillermo will permeate every frame of the movie in the same way that he can be found in every room of Bleak House, in every illustration of his journals, and on every page of this book. It's a beautiful thing to witness, and I look forward to being a part of his exceptionally imaginative world.

(OPPOSITE, TOP LEFT) A drawing of one of H. P. Lovecraft's Elder Things from del Toro's Blue Notebook, Page 151.

(OPPOSITE, RIGHT) Lovecraftian symbols from Notebook 3, Page 30A.

(ABOVE) A series of Cthulhu-like profiles from Notebook 3, Page 30A.

(ABOVE) Guillermo and Lorenza del Toro (center, always together) surrounded by family and friends at the start of the shoot for a 16mm animated short film.

ACKNOWLEDGMENTS

This book represents only a fraction of the notes in my diaries and the items in my collection at Bleak House, but it offers a great start to a dialogue with those who appreciate the work that I do. We took hours of interview tapes and spent many days archiving, photographing, editing, and designing the pages you now have in your hands. It is only proper that we thank some of the people that made this book possible.

To start, thank you to all the friends and creative confidants who contributed pieces to this book: James Cameron, Tom Cruise, Alfonso Cuarón, Cornelia Funke, Neil Gaiman, John Landis, Mike Mignola, Ron Perlman, and Adam Savage.

Without the collaboration of these artists, my films and this book would not be nearly as rich: Mike Mignola, Wayne Barlowe, Oscar Chichoni, Guy Davis, TyRuben Ellingson, Carlos Giménez, Carlos Jimenez, Rob McCallum, Raúl Monge, Sergio Sandoval, Keith Thompson, Francisco Ruiz Velasco, Raúl Villares, Tanja Wahlbeck, Simeon Wilkins, and Doug Williams. The presence of their work here, of course, does not supersede the rich partnerships I've forged with many other artists, whom I value equally as much.

At Insight Editions, I am indebted to publisher Raoul Goff, without whom this book would still be an idea. And thank you to Marc Scott Zicree, with whom I share many affinities. Behind the scenes, editor Jake Gerli and the rest of the book team—art director Chrissy Kwasnik, designer Jon Glick, translator Mike Engle, and editorial staff Chris Prince, Rachel Anderson, and Elaine Ou—did a wonderful job molding my predilections into this fine presentation.

Thank you, too, to my representatives Richard Abate, George Hayum, and Gary Ungar, for standing by me and guiding me through this book development process.

Without these kindred spirits in the world of filmmaking, there would be much less of a story to tell about the notebooks and my films: Pedro and Agustín Almodóvar, Belén Atienza, Álvaro Augustín, Arthur H. Gorson, Elena Manrique, Bertha Navarro, Bernard Nussbaumer, Alejandro Springall, Telecinco, Paolo Vasile, and Jorge Vergara.

Thank you all,

Guillermo del Toro

HANS CHRISTIAN ANDERSEN FAIRY TALES
Hans Christian Andersen La sombra y otros cuentos
IRISH FOLK & FAIRY TALES OMNIBUS
Michael Scott
PINOCCHIO
CARLO COLLODI
THE STORIES OF HANS CHRISTIAN ANDERSEN
Selected and translated by Diana Crone Frank and Jeffrey Frank
HANS CHRISTIAN ANDERSEN
THE COMPLETE TALES
II
THE FOLIO SOCIETY
HANS CHRISTIAN ANDERSEN
THE COMPLETE TALES
I